D1541444

LOGIC AND INFORMATION

LOGIC AND INFORMATION

Keith Devlin
Carter Professor of Mathematics, Colby College, Maine

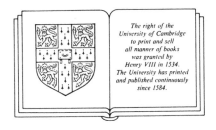

CAMBRIDGE UNIVERSITY PRESS

Cambridge

New York   Port Chester   Melbourne   Sydney

Published by the Press Syndicate of the University of Cambridge
The Pitt Building, Trumpington Street, Cambridge CB2 1RP
40 West 57th Street, New York, NY 10022–4211, USA
10 Stamford Road, Oakleigh, Melbourne 3166, Australia

© Cambridge University Press 1991

First published 1991

Printed in Great Britain at the University Press, Cambridge

British Library cataloguing in publication data available

Library of Congress cataloguing in publication data available

ISBN 0-521-41031-4

for Jon, who made it happen

CONTENTS

It is therefore quite possible that we are not too far from the limits which can be achieved in artificial automata without really fundamental insights into a theory of information, although one should be very careful with such statements because they can sound awfully silly in five years.

— *John von Neumann, 1949*

ACKNOWLEDGEMENTS

Amongst those whose conversations and suggestions proved invaluable in the preparation of this book are Jon Barwise, Mark Crimmins, John Etchemendy, Pat Hayes, David Israel, John Perry, Stanley Peters, and other members of the STASS Research Group at CSLI, Stanford University.

David Tranah, my editor at Cambridge University Press, was always very supportive, and it was he who persuaded me that I should abandon the strictly 'textbook' style I had originally adopted, in order to make the book accessible to the much wider audience he felt would be interested in the issues I raise.

Particular thanks go to Jon Barwise. Though I began to work on the material presented here in 1985, the initial development was severely hampered by the traumas resulting from the rapid contraction forced upon the British university system by the government. Trying to feel one's way forward into uncharted territories at a time when all pressures were towards the pursuit of 'useful research' (measured in terms of how many bucks will it earn by the weekend) was not easy. There was considerable pressure to abandon work regarded as 'unproductive' (read '$'). 'Pure' research was looked upon with disdain as a luxury bought at others' expense. In my own case, my then university, Lancaster, blocked any further career advancement for me there and advised (and subsequently pressured) me to seek my future elsewhere. All in all, it was not a happy time and, without Barwise's invitation for me to spend the period 1987-9 at CSLI, it is unlikely that this book would ever have been written.

The final version of the book was completed after I had taken up the position of Carter Professor of Mathematics at Colby College in Maine, and I am particularly indebted to President Bill Cotter and Dean of Faculty Bob McArthur, who facilitated the continuation of my research after I left Stanford.

Most of all, I owe an immense debt to my wife, Jan, and daughters, Naomi and Melissa, who twice suffered the trauma of being uprooted from their home and friends, first in England and then in California, as I sought to find a means by which I could pursue my work.

Should it ever come about (and I think it will) that some of the ideas developed in these pages turn out to be of real 'use', I would hope that this book serves as a testament to the stupidity, *even in those very terms of 'usefulness' that were foisted on the British university system*, of judging any intellectual pursuit in terms of its immediate cash value.

Keith Devlin
Waterville, Maine
January 1991

PREFACE

Towards a mathematics of information

In Mathematics, as anywhere today, it is becoming more difficult to tell the truth
...... Telling the truth is not quite the same thing as reciting a rosary of facts.
José Ortega y Gasset, in an admirable lesson summarised by Antonio Machado's
three-line poem, prophetically warned us that

> *the reason people so often lie is that they lack imagination:*
> *they don't realize that the truth, too,*
> *is a matter of invention.*

Sometime, in a future that is knocking at our door, we shall have to retrain
ourselves or our children to properly tell the truth. The exercise will be particularly
painful in mathematics. The enrapturing discoveries of our field systematically
conceal, like footprints erased in the sand, the analogical train of thought that
is the authentic life of mathematics. Shocking as it may be to a conservative
logician, the day will come when currently vague concepts such as motivation
and purpose will be made formal and accepted as constituents of a revamped
logic, where they will at last be allotted the equal status they deserve, side-by-side
with axioms and theorems.

The above two paragraphs were not written by me, but by Gian-
Carlo Rota.[1] The words were penned on 7 February 1985, as part of
the preface to the book *Discrete Thoughts* [11], a collection of articles
on mathematics and computing assembled by Rota together with Jacob
Schwartz and Mark Kac.

Rota's words provide a particularly apt opening to this book. And,
it is to be hoped, add weight to what I believe to be the importance to
the future of mathematics, of enterprises such as the one presented in
this volume. Without a continued supply of new areas of application,
mathematics would start to grow inwards, and eventually die. But fleshing

---

[1] Professor of Applied Mathematics and Philosophy at the Massachussetts Institute of
Technology, Fellow of the Los Alamos National Laboratory, the editor of the journal
Advances in Mathematics, and a member of the United States *National Academy of
Sciences*.

out and developing new mathematical tools is no easy matter, and the fumbling beginnings are all too easily dismissed as futile. The eloquent words of Professor Rota can remind us all, both the outside sceptics and the committed researchers (who also, let it be said, experience periodic doubts about the outcome of their work), that it is only by dreaming, and then striving to turn those dreams into reality, that mankind progresses.

None of which is to say that we can get it right first time. The theory outlined in these pages marks an attempt to develop some new mathematics, a mathematics of information, but only time will tell whether or not this is the 'right' way to do the job. It is always difficult to stride out into something new. Rota has something to say about this as well. In Chapter 1 of the same volume, he begins:

Of some fields it is difficult to tell whether they are sound or phony. Perhaps they are both. Perhaps the decision depends on the circumstances, and it changes with time. At any rate, it is not an objective fact like 'the moon is made of green cheese'. Some subjects start out with impeccable credentials, catastrophe theory, for instance, and then turn out to resemble a three-dollar bill. Others, like dynamic programming, have to overcome a questionable background before they are reluctantly recognized to be substantial and useful. It's a tough world, even for the judgement pronouncers.

What then, of the ideas set out (in a fumbling, embryonic form) in this essay? Where do they lie in Rota's spectrum: sound or phony? Obviously, it is my belief that the ideas are (or rather will evolve to be) both sound and (profoundly) useful. But I cannot claim to know this for a *fact*. The territory is uncharted, with only a handful of travellers making those first few tentative steps. But then, is that not the very nature of true research?

One further quote, this time from the great English mathematician J. E. Littlewood [6, p.144]:

Most of the best work starts out in a hopeless muddle and floundering, sustained on the 'smell' that something is there. ... In a new subject (or new to oneself) there can be a long preliminary process of getting to the essential core. At *this* process a first-rate mathematician is little, if at all, better than a PhD student. ... With a collection of really difficult problems, nothing happens in a year; much happens in ten years.

After reading this essay, the reader may judge for herself[2] how far we

---

[2] At the present time, there is always the vexing issue of how to represent the third-person singular in a gender-neutral way. In this book I take the approach of using both 'he' and 'she' interchangably in a more or less random manner.

have progressed towards the goal outlined in Chapter 1. And how much further we have still to go.

What this book is not

This book is perhaps a little out of the ordinary — certainly for a book written by a mathematician, intended to be a 'mathematics book'. (Where are the pages of symbolic expressions?) If you have picked up the book and got this far, you will, I hope, be sufficiently intrigued to proceed further. What are you likely to find? Just what nature of book do you have in your hands? The best way to answer that is to sit down and read it. But here, for the impatient, it a brief guide to what the book is not, and what it is.

This book is not intended to be a work of scholarship. That is, I did not set out to examine other work in this general area, or to compare the theory developed here with any other theories. Others are free to do that if they wish. That was not my intention.

This book is not a 'philosophy text'. True enough, a lot of the topics dealt with are regular fayre on the philosopher's table, and I pay considerable attention to many philosophical issues. But as an attempt to develop a tolerably useful piece of mathematics, the treatment of many deep philosophical issues is of necessity a 'naive' one.

This book is not a 'linguistics text'. Despite the large amount of space dedicated to natural language semantics, my interest in natural language is its great power, versatility, and robustness as a vehicle for conveying information. As with the philosophy, so too is the linguistics you will find here essentially 'naive'.

This book is not a 'computer science text'. Though the issues dealt with are all central to computer science (especially the information processing side of the subject), and though I utilize a number of concepts from computer science and occasionally use computer science examples to illustrate various points, no attention is paid to questions of implementation or computational tractibility.

This book does not pretend to present a completed body of work. It is very much an account of work in progress, work that has a long way to go until its (hoped for) completion.

What this book is

So now you know what this book is not. What then, is it?

It is a mathematics book, or at least a 'pre-mathematics' book that covers issues of crucial importance to philosophers, linguists, computer scientists, and cognitive scientists. Accordingly, it has been written in a fashion that, I hope, makes it accessible to workers in all of these areas, and possibly other fields as well.

It is applied mathematics. More precisely the book describes an instance of the important (applied) mathematical activity of *modeling*.

It is a 'research monograph' in the spirit of mathematical research. That is to say, the goal is the development of a mathematical theory, a piece of mathematics. And very much in the spirit of present-day mathematical research, little (in fact no) attempt has been made to turn it into a work of scholarship.

The overall goal is to provide the mathematics required for a science of information. I start the process of fleshing out a mathematical framework that will (I hope) form the backbone of such a science in the same way that parts of present-day mathematics support, say, physics.

It is a challenge. By sending this volume out into the world at this early stage in the development, I hope that others will be able to progress still further.

1

Information

1.1 What is information?

Imagine yourself suddenly transported back in time to (say) the Iron Age. You meet a local ironsmith and you ask him *"What is iron?"* What kind of answer are you likely to get? Very likely your craftsman would point to various artifacts he has made and inform you that each of those was iron. But this is not what you want. What you want to know is just what it is that makes iron *iron* (and not some other substance that may or may not look quite like iron). What then does your Iron Age man do in response to your persistent questioning? He is an acknowledged expert on ironship, his products sell well, and he knows a good piece of iron when he sees it. And yet he is unable to supply you with the kind of answer you are seeking. Indeed, *he has no frame of reference within which to even begin to understand what it is you are asking!* To give the kind of answer that would satisfy you, he would need to know all about the molecular structure of matter — for that surely is the only way to give a precise definition of iron. (Or maybe there are other ways, ways that require theories we ourselves are not aware of? This possibility merely strengthens the point I am trying to make.) But not only is your man not familiar with molecular theory, *he probably does not even conceive of the possibility of such a theory!*

To anyone trying to understand the nature of *information* in today's *Information Age*, the situation must surely seem not unlike that facing your Iron Age man. That there is such a thing as *information* cannot be disputed, can it? After all, our very lives depend upon it, upon its gathering, storage, manipulation, transmission, security, and so on. Huge amounts of money change hands in exchange for information. People talk about it all the time. Lives are lost in its pursuit. Vast commercial empires are created in order to manufacture equipment to handle it. Surely then *it* is there. But *what* exactly is it? The difficulty in trying to find an answer to this question lies in the absence of an agreed, underlying theory upon which to base an acceptable definition. Like the Iron Age man and his stock in trade, Information Age Man can recognize and manipulate 'information', but is unable to give a precise definition as to what exactly it is that is being recognized and manipulated.

Perhaps *information* should be regarded as (or maybe *is*) a basic property of the universe, alongside matter and energy (and being ultimately interconvertible with them). In such a theory (or suggestion for a theory, to be more precise), information would be an intrinsic measure of the structure and order in parts or all of the universe, being closely related to entropy (and in some sense its inverse). This approach would, of course, fit in quite well with the classic work of Shannon [29] on *amounts* of information.

Or perhaps you can suggest a better theory. In any event, this kind of speculation does not directly affect the discussion in this essay. What I am concerned about here is not so much the nature of information *per se*, but rather information processing and the manner in which information flows from one agent (or situation — see presently) to another, with a particular interest in the role language and 'logic' play in this. For this aim there is no need to pin ourselves down in advance as to the exact nature of *information* itself — just as it is possible to develop and study the differential calculus without having an exact conceptualization of a real number. (Indeed, historically the development of the differential calculus preceded (by some two centuries) the evolution of a rigorous theory of the real numbers, and if we pursue this analogy between a study of information flow and the development of the calculus just a little further, we might speculate that investigations such as the present one could eventually lead to an all-embracing theory of the nature of information.)

So the aim here is not to answer the question '*What* is information?' but rather to investigate the nature of information flow and the mechanisms that give rise to such flow; in short, to develop a *science* of information. The approach I shall take is in many ways a completely traditional one: namely to start with an empirical study of the phenomenon, develop a mathematical framework that seems appropriate for such a study, and then use that framework in order to construct a theoretical account that can carry the empirical study further.

The question is: just what kind of mathematical framework do we adopt in order to study information? Do we take some existing mathematical theory 'off the peg', make a few minor alterations, and then use that, or do we have to go back to basics and develop some completely new mathematics? The sensible approach is to start off with what is already available, and see if that measures up to the requirements of the task at hand. If it does not, try to see why not, and proceed from there. Maybe we will be able to get by with a few minor alterations; or perhaps more substantial changes are required; or failing that we may be forced to develop some quite new mathematics, building on the insights we gain from investigating the failure of existing mathematics.

In this essay I start with the mathematical framework most commonly used both to study information (in the sense of the 'meaning' of the information, not the information-bearing *signal* that formed the object of the well-known Shannon study [29]) and to design artificial systems to process information; namely mathematical logic.

1.2   A mathematical theory of information

As outlined above, the aim of this book is to develop a 'mathematical theory of information'. Another way to describe it would be as the development of a 'mathematical *model* of information flow'. But what exactly do I mean by these expressions?

In general by a *mathematical theory*, is meant a scientific treatment of certain real-world phenomena, carried out within the framework of mathematics, using (and developing, when required) mathematical techniques. Examples of such theories are fluid mechanics, signal processing theory, many parts of theoretical chemistry, and most branches of what is generally known as theoretical physics. By and large, I conceive of the present study as falling into this category. Thus, in particular, I regard the study of information flow as very largely a rationalist (i.e. 'scientific'), empirical investigation, albeit one where the nature of the subject provides a less firm observational and experimental base upon which to build than is the case in the other disciplines just mentioned. (Though work in linguistics, psychology, computer science, robotics, and artificial intelligence can, and does, provide data on which to base and judge our progress.)

It should be noted that this approach is quite counter to that hitherto adopted by most mathematicians in attempting to tackle the fundamental problems of information processing. By and large, the common approach has been to take the standard, formal development of mathematical logic — known variously as *classical logic*, *predicate logic*, or *predicate calculus* — and extend or modify it in various ways in order to cope with whatever issues are at hand. Thus various formal logics have been developed and studied: modal logic, temporal logic, relevance logic, deontic logic, non-monotonic logic, infinitary logic, generalized-quantifier logic, and more. However, in almost every case, the development has been approached as a strictly *mathematical* enterprise, lying clearly within the existing pure mathematics paradigm. That is to say, the emphasis has been on the specification of a formal language, the writing down of axioms, and the proof of theorems. The result of such an approach has been, to my mind, some very interesting mathematics but, at best, only modest advancement in our ability to say much about *information*.

My own view is that a completely different strategy is called for. Rather than *starting* with the formal mathematics and then trying to reach the target domain (i.e. the flow of information), we should begin by making an empirical study of information, and *then* attempt to formulate an appropriate mathematical model of that phenomenon. Such an approach would, of course, make the enterprise far more like physics or chemistry or any of the other natural sciences, rather that traditional mathematics. In particular, the familiar, comforting, absolute certainty of formal mathematical proof will be replaced by the more general kinds of scientific reasoning characteristic of the natural sciences.

To paraphrase the quotation from Rota given at the start of the preface to this book, such an approach might well be "shocking to a conservative logician," but I think it is absolutely unavoidable if we are to make any significant progress in the development of a mathematical theory of information (in the 'meaning' sense I indicated earlier). In the concluding remarks of his address to the American Mathematical Society Meeting in San Fransisco, California, in January 1991, the mathematician and physicist Sir Michael Atiyah emphasized, in reference to some startling recent work in geometry by Donaldson, Witten, and others, that it had been a historical mistake to completely separate the study of geometry from that of the physics of space, and that the deep insights that can lead to totally new developments in geometry can only come when geometry is thought of as *the geometry of space*, not just as 'abstract geometry'. In my opinion, an analogous remark applies to logic: the development of a genuinely new 'logic', which is what this book sets out to achieve, can only come about if we approach it as the development of a mathematical theory (or a mathematically-*based* theory, if you prefer) of information (flow) as it occurs in the world around us.

As with practically any new scientific discipline, an empirically-based study of information of the kind just outlined turns out to require both the application of existing mathematical techniques and the development (and subsequent application) of new mathematical tools, tailor-made for the task in hand.

Now, as is generally the case, the development of the new tools required is best carried out in an abstract ('pure mathematical') setting, removed from the complexities of the real world phenomena under examination. (A classic example of this phase is Newton's development of the differential calculus in order to provide a tool to deal with real world problems of mechanics and physics.) It is this process that is referred to as *mathematical modeling*. A precisely defined, abstract (and necessarily simplistic) 'model' of the world is set up in order to develop the mathematics in an unencumbered and rigorous fashion.

Typically, such a development is carried out using abstract mathematical 'objects' (pure sets, abstract surfaces, numbers, etc.), specified *axiomatically*, their properties being established by way of rigorously proved *theorems*. By an accident of history, this particular aspect of the mathematical enterprise has come to be *identified* with 'mathematics' by the vast majority of contemporary, practicing mathematicians. But of course, it is just that: an accident of history. An equally important part of mathematics is the initial, largely empirical work that leads to the development of new mathematical models. Indeed, in the long term this is the essential life-blood that ensures the continuation of the entire mathematical enterprise. The age of global exploration required the development of a suitable mathematics (in particular, geometry and trigonometry) in order to build ships and navigate and chart the Earth; the development of mechanical engineering and then electrical engineering each required their own particular brands of mathematics (notably, the calculus), and so too did the more recent fields of electronics and communications engineering. The information age is no different.

So this volume may not 'look' like a 'mathematics book' in the normal, present-day sense (though a planned sequel volume will), but that is purely a reflection of the early stage of the enterprise. In the sense explained above, it does constitute the beginnings of what is meant by the phrase *a mathematical theory*.

Time then to get down to business. As already mentioned, the starting point is the branch of mathematics known as logic.

1.3　Logic ≠ logic

The rapid growth of computer technology over the past three decades or so has brought to the forefront of research an area of mathematics that had hitherto been regarded as on the very edge of the subject: *logic*. The apparent contradiction in the title of this chapter should indicate that there is more to this particular word than meets the eye. Indeed, the inequality may be taken as a dramatic illustration of what is called the 'situatedness (or context dependency) of language', a topic of considerable importance in this book. The two uses of the word 'logic' in the title have quite different semantic content, as the remainder of this book makes clear.

All computers and computer languages depend, to a greater or lesser extent, on formal logic. Often this dependence is hidden, buried in either the internal circuitry of the machine or the design of the computer language being used. Occasionally the 'logic' is explicit, as occurs with the programming language *Prolog* (the name being an acronym for 'programming with logic'). The present trend is a rapid one towards an even stronger linkage between computing and formal logic, with the evolution of so-called 'formal methods' — techniques for systematically developing and proving correct (for the intended application) computer programs and complex computer systems.

Unfortunately, logic as it stands at present was not designed to handle the demands made of it by the computer designer or the software engineer. Computers are used to process *information*. Current 'logic' was developed to deal with the concepts of truth and mathematical proof, and makes no attempt to cope with information. With the only available tool not equipped for the job at hand, it is scarcely to be wondered at that ambitious aims such as the search for artificial intelligence (AI) run into such horrendous difficulties.

Genuinely intelligent systems such as Man do not operate using classical, formal logic; rather they rely upon far more sophisticated mechanisms for processing information. (Indeed, it could be argued that such is the nature of the way Man operates that the very use of the phrase 'processing information', carrying with it the computing connotations it does, is not at all appropriate to describe human mental processes.) So if there is to be any significant advance in AI (or related areas), the key surely is to be found in an analysis both of the concept of 'information' and the manner in which intelligent organisms such as Man handle and respond to information picked up from their environment.[1] What this

---

[1] In this connection the reader might like to read the quote from von Neumann (the so-called 'father of the automatic computer') given on page vi. Though as Joseph Goguen has remarked, in using the phrase *theory of information* back in 1949, von Neumann is

amounts to (at least according to my present viewpoint) is the development of a 'logic' that is far more general (and correspondingly more powerful) than that currently available.

1.4   What is logic?

But should the kind of theory asked for in the previous section be described as 'logic'? According to the definition given in the *Oxford English Dictionary* it should. *Logic*, says this source, is *the science of reasoning, proof, thinking, or inference*. And this, I maintain, is precisely what the present enterprise is all about. Disagreement with this claim can only arise, I would think, from an over-exposure to the hitherto ruling doctrine that 'logic' is the study of the properties of certain kinds of formal systems, and in particular the properties of the 'logical connectives' *and* ($\wedge$), *or* ($\vee$), *not* ($\neg$), *implies* ($\rightarrow$) and the 'quantifiers' *for all* ($\forall$), *there exists* ($\exists$), when used in conjunction with various finitary predicates and a collection of individual variables.

This was not always the case. The 'logic' developed by the Greeks, often referred to as *Aristotelean logic* after one of its more famous early pioneers, and an early precursor of present-day, 'classical' (i.e. first-order, predicate) logic, was very clearly intended to analyze rational argument, as becomes clear when we read Plato's accounts of Socrates.

Aristotle's logic attempts to reduce all rational argument to basic deductive units called *syllogisms*, the paradigm example of such a unit being:

All men are mortal
Aristotle is a man
Aristotle is mortal

Though patently inadequate for the analysis of all rational argument (at least to present-day eyes), the study of the syllogism formed the core of logic for over a thousand years. Indeed, so entrenched did syllogistic logic become in academia that as late as the fourteenth century we find in the statutes of the University of Oxford the rule "Bachelors and Masters of Arts who do not follow Aristotle's philosophy are subject to a fine of five shillings for each point of divergence, as well as for infractions of the rules of the Organon. (Traces of this kind of obstinate adherence to an inadequate and outmoded logical framework can be

unlikely to have had in mind the kind of (relatively) sophisticated semantic analysis of cognitive processes that is being attempted here.

found in some present-day university philosophy departments, where inordinate amounts of time are sometimes spent studying formal systems of propositional logic. In this case I am only objecting to the devotion of excess time to this topic, not to the topic itself.)

Logic took a step closer to mathematics with the work of George Boole in the 19th Century. The algebraic framework Boole developed in order to study the Aristotelean syllogism not only served to highlight the essential triviality of the syllogistic approach, it established logic as a branch of mathematics in the formal sense. Thus Boole's own work was published (in 1847) under the title *Mathematical Analysis of Logic*, and starting from Boole's framework, the American mathematician Schröder developed the algebraic system known as 'Boolean algebra', a system now used extensively in various parts of mathematics and computer science.

By the time of Frege, Cantor, Hilbert, Whitehead and Russell, not only was logic firmly embedded in mathematics, it was clear that the principal focus of the study was logic applied to mathematics. The analysis of mathematical truth and the notion of proof was the goal, with Hilbert's program to reduce all of mathematics to formal logic one of the main driving forces.

This thrust proved to be enormously successful. Coupled with Cantor's set theory, the predicate logic introduced by Frege provides a rigorous mathematical framework for the formulation of large parts, if not all, of mathematics. (It is all a question of how far you are prepared to stretch matters, allowing ugly circumlocutions and the like.) Moreover, predicate logic can be precisely formulated and axiomatized, and is amenable to a detailed and precise development as a mathematical discipline. It provides a rigorous definition of the notion of *mathematical proof* (albeit a definition whose idealistic nature means that it is only *in principle* that any typical, everyday mathematical proof could be made to fit its rigid strictures). And it gives rise to a highly structured and elegant study of the formal semantics (i.e. meaning) of mathematical statements (*Model Theory*), leading to the famous Completeness and Incompleteness Theorems of Gödel, the work of Tarski on truth, and Robinson's solution to the centuries old problem concerning the nature of infinitesimals. In short, mathematical logic (as it came to be known) is one of the great success stories of modern mathematics.

Faced with such credentials, few indeed would wish to rock the boat by pointing to deficiences in this particular approach to the 'science of reasoning, proof, thinking, or inference'. But deficiences there are for all that. Leaving aside the question as to whether or not first-order logic is *really* adequate for the formulation of every mathematical statement, it is clear to anyone who has ever studied first-order logic that there are fundamental problems at the most basic level, in connection with the way the logical connectives *and, or, not, implies* are defined in terms of truth values. For instance, the standard formal definition of logical implication (i.e. the material conditional) renders $p \rightarrow q$ equivalent to $\neg p \lor q$. Besides classifying the implication $p \rightarrow q$ as being true in all cases where p is false, this approach also declares that statements such as

Φ: If $2 + 2 = 4$, then for every integer $n > 1$ there is a prime number between n and $2n$.

are true. Whilst the truth of an implication $p \rightarrow q$ in the case where p is false, though worrying to most people (this author included), can be argued away on the grounds that implications with false antecedents are of no real concern in mathematics (at least), a sentence such as Φ is not so easily disposed of. Both the antecedent and the consequent are true in this case (the consequent, known as *Bertrand's Conjecture*, having been established by Chebychef in 1850). Consequently the standard definition renders the entire implication Φ true. But is this really what we want? Does anyone really believe that Φ expresses a genuine *implication*, relating the triviality $2 + 2 = 4$ with a deep result of number theory? It should be obvious by now that the standard classical-logic 'escape' that Φ is logically equivalent to its consequent will not suffice to evade the issue I am trying to flesh out here, namely the meaning of the *implication* itself. Does Φ in fact have any *meaning* (other than that it is 'true')?

For another, quite different sort of deficiency with classical logic, take any piece of simple, everyday reasoning of the sort human beings perform automatically every day, such as the reasoning process involved in understanding the following sequence of actions:

1. Jon walked into the restaurant.
2. He saw that the waitress had dirty hands.
3. So Jon left immediately.

Though you might feel that Jon's behavior here was unnecessarily fussy, I doubt very much that you would regard it as at all *illogical*. Indeed, the 'logical' path that leads from the circumstances described by 1 and 2 to Jon's action in 3 seems perfectly clear. In everyday, human terms, the passage from 1 and 2 to 3 is a sound, *logical* train. But it clearly transcends first-order logic. Unless, that is, you regard sentences 1, 2, and 3 as simply shorthand for a much longer chain of individual implications, involving various other matters, that leads from 1 and 2 to 3 via the usual rules of classical logic. That this can always be done is not in dispute (at least by me). But this is not how ordinary people regularly perform such 'deductions', and by retreating hurriedly to the seeming comfort of classical logic in this manner, the real issue is simply being evaded. Most of this book will amount to an argument to support this viewpoint.

There are then at least two sorts of major problem with classical logic: the first, which affects both mathematical and everyday uses of logic, arising from the total dependence upon truth as the basic, underlying notion; the second, perhaps not so significant as far as mathematics is concerned (though I am not so sure about even this) stemming from the inadequacy of classical logic to capture ordinary, everyday, 'people logic'. Whatever else may be said either for or against classical logic, it certainly does not fulfill the demands put upon 'logic' by the dictionary definition of the word.

Whereas this deficiency might not seem so important as far as mathematical applications of logic are concerned, when first-order logic is used both to design and to operate information processing devices (and, for that matter, to analyze the use of ordinary language in human-to-human communication), it is hardly surprising that it proves woefully inadequate for the task. For purposes such as these, a 'logic' based on truth (such as classical logic) is not appropriate; what is required is a 'logic' based on *information*. It is the aim of this book to develop just such a 'logic'.

1.5   The strategy

Here, briefly, is the approach I shall adopt in trying to develop an appropriate 'logic', a *science of reasoning, proof, thinking, or inference* as the dictionary would have it.

Information, and more specifically the flow of information, is taken as the basic, underlying (though to some extent 'undefined') concept. *Inference* is an activity whereby certain facts (items of information) about the world are used in order to extract additional information (information that is in some sense implicit in those facts). A sound inference is one whose logical structure is such as to support the role of that inference as a link in an informational chain. Truth will be a secondary notion. Classical first-order logic will be a highly restrictive, special case of our theory.

Notice that no mention was made of language in the above. This is quite different from the case of classical logic, in which language (i.e. first-order predicate language) plays a pre-eminent role. In terms of our new, dictionary-driven interpretation of the word 'logic', language is important, but by no means all-embracing. People make non-linguistic inferences every day. As you prepare to leave for work in the morning you notice the dark clouds in the sky and reach for your raincoat, having (correctly) inferred that (a) there is a strong possibility of rain, and (b) if you do not take your raincoat you may get wet. No use of language is involved in making these inferences (except subsequently, perhaps, should you have cause to reflect upon why you acted as you did). Indeed, similar kinds of inference are made routinely all the time by animals and organisms that do not have any linguistic capacities.

It should be stressed that I am not claiming that people do not sometimes think in a linguistic fashion. But I do maintain that thought is not fundamentally linguistic, and I reject the necessity of positing some form of internal language (often referred to as *Mentalese* by adherents to that school) as an underpinning of mental activity.

Two distinctive features of the present enterprise will be the concepts of an *infon* and of a *situation*. In due course I shall give a proper analysis of what is meant by these terms, but for the time being an 'infon' may be thought of as a discrete item of information and the word 'situation' may be understood in its normal, everyday sense, to refer to some part of the activity of the world, such as the *situation* that is taking place right here and now as I sit at my desk and enter these words at the keyboard. Or the *situation* that has you reading these same words. Or the larger and considerably more complex *situation* that comprises my writing these words, the internal circuitry converting each keystroke into an electrical impulse that is conveyed into the computer's memory, together with all the other steps that are involved in the transmission of this text from me to you.

In passing, notice that this last example is one that involves an explicit information flow — indeed, an information flow in which language plays a major role. As such it gives some indication as to how we may make use of situations in the study of such flow. But beware of reading too much into this remark. Though there is undoubtedly a flow of information involved, it is not at all clear just *what* information it is that is being conveyed — at least it is not obvious to me as I sit here writing. If the 'logic' of my argument is convincing, as I hope is the case, then the information conveyed to you will be the ideas about logic I am trying to put across. But the actual information you obtain may be quite different. After reading these words you may, for instance, conclude that I am confused or that what I am proposing is a hopeless dream. This

information is, of course, not at all the same as that which I am striving
to make explicit in my words. (Clearly, if it is to succeed in its stated aims,
the theory of 'logic' Idevelop here should at the very least be capable of
handling these various kinds of informational transfer. It will.)

Information flow is made possible by certain (what will be called)
constraints that link various types of situation. *Constraints* may be
natural laws, conventions, analytic rules, linguistic rules, empirical, lawlike correspondences, or whatever. Their role in the information chain is
quite well conveyed by the use of the word *means*. For instance, consider
the statement

smoke means fire.

This expresses a constraint (of the natural law variety). What it says is
that there is a lawlike relation that links situations where there is smoke
to situations where there is fire. If S is the class of all situations where
there is smoke present, and S' is the class of all situations where there
is a fire, then an agent (e.g. a person) can pick up the information that
there is a fire by observing that there is smoke and being aware of, or
(to use a suggestive term to be defined later) *attuned to*, the constraint

$$S \Rightarrow S'$$

that links the two kinds of situation. It should be noted that his use of
the symbol $\Rightarrow$ is not at all the same as its usage in classical logic, where
it is sometimes used to denote the material conditional (i.e. truth-value
implication) for which I use the symbol $\rightarrow$. Here the expression $S \Rightarrow S'$
means that there is a systematic, informational link between situations in
the class S and situations in the class S'. A more complete explanation
of this notion will be given in due course.

Note that the above example did not depend upon language. Indeed,
that particular constraint is one that holds regardless of the presence or
absence of any cognitive agent. For an example of a constraint that does
involve language, consider the assertion

FIRE *means fire.*

(Here and throughout I use the linguist's convention whereby capital
letters indicate the *word* itself, rather than its meaning.) This assertion
describes the constraint

$$S' \Rightarrow S'$$

that links situations (of type S') where someone yells the word FIRE to
situations (of type S') where there is a fire. Awareness of this constraint
involves knowing the meaning of the word FIRE and being familiar with

the rules that govern the use of language. Because these rules may be broken (a person might yell FIRE when there is no fire), this constraint is not as reliable as the one before. *Misuse* of constraints can result in the conveyance of *misinformation*.

Logic, in our sense, is the study of such constraints. As such it may be regarded not as an *alternative* to classical, first-order, predicate logic, but as an *extension* of it, with first-order logic being the study of just those particular constraints established by the axioms of first-order logic. Just how far this extension can be taken within the framework of a mathematical study is an interesting question. One that can only be answered by making the attempt.

2

Information, Situations, and Infons

2.1 The nature of information

I start off with the assumption that there is such a thing in the world as *information*. *Cognitive agents* (people, various kinds of organism, certain mechanical or material devices — see later for a discussion of just what is meant by the term 'cognitive agent') generally make their way in the world by being able to pick up certain of that information and react accordingly. A human being, on seeing flames all around, will take flight, having extracted the information that there is a fire and being already in possession of the previously acquired information that fires are life-threatening; a cat, on seeing a mouse, will pounce, knowing that there is fun to be had, if not food; a flower, on detecting the sun's rays in the morning, will open; a thermostat, on sensing a drop in temperature, will switch on the heating; and so on.

Already these few examples indicate one significant factor that we shall have to consider right at the outset: the fact that different agents are capable of extracting different information from the same source (situation). A person can pick up a great deal of information about the surrounding air — its cleanliness, the presence or absence of any smells, whether it is stationary or moving, whether it is warm or cool, how humid it is, and so on. A simple, mechanical thermostat on the other hand can only pick up one piece of information, though it is a piece of information that few humans are capable of picking up in all circumstances: namely the information whether the temperature is above or below the value set, say 21 °C. Just what kind of information may be picked up depends upon just what kind of device the agent is, and in particular upon the *state* of that agent *vis á vis* the extraction of information.

For a richer example, consider Barwise's tree stump as described in [1]. You come across a tree stump in the forest. What information can you pick up from your find? Well, if you are aware of the relationship between the number of rings in a tree trunk and the age of the tree, the stump can provide you with the age of the tree when it was felled. To someone able to recognize various kinds of bark, the stump can provide the information as to what type of tree it was, its probable height, shape, leaf pattern, and so on. To someone else it could yield information about the weather the night before, or the kinds of insects or animals that live in the vicinity; and so on. (As an exercise, you might like to think of, say, three further items of information the tree stump may be capable of providing.)

What the above examples indicate above all is that the acquisition of information from a situation depends upon those *constraints* of which the agent is aware, or to which the agent is *attuned*. Constraints? Attunement? Proper definitions will be given in due course. In the meantime, the discussion of Section 1.5 will suffice to indicate what a *constraint* is, and attunement to a constraint may be understood as systematically acting in accordance with that constraint. Information is obtained from a situation by means of some constraint, and awareness of, or attunement to, that constraint is what enables the agent to acquire that information. Thus the simple thermostat is, by its construction, attuned to a certain physical relationship between temperature and the expansion rates of various metals, whilst the forest ranger is aware of the relationship between the number of rings in a tree trunk and the age of the tree. (But note that this is not to say that the thermostat is in any sense 'aware' of how and why it operates the way it does. Nor does the forest ranger need to have a deep knowledge of tree biology. 'Attunement'

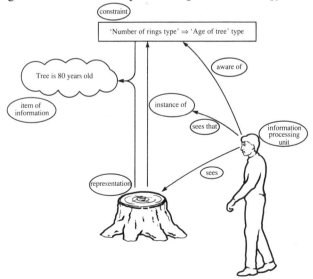

to, or behavior-guiding awareness of, a particular constraint may be an essentially *empirical* phenomenon.)

The example of the tree stump also highlights another aspect of information acquisition: there is never just a single item of information to be obtained from a given situation. For one thing, different constraints will give rise to different (kinds of) information being picked up. And, besides that, there is the phenomenon of 'nested' information. (See Dretske [8, p.71].) Given the possession of prior information and/or attunement to other constraints, the acquisition by an agent of an item of information Φ can also provide the agent with an additional item of information Ψ. For instance, if I tell you that a certain geometric figure (hidden from your view) is a square, then you also gain the (different) information that the figure is a rectangle. (This is by virtue of the 'analytic' constraint that all squares are rectangles.) You also learn that the figure is a parallelogram, that all its internal angles are 90 degrees, that it is a planar figure, and so on. Each of these additional items of information is *nested* (by way of certain constraints) in the information that the figure is a square. Thus information, when it comes, tends to do so in large, structured amounts. The acquisition of certain specific items of information from the mass available is part of the process known as *cognition*.

2.2   Cognition

Information, as we usually encounter it, is not unlike a 'bottomless pit', seemingly capable of further and further penetration. To borrow a term from another fairly new area of mathematics, we might say that information has what appears to be a *fractal* nature.[1] On the other hand, cognitive agents deal (at any one moment) with a relatively small collection of specific *items* of information extracted from that fractal-like environment. The acquisition of information from the environment by a cognitive agent is a process analogous to, though not necessarily the same as, going from the infinite and continuous to the finite and discrete.

---

[1] Both of these analogies have a potentially misleading aspect, in so far as they might suggest that information is capable of *endless* refinement. Whether this is in fact the case — and for the record I myself think that it is not — is not an issue that needs to be decided for the present study. Rather the distinction to be drawn in this section is between information in the world, which to the agent has the *appearance* of further and further penetrability and/or refinability, and the discrete *items* of information that the agent acquires from that available mass in order to function in a cognitive manner.

Dretske [8, pp.135-141] has used the terms *analog* and *digital* coding to facilitate discussion of this process.[2]

Consider the most basic kind of informational item: the possession or otherwise by an object s of a property P. Such an item of information will be conveyed to an agent by means of some kind of signal. That signal is said to carry the information that the object s has the property P in *digital* form, if that signal carries no additional information about s other than that which is nested in s being P. Otherwise the signal is said to carry the information that s is P in *analog* form. Thus if I tell you that Jon is taller than Fred, that piece of information is conveyed to you in digital form. You learn nothing more about Jon and Fred other than that one single fact (plus anything nested therein, such as Jon's being able to reach a higher shelf in the library than Fred, and so on). You do not, for instance, pick up the information that Jon has a beard and Fred does not. If, on the other hand, I show you a photograph of Jon and Fred standing side by side, that photograph will also convey to you the information that Jon is taller than Fred, but it does so in analog form. By looking at the photograph, you are able to pick up all kinds of information about these two characters, information more specific than the mere fact as to who is the taller. For instance, you learn something about the *extent* by which Jon is taller than Fred, something that my simple utterance does not convey to you. Information received in analog form is always capable of yielding more specific details. Information received in digital form is not capable of such refinement. (It should be noted that all of this is relative to the item of information concerned. The terms analog and digital are not 'absolute' as used here. The photograph conveys in analog form the information that Jon is taller than Fred, but it stores in digital form the information of what the photographer saw through the camera lens at the time the picture was taken.)

Now, what Dretske is concerned with when he makes the analog/digital

---

[2] It should be stressed that I am using the analogy with Dretske's work here in order to motivate a particular approach to the development of a mathematical framework within which to study information. This is not Dretske's intention. Rather he makes the analog–digital distinction in a formal way, *within* a theory of information, whereas I am taking it to guide the step from an intuitive, *pre-theoretic* notion to a formal, *theory-defined* notion. This point has also been observed by Seligman and Chater [28]. Another difference between my motivation and Dretske's, is that he is not attempting to give an ontological *definition* of information in the way that our theory does — see presently — but rather is concerned with the *flow* and *utilization* of information, accessed using Shannon's ideas of 'surprisal value'.

distinction, is the *representation* of information, whereas in this essay I am taking *information* itself as the basic entity under consideration. More precisely, I am seeking a specific conceptualization of 'information' as a theoretical 'commodity' that we can work with, analogous to (say) the *numbers* that the number-theorist works with or the *points, lines* and *planes* the geometer works with. At the moment, all we have is a name: 'information'. This name may *mean* something to us, but it is not a formally defined mathematical concept that can form the basis of a scientific study. I shall use Dretske's ideas in order to obtain the kind of precisely defined conceptualization of information we need.

We may regard the extraction of information from the environment by an agent as taking place in two separate stages, corresponding to the analog/digital distinction. The first stage is *perception*, where the information in the environment becomes directly accessible to the agent by way of some form of sensor (seeing, feeling, smelling, hearing, etc. in the case of a person or animal, or by the molecular agitation of the air impinging on the bimetallic strip in the case of a thermostat). At this stage the information flow is analog, relative to whatever information we are concerned with. The second stage, if there is one, involves the extraction of a specific item (or items) of information from that perceived 'continuum'; that is to say, it involves the conversion from analog to digital information. This stage is *cognition*. In the case of a person, this could be the recognition from the photograph of the fact that Jon is taller than Fred; for a thermostat, it is the discrete behavior between open and closed. A *cognitive agent* is an agent that has the capacity of *cognition* in this sense; i.e. the ability to make the analog to digital conversion.

It should be emphasized that the last sentence above is not intended to constitute a *definition* of a cognitive agent. Rather it enunciates one of the attributes an agent must possess in order to justify the description *cognitive*. My only aim at this stage in the proceedings is to motivate intuitively the model of the world I intend to work with. (A more detailed investigation of the notion of cognition is presented in Chapter 6.) The 'cognitive agent' I have at the back of my mind is Man, though it seems clear that much, if not all, of what I say will have much wider application.

For the undecided, Dretske has something to say on both sides of the matter. On page 142 of [8] he says, *apropos* cognition:

It is the successful conversion of information into (appropriate) digital form that constitutes the essence of cognitive activity ... Cognitive activity is the *conceptual* mobilisation of incoming information, and this conceptual treatment is fundamentally a matter of ignoring differences (as irrelevant to an underlying sameness) ... It is, in short, a matter of making the analog–digital conversion.

This much would appear to support use of analog–digital conversion as a working definition of 'cognition'. But in a footnote to the above quoted passage, Dretske goes on to say:

It is not *merely* the conversion of information from analog to digital form that qualifies a system as a perceptual–cognitive system ...To qualify as a genuine perceptual system, it is necessary that there *be* a digital-conversion unit in which the information can be given a cognitive embodiment, but the cognitive embodiment of information is not *simply* a matter of digitalization.

Basically, the point Dretske is making is that, *provided* the agent has the means of manipulating and utilizing the information it obtains, *then* the digitalization of perceived information is the essence of cognitive activity [9].

Notice that the process of cognition (i.e. at the very least an analog–digital conversion) involves a loss (often a huge loss) of information. But this is compensated for by a very definite gain, in that there occurs a *classification* of the perceived information. A thermometer simply registers the temperature (analog coding of information) and hence is a perceiving agent but not a cognitive agent (in even the most minimal sense suggested above); the thermostat classifies the temperature into two classes ('warm' and 'cold'), and thus exhibits a form of cognition.

A suggestive term to use in this discussion would be *concept*. The thermometer has no *concept* of warm and cold, the thermostat does. It is by the use of concepts to classify perceived (i.e. incoming) information that such information becomes available for (semantic)[3] processing. And it is with such *conceptual* information in digital form that I shall be primarily concerned in this essay.

2.3   Schemes of individuation

Having sketched the considerations that are both to motivate and guide the development of a proposed *mathematical theory of information flow*, the next step is to try to flesh out just what kind of framework will support such a study. As a first step, we need to have available some formally defined, standard way to represent conceptual information —

---

[3] The parenthesized adjective is to distinguish between the kind of content-oriented manipulation usually referred to as 'information processing', which is what is meant here, as opposed to some kind of quantitive signal manipulation such as volume or frequency control.

a way that should correspond tolerably (and consistently) well to what we feel is actually involved in the acquisition, storage, and manipulation of information by an agent (and which is at the same time amenable to a precise, mathematical development and study). In this chapter and the next, I shall set about this task in a fairly naive fashion, making a number of simplifying assumptions along the way. Later on, as our study progresses, we shall encounter a number of issues that require modification to the way I set things up initially.

Consider an agent, $\mathscr{A}$, that has sophisticated cognitive abilities; call it Man. Later on I shall consider the case of more simple agents. As Man goes about in the world, he extracts information from the environment, that is, he makes the basic analog to digital conversion of perceived information as discussed in the previous section. What cognitive abilities does he need in this regard?

One of the most important (and fundamental) cognitive abilities possessed by Man is the facility to *individuate* 'objects', that is to say, to see objects *as objects*. For example, when you see a table before you, you recognize it as *a table*, that is, as a single object, not as some huge collection of molecules or (on a different scale) an assembly of wood, steel, glue, and whatever; when I look at the computer screen in front of me as I type these words, I see (*recognize*) a single object, a terminal; and so on. Of course, this is not to say that you or I are at all unaware that these individual objects are made up of many other, smaller objects. To you as you eat your lunch, the table is a single object. To the worker who made it, the single, individuated objects that mattered were not only the table, but also its various components, the legs, the top, the screws that hold it together, and so forth. And though I never regard my computer terminal as anything other than a single, incomprehensible entity, I realize that to the computer engineer it has a fascinating and complex structure, involving many component objects.

It is, by and large, a matter of the agent's purpose (and to some extent of scale) just what parts of the world are individuated as 'single objects'. But whichever way the cake is cut, it seems clear that in order to make its way in the world, a cognitive agent such as Man makes constant use of the ability to individuate 'objects'.

The notion of individuation will occur frequently in my account, this being the way the agent carves up the world. But for many of our purposes, the somewhat less restrictive notion of *discrimination* turns out to be more appropriate. To explain what this means, consider my dog, Sam. As a result of observing Sam's behavior, it seems reasonable to assume he has a number of individuation capacities; for instance he appears to individuate balls, sticks, our two cats, his water bowl, and many other objects. Far less clear is whether he *individuates* our house or the local wood. And yet his behavior varies in a systematic way according to whether he is in the house, outside the house in the garden, or in the local wood. That is to say, he *discriminates* (by his behavior) the house, the garden, and the wood.

Thus in describing the dog's cognitive behavior, it seems appropriate to classify his actions in terms of the house, the garden, and the wood, and yet there seems no reason to suppose that he *individuates* these objects the way he does (it seems) his ball, sticks, the cats, and his water bowl. There is of course an act of individuation going on here: *we as theorists* studying the dog's behavior individuate the house, the wood, etc. Our theory can treat these as single entities. But there seems to be no reason to assume that Sam, the agent, has similar individuation capacities.

Enitities that are individuated (by the agent or the theorist) as 'objects' will be referred to as *individuals*, denoted by $a, b, c, \ldots$

Our theory takes these *individuals* as given. That is to say, among the objects discussed by the theory there are individuals. A formal mathematical development might wish to model these individuals by means of mathematical objects of some form or other. Exactly *what* mathematical objects are chosen for such a task is not important. If a set-theoretic development were followed, there is a rich structure of abstract objects available. For instance, any collection of 'pure sets' may be taken to represent the *individuals*. Alternatively, the formal 'individuals' may be taken as a collection of (unanalysed) *ur-elements* or *atoms* that form (part of) the ground level of some set theory with ur-elements. This issue will only be of relevance when it comes to dealing with the mathematical modeling of our theory. For the rest of the present development, individuals are just that: individuals, as *individuated*, either by the agent or the theorist.

It should be noted that individuation of individuals does not at all require them to be *atomic* entities, incapable of subdivision within the scheme of individuation. For instance, both the table and the computer terminal mentioned a moment ago, are *individuals* that have other *individuals* as components.

In addition to the individuation of individuals, an agent such as Man will be able to recognize that various *properties* hold or fail to hold of some or all of those individuals, and that various *relations* hold or fail to hold between some of those individuals.

I shall use $P, Q, R, \ldots$ in order to denote the properties and relations the agent recognizes or discriminates. Just which properties and relations these are is determined by the agent or species of agent. This is not an issue that greatly affects the development of our calculus of information flow. I shall assume that each property or relation has a fixed, finite number of argument places that may be filled by objects of appropriate kinds. (The issue of the *appropriateness* of the objects that fill the various argument roles of a property or relation will be considered at length in due course, when we investigate the nature of properties and relations more fully.) Again, a formal mathematical development might require these properties and relations to be modeled by certain sets. These need not be properties and relations in the set-theoretic sense, but they should be distinct from the objects used to model individuals.

The notion of *information* that I shall adopt in our study is:

objects $a_1, \ldots, a_n$ do/do not stand in the relation P.

Here P is some property in the ontology (about which more later) that applies to n or more objects of certain kinds (see later), and $a_1, \ldots, a_n$ are objects in the ontology that are *appropriate* (see later) for the respective argument places of the relation P. The identification of the objects $a_1, \ldots, a_n$ is *not* assumed to be part of the information. That is to say, information is taken to be in an *itemized*, conceptual form, and each item of information pertains to certain *given* objects.

If P is an n-place relation and $a_1, \ldots, a_n$ are objects appropriate for the respective argument places of P, then I shall write

$$\ll P, a_1, \ldots, a_n, 1 \gg$$

to denote the informational item that $a_1, \ldots, a_n$ stand in the relation P, and

$$\ll P, a_1, \ldots, a_n, 0 \gg$$

to denote the informational item that $a_1, \ldots, a_n$ do not stand in the relation P.

Noting that these objects represent the basic informational unit of our theory, I adopt the word *infon*[4] to denote an object of the form

$$\ll P, a_1, \ldots, a_n, i \gg$$

---

[4] Our subsequent analysis will reveal that only in a restricted sense are these the basic informational units of the theory, and accordingly I shall have cause to modify this definition of the word *infon* as our development proceeds, but the present definition will suffice for now.

where P is an n-place relation (for some n), $a_1, \ldots, a_n$ are objects appropriate for the respective argument places of P, and i is equal to 0 or 1. The notation and the name are intended to emphasize the fact that 'infons' are *semantic* objects, not syntactic representations. The 'truth value' i is called the *polarity* of the infon. In Dretske's terminology, an infon is a *digitalization* of information.

An infon that corresponds to the way things actually are in the world is called a *fact*. More on this later.

Again, for a set-theoretic development it would not matter just what kinds of set-theoretic object were taken to represent infons. The notation used is suggestive of an ordered $(n+2)$-tuple for an infon that involves an n-place predicate, with the use of the double angular brackets as simply a notational device to emphasise the particular usage for an infon. (Readers unfamiliar with the mathematical notion of a 'tuple' can simply ignore this remark. It plays no role in the development presented in this book.)

Examples of infons are:

$$\ll L, 2, \pi, 1 \gg$$

$$\ll S, 7, 3, 5, 0 \gg$$

where L is the relation *less than* (so L, x, y means x is less than y) and S, x, y, z means that x is the sum of y and z. Both of these infons are *facts*, of course; i.e. they provide true information about numbers. Notice also that each infon supplies a single item of information about the numbers involved (i.e. digital information). Observe too that this example indicates that the 'individuals' individuated by the agent Man can include highly abstract entities such as numbers.

One important fact to notice about the two examples given above is that they are mathematical. As far as a general study of information flow is concerned, such examples are by no means typical. Mathematical facts have a timeless, universal nature that most other informational items do not. The majority of real life 'facts' pertain only to a certain region of space and a certain interval of time. In order to deal with these kinds of facts, I need to introduce both spatial and temporal *locations* and to allow locations to figure in the argument places of relations.

(Spatial) *locations* will be denoted by $l, l', l'', l_0, l_1, l_2$, etc. They are not necessarily like the 'points' of mathematical spaces, though they may be so; locations can have spatial extension. Thus a location l may be either a point in space or a *region* of space. (Usually a connected region, though I do not demand this restriction.) This, of course, endows the collection of all locations with a fairly complex structure: one location may be a point within another, two (regional) locations may overlap in space, and so on. This structure will clearly play a significant role in any theory of information flow.

Temporal locations will be denoted by $t, t', t_0, \ldots$. As with spatial locations, temporal locations may be either points in time or regions of time. And once again, temporal locations come with a complex structure that relates them in various ways.

As an example of an infon that involves a temporal argument, consider

$$\ll \text{married-to, Bob, Carol, } t, 1 \gg$$

This provides the information (in digital form) that Bob is married to Carol at time t. (Presumably t is some *interval* of time here, though this is not necessarily the case — recall my assumption that each relation comes with a fixed set of argument places, each of which may only be filled with objects of a certain kind.)

For an example involving a location argument, at some time t' prior to the time t of the above example, it must have been the case that

$$\ll \text{marries, Bob, Carol, } l, t', 1 \gg$$

where l is the location where the marriage took place.

Because the relation of one temporal location preceding another (in time) is such a common one, I introduce a special notation for it. I write $t < t'$ to indicate that t temporally precedes t'. (Each of t, t' may be either a point or a region here.) Likewise I introduce the notation $t \circ t'$ to indicate that the temporal regions t and t' overlap, and $l \circ l'$ for overlap of the spatial regions l, l'.

Notice that some relations take other relations as arguments, and hence give rise to infons having relations in their argument places. The above example of *married-to* is a case in point. The following infon is a fact:

$$\ll \text{legal-relation, married-to, } l, t, 1 \gg$$

where l is the USA and t is the period 1900–1989 (say), and the property of being a legal relation refers to the laws of the United States.

The introduction of spatial and temporal locations raises an issue that can be significant in applications of our theory, both in the design and construction of information processing devices (such as robots) and in the domain of natural language semantics.

I have assumed that the cognitive activity of an agent such as Man depends upon that agent being equipped with the capacity to *individuate* various (what I will call) *uniformities* in the world, among them the individuals and relations mentioned so far. But does such an agent have equal need to individuate spatial and/or temporal locations?

Certainly, Man, in particular, has the *ability* to individuate uniformities of these kinds, but this is not the present issue. The question is, whether Man's cognitive activity *requires* such individuation, in the same way it requires the individuation of individuals and relations? And here it seems, the answer is "Not always." Rather, for a great many (though not all) instances, all that is required is that Man's behavior be *discriminatory* of space and time, to account for the fact that the various relations he individuates are, in the main, both location and time dependent.[5] Such dependency on being discriminatory of space and time is considerably less than *individuating* spatial and temporal locations.

But as *theorists* setting out to study the cognitive behavior of agents such as Man, in order to take account of the time and location dependency of the various relations that arise, *we* require both spatial and temporal locations having a similar ontological status (within the theory) to that of the agent-individuated uniformities of individuals, relations, and what-have-you; and, accordingly, these entities do form part of the ontology of our theory. But note that by allowing these locations to figure as arguments in the basic relations in our ontology, we are, or at least may be, passing from relations-as-they-are-individuated-by-the-agent, to theorist's extensions thereof.

In cases where the agent *is* able to individuate spatial and temporal locations, it may be the case that the spatial and temporal locations utilized by our theory are identical to those individuated by the agent. But in general this will not be the case. For instance, it is often convenient to make use of *point* locations of space or time, but no agent is capable of individuating such idealized (mathematical) locations.

What *is* usually the case is that the spatial and temporal locations in the theory's ontology should be *appropriate* for a study of that agent. For example, in a study of human–human communication, temporal locations of extremely long duration (say a million years) or of very short duration (say a millionth of a second) are unlikely to be of much use, and similarly for spatial locations of extreme magnitudes. Rather the spatial and temporal locations should correspond to the way in which the agent's activity is discriminatory of space and time. In this way, though they may not be *individuated* by the agent, the spatial and temporal

---

[5] This says rather more than the truism that any agent is of necessity located in both space and time.

locations used in our study do *depend* upon what kind of agent it is, and this *agent-dependency* they have in common with the agent-individuated uniformities (individuals, relations, and whatever).

What has just been said in the case of an agent such as Man holds even more for less sophisticated agents, such as lower creatures or simple robotic devices. An unsophisticated information-processing agent might only be capable of quite rudimentary individuation capacities, but the study of such an agent could require a fairly rich ontology of individuals, relations, locations, and whatever.

For example, in the present-day automobile industry, fitting a car windshield is generally done by means of a robot. This device picks up the windshield from a suitably located supply, orientates it correctly, applies the bonding material to the rim, and fits the windshield into the car as it passes along the conveyor line. In order to perform this task, such a robot does not need to individuate either the car or the windshield.

Typically, it picks up and orientates the windshield by means of an electronic 'eye' that seeks a particular feature of the windshield, say a certain corner or else a specially affixed marker, and simply 'fits' it to a car frame that is 'assumed' to be in the right location. That is to say, the robot is designed to position the correctly orientated and bonded windshield at a certain location, and apply pressure to it at a certain time. The conveyor-line is organized so that the incoming car is always at the correct location at precisely the correct time. If something goes wrong and there is no car on the line, then the robot simply 'fits' the windshield to thin air and lets it fall to the ground.

Clearly, the only thing such a device can be said to *individuate* is that feature of the windshield it is designed to pick out. (Though some might feel that this is a very generous use of the word 'individuate'.) It does not individuate the car at all. Nevertheless, in both the design and the study of this device, we, as theorists and designers, would clearly treat (in particular) both the entire windshield and the car as *bona fide* individuals.

By a *scheme of individuation*, I mean a way of carving up the world into the various 'uniformities' that form the basis of our study: individuals, relations, spatial and temporal locations, and further entities to be introduced in due course.

Such a scheme of individuation will be determined by a particular agent or, more commonly, though the discussion will not consider this case explicitly, a species of agent. In fact, associated with any particular agent (or agent-species) will be not one but two, related schemes of individuation that will be of relevance to us.

First of all, there is what I shall call the *agent scheme*. This carves the world into those uniformities that, from the theorist's standpoint (see presently), the agent either individuates or else at least discriminates. Secondly, there is what I call the *theorist's scheme*, an extension of the agent scheme that provides for a mathematically idealised ontology appropriate for the objective study of the information processing activities of the agent.

For example, it is very often convenient to examine the agent's behavior in terms of idealized, point locations of time and space — indeed, *mathematical* studies do this all the time. In this case, these idealized uniformities are provided by the theorist's scheme. However, no agent is capable of individuating point locations in time or space, nor of behaving in a manner that *discriminates* such entities, so these will not be picked out by the agent scheme.

As should be fairly evident from my nomenclature, practically all of the development will be carried out using the theorist's scheme of individuation and, in general, when I refer to 'the scheme of individuation' without further qualification, it is the theorist's scheme that I mean. But there are occasions when it can be advantageous to consider the two individuation schemes at the same time. For instance, examination of the agent scheme of individuation from the perspective of the theorist's scheme, could lead to explanations of why the agent succeeds or fails at various tasks.

It should be pointed out that my use of the term '*agent* scheme' is not intended to imply that this scheme in any way represents the way the agent *actually* individuates the world. (It is not, therefore, the 'agent's scheme', meaning the scheme used by the agent.) After all, in general, how can we know how a particular agent sees the world? Maybe in the case of agent Man we can, so in this case the 'agent scheme' of our theory might well be the same as the scheme that we actually use as agents in the world. Likewise in the case of a man-made device, where we design and build the various input and processing mechanisms, we might have some insight into the connection between the way the device actually individuates the world (assuming the device is such for this notion to be at all meaningful) and the 'agent scheme' that our theory adopts in order to study that agent. But in all other cases, the agent scheme at best provides *a theorist's ascription* of a scheme to that agent, one that accords with our observations of that agent. It could be that the way the agent actually does individuate the world is quite different from the 'agent scheme' we introduce in order to study that agent. (Thus there is in fact a third individuation scheme floating about: the scheme of individuation that the agent actually uses. But as I have just indicated, in general we have no access to this scheme, and accordingly it will play virtually no part in our development.)

Use of the word 'scheme' in the phrase 'individuation *scheme*' is meant to emphasise the fact that it is not claimed that entities in our ontology are constrained to be within the agent's immediate environment, or accessed by the agent in any way, either perceptually or conceptually. Rather, in speaking of a *scheme of individuation* corresponding to some particular agent, we conceive of an idealized ontology that is not in any way restricted to, say, some particular spatial region or time.

For example, it is part of our own perceptual–cognitive abilities that we individuate stars as individuals. Consequently, our own (i.e. Man's) agent *individuation scheme* admits stars into the ontology (as individuals). This ontology may include a great many stars that never have been, nor ever will be, either seen or otherwise detected by, or even thought about by, any human. Nevertheless, their presence in the ontology, that is to say, their *being* individuals, is a direct consequence of the fact that they are picked out by the *scheme* of individuation that is determined by our very individuation capacities.

A possibly helpful (though not at all literal) illustration of what is meant by the word 'scheme' in the phrase 'individuation scheme' can be obtained by considering the individuation capacities of a particular agent. Picture the agent's individuation mechanism as consisting of a family of *grids* through which the agent can 'view' an otherwise indiscernible world. These grids pick out (or determine) the individuals, relations, locations, etc. that constitute the ontology of our theory (for that agent). Only parts of the world of the appropriate size and form to be picked out by the grid will qualify as entities within the ontology. Passing from the agent's actual individuation capacities to the corresponding individuation *scheme* is then analogous to imagining each of the grids in this family being extended indefinitely in all directions.

Thus, we are very free as to the extent of those entities that an individuation scheme admits into our ontology. Nevertheless, they are, in a very specific sense, agent-relative: for all that they may in fact be well out of the range of perception or conceptualization by any particular agent of the species, what counts as an individual, relation, location, etc. does *depend* on the agent.

To sum up then, associated with a particular agent are two *schemes of individuation*, the *agent scheme* and the *theorist's scheme*. The former provides what we can regard as a theorist's conceptualization of the way the world is carved up by the agent; the latter is an idealized extension of the agent scheme designed to facilitate a smoother mathematical study.

In the case of fairly simple agents, where the agent scheme gives rise to a fairly impoverished ontology, the distinction between the two schemes might seem self-evident. (The study of simple mechanical devices can involve some quite sophisticated theorist's concepts.) In the case where the agent is Man, the distinction can be less clear, but nevertheless is usually present, manifesting itself through such entities as point locations in space and in time, which are picked out by the theorist's scheme but not the agent scheme. In general, our development is carried out using the ontology provided by the theorist's scheme.

Finally, I remark that as theorists trying to understand the behavior of some particular agent, we impose upon the world a particular scheme of individuation that we judge to be appropriate to that agent. But, of course, that very act of imposing a scheme is a cognitive act carried out by certain agents in the world, namely ourselves, and consequently is inescapably dependent upon our own individuation capacities. Thus, whereas our standpoint is, as always in mathematics, that of the priviliged 'observer' (the so-called 'God's eye view'), this is essentially a matter of stance not of fact.

Though this issue is not one that affects the mechanics of our development, I do feel it worthwhile emphasizing the point by quoting the following passage from Searle [24]:[6]

I am not saying that language creates reality. Far from it. Rather I am saying that *what counts as* reality — what counts as a glass of water or a book or a table, what counts as the same glass or a different book or two tables — is a matter of the categories that we impose on the world ... And furthermore, when we experience the world, we experience it *through* [linguistic] categories that help shape the experiences themselves. The world doesn't come to us already sliced up into objects and experiences: what counts as an object is already a function of our system of representation, and how we perceive the world in our experiences is influenced by that system of representation. The mistake is to suppose that the application of language to the world consists of attaching labels to objects that are, so to speak, self identifying. On my view, the world divides the way we divide it ... Our concept of reality is a matter of our [linguistic] categories.

---

[6] In this particular passage, Searle is concerned with language and the linguistic categories language imposes on the world. Though the point I am making here is in fact the same one, the present discussion is not explicitly linguistic, and consequently I have used omission and bracketing to emphasise the main issue.

2.4   Situations

So far,my basic ontology for the study of information and cognition has a fairly traditional look to it: individuals, relations, spatial and temporal locations. One thing that is novel about this particular approach, and what is characteristic of 'situation theory', is the inclusion in the ontology of what are called *situations*.

In *situation* theory, we take note of the fact that an agent's world divides up into a collection, or succession, of situations: situations encountered, situations referred to, situations about which information is received, and so on. That is to say, our theory reflects the fact that agents discriminate (by their behavior) situations.

Thus, the behavior of people varies systematically according to the kind of situation they are faced with: threatening situations, spooky situations, pleasant situations, challenging situations, conversations, and what-have-you, all evoke quite different responses. And likewise at the other end of the cognitive spectrum, the behavior of mechanical devices can depend quite dramatically on the situation in which the device is located: a computer will generally function quite differently in my office than it will when placed in a tub of water, and a moon buggy that moves smoothly on the surface of the Moon may not move at all when placed on Earth.

In order to take account of this 'situation-dependency' of various agents, the agent's scheme of individuation is taken to provide us with a collection of *situations*, highly structured (in general) parts of the world that the agent's behavior discriminates.

Exactly what does and what does not constitute a situation is largely a matter of what agent is under discussion — as with everything else in our ontology so far, as products of the theorist's individuation scheme, situations are agent-relative. It may or may not be the case that the agent itself can *individuate* situations (i.e. regard and treat them as single, identifiable entities). Simple agents probably do not individuate any situations, though, if they are to be the kind of agent of interest to us here, their behavior does discriminate them. In the case of sophisticated agents such as Man, it seems that we do often *individuate* situations. For example, when we attend or talk about a football game, or when we refer to, say, "the situation in the Middle East." But in many cases our behavior simply discriminates situations, without there being any act of *individuation* going on. For example, we rarely think of the climatic region we are in as a single entity, that is as a situation, but our behavior changes when we travel from Florida to Alaska in January.

Regardless of their status regarding individuation by agents, within our theory situations are regarded as first-class members of the ontology, alongside the individuals, relations, locations, and all the rest of the ontology to be introduced later, and is really this move that distinguishes situation theory from other theories that take account of context or other environmental effects. In particular, situations are allowed to fill (appropriate) argument roles of relations, and thus to appear as constituents of infons. (This amounts to the first of the succession of modifications to the notion of an infon, mentioned earlier.)

Notice however, that, even in the case of agent-individuated situations, their status alongside individuals does not mean that situations are at all the same as individuals. An important feature of situations that our theory reflects, is that the structure of a situation is significant to the agent, in a way that the internal structure of an individual is not.

On the other hand, it may be that an agent can individuate the same entity both as an individual and a situation. For example, a steel ball (an 'individual' if ever there was one), when examined through a microscope, is individuated as a situation. And again, I generally regard my computer as an individual, but to the computer engineer who repairs it, it can be regarded both as an individual and as a situation.

The status of situations in our theory is, then, clear cut. They are first-class citizens alongside the rest of the theorist's ontology. But in what sense does an agent *individuate* a situation (when it does)? Not, in general, as an individual. Rather, the agent individuates a situation *as a situation*, that is to say, as a structured part of Reality that it (the agent) somehow manages to pick out. There are a number of ways an agent can 'pick out' (that is, individuate) a situation. Two obvious examples are direct perception of a situation, perhaps the immediate environment, or thinking about a particular situation, say last night's dinner party.

In any event, it should be pointed out that the individuation of a situation by an agent does not necessarily entail the agent being able to provide an *exact* description of everything that is and is not going on in that situation.

For example, suppose John and David are having a conversation about a particular football game, say one they have both seen. Then they are both referring to a very definite *situation* — namely that particular game. This is a situation that they both individuate (as a *situation*, not as an individual). A long, informative, and confusion-free discussion can take place. And yet neither John nor David would be able to list every single event that formed a part of that game, or every item of information that related to it in some essential way. Indeed, it is highly likely that what makes their conversation about the game of interest to both parties is the fact that each one acquires from the other *new* items of information about the game, information that the one picked up but the other did not. The fact that each person left the game with some information that the other did not, does not mean that their subsequent conversation is about two different games. The situation is the same for both individuals, a highly structured part of the world, having a fixed duration in time. What differs is what each knows about that situation.

People who have met the notion of a situation for the first time are often very reluctant to accept situations as genuine *objects*, things to be studied alongside individuals, relations, locations, and so forth. I believe such unease stems in part from the novelty of the notion, but to a larger extent has to do with our inability to reduce situations to a composite of other, more familiar objects. But it seems to me that if a proper study is to be made of information flow, and in particular communication, then situations cannot be avoided. After all, if you were to interrupt John and David in the middle of their conversation and ask them *what* they were talking about, they would reply "Last night's football game." Are we then to conclude that they were in fact talking about nothing; or that neither was really sure *what* it was they were discussing? Clearly not. But this example is not an unusual one; rather this is typical of many instances of human–human linguistic communication. The ability to *individuate* a 'situation' is a fundamental one that humans, and possibly only humans, come equipped with, as part of the behavior-guiding apparatus that enables them to function in a large and complex society.

What is new and distinctive about situation theory is that it takes the bull by the horns and tackles this issue head-on, by admitting situations into the ontology from the very start, alongside the more familiar (to scientists) entities such as individuals, relations, locations, and the like. For John and David, it may well be that the *only* way to specify the situation under discussion is as 'last night's football game'. The development of situation theory has to proceed under the realization that techniques that are useful in dealing with individuals, locations, and so on, may well not be appropriate for situations. Situations are, for the theorist, a quite new kind of entity, that will probably require quite new techniques to handle.

As mentioned earlier, since situations are members of the ontology just like anything else, situations may be constituents of infons. For an example of an infon that involves a situation as an argument of a relation, I suggest

$$\ll \text{sees, David, } s, l, t, 1 \gg$$

where s is the football match referred to a moment ago, l is the location of David and the match, and t is the time interval during which David sees s.

Let s be a situation. Given an infon σ, we shall need to consider the fact that σ is 'made true by' s, which I shall write

$$s \models \sigma$$

Another way to express this is to say that σ is an item of information that is true of s. The official terminology is that s *supports* σ.

Note that this notion is fundamental in the sense that, given an infon, σ, it is a fact of the world that the relation $s \models \sigma$ either holds or does not hold.

If I is a set of infons and s is a situation, I write

$$s \models I$$

if $s \models \sigma$ for every infon σ in I.

I assume that among the situations available to our study is a unique, maximal situation, *the world*, of which every other situation is a part. It may or may not be the case that the species of agent under consideration can individuate this situation. In the case of Man, it seems to me that we can individuate such a totality. But in any event, from the theorist's point of view it is extremely convenient to have this situation as part of our ontology. I generally denote this 'world' situation by w.

Our previous definition of a *fact* can now be reformulated as an infon, σ, such that

$$w \models \sigma$$

2.5 Abstract situations

In certain contexts, notably the construction of mathematical models of situation theory, it is convenient to have available abstract analogs of real situations, set-theoretic entities that have some of the features of real situations, but which are more amenable to standard mathematical manipulations than are the intrinsically 'fuzzy' real situations. One such analog is provided by what we shall call *abstract situations*.

Formally, I make the definition

an abstract situation *consists of a set of infons.*

And in order to emphasize the distinction (whenever such emphasis is required) let us agree to use the term *real situation* for the kind of 'in-the-world' situation picked out by the individuation scheme, as considered hitherto.

Thus *real* situations are the 'parts of the world', picked out by some individuation scheme; *abstract* situations are mathematical constructs built out of the relations, individuals, and locations of our ontology.

There is an intuitive sense in which, to every real situation s, there corresponds a particular abstract situation, namely the set

$$\{\sigma \mid s \models \sigma\}$$

but, as I indicated in our discussion of the football match situation in the previous section, the present framework does not in general enable us to provide a useful alternative description of this set.

What is the case is that the definition of an abstract situation gives us a great deal of freedom to construct 'situations' of sufficient simplicity and precision to facilitate extensive mathematical modeling. For this reason, a great deal of the technical, mathematical modeling work in situation theory is carried out in terms of abstract situations. The following brief discussion provides some examples of abstract situations.

Situations (either real or abstract) may be *static*, involving either just one spatial location or a number of contemporary spatial locations, or they may be *dynamic*, possibly spread over a time-sequence of locations.

An example of an abstract situation involving just a single location would be:

$$s = \{\ll \text{lecturing, Jon, } l, t, 1 \gg, \ll \text{listening-to, Carol, Jon, } l, t, 0 \gg\}$$

Obviously, s may be part of a great many larger abstract situations; for example:

$$s' = s \cup \{\ll \text{barking, Max, } l', t', 1 \gg\}$$

where as usual $\cup$ denotes set-theoretic union. If the locations l, t and l', t' are totally unconnected, then this abstract situation may only qualify as such in a purely formal way, having little to do with the real world. But if there is a locational overlap (both spatially and temporally), then the dog's barking may, of course, explain Carol's lack of attention to the lecture.

For an example of an abstract situation involving a time-sequence, how about the moralistic novelette:

$$s' = s \cup \{\ll \text{fails, Carol, the exam, } t', 1 \gg\}$$

where t' is a temporal location subsequent to t. A better way of denoting the situation s' would be:

$$s' = \{\ll \text{lecturing, Jon, } l, t, 1 \gg\} \cup$$
$$\{\ll \text{listening-to, Carol, Jon, } l, t, 0 \gg\} \cup$$
$$\{\ll \text{fails, Carol, the exam, } t', 1 \gg\}$$

(where $t < t'$).

Notice that, in the case of an abstract situation, the supports relation reduces to simple set-theoretic membership:

$$s \models \sigma \quad \text{if and only if} \quad \sigma \in s$$

for any abstract situation, s, and any infon, σ.

However, even on those occasions when we are engaged in mathematical modeling, and are thus working with abstract situations, a great many of the examples will be of a 'real life' variety, where situations are referred to using everyday language, such as 'conversation', 'utterance', 'football game', etc. In such cases, as has been noted already, there is usually no means available to provide any specification of the set of infons that constitutes the abstract situation other than that everyday description. Consequently, I always use the $\models$ notation in preference to the set-membership symbol $\in$.

To sum up, I have distinguished between *real* and *abstract* situations. A *real situation* is a part of reality, individuated as a single entity according to some scheme of individuation. An *abstract situation* is a set-theoretic construct, a set of infons, built up out of entities called *relations, individuals, locations*, and *polarities*.

It should be emphasized that I do not assume a one-to-one correspondence exists between the real situations given by a scheme of individuation and the set-theoretic constructs we call abstract situations. Given a real situation, s, the set

$$\{\sigma \mid s \models \sigma\}$$

is a corresponding abstract situation. But, going in the other direction, not all abstract situations have *any* real counterpart. Because of the freedom we have (by default) allowed ourselves in constructing abstract situations as sets of infons, there may be abstract situations for which there is no corresponding real situation. For instance, there can be *incoherent* abstract situations involving contradictory facts, such as

$$s \models \{\ll R, a_1, \ldots, a_n, 1 \gg, \ll R, a_1, \ldots, a_n, 0 \gg\}$$

Not surprisingly, there are many occasions when we wish to exclude such incoherent situations from our discussion, and accordingly I make the following definition.

An abstract situation s is said to be *coherent* if it satisfies the following three conditions:

(i)   for no $R, a_1, \ldots, a_n$ is it the case that

$$s \models \ll R, a_1, \ldots, a_n, 1 \gg$$
$$s \models \ll R, a_1, \ldots, a_n, 0 \gg$$

(ii)   if for some a, b it is the case that

$$s \models \ll \text{same}, a, b, 1 \gg$$

then $a = b$

(iii)   for no a is it the case that

$$s \models \ll \text{same}, a, a, 0 \gg$$

This definition assumes a two-place relation *same* that is location independent. Conditions (ii) and (iii) imply that this relation corresponds to genuine equality.

Notice that the above definition was only made with regard to abstract situations, such a concept being unnecessary in the case of real situations, all of which are 'coherent' by virtue of the way things are.

Notice also that I am not proposing that incoherent, abstract situations be banned from consideration. Indeed, they can play a significant role in analyzing how inconsistencies may arise in the everyday use of language.

Two abstract situations s and s' are said to be *compatible* if their union is a coherent situation. Again this definition is only significant with regards to abstract situations, since any two real situations will be 'compatible'.

Of course, simply being coherent does not on its own guarantee that an abstract situation will correspond to some real situation. The abstract situation might just get some piece of information (*infon*) wrong, perhaps classifying Bob as being married to Alice when in fact he is married to Carol. I call an abstract situation s *actual* if:

(i)   whenever

$$s \models \ll R, a_1, \ldots, a_n, 1 \gg$$

then in the real world it really is the case that $a_1, \ldots, a_n$ stand in the relation R, and

(ii)   whenever

$$s \models \ll R, a_1, \ldots, a_n, 0 \gg$$

then $a_1, \ldots, a_n$ really do not stand in the relation R.

Clearly, any actual abstract situation is coherent.

2.6   The nature of infons

So far our theory has involved two new kinds of objects: (real) situations and infons. The nature of situations has already been discussed: they are structured parts of reality that the agent discriminates, or possibly even individuates. But what of infons?

The name suggests a parallel with the fundamental particles of physics, the electrons, protons, neutrons, photons, (gravitons?), and so forth. This was a deliberate choice on my part, designed to emphasise the importance I attach to approaching the study of information as an empirical science.

But this is not to say that I regard infons as having some form of physical existence (whatever you take that to mean). Nor that my intention is to study information flow as the motion of particles of information along some kind of 'information field'. Rather I am following a long established trend in mathematics, of introducing a collection of abstract objects with which to reason. Mathematicians work with many kinds of abstract object: natural numbers, rational numbers, real numbers, imaginary numbers, groups, rings, fields, topological spaces, metric spaces, Banach spaces, geometric spaces, and so on. None of these have any form of physical existence, but all play crucial roles within mathematics.

The present aim is to develop a mathematical theory of information. Mathematics deals with mathematical *objects*. A definite ontology is essential to the thinking process of most, if not all, mathematicians. The objects they deal with have to have an 'existence' within the mathematical realm. This may or may not be the same kind of existence ascribed to the particles of physics — that is besides the point. What matters is that, in order to develop a mathematical theory of information, it is necessary (from a practical viewpoint) to have available some definite 'informational object'.

From a mathematical point of view, such an object will have the same form of 'existence' as any other mathematical object, such as a natural number, a real number, an imaginary number, or a topological space.

Which is not to say that one can simply say "Let there be infons" and proceed to develop a theory. They have to fulfill the role we have in mind. Just as the physicist's particles have to accord with observation of the physical world and the number systems of mathematics have to accord with their intended uses in the world, so too our 'infons' have to fit in with our picture of the way information flows in the cognitive world.

This then is the way I think of infons: artifacts of a theory that enable us to proceed. It is not a question of whether infons 'physically exist'. The aim in choosing the name 'infons' is to emphasise by analogy with physics the fundamental role these abstract objects play in our theory as *items* of information.

Now, it is possible to dispute the *existence* of the particles of physics. Do they 'exist' (as particles) except as an artifact of one of our theories of the world? The question is a deep one with many ramifications, not the least being what do we mean by 'exist' anyway? But such questions do not really affect the way physicists go about their work (at least not at the present time). Thinking of matter in terms of particles provides a useful framework in which to operate, that seems to be consistent with our observations, so why not? Hitherto this approach has proved extremely fruitful, so it makes sense to continue in this manner until evidence arises to the contrary. (Of course, evidence did arise to contradict the original picture whereby the electrons and protons are 'fundamental particles', but this did not lead to an abandonment of the particle approach. Rather the fundamental particles simply got smaller, with the electrons, protons, etc. regarded as composites of other particles.)

Having decided on an approach to a theory of information that takes information in the form of 'items' of information, how do we go about providing the appropriate concept of an 'infon'?

Well, the ontology introduced so far reflects the manner in which the agent *classifies* the world, either by cognitive individuation or by behavioral discrimination. In particular, its behavior may be affected by whether or not certain objects $a_1, \ldots, a_n$ stand in the relation P (which may have more than n argument places). Thus a fundamental form of *information* of relevance to that agent is information of the form

$$objects\ a_1, \ldots, a_n\ have/do\ not\ have\ property\ P,$$

what I have referred to as *conceptual information*. This is the form of information considered in our study. It accords with Dretske's theory of information and cognition [8], outlined in Section 2.2.

The next step is to introduce appropriate mathematical objects to represent (or, if you prefer, *be*) such items of conceptual information. This is analogous to, say, the introduction of the real numbers to enable numbers such as 2 to have a square root, or of the imaginary numbers to provide mathematical objects that are the square roots of negative numbers.

In order to carry out this step, we must first ask ourselves what phenomenon in the world the proposed objects are intended to correpond to or represent.

The first thing to observe is that information is 'carried' or 'arises from' a representation (by way of certain constraints). Without some form of representation, there can be no information. But just because the information cannot 'exist' without the representation, it does not follow that the representation is all there is — that the information is somehow *contained in*, or *part of* the representation. The information arises by virtue of what I am calling the *constraints*, and they are separate from the representation that carries the information.

The representation has some form of physical realization — an ink pattern on paper, an electro-chemical configuration in the brain, an optical or magnetic pattern on a disk, a sound wave in the air, a sequence of electrical pulses in a wire, or more generally any configuration of objects in the world.

The representation can thus be *measured*, either in actuality or in principle, by physical means. But what about the *information*? Well, there is no fixed amount of 'the information' that is represented by any particular configuration of objects. Relative to different constraints, the same configuration can encode quite different information, so the 'amount' of information that can be represented by a particular configuration is, in principle, infinite. (It is certainly unbounded.)

But what if we fix some particular constraint? Well, then it makes sense to talk about *the* information represented by a configuration. But notice that the information is *not* the representation, it is something that results from the combination of the representation *and the constraint*.

How then does a mathematical theory deal with this kind of situation? Well, one possible approach would be to take the information content of a representation, R, relative to a constraint, C, to be (modeled by) the ordered pair $\langle R, C \rangle$. But this is not what we want, since different representations can give rise (via different constraints) to the same information. That is, we can have distinct R, R' and distinct C, C' such that $\langle R, C \rangle$ and $\langle R', C' \rangle$ denote the same item of information.

For example, relative to two linguistic constraints, one pertaining to the English language and the other to German, utterances of the two sentences

It is cold

Es ist kalt

both represent the same item of information, namely that it is cold. So too does frost on a windowpane or the sight of snow on the ground (relative to the appropriate constraints).

Now, to the mathematician, this kind of situation is not at all uncommon. Indeed, it arises all the time. The pseudo-identity

$$\langle R, C \rangle \approx \langle R', C' \rangle$$

that means $\langle R, C \rangle$ and $\langle R', C' \rangle$ denote the same item of information, is an instance of what is known as an *equivalence relation*.

An equivalence relation is a two-place relation, E say, defined on some set, A, of objects, that satisfies the three properties:

(i) E relates everything in A to itself, i.e. aEa for all a in A ;

(ii)   if E relates a to b, then E relates b to a, i.e. aEb implies bEa for all a, b in A ;

(iii) E is *transitive*, i.e. if aEb and bEc, then aEc .

One obvious example of an equivalence relation is equality ($=$). Intuitively, an equivalence relation can be thought of as a sort of 'pseudo-identity', a 'loose' equality, a kind of 'roughly equal' (in some sense).

Now, there is a standard operation you can perform on an equivalence relation, known as 'factoring out', and the result of factoring out is that the original collection of objects is partitioned into distinct subcollections known as 'equivalence classes'. In a moment, I shall give an example that should help clarify these notions, but first let me indicate what all of this has to do with infons.

By factoring out the equivalence relation $\approx$, the pseudo-identity between pairs of the form $\langle R, C \rangle$ can be reduced to a genuine identity between the *equivalence classes* of such pairs. These equivalence classes are what I propose to call *infons*.

But does this not mean that, far from being the *basic items of information* I initially claimed them to be, the infons are in fact rather complex objects that incorporate both representations and constraints? The answer is "No." In order to explain why, and to provide a more detailed explanation of infons, I shall consider, in brief detail, some analogous situations in classical mathematics.

2.7   Number systems

The natural number system is our first encounter (as small children) with the world of mathematics (as it is usually thought of). More precisely, the natural numbers (i.e. the positive, whole numbers, 1, 2, 3, ...) constitute the first instance of a mathematical abstraction. At a fairly early stage in our development, we make the leap to accepting 'numbers' as some kind of entity. This despite the fact that we can neither see nor feel a single number. Numbers are somehow 'there'. They form a significant and influential part in the life of human beings.

But what *are* the whole numbers? One answer is that they are *intentional objects*, entities that arise by being individuated by the intentional minds of people — constructs of the human intellect. Irrespective of philosophical questions as to what exactly this form of 'existence' amounts to, it certainly accords with our everyday experience. Simple observation indicates that the notion of number is common to practically every adult member of the species, and that everyone's concept of, say, 'the number two' or 'the number ten' is, to all practical purposes, the same.

The mathematician looks for a different answer, one that provides numbers with an *objective* status within the rigorous framework of mathematics. There are several ways to do this, the most common being along the following lines, which assumes a set-theoretic foundation for mathematics.

Two sets of objects, A and B, are said to be *equipollent* if there is a bijection $f : A \leftrightarrow B$ that puts the members of A into a one-to-one correspondence with the members of B. If we write

$$A \equiv B$$

to denote that A and B are equipollent, then the relation $\equiv$ between sets is an *equivalence relation*.[7] For any set, A, the collection

$$[A] = \{B \mid B \equiv A\}$$

is called the *equivalence class* of A. Using the properties of an equivalence relation, it is a routine exercise to show that:

(i) no two distinct equivalence classes have a common element;

(ii) $A \equiv B$ if and only if A and B are members of the same equivalence class;

(iii) $[A] = [B]$ if and only if $A \equiv B$.

The natural numbers are then *defined to be* the equivalence classes of sets under the equivalence relation of equipollence. Thus, for example, the *number* 3 is defined to be the class of all sets having three elements. This way of putting it is a bit misleading, since we refer to 'three' in

---

[7] That is, it satisfies the three requirements: (i) $A \equiv A$ for all sets A, (ii) if $A \equiv B$ then $B \equiv A$ for all sets A, B, and (iii) if $A \equiv B$ and $B \equiv C$ then $A \equiv C$, for all sets A, B, C.

the definition of the number 3 itself. The complete story takes a bit longer to tell. In essence, what is done is to define (in a natural way) a total ordering on the set of equivalence classes, and operations of 'addition' and 'multiplication' on pairs of equivalence classes, so that the resulting system has all the properties we usually associate with the natural numbers.

Thus the mathematician's *definition* (or *construction*) of the natural numbers is somewhat sophisticated. But this clearly does not mean that a small child has to master the basics of set theory and equivalence relations in order to learn how to count and perform elementary arithmetic. The natural numbers and their arithmetic arise in a very natural way by abstraction from our everyday experience. As 'uniformities' individuated by the human mind, the natural numbers are pretty basic as abstract entities go. It is just that some effort is required in order to construct a *mathematical model* of these numbers.

The last paragraph might seem to be laboring the obvious, but it is easy (and not uncommon) to confuse abstract entities and their mathematical models. Mathematics texts often include definitions such as "A relation is a set of ordered pairs," or "A function is a set or ordered pairs such that any first element is paired with just one second element." The mistake in both cases is that word 'is'. A relation, surely, is just what the word means to practically every living English speaker, and likewise for a function. That both may be *modeled* by sets of ordered pairs is not in dispute (at least by me). Indeed, in a treatise on set theory one might even provide formal *definitions* of relations and functions as sets of ordered pairs. But this does not usurp the fundamental nature of the two concepts of relation and function within the realm of human mental activity. So too with natural numbers. They arise in a quite natural way as intentional objects in the human domain. That mathematics is able to provide a set-theoretic *model* of such entities is a reflection of the power of mathematics. What structural complexity arises in this modeling process is a feature of the model, not the thing being modeled.

The system of rational numbers (i.e. numbers formed by the division of one whole number by another) may be constructed (modeled?) in a fashion very similar to the natural numbers. Given the natural number system, one 'defines' a rational number as follows. Two ordered pairs, $\langle m, n \rangle$ and $\langle p, q \rangle$, of whole numbers are said to be *equivalent* if and only if $mq = pn$. This gives an equivalence relation on the set of all ordered pairs of numbers. The equivalence classes are taken to be the 'rational numbers'. It is easily seen that the members of any given equivalence class are precisely the pairs $\langle m, n \rangle$ such that the 'quotient' m/n is a representation of that particular rational number.

As in the case of the natural numbers, the full story involves a definition of a total ordering on the equivalence classes and of operations of 'addition' and 'multiplication' on pairs of equivalence classes, so that the resulting system has all the properties we associate with the rational-numbers-*qua*-intentional-objects.

But once again, it should be noted that there are two quite distinct things going on here. Rational numbers are abstract objects in the human intentional realm, with both geometric and quantitive-proportional aspects. Thus their 'existence' does not require any fancy set-theoretic construction. It happens that there is an elegant way to *model* rational numbers within set theory, and that construction can add great weight to the confidence we have with regards to our understanding of the deeper properties of rational numbers. But again the model is not the same as that which is being modeled.

The situation is also similar with regards to the real number system.[8] But notice that the real numbers represent a further step into the abstract. The natural and rational numbers arise in a natural way as part of the process of individuating the world (by humans).[9] The real numbers, on the other hand, result from purely mathematical considerations of *continuity*, whereby one 'fills in' the infinitely small 'holes' in the rational number line, a process known as *completion*. However, for all their high level of abstraction, the real numbers seem sufficiently intuitive for most high school science students to feel perfectly familiar with them.

There are two popular ways to construct (or model) the real numbers within set theory. One takes the real numbers to be equivalence classes of certain pairs of infinite sets of rational numbers, known as 'Dedekind cuts'. The other takes the real numbers to be equivalence classses of certain infinite sequences of rational numbers, called 'Cauchy sequences'. The thing to notice here is that there are *two* distinct constructions. Different textbooks give different 'definitions' of real numbers. Sometimes a textbook will give *both* definitions. So which one is the 'right one'? Are

---

[8] *Real numbers* are all numbers that can be represented by means of an *infinite* decimal expansion. Besides the rational numbers, this also allows for numbers such as $\sqrt{2}$ and the mathematical constants π and e, none of which can be expressed as a quotient of two whole numbers.

[9] Actually, this may be only true with regards to relatively small numbers, but the step to the potential infinity of the two systems seems to be one that causes few people any difficulty these days.

the real numbers equivalence classes of pairs of sets of rational numbers or equivalence classes of infinite sequences of rational numbers? The answer should be obvious by now. (Though it is not at all obvious from reading most of the textbooks!) The real numbers are the real numbers, abstract objects created by the human mind. Their existence is useful and their properties worth detailed investigation because they are a part of the *common* domain of abstract objects in the world of Man, rather than just the arbitrary creations of a single mind. These abstract objects can be modeled mathematically in at least two distinct ways. Neither approach gives rise to 'a genuine real number', though in mathematical investigations it is often useful to adopt one of these constructions as a 'formal definition' of real numbers.

The complex numbers[10] are even further into the realm of the abstract, in that for most people they have no 'existence' outside of mathematics. Indeed, the very terminology reflects this fact. The real numbers are *'real'* numbers, whereas the complex numbers are a combination of real and *imaginary* numbers, numbers that involve the square root of minus 1. The standard mathematical construction (model) of the complex numbers is as ordered pairs of real numbers, and is mathematically the simplest of the various number-system constructions. But for all the simplicity of the mathematics, the step from the real number system to the complex numbers is the one that causes most people the greatest qualms. "The complex numbers are not 'real' (i.e. genuine) *numbers*," is the response of most students. This is not because of the difficulty or sophistication of the mathematics required to model these two number systems. Indeed, the real numbers are hard to model whereas the complex numbers can be modeled using quite trivial mathematics. Rather it is because the step from the real numbers to the complex numbers is a genuine step from the world of abstract objects common to a large section of mankind, to the world of abstract objects common only to the trained scientist.[11]

One final remark. Though I did not make explicit mention of the fact, throughout the above discussion I was really thinking primarily of *positive* numbers. The step from the positive whole numbers (the natural

---

[10] The *complex numbers* are numbers of the form $a + b\sqrt{-1}$, where a and b are real numbers. Numbers that are of the form $b\sqrt{-1}$ are known as *imaginary numbers*, since the square root of minus 1 only 'exists' in 'the imagination', or so at least was the derivation of this terminology.

[11] Mathematicians feel as much at home with complex numbers as they do with real numbers.

numbers) to all whole numbers (the integers) and from the positive rational numbers to all rational numbers involves nothing more than a simple wrinkle in the modeling process. It causes the mathematician hardly a pause for breath during the construction.

Negative numbers were, however, ontologically problematical, even to mathematicians of world class. Though European mathematicians of the Renaissance period were content to follow the Greek tradition of allowing minus signs in their arithmetic, they did not recognize 'negative numbers' as such, and referred to negative 'solutions' of equations as 'fictitious roots'. In the seventeenth century, René Descartes spoke of negative roots as 'false roots' and Blaise Pascal also thought there was no such thing as a negative *number*. Indeed, it was only during the eighteenth century, with the increasing emphasis on the axiomatic approach to mathematics, that a general acceptance grew, that there were such entities as 'negative numbers'.

So with negative numbers we have a clear example of the mathematical concept *preceding* the inclusion of that object in the world of human abstract objects. At which point it is time to turn our attention back to infons.

2.8 So what exactly are infons?

I start from the premise that agents carve up the world in a certain way, both by cognitively individuating various uniformities and by behaviorally discriminating various uniformities. These uniformities include, in particular, individuals, relations, and spatial and temporal locations.

Information flow is made possible by a network of abstract linkages (called constraints) between higher-order uniformities known as *types*. Thus, for example, if you see smoke you can conclude that there is (some kind of) fire, since there is a constraint that provides a systematic link between situations where there is smoke and situations where there is fire. This constraint is not particular to one instance where there is smoke and fire, but obtains in general: *whenever* there is smoke there is fire. The constraint links not the actual situations but *types* of situations, smokey-type situations to firey-type ones.

Since I have spent time discussing number systems, it is perhaps instructive to mention at this juncture, the similarity between types and natural numbers. *'Having three elements'* (say) is a uniformity across sets of objects, a uniformity that humans learn to individuate at a fairly early age. Sets can be 'typed' or classified according to whether or not they have three members. All sets with three members have something in common, the uniformity of 'threeness'. Once this uniformity has been recognized, the next step (at least for people) is to formulate the abstract concept of 'the number three'. An abstract object is 'created' that *is* the thing all sets with three members have in common. Types are essentially the same in nature, only more general in scope. Indeed, having three elements is a particular instance of a type for sets. Regarding a type as an *object* is analogous to regarding a number as an object.

The constraints that link types are themselves uniformities, regularities in the world that an agent can either cognitively individuate or else behaviorally discriminate. They are clearly of an order of abstraction one higher than the types that they link, and whereas the types are probably accepted as genuine abstract *objects* by those people who pause to think about the matter, the constraints seem to be very definitely objects within the domain of the cognitive scientist, a situation analogous to the difference between real and complex numbers, both of which are regarded on equal terms by the mathematician but only the former of which are accepted as genuine 'numbers' by the man-in-the-street.

The infons come into the picture not because agents necessarily individuate them, rather as artifacts of our theory, a situation having *some* parallel to the introduction of elementary particles in physics. The types and the constraints that link them seem to be part and parcel of the everyday life of cognitive agents, who make their way in the world by picking up and acting in accordance with various information. The world does not operate randomly from one moment to the next (at least not on the scale of interest to us here), but rather exhibits a great deal of regularity, a regularity that the agent becomes attuned to and possibly even aware of. Above the abstraction levels of individual objects, locations, and relations, are types and a network of constraints that connect them. All of this is surely 'there'. As theorists we are not 'inventing' these entities. Rather the only move we are making is to accord these entities an objective status.

But the infons are purely an artifact of the theory. A mathematical theory of information needs some specific notion of an 'informational object' or an 'item of information' to work with. It may or may not be the case that cognitive agents actually function by handling 'information' in an 'infonic' form, though it is an underlying thesis of this work that the concept of an 'item of information' does seem to be an intuitive one. Information arises by virtue of a representation and a constraint. Simple observation indicates that different constraints enable the same world configuration to represent different pieces of information, and that different configurations can, via different constraints, represent the same piece of information. To handle such diversity, we introduce a theory-absolute (i.e. representation-independent) notion of 'item of information', namely the infons. We do this in a manner analogous to the introduction of the various (models of) number systems in classical mathematics.

That is, an infon is defined to be an equivalence class of a pair $\langle R, C \rangle$ of a configuration, R, and a constraint, C. This assumes an agent-discriminated (and theorist-individuated) notion of equivalence that two pairs $\langle R, C \rangle$, $\langle R', C' \rangle$ 'give rise to the same item of information'. We do not attempt (here) to reduce this equivalence relation to anything more 'basic', any more than we try to define the other uniformities in our theory. We simply take it as one of the starting points for any theory of information that there is *something* that can arise from a combination of a configuration and a constraint that is not necessarily unique to that particular pair. We objectify that 'something' as an infon.

This process is no more circular than any of the number system constructions described earlier, and indeed the analogies are good ones. Just as the irrational numbers fill in the 'infinitesimal holes' in the rational number system that we 'observe' to be there, and the introduction of the imaginary numbers, $a\sqrt{-1}$, provides us with a system of numbers having more expressive power than the real numbers, so too the infons provide the object that results from the combined effect of a representation and a constraint.

And just as the mathematician, having completed the complicated construction of, say, the real numbers, promptly turns matters on their head by henceforth regarding the real numbers as 'point-like, atomic objects', rather than the complex mathematical structures she has just defined, so too our theory regards infons as entirely basic objects — indeed as one of the starting points of our theory of information.

Thus, for instance, in the development in the following chapter, the various types and constraints are defined *using* infons, exactly the opposite of the above process of derivation. Given that our theory is striving for a mathematical development using ideas of, in particular, set theory, this approach is unavoidable. In set theory, a relation is an extensional entity that has to have a domain of objects upon which to operate: it is a relation between objects, indeed it is generally taken to be a set of ordered tuples of objects. So the objects ontologically precede the relation.

But the relations that agents individuate and discriminate are essentially *intensional*, and can be regarded as themselves *leading to* the 'objects' they relate. Thus the types and constraints arise (i.e. exist as abstract objects) by virtue of the agent's cognitive behavior, as does a certain equivalence relation that we find helpful to describe as 'giving the same item of information', and this leads to the (mathematical) objectification of a new realm of theorist's abstract objects that we call 'infons'.

That is the sense in which I regard infons as 'existing'. Thus infons are semantic objects within the framework of our theory. That is, their status is the same as, say, the real numbers within mathematics. This gives them an 'absolute' nature, independent of representation. (Though this absoluteness is relative to an original ontology of individuals, locations, relations, and what have you, that is essentially dependent on the agent or species of agent under consideration.) Their status as abstract objects within our theory does not preclude their corresponding to abstractions recognized by agents in the world. Indeed, I feel that there is a strong intuition of an 'item of information' that corresponds fairly closely with the notion of an infon. But the present theory does not require any commitment to such a view. Indeed, given the vagueness inherent in our current usage of the word 'information', it seems unlikely that *any* formal definition could meet all demands.

Note that their status as 'abstract objects' does not mean that infons have any kind of physical existence. Being an intentional, abstract object is not the same as being a part of the physical world. Numbers are abstract objects in the world, be they positive or negative, whole, rational, real, or complex. The *number three* is a particular abstract object in the world. It does not depend upon representation. (The words 'three', 'drei', and 'trois' all represent the same entity, relative to various constraints.) Infons are, I maintain, entirely similar in this respect.[12] As abstract objects, infons may be regarded as being as much a part of our world as numbers. True enough they are a highly abstract part of the world. But then so too is the very notion of information in the first place.

---

[12] The analogy is perhaps better when made to real and complex numbers, rather than the natural or rational numbers.

3

Situation Theory

3.1   Situations and situation-types

Our aim is to use the situational perspective on the world (outlined in the previous chapter) to study the flow of information. In order to do this we need to be able to classify situations, to pick out features that situations may or may not have in common. That is to say, we need to extend our ontology to include certain 'higher-order' uniformities that cut across situations. I call these higher-order uniformities *types* of situations (or *situation-types*).

As members of our ontology, situation-types will be provided (indirectly) by our scheme of individuation, and thus will be agent-relative. It will be inherent in the nature of situation-types (and in particular their role in information flow) that agents discriminate such uniformities. In the case of the agent Man, it is arguable that we do in fact individuate certain *types*, albeit in a less concrete fashion than we individuate individuals or situations.

Roughly the idea is this. Suppose there are two situations, s_0 and s_1, such that

$$s_0 \models \,\ll \text{running, Jon, Palo Alto, 1.1.88, 1} \gg$$

$$s_1 \models \,\ll \text{running, Fred, Menlo Park, 3.7.88, 1} \gg$$

Clearly there is a great deal of difference between these two situations: they involve different people, at different locations and different times. Moreover, both s_0 and s_1 may each involve a great many other activities (not mentioned above) that also serve to distinguish them. But there is obviously something that is common to both these situations, a feature they both share: in each situation, some person is running. It is this common feature that we referred to above as a 'higher-order uniformity'. In order to carry through our intended study of information flow, our theory has to provide some mathematical representation of such a uniformity.

That representation is what I shall call a *situation-type*. In the case of
the situations s_0 and s_1 above, what they both share is the situation-type
of those situations in which some person is running. This particular
type (when it has been defined within our theory) will be common to all
situations in which there is a person running.

An obvious analogy to this is the concept of *number* (more precisely,
positive whole number). The number 7 (say) is that abstract entity that is
common to all sets of seven objects. By saying that a particular set has
seven members, one is presenting one feature that this set has in common
with any other set of seven objects. And just as a careful development
turns this apparently circular proposition into a genuine definition of
(natural) number, so too the concept of a situation-type may be properly
defined. This is the task I turn to next.

3.2   Types, parameters, and anchors

Motivation for introducing *situation-types* was given in the previous
section. In fact it turns out to be more useful to develop a complete
theory of *arbitrary types*, not just types of situations. Because of the
higher degree of abstraction involved in this step, the mathematics I
am using to carry out our study will now of necessity be a little more
prominent than hitherto. (As usual, the mathematics may be formalized
in some underlying set theory.)

The overall idea is to put into our ontology further uniformities that are
discriminated by cognitive agents, uniformities in addition to the spatial
locations, temporal locations, individuals, relations, and situations that
have already been identified. A particular consequence of this extension
is that we need to modify our conception of relations (and hence of
infons) to allow for these extra uniformities.

In our new framework, the relations R, S, P, etc. may have their
argument places filled (according to the nature of the relation) with
either individuals, situations, locations, and other relations (as before),
or with types for individuals, situations, locations, and relations.

Under certain special circumstances, we also need to consider relations
that can take infons as arguments. In particular, the *supports* relation, $\models$,
takes an infon as one of its arguments. Accordingly, let us also amend
our notion of relation to allow for relations taking infons or types for
infons as arguments.

Notice that some relations can take different kinds of argument, according to use. For example, the relation *sees*. (A fuller discussion of this

particular relation is given in Chapter 7, when I will present a somewhat
different analysis to the somewhat simplistic one given here.) This may
be used with individuals as arguments, as in

Jon sees Mary

or with a situation as second argument, as in

Jon sees Mary run

A situation s in which Jon sees Mary would be described by

$$s \models \ll \text{sees, Jon, Mary, } l, t, 1 \gg$$

and a situation s' in which Jon sees Mary run would be indicated by

$$s' \models \ll \text{sees, Jon, } e, l, t, 1 \gg$$

where e is the situation that Jon sees, a situation such that

$$e \models \ll \text{runs, Mary, } l', t, 1 \gg$$

where the temporal location t of the running is the same as that of the
seeing. (The spatial locations may be quite far apart, of course. Perhaps
Jon sees Mary run on (live) TV.)

The *types* of our theory will be defined by applying two forms of
type-abstraction, starting with an initial collection of *basic types*. The
basic types correspond to the cognitive process of individuating or discriminating uniformities in the world at the most basic level. The first of
these *basic types* are:

TIM : the type of a temporal location;
LOC : the type of a spatial location;
IND : the type of an individual;
REL^n : the type of an n-place relation;
SIT : the type of a situation;
INF : the type of an infon;
TYP : the type of a type (see later);
PAR : the type of a *parameter* (see later);
POL : the type of a polarity (i.e. the 'truth values' 0 and 1).

For each object x of our theory, there is at least one type such that x
is of that type. For instance, if l is a location, then l is of type LOC, and
the infon

$$\ll \text{of-type, } l, LOC, 1 \gg$$

is a fact (i.e. an infon that is supported by the world). Again, for any
situation s, the infon

$$\ll \text{of-type, } s, SIT, 1 \gg$$

is a fact.

Every basic type (indeed, every type) T is of type TYP, expressed by the fact

$$\ll \text{of-type}, T, TYP, 1 \gg$$

In particular, the infon

$$\ll \text{of-type}, TYP, TYP, 1 \gg$$

is a fact.

If an object x is not of basic type T, then the infon

$$\ll \text{of-type}, x, T, 0 \gg$$

is a fact.

Further technical development of our theory requires the availability of some device for making reference to arbitrary objects of a given type. The device we adopt is that of *parameters*.

For each basic type T other than PAR, I introduce an infinite collection $T_1, T_2, T_3, \ldots$ of *basic parameters*, used to denote arbitrary objects of type T. The parameters T_i are sometimes referred to as T-*parameters*. Thus, for example, IND_3 is an IND-parameter, and SIT_{56} is a SIT-parameter.[1]

I use the notation $\dot{l}$, $\dot{t}$, $\dot{a}$, $\dot{s}$, etc. to denote parameters (in this case of type LOC, TIM, IND, SIT, respectively).

For technical reasons connected with the mathematics of our theory, I also need to have available a formal means of assigning 'values' to parameters. I refer to the appropriate mechanisms as 'anchors'. Formally, an *anchor* for a set, A, of basic parameters is a function defined on A, which assigns to each parameter T_n in A an object of type T. Thus, if f is an anchor for A and T_n is an parameter in A, then the infon

$$\ll \text{of-type}, f(T_n), T, 1 \gg$$

is a fact.

So far so good. But, as they stand at the moment, the parameters (i.e. the basic parameters) are far too general for all but the most elementary of discussions. What is required are parameters that range over uniformities much finer than those captured by the basic types. Rather than having to work with parameters ranging over all individuals, for example, it would be useful to have parameters that range over various subclasses of IND, say the class of all persons, the class of all speakers, the class of all footballs, the class of all men kicking footballs, and so on. Similarly for locations and relations. Officially, such particularized parameters are

---

[1] Parameters for infons are only required in highly technical discussions.

called *restricted* parameters, though in practice I refer to them simply as *parameters*.

The formal definition of a *(restricted) parameter* will be given presently, but briefly the idea is this. Suppose $\dot{p}$ is to be a parameter for a person. Then $\dot{p}$ should be a restricted form of parameter such that whenever f anchors $\dot{p}$ to an object a in a situation s, then (in s) a is a person. (Thus parameters will work by placing restrictions on anchors.) Roughly speaking, a parameter such as $\dot{p}$ will be obtained by tagging a parameter IND_i by the 'condition' C of being a person, writing $\dot{p} = IND_i \upharpoonright C$. The question now is how do we realize this requirement within our mathematical framework?

Our first step is to modify our previous definition of infons so that for any of the basic types *TIM, LOC, IND, REL^n, SIT, INF*, and *TYP* (but not *PAR* or *POL*), a parameter for a type T object is allowed to appear wherever a type T object may itself appear.

Thus we now have: if

$$\ll R, a_1, \ldots, a_n, i \gg$$

is an *infon* then R is either an *n*-place relation or a *REL^n*-parameter, and each a_k is one of the following:

an individual or an *IND*-parameter;
a situation or a *SIT*-parameter;
a spatial location or a *LOC*-parameter;
a temporal location or a *TIM*-parameter;
a relation or a *REL*-parameter;
an infon or an *INF*-parameter;
a type or a *TYP*-parameter.

(The i is a polarity, just as before.)

In general then, infons (and hence types) may involve parameters. But notice that the recursive nature of the various definitions means that a parameter may occur buried one or more levels inside an infon or a type. That is to say, the notion of an *occurrence* of a parameter in an infon or a type is a hereditary one. More precisely, I make the following definitions.

A parameter $\dot{r}$ is said to *occur* in an infon $\ll R, a_1, \ldots, a_n, i \gg$ if and only if either $\dot{r}$ is equal to one or more of $R, a_1, \ldots, a_n$ or else $\dot{r}$ *occurs* in one or more of $R, a_1, \ldots, a_n$; $\dot{r}$ is said to *occur* in a parameter $\dot{v} \upharpoonright C$ (see presently) if and only if $\dot{r} = \dot{v}$ or $\dot{r}$ occurs in $\dot{v}$ or $\dot{r}$ occurs in some infon in C; $\dot{r}$ is said to *occur* in a type-abstraction $[\dot{v} \mid P]$ (see presently) if and only if $\dot{r}$ occurs in $\dot{v}$ or in (some constituent of) P.

Broadly speaking, occurrences of parameters in infons and types fall into one of two categories, analogous to (though not exactly the same as) the distinction made in classical first-order predicate logic between *free* and *bound* occurrences of variables in formulas.

Consider for instance, the infon

$$\sigma = \ll \text{kicks, Bob, } \dot{b}, \text{ Palo Alto, noon.1.1.1988, 1} \gg$$

(where $\dot{b}$ is a parameter for a ball).

As it stands, this infon is not enough to provide us with information about the world. More formally, if e is some situation, then an assertion of the form $e \models \sigma$ does not give us any information about e. (Existentially quantifying out the parameter $\dot{b}$ does yield information, namely the information that Bob kicks some ball in Palo Alto at noon on January 1, 1988, but that is another matter, to be taken up later.) Only when the parameter $\dot{b}$ is anchored to some specific ball, b, does σ become informational, namely it is then able to supply (in some sense *is*) the information that Bob kicks b in Palo Alto at noon on January 1, 1988. But with the parameter, $\dot{b}$, unanchored, the infon σ is only a kind of 'template' for an item of information.

The occurrence of the parameter $\dot{b}$ in the infon σ is an example of what I call a *free* occurrence, in that $\dot{b}$ may be anchored to an actual object of the appropriate type. On the other hand, the occurrence of the parameter $\dot{v}$ in the type-abstraction $[\dot{v} \mid P]$ (see presently) is what I call a *bound* occurrence, in that the parameter here plays an internal, structural role in the formation of the type, rendering it unavailable for anchoring to any particular object.

Unfortunately, the above remarks do little more than provide a suggestive pointer towards what turns out to be quite a tricky (and certainly subtle) issue, that cannot be properly dealt with until our theory is developed much further than in the present book. Which means that once again the reader will have to get by as best she can relying upon her intuition — in this case the analogy with free and bound variables in predicate logic.

In cases where I wish to emphasize that a particular infon or type has one or more free occurrences of one or more parameters, I shall use the phrase *parametric infon/type*. Infons/types that have no free parameters will be called *parameter-free*. Some authors use the term *state of affairs* to mean a parameter-free infon. The motivation for the phrase 'state of affairs' will be provided in Chapter 5, when the issue of free and bound occurrences of parameters will also be properly dealt with.

If σ is a parametric infon and f is an anchor for some or all of the parameters that occur free in σ, I denote by $\sigma[f]$ the infon that results by replacing each v in the domain of f that occurs free in σ by its value $f(v)$. Thus in particular, if f is defined on all parameters that occur free in σ, then $\sigma[f]$ will be a parameter-free infon (or state of affairs).

If I is a set of parametric infons and f is an anchor for some or all of the parameters that occur free in infons in I, I define

$$I[f] = \{\sigma[f] \mid \sigma \in I\}$$

Mathematicians among my readers will at once recognize the similarity between the introduction of parameters into infons and types and the formation of polynomials over a field.

I turn now to the task of providing a formal development of the machinery I shall use in order to form parameters.

Let v be any basic parameter of type *LOC, TIM, IND, REL^n*, or *SIT*.[2] By a *condition* on v I mean any finite set of (parametric) infons. (At least one of these should involve v, otherwise the definition is degenerate.)

Given such a basic parameter, v, and a condition, C, on v, I define a new (*complex*) parameter, $v \upharpoonright C$, called a *restricted parameter*. (In the case where C consists of a single parametric infon, σ, I write $v \upharpoonright \sigma$ instead of $v \upharpoonright \{\sigma\}$.) The idea is that $v \upharpoonright C$ will denote an object of the same basic type as v, that satisfies the requirements imposed by C (*in any situation where this applies*). This amounts to our putting a requirement on anchors more stringent than the mere preservation of basic types that applied to anchors for basic parameters.

Let $\dot{r} = v \upharpoonright C$ be a parameter. Given a situation, s, a function, f, is said to be an *anchor* for $\dot{r}$ in s if:

(i) f is an anchor for v and for every parameter that occurs free in C ;

(ii)   for each infon σ in C: $s \models \sigma[f]$;

(iii) $f(\dot{r}) = f(v)$.

I give a couple of examples. Consider the parameter:

$$\dot{r}_1 = IND_1 \upharpoonright \ll\text{speaking}, IND_1, LOC_1, TIM_1, 1 \gg$$

(Presumably we are referring to a person here. In which case we should perhaps add to the condition the extra parametric infon

$$\ll\text{person}, IND_1, 1 \gg)$$

Suppose f anchors $\dot{r}_1$ in some situation s_1. Then each of $f(IND_1) = a$, $f(LOC_1) = l$ and $f(TIM_1) = t$ are defined and are constituents of s_1. Moreover, $f(\dot{r}_1) = a$ and

---

[2] I shall not have need for restricted parameters of type *INF*.

$$s_1 \models \ll\text{speaking}, a, l, t, 1 \gg$$

Thus, in the situation s_1, the individual $f(\dot{r}_1) = a$ is speaking at the location $l = f(LOC_1)$ at the time $t = f(TIM_1)$.

Similarly, the parameter

$$\dot{r}_2 = LOC_1 \upharpoonright \ll\text{speaking}, IND_1, LOC_1, TIM_1, 1 \gg$$

will only anchor to a location at which some individual is speaking. (The part played by the basic parameter TIM_1 in a parameter such as this will become clear later, when the theory is developed more fully.)

And the parameter

$$\dot{r}_3 = SIT_1 \upharpoonright \ll\text{sees}, \text{Jon}, SIT_1, LOC_1, TIM_1, 1 \gg$$

will anchor (in some situation s_3) only to a situation that is seen by Jon (at some location in s_3).

So far so good. But suppose now that we wanted to form a parameter that denotes any individual that is kicking a ball. Obviously, one way to do this would be by using the condition

$$C = \{\ll\text{kicking}, IND_1, IND_2, LOC_1, TIM_1, 1 \gg, \ll\text{ball}, IND_2, 1 \gg\}$$

to form the parameter $IND_1 \upharpoonright C$. But suppose we are in the middle of a long and involved discussion of balls and have already introduced a parameter $\dot{b}$ to denote a ball. Then it would be more natural to use instead the construction:

$$\dot{r}_4 = IND_1 \upharpoonright \ll\text{kicking}, IND_1, \dot{b}, LOC_1, TIM_1, 1 \gg$$

(Again it is arguable that we need an extra parametric infon to the effect that IND_1 denotes a person. This kind of problem will be dealt with once and for all in just a moment.) This definition requires a notion of 'parameters' that allows 'nesting', i.e. the appearance of already defined parameters in the construction of new parameters. This is easily achieved. All we need to do is regard the previous definitions of both *parameters* and *anchors for parameters* (in a situation) as the clauses of a recursive definition, the recursion starting from the basic parameters and anchors thereof.

With this extended notion of a parameter, the above definition of $\dot{r}_4$ is legitimate, and the amended definition of an anchor will ensure that $\dot{r}_4$ can only be anchored to individuals that are kicking some ball (in a situation). Moreover, the problem with both $\dot{r}_1$ and $\dot{r}_4$ concerning the 'missing infon' that I alluded to may now be overcome by the more natural means of replacing the parameter IND_1 in each case by a parameter for a person.

To take a slightly different example, suppose now we want a parameter to denote all those situations that cause an alarm bell to ring. This may be done as follows.

Take

$$\dot{r}_5 = SIT_1 \restriction \ll \text{causes}, SIT_1, SIT_2 \restriction \tau, 1 \gg$$

where

$$\tau = \ll \models, SIT_2, \sigma, 1 \gg$$
$$\sigma = \ll \text{rings}, IND_1 \restriction \nu, LOC_1, TIM_1, 1 \gg$$

and

$$\nu = \ll \text{is a bell}, IND_1, 1 \gg$$

What is novel about this particular construction is that it involves the appearance of the *supports* relation, $\models$, within an infon. Hitherto, all relations that have occurred in the head position of an infon have been relations determined by the *agent* scheme of individuation. The *supports* relation is, presumably, one that would normally be regarded as produced by the theorist's scheme.

It is worthwhile working through the particular example of the parameter $\dot{r}_5$ in some detail, to see that it does indeed anchor only to situations that cause an alarm bell to ring.

Following through the recursive definition that leads to this parameter, we start with the parameter

$$\dot{b} = IND_1 \restriction \ll \text{is a bell}, IND_1, 1 \gg$$

Then we form the parameter

$$\dot{s} = SIT_2 \restriction \ll \models, SIT_2, \sigma, 1 \gg$$

where

$$\sigma = \ll \text{rings}, \dot{b}, LOC_1, TIM_1, 1 \gg$$

Finally, we obtain

$$\dot{r}_5 = SIT_1 \restriction \ll \text{causes}, SIT_1, \dot{s}, 1 \gg$$

Suppose now that f anchors $\dot{r}_5$ in some situation s_5. Then f must anchor both SIT_1 and $\dot{s}$, $f(\dot{r}_5) = f(SIT_1)$, and

$$s_5 \models \ll \text{causes}, f(SIT_1), f(\dot{s}), 1 \gg$$

In order for f to anchor $\dot{s}$, f must anchor SIT_2, $\dot{b}$, LOC_1, and TIM_1, and it must be the case that $f(\dot{s}) = f(SIT_2)$ and

$$s_5 \models \ll \models, f(SIT_2), \ll \text{rings}, f(\dot{b}), f(LOC_1), f(TIM_1), 1 \gg$$

Moreover, f has to anchor $\dot{b}$, with $f(\dot{b}) = f(IND_1)$ and

$$s_5 \models \ll \text{is a bell}, f(IND_1), 1 \gg$$

Thus if $f(IND_1) = b$, then b is a bell, and if $f(SIT_2) = s$, $f(LOC_1) = l$, and $f(TIM_1) = t$, then

$$s_5 \models \ll \models, s, \ll\text{rings}, b, l, t, 1 \gg, 1 \gg$$

If $f(SIT_1) = e$, then

$$s_5 \models \ll\text{causes}, e, s, 1 \gg$$

But $f(\dot{r}_5) = e$. Since, in s_5, e causes a bell to ring, this means that $\dot{r}_5$ is anchored as intended, to a situation that causes a bell to ring.

In general then, a parameter 'carries with it' certain information, in that it is constrained as to the sort of object to which it may be anchored. Anticipating topics to be considered more fully later, it is worth remarking at this stage that such 'information constrained indeterminates' are common in natural language.

For example, the pronoun *he* 'carries' the information that the individual denoted by this token (parameter) is an animal — human in many contexts — and is male. That is to say, the pronoun *he* corresponds to the parameter

$$IND_1 \restriction \{\ll\text{animal}, IND_1, 1 \gg, \ll\text{male}, IND_1, 1 \gg\}$$

(I have ignored possible location and time arguments here.)

Likewise, a proper name such as *John* carries with it the information that the individual the name is used to depict is (usually) human, male, and named 'John'.

Notice that, as a consequence of the manner in which I defined parameter-restriction and anchors of restricted parameters, an anchoring, f, of a restricted parameter, $v \restriction C$, to some object a, also anchors the parameter v to a. Thus the formation of $v \restriction C$ from v prevents any further use of v as a parameter 'in its own right'. If both v and $v \restriction C$ occur in the same context, this could lead to some confusions. In the case of theoretical work, this problem is easily avoided. Since we have infinitely many parameters available, we can always ensure that no pair v, $v \restriction C$ ever occur in the same context. In the case where a computer implementation of parameter-restriction was being designed (say as part of a natural language system), an obvious solution would be parameter duplication, by which I mean something along the following lines.

Parameter-restriction of v by C would presumably involve linking the parameter v to those entries in a database corresponding to the restriction conditions, C. To avoid possible v, $v \restriction C$ clashes, instead of simply linking v to the C-data, first of all make a duplicate, v', of v (suitably flagged to ensure the distinction), replace all occurrences of v in C by v' to give a duplicate C' of C, and take $v' \restriction C'$ as the new restricted parameter. Thus

$v \upharpoonright C$ is never actually formed. Linking of a parameter to restriction data is always preceded by the formation of a duplicate of that parameter and the restriction data.

Turning now to the notion of *types*, the standpoint of our theory leads to two kinds of type, though as we shall see presently, there is a level of abstraction at which these two forms of type arise from the same procedure.

First of all there are the *situation-types*. Given a *SIT*-parameter, $\dot{s}$, and a set, I, of infons, there is a correponding *situation-type*

$$[\dot{s} \mid \dot{s} \models I \,]$$

the *type* of situation in which the conditions in I obtain.

This process of obtaining a type from a parameter, $\dot{s}$, and a set, I, of infons, is known as *(situation-) type-abstraction*. I refer to the parameter $\dot{s}$ as the *abstraction parameter* used in this type-abstraction.

For example,

$$[SIT_1 \mid SIT_1 \models \ll \text{running}, \dot{p}, LOC_1, TIM_1, 1 \gg]$$

(where $\dot{p}$ is a parameter for a person) denotes the type of situation in which someone is running at some location and at some time. (Strictly speaking, this is an example of what will be called a *parametric type*. Replacing each of the parameters $\dot{p}$, LOC_1, TIM_1, by specific objects of the respective types, would produce a *parameter-free* type.) A situation s will be of this type just in case someone is running in that situation (at some location, at some time).

Again, if $\dot{s}$ is a parameter denoting a football game, then

$$[\dot{s} \mid \dot{s} \models \ll \text{winning}, \text{the 49ers}, \dot{l}_{game}, \dot{t}_{now}, 1 \gg]$$

denotes the type of game situation in which the (San Fransisco) 49ers are winning — a situation-type that is highly abstract but which at the time of writing is recognized by an enormous number of people of widely differing intellects. For a game situation s to be of this type, it is necessary and sufficient that the game s involves the 49ers, and moreover that the 49ers are winning (at the time of reference).

Exactly what mathematical objects will be taken to represent types is not, at this stage, important. 'Obvious' ways to proceed would be to take as types the (possibly proper) classes of objects being typed, or else to take 'canonical members' of those classes. But however they are modeled mathematically, situation-*types* are definite, higher-order uniformities across situations that are discriminated, if not individuated, by cognitive agents such as ourselves, and presumably a great many other animals and cognitive devices as well.

As well as situation-types, our theory also allows for *object-types*. These include the basic types *TIM, LOC, IND, REL^n, SIT, INF, TYP, PAR,* and *POL*, as well as the more fine-grained uniformities described below.

Object-types are determined over some initial situation. Let *s* be a given situation. If $\dot{x}$ is a parameter and *I* is some set of infons (in general involving $\dot{x}$), then there is a type

$$[\dot{x} \mid s \models I\,]$$

the *type* of all those objects *x* to which $\dot{x}$ may be anchored in the situation *s*, for which the conditions imposed by *I* obtain.

I refer to this process of obtaining a type from a parameter, $\dot{x}$, a situation, *s*, and a set, *I*, of infons, as *(object-) type-abstraction*. The parameter $\dot{x}$, is known as the *abstraction parameter* used in this type-abstraction. The situation *s* is known as the *grounding* situation for the type. In many instances, the grounding situation, *s*, is 'the world' or 'the environment' we live in (generally denoted by *w* in our account). For example, the *type* of all people could be denoted by

$$[IND_1 \mid w \models \ll \text{person}, IND_1, l_w, t_{now}, 1 \gg]$$

Again, if *s* denotes Jon's environment (over a suitable time span), then

$$[\dot{e} \mid s \models \ll \text{sees}, \text{Jon}, \dot{e}, LOC_1, TIM_1, 1 \gg]$$

denotes the type of all those situations Jon sees (within *s*). (Again these examples are, strictly speaking, *parametric* types.) Notice that this is a case of an object-type that is a type of situation. This is not the same as the *situation-types* described a moment ago. Situation-types classify situations according to their internal structure, whereas in this case the situation is typed from the outside.

Another 'duplication' in the way types arise in our theory concerns the manner in which parameters operate. For instance, with *w* denoting the 'world' still, the type of all persons may be derived using a vacuous condition, as

$$[\dot{p} \mid w \models \emptyset],$$

where $\dot{p}$ is a parameter for a person. (As usual, $\emptyset$ denotes the empty set.) In such a case (in particular, where the underlying reference situation is clear, as with *w* here) we may adopt the abbreviated notation $[\dot{p}]$ for such a type. But it should be noted that there are two quite different notions involved here. Parameters act as 'variables' that are constrained with regard to what they may depict (i.e. the objects to which they may be anchored), whilst types are higher order uniformities given by a scheme of individuation. The former are merely artifacts of our theory (albeit artifacts that correspond to various features of natural language and mental activity), whilst the latter are amongst the fundamental uniformities that our theory sets out to study. Though there is a quite clear connection between these two notions, the distinction between them should be borne in mind.

One particular remark that should be made concerning the above is that it is only when the grounding situation is 'the world' (or some other suitably 'large' situation) that parameters can give rise to types in the fashion described. This is because there is in general no requirement for the situation in which a parameter $\dot{p}$ is anchored (i.e. the situation in which the various restrictions on the anchor obtain) to be the same as the grounding situation for the type.

For instance, consider the type

$$T = [\dot{p} \mid s \models \ll \text{the winner}, \dot{p}, l, t, 1 \gg]$$

where

$$\dot{p} = IND_1 \upharpoonright \{\ll \text{person}, \dot{p}, 1 \gg, \ll \text{named}, \dot{p}, \text{JOHN}, 1 \gg\}$$

and where s is a race situation.

Clearly, the situation s is unlikely to have anything to say concerning the properties of being a person or of being named 'John'; s is just a race (situation). Rather any particular use of the parameter $\dot{p}$ will refer to some particular *resource situation*, e, a situation in which there is an individual a to which $\dot{p}$ may be anchored. Then

$$e \models \{\ll \text{person}, a, 1 \gg, \ll \text{named}, a, \text{JOHN}, 1 \gg\}$$

An object a will be of type T just in case there is such a resource situation e and an anchor f of $\dot{p}$ to a in e, such that

$$s \models \ll \text{the winner}, a, l, t, 1 \gg$$

(As a race situation, s does of course have things to say about particular individuals being winners, etc.)

This issue of resource situations is one that will be considered in much greater detail in the chapters on situation semantics, but it does serve to illustrate the difference between parameters and types.

Another distinction between the way that parameters and types function concerns their respective identity conditions. If $\dot{v}_1$ and $\dot{v}_2$ are distinct parameters, and if $I(\dot{v}_1)$ is a set of infons involving $\dot{v}_1$ and $I(\dot{v}_2)$ is the same set with $\dot{v}_2$ in place of $\dot{v}_1$ (whenever $\dot{v}_1$ occurs in $I(\dot{v}_1)$), then the two parameters $\dot{v}_1 \upharpoonright I(\dot{v}_1)$ and $\dot{v}_2 \upharpoonright I(\dot{v}_2)$ are distinct, whereas the types $[\dot{v}_1 \mid s \models I(\dot{v}_1)]$ and $[\dot{v}_2 \mid s \models I(\dot{v}_2)]$ are identical, i.e.

$$[\dot{v}_1 \mid s \models I(\dot{v}_1)] = [\dot{v}_2 \mid s \models I(\dot{v}_2)].$$

Taking the above observation a step further, notice that the abstraction-parameter used in the type-abstraction no longer figures in the resulting type; that is to say, given the type, it is not possible to recover 'the' abstraction parameter. Indeed, though type-abstraction is a process that involves an abstraction-parameter, the resulting type involves no 'abstraction-parameter' to be recovered. Rather the type is a structured object, part of whose abstract structure is an *argument role* (or several argument roles in the case of more complex types, considered later). I denote the argument role of a one-place type, T, by arg_T (those of an n-place type, T, by $arg_T^1, \ldots, arg_T^n$).

In case the definition of a type involves the occurrence of one or more (unanchored) parameters other than the abstraction parameter, then (unlike the abstraction-parameter) these parameters retain their parametric role in the resulting type, which is then known as a *parametric-type*. For example, if $\dot{s}$ is a parameter for a chess tournament and $\dot{p}$ is a parameter for a person, then

$$[\dot{p} \mid \dot{s} \models \ll \text{winner}, \dot{p}, LOC_1, TIM_1, 1 \gg]$$

denotes the (parametric-) type of a winner in *any* chess tournament. Given an anchor for the parameter $\dot{s}$ to a particular chess tournament, we obtain the type of a winner in *that* chess tournament.

If T is a parametric type and f is an anchor for some or all the parameters in T, I denote by $T[f]$ the type that results from replacing each parameter, $\dot{x}$, in the domain of f by its image, $f(\dot{x})$.

This is consistent with the previous definition of $I[f]$ in the case of a set, I, of infons.

Following the usage in computer science, I shall write

$$x : T$$

to indicate that object x is of type T. A construct of the form $x : T$ is said to be a *proposition*. Thus, a proposition is a claim about the world to the effect that a certain object is of a certain type.

If T is a parametric type, then a construct $x : T$ will be what we shall call a *parametric proposition*. In this case, if f is an anchor for the parameters of T, then

$$x : T[f]$$

will be a proposition.

Notice that if T is the situation-type

$$T = [\dot{s} \mid \dot{s} \models \sigma]$$

then for a situation s we will have

$$s : T \quad \text{if and only if} \quad s \models \sigma$$

Again, if T is the object-type

$$T = [\dot{r} \mid s \models \sigma]$$

then for an object x we will have

$$x : T \quad \text{if and only if} \quad s \models \sigma[f]$$

where $f(\dot{r}) = x$.

There is one caution. Though technically correct *as a description*, the above explanation of the typing relation is a little misleading, since it does not constitute a general *definition* of typing. Strictly speaking, if T is an arbitrary one-place type, then an object, x, will be of type T if and only if x can *fill* the argument role, arg_T, of T. To make this precise, I need to describe what is required in order for an object to *fill* the argument role of a one-place type. Since we shall, at this stage in our development, only encounter types via some explicit type-abstraction, where we have an abstraction parameter available, I choose to avoid the introduction of further technical machinery by using instead our existing framework of parameters and anchors, as above. This amounts to our providing an implicit definition of what is required in order for an object to *fill* an argument role of an abstraction type.

Notice that, although our definitions allow for the possibility, none of the examples I have given involve parameters or types for objects of type *REL*. This is in keeping with the viewpoint implicit in what was said in Chapters 1 and 2, that the (basic) relations of an informational theory are fixed by the agent or species of agent, with the main thrust of the theory being the manner in which information is manipulated within that initial framework.

I finish by showing how it is that situation-type abstraction and object-type abstraction may be regarded as two instances of a single phenomenon. The linking notion is the fundamental one of what I shall call an *infonic proposition*.[3] The adjective 'infonic' is to distinguish these propositions from those of the form $s : T$, where T is an object-type.

An *infonic proposition* is a claim of the form

$$s \models I$$

where s is a situation and I is a finite set of infons. (In the case

---

[3] In due course we shall be in a position to view propositions as uniformities across intentional mental states. That will be after the discussion of mental states in Chapter 6. In the meantime, the definition given here should be sufficient, though it does not, of course, accord propositions any ontological status within our theory.

where parameters are involved I sometimes speak of a *parametric infonic proposition*.) Since this may be re-written as $s : T$ where T is the type

$$T = [\dot{s} \mid \dot{s} \models I\,]$$

we see that the previous usage of the word 'proposition' is essentially the same as the present one.

It is clear that, from the standpoint of our theory, where infons are the basic units of (digitalized) information, infonic propositions play a fundamental role in the way information arises in the world. When developed in a more rigorous way, *types* are taken to be uniformities that arise (or can be regarded as arising) by means of a process of abstraction across parametric infonic propositions. In case the abstraction is across the situation parameter $\dot{s}$ in a parametric infonic proposition

$$\dot{s} \models I(\dot{x}, \dot{y}, \dot{z}, \ldots)$$

the result is what I called a *situation-type*; abstraction across one of the parameters in the set I (which may be a parameter for a situation) produces an *object-type*. (Strictly speaking, in both cases here, what results is a *parametric* type.)

In a more rigorous, mathematical development, I would allow for the formation not just of unary types as here, but types of any finite arity. Thus, for instance, we would be able to form the type

$$[\dot{s}, \dot{x}, \dot{z} \mid \dot{s} \models I(\dot{x}, \dot{y}, \dot{z}, \ldots)]$$

Such generalised types are useful in more advanced mathematical discussions.

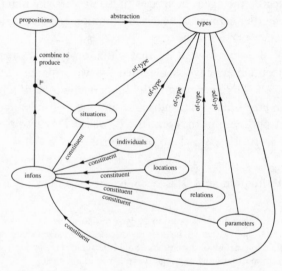

One final remark for the benefit of readers who skip ahead. Later on in our development I introduce a logical calculus of infons. This will enable us to form abstraction types of greater complexity than those indicated above. (It will also mean that we can abstract over a finite conjunction of infons rather than a finite set of infons.) However, the whole question of the logical combination of infons requires careful development, which is why we do not deal with it at this early stage in the development.

3.3 The nature of the ontology

I continue the discussion begun in Sections 2.6 and 2.8.

Most present-day mathematicians, myself included, have learnt our mathematics in a mathematical environment in which abstraction, formal definition, and proof are not only pre-eminent, but almost taken to be synonymous with the word 'mathematics'. Thus, the Gödel results notwithstanding, we are almost all brought up in a tradition of axiomatic mathematics, and the underlying philosophy we profess in public is essentially that generally known as formalism, which maintains that, ultimately, mathematics is nothing more than a highly structured, syntactic 'game' played according to specific rules. For the most part, this is the tradition we pass on to our students in our lectures and our books.

Now the truth is that, for the majority of mathematicians, a formalist-based approach is only adopted when it comes to their published papers and their publically acknowledged work. At heart, on a day-to-day basis, practically all mathematicians work in a highly intuitive fashion built on an out-and-out Platonistic philosophy. Abstract mathematical entitites such as numbers (natural, integer, rational, real, complex, infinite cardinal and ordinal) and spaces (geometric, metric, topological, linear, normed, etc.) are regarded as 'real objects' in a world that the mathematician sets out to *discover*. They are part of a mental world the mathematician learns to live in and become familiar with. Indeed, it is this intimate familiarity with an idealized, highly-ordered, abstract world of great simplicity that makes mathematics such an incredibly powerful tool with which to study certain aspects of the world.

So why then is there such a pretence of a formalistic philosophy, if such it is? Well, it certainly gets the mathematician off a thorny philosophical hook with very little effort. She may describe her work quite simply as "deriving logical consequences of certain axioms." Now, for the mathematician whose primary concern is to solve mathematical problems and prove mathematical theorems, this kind of 'Sunday-best formalism' is all well and good. But as soon as the mathematician starts to investigate matters that arise in real life, the situation changes dramatically. For instance, as Putnam points out in [19, p. 347]

... [talk about] mathematical entities is indispensible for science ... therefore we should accept such [talk]; but this commits us to accepting the existence of the mathematical entities in question. This type of argument stems, of course, from Quine, who has for years stressed both the indispensibility of [talk about] mathematical entities and the intellectual dishonesty of denying the existence of what one daily presupposes.

Of course, the issue of intellectual dishonesty aside, a strict adherence to a formalist philosophy leaves the mathematician unable to explain just why it is that his 'formal game' invariably turns out to be extremely useful in everyday life, in a manner that other formal games (such as chess) do not. On the other hand, the applicability of mathematics, what has sometimes been called its 'unreasonable usefulness', is not at all hard to explain for the mathematician who claims to be investigating the properties of various abstract features of the world.

I have already stated that, in my view, the search for a mathematical theory of information should be carried out in an empirical fashion, in much the same spirit as contemporary physics. I agree with Putnam that such an approach likewise leads to an 'indispensible' need for mathematical entities, in this case the infons (among other objects).

Recall the argument for infons presented in Section 2.6. This runs roughly as follows. Information (in the form considered in this book) arises by way of intentional representations in cognitive devices such as the brain. A particular cognitive state represents a certain piece of information by means of a constraint. Effective communication between cognitive agents requires that there be an empirical equivalence relation between two representations, an equivalence that can best be described as 'representing the same item of information'. If you factor out the set of all representations by this equivalence relation, the equivalence classes you obtain are what I call the infons — the 'fundamental items of information' of the theory.

In my discussion of infons, I pointed out the similarities between this process and the standard mathematical constructions of the various number systems of mathematics, from the natural numbers (equivalence classes of finite collections under equipollence) through to the imaginary and complex numbers. In particular, this analogy indicates how the process avoids being circular, even though the most natural description using ordinary language involves the apparent circularity of using the phrase 'represent the same item of information' in order to define the equivalence relation that produces those *items* of information. Just as the standard definition of natural numbers involves reference to the equivalence relation of two sets having the same *number* of elements.

Now, the representations and the equivalences are surely *there* in the world, for otherwise how could we ourselves function and communicate in our society? So why not work directly with them? Why go to the additional step of introducing a realm of abstract objects?

The answer is that it is far, far easier to reason using such entities. I happen to think that our intellectual devlopment does not progress very far beyond our childhood manipulations of marbles, sticks, counters, beans, and what-have-you. We reach a stage of maturity when we can reason using abstract objects created by the mind, in place of the physical objects of our earlier years. But our reasoning is still in terms of 'objects'. We do of course develop the facility for far more complex patterns of reasoning. Indeed, the use of *abstract* 'objects' greatly facilitates this increased logical complexity. But it is still reasoning *about objects*.

Certainly this is true in my own case. And I can only understand and appreciate the mathematics produced by other mathematicians under the assumption that this is how they too operate.

The axioms that we (mathematicians) develop for our Sunday-best formalism thus amount to the product of a carefully reasoned analysis of the most basic properties of those abstract objects that we 'create'. The fact that we appear to end up with just one common 'mathematics' about one particular collection of shared 'mathematical objects', follows from the common experience upon which we draw in order to make the various abstractions.

To anyone who objects to such an anthropological description of the mathematical enterprise, and I know there are such objectors, let me pose the following question: How else was it that many generations of mathematicians were able to develop some very sophisticated, and ultimately useful, mathematics, prior to the formulation of the axioms for that mathematics? Indeed, how is it that in practically all useful branches of mathematics, the axiomatization invariably came some time *after* the main ideas of the theory were worked out?

It is one of the aims of this book to convince you that a potentially useful mathematical theory of information, including the ability to handle the role played by language in the communication of information, is greatly facilitated by the introduction of certain abstract objects, in particular, but not exclusively, infons and situations.[4] Indeed, given the belief I expressed above that the human mind is only capable of mathematical reasoning in terms of the mental 'manipulation' of abstract *objects*, I claim that a useful theory of information *necessitates* the introduction of such mathematical objects. The complexity that would result were such a study attempted using only what is, in a sense, actually *there*, namely the various representations, would, I maintain, prevent any significant progress.

In trying to make my case for this view, there are in fact two issues I must address. First of all, the requirement for abstract objects at all in the intellectual activity of mathematicians. And secondly, the necessity of some *new* abstract objects in the case of a theory of information.

The first issue has already been addressed. To those who maintain that strict formalism is all that is required for mathematics, there is little more I can say. I simply cannot imagine what such people are *doing* (mentally) when they perform an arithmetic computation in their heads or seek a new theorem of number theory, field theory, algebraic topology, or whatever. Certainly, in performing positive whole number arithmetic for instance, they cannot surely be formally deriving some consequences of the Peano axioms, can they?

What seems to single out the truly great mathematicians of any age is the incredible 'familiarity' they develop with the 'domain of objects' they generally work with. They might indeed have little else other than this familiarity. Such was the case with the Indian mathematician Ramanujan, who was able to make wonderful *discoveries* about numbers, but lacked the knowledge or training required to 'deduce' those results from 'axioms'. Likewise Fermat, Gauss, and Euler appeared to have a deep understanding of the natural numbers *qua* objects, rather than as some formal system determined by axioms.

Indeed, my own experience some years ago as a young mathematician working alongside a mathematician of world class, the set-theorist Ronald Jensen, was that his mathematical *discoveries* generally preceded his construction of a 'proof' by some considerable time. In fact, on several

---

[4] David Israel has questioned whether situations should be described as *abstract*. Some of them are, after all, pretty concrete, in that they are parts of the physical world. He has a point, but I think most people would still regard situations as pretty 'abstract' sorts of entities, and in any event the mathematical theory we develop will involve abstract mathematical objectifications of situations having the same sort of ontological status as numbers. So the adjective 'abstract' is not entirely inappropriate.

occasions he never did work out a *correct* proof, that part of the process being accomplished by others (myself included). He *knew* a certain result was true (*in his abstract world of infinite sets*), and his understanding was such as to provide him with the general idea for a proof, but the details often came much later, as a result of the efforts of others. And this was in the field of transfinite set theory, a field of high abstraction if ever there was one.

From now on, I shall assume that the reader either agrees with me that mathematical thought requires a realm of abstract objects, or at least grants me this assumption for the sake of argument. The question then is, why does a mathematically based study of information and natural-language communication require a *new* collection of abstract objects?

A great deal of the basic, situation-theoretic ontology for the study of information and cognition has a fairly traditional look to it: individuals, relations, spatial and temporal locations, parameters and anchors, types. One thing that is novel to the situation-theoretic approach, and what gives rise to the name of this theory, is the inclusion in the ontology of what we call *situations*.

Situations are the theory's way of handling *context*. But what exactly *is* a situation? In many of the examples given in this book, the situations that occur are determined by (what goes on in) simply-connected[5] regions of space–time. But this is purely because these provide a natural class of examples that are easily understood. Space–time regions certainly do provide examples of situations, but they by no means exhaust all possibilities.

A slightly more complex case arises in the semantic analysis of a telephone conversation between someone in, say, New York and someone in San Francisco. The 'telephone-call situation' then involves two connected regions of space over the same time interval, and possibly also the communication link between them, be it a landline, a satellite link, or whatever.

Again, the constraints that allow one situation to provide information about another, and which serve as the link between representations and the information they represent, are generally dependent on a whole range of 'background conditions' that our theory takes in the form of *background situations*. (See Section 4.5.)

The inclusion of *situations* in our ontology, then, serves to take account

---

[5] In the topologist's sense of this phrase.

of the critical role played by context in practically all forms of behavior and communication, and by the background that governs the reliability of constraints.

But what kind of entitites are these situations? This question is a natural one for us humans to raise, since it arises from the desire mentioned earlier, always to understand, and if possible *define*, the new in terms of the old and familiar. But, as should by now be obvious from my drift so far, it is simply not possible to give a precise definition of situations in terms of familiar mathematical concepts. Situations are a quite new kind of object. They can be *modeled* using standard techniques, say as sets of infons, along the lines outlined by Barwise and Etchemendy in [4]. Indeed, in a forthcoming companion to this book, I intend to present just such a model. But this is just a modeling process. As such it can provide *some aid to the intuition*, but not a *definition* of what a situation *is*. Situations are just that: situations. They are abstract objects introduced so that we can handle issues of context, background, and so on.

Situations are abstract objects in their own right, distinct from all the other entities in the ontology of situation theory, or indeed the rest of mathematics for that matter, and some questions that are meaningful when asked of, say, individuals, locations, or sets, are simply not appropriate for situations, any more than it is appropriate to ask what color the number 7 is, or how hot a given Banach space is. In particular, it is in general not appropriate to ask for an 'extensional definition' of a situation — even in the case of a situation that is determined by (what goes on in) a connected region of space–time.

For example, recall the example from Section 2.4 of the discussion between John and David about a particular football game they have both seen. In their conversation, they both refer to a very definite *situation* — namely that particular game. This is a situation that they both individuate (as a *situation*). A long, informative, and confusion-free discussion takes place. And yet neither John nor David is able to list every single event that formed a part of that game, or every item of information that related to it in some essential way. Indeed, what makes their conversation about the game of interest to both parties is the fact that each one acquires from the other, *new* items of information about the game, information that the one picked up but the other did not. The fact that each person left the game with some information that the other did not does not mean that their subsequent conversation is about two different games. The situation is the same for both individuals, a highly structured part of the world, having a fixed duration in time. What differs is what each knows about that situation.

It is characteristic of our entire theory that an agent may obtain more and more information about a particular situation. The more infons, σ, that can be found for which

$$s \models \sigma$$

the more we know about the situation *s*. Indeed, our theory can be viewed as a study of how agents can acquire more information about particular situations. Without the situations to refer to, we would be forced to make theorist's assertions of the form

The agent acquires additional information about whatever in the world it is that the agent acquires that additional information about.

By putting *situations* into our theorist's ontology, we avoid such awkward circumlocutions, but we must accept that these new abstract objects might not behave as do the ones more familiar to us. The agent will in general only have partial information about a given situation, and hence can only access or talk about that 'situation' by some intensional, roundabout means, and our theory will reflect that partiality.

But if it is not possible to get a complete definition of situations in terms of more familiar notions, how then are we to deal with them? How can we develop our intuitions and our understanding of situations? Well, that is something for situation theory itself to answer. But the answer will of necessity be an *internal* one, one within the framework of situation theory.

As mentioned before, exactly what does and what does not constitute a situation is largely a matter of what agent is under discussion. It may or may not be the case that the agent itself can *individuate* situations (i.e. regard and treat them as single, identifiable entities). Simple agents probably do not individuate any situations, though, if they are to be the kind of agent of interest to us here, they do discriminate them. In the case of sophisticated agents such as Man, though we do often *individuate* situations (for example, we often individuate the situation that we *see*), in many cases our behavior also simply discriminates situations, without there being any act of *individuation* going on.

Then too there are the situations that are required by the internal mechanics of the theory. These often consist of finite sets of infons — what I have referred to as *abstract situations* (Section 2.5). One instance involves the manner in which the theory treats causality. For details, I refer the reader to Chapter 7.

Regardless of their status regarding individuation or discrimination by agents, within our theory situations are regarded as first-class members of the ontology, alongside the individuals, relations, locations, and all the rest of the ontology. In particular, we allow situations to fill (appropriate) argument roles of relations, and thus to appear as constituents of infons.

Since we do not generally regard situations *extensionally*, the question arises as to exactly what we mean by the equality of two situations. The strict answer is that an equality

$$s_1 = s_2$$

between two situations means that these are in fact one and the same situation. However, our only means of distinguishing between two distinct situations is by means of an item of distinguishing information. That is to say, we can only know that the situations s_1 and s_2 are distinct if we can find an infon, σ, such that

$$[s_1 \models \sigma \text{ and } s_2 \not\models \sigma] \quad \text{or} \quad [s_2 \models \sigma \text{ and } s_1 \not\models \sigma]$$

Thus to all intents and purposes we have an 'extensionality principle'

$$s_1 = s_2 \quad \text{if and only if} \quad (\forall \sigma)[s_1 \models \sigma \Leftrightarrow s_2 \models \sigma]$$

(As usual, $\Leftrightarrow$ means 'if and only if'.)

Again, there is a fundamental notion of one situation being *part of* another. I write

$$s_1 \subseteq s_2$$

to indicate that the situation s_1 is *part of* the situation s_2. Since situations are not in general sets, this should be regarded as simply a new (and suggestive) use of existing notation. It does not indicate set-theoretic inclusion.[6] In the case of two situations that are determined by space–time regions, the *part-of* relation will imply 'space–time inclusion'.

The *part-of* relation between situations is anti-symmetric, reflexive, and transitive, and consequently provides a partial-ordering of the situations.

As in the case of situation identity, since our only means of identifying situations is in terms of infonic 'information', we have another *de facto* 'extensionality principle':

$$s_1 \subseteq s_2 \quad \text{if and only if} \quad (\forall \sigma)[s_1 \models \sigma \Rightarrow s_2 \models \sigma]$$

The introduction of situations, then, is not unlike the step from the rational numbers to the real numbers, when viewed from a finitist position. The normal means of specifying rational numbers by giving their

---

[6] In the case of abstract situations (Section 2.5), the *part-of* relation does of course reduce to set-theoretic inclusion.

decimal expansion does not prevent us from constructing the *completion* of the rational number system, namely the real numbers, a process that consists of *introducing* a new realm of abstract objects that, from the original, finitist standpoint, may only be *partially* specified, by giving the decimal expansion to a certain finite number of places.

In fact, a better analogy is the step from the rational numbers to the *algebraic* real numbers.[7] Irrational algebraic numbers are idealized entities that require an infinite amount of decimal information to be completely specified, but admit of an alternative, 'higher-order', finite definition (as a solution to a certain polynomial equation with rational coefficients). Analogously, situations are idealized entities that cannot be completely specified by extensional, infonic means, but they find their way into the ontology because the agent somehow picks them out, either by cognitive individuation of some higher-order fashion (such as the football game example of Section 2.4) or else by behavioral discrimination.

Just as the step from the rational numbers to the real numbers involves a definite commitment to the 'uncertainty' (when viewed 'from below') of the completed infinite, so too the step from the individuals, locations, relations, and infons to the situations requires a definite commitment to dealing with entities that can only be understood *in terms of the system that thereby results*.

As with the situations, so too with the *types* and all the machinery that goes with them. These also seem to me to be unavoidable. Consider the following scenario.

You are driving in (say) Cincinnati for the first time in your life. You come to a red stop-light. What do you do? You bring your car to a halt. After a few moments the light changes to green and you continue your journey. You probably do not pause to reflect on your actions. Your training and experience as a driver have conditioned you to act in this way so as to avoid injury, death, fine, imprisonment, or at the very least damage to your vehicle. And yet you have never before encountered *this particular* stop-light. This particular situation is quite new to you — the precise layout of the intersection, the buildings on the corners, the particular configuration of other vehicles in your vicinity. Indeed, you have never been in Cincinnati before in your life! So what exactly causes you to act the way you do?

Well, though the actual situation you encounter is brand new to you,

---

[7] Algebraic numbers are real numbers that are the roots of polynomial equations having rational coefficients.

it is of a *type* you are familiar with. And it is this *type* that affects your behavior. Indeed, learning to drive consists in large part of training the mind and the body to recognize various types and act accordingly.

To take another example, learning to ski consists of a (generally) lengthy process of training the body to discriminate various *types* and react automatically to situations of different types: you do one thing in bumpy situations, another in steep situations, another in icy situations, and so on. Though in the case of the stop-light example one could argue (wrongly in my opinion) that there is some form of logical reasoning involved in your first stopping and then moving forwards again when the light changes to green (i.e. rule-based behavior), this is not the case in skiing. Here the behavior is clearly automatic, and is in response to situation-*types*.

In a similar vein, when analyzed from a logical viewpoint, much of the recent work in neural networks clearly involves a 'logic' at the type level. The training cycles that are required in order to 'program' a neural network to perform some action amount to a process whereby the network formulates some form of *type*, and the subsequent behavior of the trained network then consists entirely of type-based activity. Put simply, the trained neural network recognizes *types*.

3.4   Learning to live with abstraction

There is a natural tendency in humans to resist change. When something new comes along, we try to explain or understand it in terms of, or even reduce it to, concepts with which we are familiar. This is true both in real life and in the more esoteric pursuit of mathematics.

For example, in mathematics there was for a long time a considerable reluctance to accept the concept of negative (whole) numbers. Indeed, these were only accepted as genuine 'numbers' by the mathematical community as recently as the eighteenth century, despite mathematicians as long ago as the time of the Ancient Greeks having had a considerable facility with the algebraic manipulation of expressions involving minus signs. Such acceptance only came with a *geometric* picture of a number line, whereby negative whole numbers can be thought of as counting to the left from zero (i.e. counting in the *negative direction*), with the more familiar positive whole numbers being counted to the right (i.e. in the *positive direction*).

The discovery by the Greeks that not all lengths were expressible in terms of rational numbers led to an unease concerning the real number system that lasted until the nineteenth century, when Weierstrass, Dedekind, Cauchy, and others developed the modern theory of the real number continuum.

Again, complex numbers were regarded with considerable scepticism until the Norwegian mathematician Argand proposed the now familiar picture of the complex plane, whereby complex numbers are represented by the points of the two-dimensional Euclidean plane.

In each case, what happened was that something new was *modeled* in terms of something more familiar: geometric (and also algebraic) models in the case of negative and complex numbers, set-theoretic models (Cauchy sequences, Dedekind cuts) in the case of the real numbers. The process of modeling something new in terms of established notions is a powerful device on two counts. First of all it removes all worries about any formal inconsistency in the new notion. (Or rather, it throws any such worries back to a concern for the consistency of the previous notion.) Secondly, by providing a bridge from the familiar to the new, it usually assists in the process of understanding the new concept.

The two potential dangers that accompany the modeling process are firstly that it can obscure the fact that a genuinely new collection of abstract objects is involved. Modeling something is just that: *modeling*. The real numbers are neither Dedekind cuts nor equivalence classes of Cauchy sequences of rationals; they are *real numbers*, abstract mathematical objects in their own right. The complex numbers are *not* points in the complex plane — numbers and points are not at all the same kind of object.

The second danger is that any model invariably brings with it features not only of the thing being modeled, but also the structure in which the modeling is done, and it is often quite difficult to decide if a particular aspect of the model says something about the thing being modeled or the theory providing the model. A particular example of this within situation theory itself is provided by early attempts of Barwise and Perry in [5] to model situations in classical set theory. The well-foundedness axiom of set theory, in particular, led to a number of difficulties in trying to understand situations, that turned out to be not issues concerning situations at all, but rather were a feature of that particular means of modeling.

As with the various number systems of mathematics (and other examples that I could have given), so too with situations. In a sequel to this book, I intend to present a set-theoretic model of situations (and various other aspects of situation theory), along the lines outlined by

Barwise and Etchemendy in [4]. But this does not mean that situations *are* certain sets. Rather they are *situations*, abstract objects in their own right, as suggested in the earlier parts of this paper.

The reason for any unease the reader might have about the status of infons, situations, and the rest of our ontology is, I suggest, entirely one of novelty. Human beings do not, it appears, have an innate ability to handle abstract concepts. Rather, as is suggested by some contemporary work in anthropology and linguistics, a facility with abstraction seems to be something we acquire, often with great difficulty, as part of our intellectual development.

For instance, the work of the cognitive psychologist Jean Piaget suggests that the abstract concept of volume is not innate, but is learnt at a quite early age. Young children are not able to recognize that a tall, thin glass and a short, stout one can contain the same 'volume' of liquid, even if they see the one poured into the other. For a considerable time they will maintain that the quantity of liquid changes, that the tall glass contains *more* than the short one.

Likewise with the concept of abstract number. The ability to count appears to precede the formulation of the number concept. When asked to count the pencils in a pile of red and blue pencils, young children will readily report the number of blue or red pencils, but must be coaxed into reporting the total. The level of abstraction involved in the latter seems to be just beyond their capabilities.

Further evidence that even such basic (to us!) abstract concepts as natural numbers are not innate comes from the study of cultures that have evolved in isolation from modern society.[8]

Anthropologists have found that when a member of the Vedda tribe of Sri Lanka wants to count coconuts, he collects a heap of sticks and assigns one to each coconut. Each time he adds a new stick, he says "That is one." But if asked to say how many coconuts he possesses, he simply points to the pile of sticks and says "That many." The tribesman thus has a form of number system, but far from consisting of abstract *numbers*, his numbering is in terms of entirely concrete sticks.

In our Western culture, children typically form the concept of abstract

---

[8] The following discussion is based on the fascinating article [23] by Denise Schmandt-Besserat, of the Middle-Eastern Studies Department of the University of Texas at Austin. I am grateful to Adrienne Diehr, the Administrative Associate at the Center for Cognitive Science at the University of Texas at Austin, for bringing this article to my attention.

numbers at around the age of six. But this appears to be not an innate development; rather it is a result of childhood conditioning.

It is only recently that evidence has been uncovered concerning the actual origins of our abstract number concept.

The earliest Middle East artifacts connected with counting that have been discovered are notched bones found in caves in present-day Israel and Jordan, dating from the Paleolithic period (15,000 to 10,000 B.C.). The bones seem to have been used as Lunar calendars, with each notch representing one sighting of the moon. Similar instances of counting by means of a one-to-one correspondence appear again and again in preliterate societies: pebbles and shells were used in the census in early African kingdoms, and in the New World, cacao beans and kernels of maize, wheat, and rice were used as counters.

Any such system suffers from an obvious lack of specificity. A collection of notches, pebbles, or shells indicates a quantitity but not the items being quantified, and hence cannot serve as a means of storing information for long periods. The first known enumeration system that solved this problem was devised in the Fertile Crescent, the rich lowland area stretching from Syria to Iran. Clay tokens an inch or less across, were used to represent specific commodities according to their shape. For example, a cylinder stood for an animal, cones and spheres referred to two common measures of grain (approximately a peck and a bushel). This still did not amount to a system of abstract numbers, of course, but it did ensure an enduring method of counting.

By 6,000 B.C., clay tokens had spread throughout the Middle East. Their use persisted largely unchanged until around 3,000 B.C., when the increasingly more complex societal structure of the Sumerians led to the development of more complex forms of token, involving both a greater variety of shapes (ovoids, rhomboids, bent coils, parabolas, etc.) as well as markings on the tokens.

This development set the stage for the evolution of abstract numbers. It became common to store clay tokens in clay envelopes, each one imprinted with a mark indicating the owner or government agency whose account the envelope contained. Sealed clay envelopes thus served as accounts or contracts. Of course, one obvious drawback of a clay envelope is that the seal has to be broken open in order to examine the contents. So the Sumerian accountants began to impress the tokens on the soft exteriors of the envelopes before enclosing them, thereby leaving a visible exterior record of the contents of the envelope. But then, of course, the contents become largely superfluous. All the requisite information is stored on the enevelope's outer markings. And in this way the clay tablet was (after some time) born, with marks on a single tablet used to denote numbers of items. The intermediate clay tokens were discarded. In present-day terminology we would say that they had been replaced by the abstract numbers that were left when the tokens were taken away.

Now, the formalist reader of this article might claim that the above discussion does not prove the 'existence' of abstract numbers *qua* abstract objects. That is an objection I have already suggested be set aside. But the interesting thing is that the step from using physical tokens set in a one-to-one correspondence to whatever was being counted, to using markings on a single tablet, *did not take place immediately*. For some time the marked clay envelopes redundantly contained the actual tokens the outer markings depicted. This would suggest that going from physical tokens to an abstract, two-dimensional representation was a considerable cognitive development.

So what do these considerations tell us about the future status of situations within the realm of mathematical abstract objects? Certainly nothing I have said will guarantee that situations (or infons) will eventually take their place alongside the various number systems and spaces that are already an established part of mathematics. That will depend partly upon the way these putative new objects come to be regarded in the light of greater familiarity and use. Partly too upon how effective they prove to be in the study of information and communication. But if the arguments presented in this volume in support of infons, situations, etc. prove to carry sway, and if their adoption proves of use, then I see no reason why these new abstract objects should not achieve a mathematical status equivalent to, say, the real or the complex numbers. I do not believe there are any 'absolutes' in mathematics; just intuition (an intuition that is subject to development and evolution) and utility. Had Abraham Robinson been alive a century earlier and developed his 'non-standard analysis' prior to the invention of the familiar ϵ, δ theory of the real line, I am sure that infinitesimals would now rank alongside the real numbers as abstract objects of equal ontological status.

The introduction and acceptance of abstract objects does not, I believe, follow some pre-ordained sequence of discoveries of an abstract world that awaits our investigation, but rather is a pragmatic matter of cognitive development, motivated and spurred on by necessity, utility, and intuition, guided by logic. In the meantime, it is our task as mathematicians simply to investigate the issues of the age we live in, and leave it to future generations to judge if we are successful in the long run.

3.5 Oracles

A collection of situations of particular importance in the situation-theoretic analysis of natural language are the *oracles*. Though I shall not have occasion to make significant use of these situations until Chapter 8, the above discussions make this an ideal moment to introduce the concept.

By a *set of issues* I mean a collection of parametric infons. The idea behind this definition is that a set of issues provides us with an information-theoretic framework for discussing the world or some part thereof. By anchoring the parameters in an infon in the set, we obtain an item of information. Clearly, different sets of issues will enable us to talk about, and obtain information about, different aspects of the world.

I fix some particular set of issues Γ. By a Γ-*infon* I mean any infon that results from anchoring the parameters in an infon in Γ.

Given an individual (animate or inanimate) or a situation a, the Γ-*oracle* of a, $Oracle_\Gamma(a)$, is the situation comprising that part of the world and the entire 'body of knowledge' that, within the framework provided by Γ, concerns a. That is to say, $Oracle_\Gamma(a)$ is the 'minimal' situation, s, such that

$$s \models \sigma$$

for any factual, parameter-free Γ-infon, σ, that 'genuinely' involves a.

So far this is, of course, very vague. For one thing, what do those enquoted terms mean? The problem is that this notion is both new and highly intensional, and can really only be understood in terms of the situation theory we are currently developing.

An analogy from first-order model theory that might be helpful is the smallest Σ_n-elementary submodel of the universe containing the object a. (Readers unfamiliar with model theory can skip this section. Its inclusion is purely motivational.)[9] By the very nature of Σ_n-elementary submodels, if

$$M \prec_{\Sigma_n} V$$

---

[9] For the benefit of readers with only a cursory familiarity with logic, let me remark that a Σ_n formula is one consisting of a quantifier-free body, prefixed by n alternating blocks of quantifiers, starting with a block of existential quantifiers, then a block of universal quantifiers, etc. By restricting to the set of Σ_n formulas of the language, it is possible to construct elementary submodels of the set-theoretic universe.

(i.e. if M is a Σ_n-elementary submodel of V) and if the only information available about V is that given by first-order, Σ_n formulas then, starting from a point inside M, it is not possible to distinguish M from V. For all Σ_n formulas $\phi(v_1, \ldots, v_n)$ and all $a_1, \ldots, a_n$ in M,

$$M \models^T \phi[a_1, \ldots, a_n] \text{ if and only if } V \models^T \phi[a_1, \ldots, a_n]$$

where the symbol $\models^T$ denotes model-theoretic satisfaction in the sense of Tarski.[10]

Likewise in the case of oracles. If the only kind of information available is that provided by the set of issues Γ, then, starting with the object a, there is no way to distinguish $Oracle_\Gamma(a)$ from w, the world. For any Γ-infon σ in which only objects that are constituents of $Oracle_\Gamma(a)$ occur,

$$Oracle_\Gamma(a) \models \sigma \text{ if and only if } w \models \sigma$$

For example, given an appropriate set of issues Γ, if a were a rock, then $Oracle_\Gamma(a)$ would involve a time-span stretching backwards to the origins of the rock and forwards at least to the moment (if such a moment exists) the rock ceases to exist (as such), and would support all the facts that pertain to that rock: its composition, color, mass, volume, shape, melting point, any names it has, the various locations it has occupied, who or what has touched it, etc. Clearly this is a long and varied list, that involves a great many properties and relations and a great many other objects. But note that by no means all properties and relations will be involved, nor all other objects. For instance, the property 'happy' is unlikely to figure in any infon supported by $Oracle_\Gamma(a)$, and since I am assuming a is a rock I myself have not encountered, nor ever will encounter, neither will I figure in $Oracle_\Gamma(a)$. (Of course, having now discussed the rock, a, in this book, a now figures in *my* oracle, $Oracle_\Gamma(\text{Keith\_Devlin})$, as an object I have thought about and discussed in print. But this does not necessarily put me into $Oracle_\Gamma(a)$)

To move on to a more interesting example, what about that oracle

$$s = Oracle_\Gamma(\text{Keith\_Devlin})$$

just mentioned? What kinds of objects will be constituents of s and what infons will be supported by s ?

Well, for an appropriate set Γ, s will stretch back in time far enough to include all my ancestors and forward in time to include my descen-

---

[10] The standard symbol used to denote the Tarski satisfaction relation is $\models$. But in this book I am using this symbol to denote the situation-theoretic *supports* relation. Though the two notions are really quite different, in this instance the commonality of the notation serves to highlight the analogy I am trying to make.

dants; it will contain me, my birthplace, my parents, grandparents, etc., my wife, my children, any grandchildren, etc., several dogs, even more cats, and various apartments, houses, and automobiles (associated with different times, I should add); it will support the infons that provide the information that I am human, male, a mathematician, married, a father, of British nationality, named KEITH DEVLIN, and so on.

Clearly, s has a considerably larger reach, both in time and in space, than the individual Keith Devlin. (Unless one wanted to take an extreme philosophical stance concerning the 'extent' of individuated objects, and identify $Oracle_\Gamma(a)$ with a for every object a.) But again, there will be far more things *not* in $Oracle_\Gamma(\text{Keith\_Devlin})$ than are included, so for all that $Oracle_\Gamma(\text{Keith\_Devlin})$ seems unmanageably large, it has far less extent than w.

As will be demonstrated in Chapter 8, oracles play a significant role in natural-language communication (or at least, they are our theory's counterpart to a crucial feature of such communication). By way of a foretaste of things to come, suppose I say to you

Jon Barwise was the first director of CSLI.

First of all, how do I know this? Well, over the years I have acquired more and more information about the situation

$$s = Oracle_\Gamma(\text{Jon\_Barwise})$$

where Γ is, say, the set of all parametric infons in the informational ontology of any of the people who have heard of Jon Barwise. Among my current stock of information is the information, supported by s, that Jon Barwise was the first director of CSLI. I acquired this particular item of information some time in 1985. By then I knew Barwise moderately well, and my information concerning him was already quite extensive, though it did not at that time include any information about his family, as it does today. Prior to 1971, however, when I met Barwise for the first time, my knowledge of s was very miminal, amounting to little more than that this character Jon Barwise was an American, male mathematician at the University of Wisconsin, who had proved a famous result called the *Barwise Compactness Theorem*. The point to note is that it was the same situation, s, throughout this twenty year time span. What changed over time was the information I have concerning s.

So much for me, the speaker of the above sentence. What about you, the listener? You may, of course, already have considerable knowledge about the situation s. Maybe you are a close friend of Barwise of many years' standing; or maybe just an acquaintance; or perhaps you have never met the guy, but have long been an avid follower of his exploits. In any event, let us suppose that you already know that Jon Barwise was the first director of CSLI. Then, of course, my utterance does not provide you with any new information. Nevertheless, upon hearing the name JON BARWISE, your mind immediately conjures up a host of facts and/or images you associate with this name — facts and/or images that are part of, or supported by, the situation *s*.

Alternatively, it could be that although you have considerable knowledge about *s*, you were not previously aware that the person Jon Barwise was the first director of CSLI. So you now add this to your stock of information about *s*. You now know *more* about *s*. (Though unless you know what 'CSLI' refers to, your new information amounts only to the fact that Jon Barwise was the first director of *something*.)

At the other end of the spectrum, suppose you have never before heard of Jon Barwise. Then my utterance nevertheless still serves to convey information to you. From now on, you know that there is someone called JON BARWISE, and moreover you have some information about the associated situation $s = Oracle_\Gamma(\text{Jon\_Barwise})$, namely you know that:

$$s \models \ll\text{named}, a, \text{JON BARWISE}, t_{JB}, 1 \gg$$
$$\land \ll\text{human}, a, t_{JB}, 1 \gg \land \ll\text{male}, a, t_{JB}, 1 \gg$$
$$\land \ll\text{first-director-of}, a, \text{CSLI}, 1 \gg$$

You know this because of what you hear me say, coupled with your prior knowledge of the world: the kinds of objects that can be directors of things, and the way the English language operates, in particular its conventions concerning proper names. This would not, of course, enable you to recognize this guy Barwise if you saw him in the street. Nor do you know exactly what sort of an institution CSLI is, though you have also just learnt of another situation, $Oracle_\Gamma(\text{CSLI})$, about which you know it is some form of human organization, whose first director was called JON BARWISE.

Though the amounts of information that are known and/or learnt about the Jon Barwise situation, *s*, can vary enormously from case to case, the situation is *one and the same*: it is $Oracle_\Gamma(\text{Jon\_Barwise})$. Different people at different times have access to vastly different information about *s*. Barwise's friends will likely know more about *s* than strangers who have never met him but have simply read *Situations and Attitudes*. Barwise himself will know considerably more about *s*, though not everything. His physician will have access to information about *s* quite different from that known to his friends, or even to Barwise himself. Various government agencies will have files of information about *s*. Future biographers of mathematics may spend several months investigating the situation *s*.

Communication, in particular linguistic communication, can be considered as the transmission of information about various situations. Indeed, we may regard the enormous efficiency of natural language as a carrier of information as stemming in large part from the fact that a single word or phrase can bring into focus an entire oracle situation. The more information about that oracle that the speaker and listener share, the more efficient can be the communication between them.

It should be emphasized that $Oracle_\Gamma(a)$ is *not* some kind of file or database of information concerning the object *a*, through which speakers and listeners search when discussing *a*. Rather, oracles are *situations*, objects about which it is possible to acquire and/or pass on information. It is highly unlikely that an agent ever has more than *partial* information about a particular oracle, $Oracle_\Gamma(a)$. And that information might not have *a* as its main focus. (For instance, my knowledge about Benjamin Franklin is almost exclusively concerned with those scientific facts supported by his oracle situation; about the man himself I know very little.)

Of course, in the above discussion I have been very vague about the underlying set of issues Γ in each case. At the present level of analysis, such vagueness seems appropriate. Accordingly, when I use oracles in later parts of this book, I shall generally drop all mention of the set Γ, writing simply $Oracle(a)$, and leave it to the reader to supply an appropriate set of issues.

Given the comparison between infons and number systems developed in Section 2.8, and the general discussion of the number concept in the preceding section, it should be helpful to draw an analogy between oracle situations and numbers. The analogy concentrates on the real number system, and in particular the irrational numbers.

As discussed in Section 3.4, the evolution of even the abstract natural number system was a long and slow one, and the development of the real number system was not fully completed until the latter part of the nineteenth century. I shall consider the latter — the real numbers — in terms of the former — the natural numbers. For convenience, I restrict attention to positive numbers.

Rooted as they are in our intuitions, the natural numbers have a certain *concreteness*. They are, in a sense, *individuals*, each of which we can completely identify (as the *first*, the *second*, the *third*, and so on).

Consider now the problem of specifying other kinds of numbers — that
is to say, providing information that determines numbers of other kinds.

Starting with the natural numbers, *decimal representations* provide us
with a means of specifying (in principle) all rational numbers. And given
the finite nature of the world, the rational numbers clearly suffice for all
counting and measurement purposes. The one thing they do not provide
is a number system that alllows the development of powerful and elegant
mathematical theories such as the differential and integral calculus. The
problem is, as the Greeks discovered, that there are 'infinitesimal gaps' in
the rational number system. 'Filling in' these gaps by the introduction of
the irrational real numbers requires some significant mathematical effort.

Viewed from the informational standpoint of decimal representations,
it seems impossible to specify even a single irrational number. The
specification of an irrational number would require an infinitely long
string of decimals — an infinite amount of information in our present
sense — and thus the irrationals seem to be nothing more than conceptual
idealizations that are postulated to exist. An irrational can only be
approximated, albeit with as much finite accuracy as we desire.

The oracle situations are a situation-theoretic analogue of the irrational
real numbers: idealized objects about which we can acquire arbitrarily
large finite amounts of information (infons), but which cannot in general be uniquely specified in such a fashion. The only way to identify
a particular oracle is in terms of a higher-order (i.e. higher than infonic) description, namely *as Oracle(a)* for some object *a* (more precisely
$Oracle_\Gamma(a)$ for some set of issues Γ), a definition that has no meaning at
the level of infons.

Analogously, it is of course possible to specify certain irrational real
numbers in higher-order terms than at the level of decimal representations. For example, the algebraic irrational numbers (such as $\sqrt{2}$) can be
specified as the solutions to rational polynomial equations, the irrational
number π can be specified in geometric terms as the ratio of the circum-
ference of any circle to its diameter, and the irrational constant *e* can be
defined by analytic means. Indeed, given that oracle situations are, by
virtue of *being* oracles, definable in situation-theoretic terms, the closest
analogy would seem to be between the oracles and (say) the algebraic
numbers, with arbitrary situations being the situation-theoretic analogue
of arbitrary real numbers.

Oracles make no sense if you try to pin them down in terms of which
infons they support. Just as irrational numbers make no sense if you
try to specify them using decimal representations. Only in terms of the

appropriate higher-order theory do oracles and irrational numbers make sense. The higher-order theory appropriate for the irrational numbers was fully worked out over a century ago (a fairly short time in the history of mathematics). We are still working on the theory appropriate for situations.

4

Meaning and Constraints

4.1 Situation semantics

In *situation semantics*, the theory of situations is used to provide a semantic account of language — either a formal language of the kind traditionally studied in logic, or else a fragment of natural language. It does so by starting from the premise that the most significant aspect of language, at least as far as simple assertive[1] uses of language are concerned, is the conveyance of *information*. Since the information conveyed by the utterance of an assertive sentence is almost invariably dependent on a variety of contextual factors, as well as depending on the actual sentence used, this means that it is with *utterances* of sentences that the theory is principally concerned. The utterance of an assertive sentence will be referred to as a *statement*.

As far as statements are concerned, the most basic questions to be answered are:

What is the *propositional content* of a given statement, i.e. what claim does it make?[2]

What is the *meaning* of the sentence uttered?

Though these questions will be examined more fully in the chapters on situation semantics proper, it will be useful to provide some answers here and now, in order to motivate and exemplify the study of meaning.

Suppose Jon utters the sentence

$$\Phi : \textit{Mary is running.}$$

There are two situations involved here. One situation, call it u, is the one where Jon makes this utterance. This is what I shall refer to as the *utterance situation*. (Often I refer simply to 'the utterance' when I

---

[1] Also referred to as indicative use by some authors.

[2] Recall that, in general, by a *proposition* we mean a claim of the form $x : T$, where T is a type and x is an object.

mean the utterance situation. In general, the context should make the particular usage clear but, when the distinction is important, I shall strive to be precise in this regard.) Factors about the utterance situation will determine, in particular, just which of the many Marys in the world this particular use of the name 'Mary' denotes.

The other situation is what I shall call the *described situation*. In making the utterance, Jon makes a claim about some particular situation e, a situation such that

$$e \models \ll \text{running, Mary, } t, 1 \gg$$

(I am suspending any mention of the location of Mary's running. The justification for doing this will be provided in Chapter 5, when I discuss saturated and unsaturated infons.) There are a number of specific objects involved here. The time t is a specific time, namely the present time (Mary *is* running); the property *running* is a specific property; the individual *Mary* is a specific person; and the situation e is a definite situation. Each one of these objects is fixed by features of the utterance situation, u. This is not to say that Jon is able to provide uniquely identifying descriptions of each of these objects when he makes his utterance. Though his use of the word 'Mary' might be enough to identify uniquely the person who is running, he may well be unable to specify the time in any way, other than that it is 'now'. Referring to a particular instant or period of time does not require a specific identification of that time in terms of some scale of measurement.

Exactly how the described situation e is picked out depends on the particular circumstances of the utterance. Suppose u is a conversation of which Jon's utterance of the sentence "Mary is running" is part of a discussion of some children's game. Then that game will constitute the situation e. In this case, various features of the overall conversation could serve to identify e. Or perhaps Jon is providing a live radio commentary of some sporting event, in which case e is that event, a situation that is *seen* by Jon but only identified by some remote listener by means other than direct perception — say by the announcement Jon makes at the start of his broadcast. Again, if Jon's utterance is in reply to the question "What is Mary doing now?" with the focus entirely on Mary and not some larger context, then e could be pretty minimal, being just that part of the world that is sufficient to support Mary's running, namely Mary's immediate environment. In this case, Jon himself may have no thoughts whatsoever about e as a situation. No individuation of e by

Jon is required here. It is just a feature of his utterence that it is about a part of the world, and our theory reflects this by means of a situation.

Even in the case where Jon does individuate e, it is highly unlikely that he, let alone anyone else, would be able to say of every given infon whether or not that infon is true of e (i.e. is supported by e). There may be a great many features of this situation that he is aware of, and likewise many he is not aware of. Perhaps Mary is running alongside someone else. Or maybe she is being chased by a dog not yet within Jon's view. There is a whole range of possibilities. Individuation of the situation e does not require recognition of all the facts it supports. Indeed, one of the main tasks of situation theory is to study the way in which information may be accumulated to provide an increasingly rich description of an epistemically 'vague' situation such as e.

I return to these issues again later.

The *propositional content* of Jon's utterance u provides one instance of how information concerning the situation e may be conveyed. Indeed, the propositional content is the most important instance as far as our semantic study is concerned. What Jon is claiming (about e) is that:

$$e \models \ll\text{running, Mary}, t, 1 \gg$$

To put this another way, Jon provides the information that the situation e, to which his utterance refers, is of *type E*, where

$$E = [\dot{e} \mid \dot{e} \models \ll\text{running, Mary}, t, 1 \gg]$$

I shall in fact define the *propositional content* of Jon's utterance u to be precisely the claim

$$e : E$$

Thus, supposing we have a case of a genuine exchange of information (i.e. what Jon says is true, he knows it, and he makes his utterance with the intention of conveying this information), then the *propositional content* of the utterance is that item of information contained in the utterance in the most intentional manner, as opposed to any other information that the utterance might convey, such as the speaker's ability to speak English, the fact that the speaker has certain knowledge about the events described by the utterance, and so on.

To any listener who is aware, by whatever means, just which particular Mary is a constituent of the situation e, this *propositional content* is precisely the informational item about that person that would normally be regarded as the information the speaker intends to convey by the utterance. To a listener not able to identify the individual concerned, the utterance conveys less information, namely just the information that the person Jon is referring to, *whichever Mary it may be*, is running. In any event, the propositional content is meant to pick out just what it is about the world that the utterance claims to be the case.

Turning to the second of my two questions,[3] what is the *meaning* of the sentence Φ that Jon utters in the situation u ? Presumably this is not tied exclusively to the specific situation u. After all, there will be a great many utterance situations, involving a great many speakers, referring to a variety of Marys, each consisting of the utterance of this one sentence Φ. The *meaning* of Φ should surely be some form of uniformity across these various utterances. (If this were not the case, what would be the justification for our using the word *meaning* ?) That is to say, the *meaning* of Φ, whatever it is, should be such that, given a particular utterance u of Φ, and in particular a specific reference for the name MARY, the meaning plus the utterance situation together yield the content.

A natural step then, would be to take this requirement and turn it into a formal definition of what I shall call the *meaning* of Φ. Thus, according to this strategy, the *meaning* of Φ can be *defined* to be the abstract linkage, let us denote it by $\|\Phi\|$, between the two situation-types

$$U = [\dot{u} \mid \dot{u} \models \{\ll\text{speaking}, \dot{p}, \dot{l}, \dot{i}, 1 \gg, \ll\text{saying}, \dot{p}, \Phi, \dot{l}, \dot{i}, 1 \gg,$$
$$\ll\text{refers-to}, \dot{p}, \text{MARY}, \dot{q}, \dot{l}, \dot{i}, 1 \gg\}]$$

(where $\dot{p}$ and $\dot{q}$ are parameters for persons), and

$$E = [\dot{e} \mid \dot{e} \models \ll\text{running}, \dot{q}, \dot{i}, 1 \gg]$$

Thus, if u is a situation of type U, there must be some person, Jon, say, that fulfills the role of the speaker (i.e. the parameter $\dot{p}$ anchors to Jon), and that person Jon is saying (at the location l and time t to which the parameters $\dot{l}$ and $\dot{i}$ anchor) the sentence Φ. Furthermore, in making this utterance, Jon is using the word 'Mary' to refer to some particular individual a to whom the parameter $\dot{q}$ anchors. (Presumably this will be someone named Mary, though there is nothing in what has been specified so far to ensure this.) Then, provided Jon has the information that this person Mary is running, and utters the sentence Φ with the intention of conveying that particular piece of information (relying upon the rules that govern language use), a listener hearing this utterance will thereby acquire the information that the situation e to which Jon's utterance refers is such that person a is running (at time t) in e; that is to say, the listener learns that the situation e is of type E modulo the determined

---

[3] This is not to say that we are finished with the first one. Not by a long way.

anchoring. The utterance carries this information about the described
situation *e*. Thus the *meaning*, $\|\Phi\|$, of the sentence Φ provides the link
between the utterance situation and the described situation, enabling an
utterance of Φ to be informational.

Notice that the meaning itself is a linkage between *types*, not between
situations. The sentence Φ is fixed, but the parameters of the speaker,
the name-referent, the location, and the time, are all left open. Thus the
meaning transcends any particular usage of the sentence.

Given such a definition, *situation semantics* can be regarded, at least as
a first approximation and when restricted to simple assertive sentences,
as a study of the linkages $\|\Phi\|$ for various sentences Φ, and of the related
'meanings' $\|\alpha\|$ of expressions α that are only parts of sentences (nouns,
pronouns, verbs, etc.).[4] According to this approach, 'meaning' is regarded
as a three-place *relation* that connects syntactic objects (words, phrases,
sentences, etc.) with pairs of types.

But our overall interest is in information and its transfer, and linguistic meaning is only one of the many ways in which information may
be conveyed. Accordingly situation semantics forms only a part of our
overall study, albeit a large and significant part. The most general question to ask is how one situation can contain information about another,
regardless of whether or not the linkage between the two situations involves language. In the example above, where Jon utters the sentence
Mary is running, the utterance contains as its propositional content the
information that the person named Mary is running, and in this case
language plays a crucial role in carrying the information from Jon to the
listener. But we can imagine that Jon himself obtained this particular
item of information by virtue of seeing the event *e* concerned, in which
case the flow of information from *e* to Jon involves no use of language.

So what, then, can be said about meaning and information in general,
not restricting to linguistic meaning and the conveyance of information
by language? This forms the main topic for the remainder of this chapter.

4.2   Meaning

Barwise and Perry [5] give four simple examples to illustrate the diversity
that exists in the way one situation can *mean* another. I shall give the
four examples in this section, then in the next I shall examine the way

---

[4] Indeed, historically this was pretty well the approach originally taken by Barwise and
Perry in their book [5].

in which the notion of *constraint* introduced can give rise to a flow of information.

Smoke means fire. There is a regular relation between smoke and fire: situations where there is smoke are linked to situations where there is a fire. This linkage, which arises from the way the world is, is an example of what I shall call a *constraint*. If we let S_0 be the type of all situations where there is smoke and S_1 the type of all situations where there is fire, in symbols

$$S_0 = [\dot{s}_0 \mid \dot{s}_0 \models \ll\text{smoke-present}, \dot{l}, \dot{t}, 1 \gg]$$

$$S_1 = [\dot{s}_1 \mid \dot{s}_1 \models \ll\text{fire-present}, \dot{l}, \dot{t}, 1 \gg]$$

then this particular constraint will be denoted by the expression

$$S_0 \Rightarrow S_1$$

This is read as S_0 *involves* S_1, and represents a fact (i.e. a factual, parameter-free infon):

$$\ll\text{involves}, S_0, S_1, 1 \gg$$

Awareness of, or *attunement* to, this constraint is what enables a cognitive agent that perceives smoke in a situation to infer that the situation is part of a larger actuality in which there is a fire. Exactly what is involved in *awareness* or *attunement* here will be considered presently, but notice that it does not require language. Rather it amounts to a form of familiarity with, or behavioral adaptation to, the way the world operates *vis à vis* smoke and fires. A great many living creatures are aware of, or attuned to, this particular constraint, and make use of it in order to survive, though only humans have the linguistic ability to describe it with an expression such as SMOKE MEANS FIRE, and to use this expression to create a state of awareness of the constraint in others not yet familiar with smoke and fire, such as very young children.

It should be noted that, although the types S_0 and S_1 involve parameters $(\dot{l}, \dot{t})$, the constraint is a parameter-free infon that links two specific (parametric-) types. The role played by the various parameters in a constraint of this form will be considered in a moment.

Constraints of the above kind, corresponding to some natural law, are often referred to as *nomic constraints*.

Kissing means touching. If I tell you that Bob kissed Carol, then you may correctly infer that Bob touched Carol. The constraint in this case is a consequence of the original act of individuating (relational) uniformities, whereby kissing is a finer uniformity than touching. Awareness of this basic constraint is what enables you to obtain the information that Bob touched Carol, from being informed that Bob kissed Carol. Again, no use of language is involved in the inference mechanism (though in the case of the scenario described there is a use of language in conveying the original information about the kissing).

In this case, the constraint operates in a slightly different manner from the one above. Whereas it is not necessarily the case that the situation in which there is smoke is the same as the situation in which there is a fire (though the two may in fact be one and the same), it is surely the case that if *s* is a situation in which (say) Bob is kissing Carol, then in *that very same* situation, *s*, Bob is touching Carol.

I refer to such a constraint, that provides more information about *the same* situation, as a *reflexive constraint*. The reflexivity of the constraint may be represented in this notation by using the same situation parameter in the two type-abstractions. Thus:

$$S_2 \Rightarrow S_3$$

where

$$S_2 = [\dot{s} \mid \dot{s} \models \ll \text{kisses}, \dot{a}, \dot{b}, \dot{l}, \dot{t}, 1 \gg]$$

$$S_3 = [\dot{s} \mid \dot{s} \models \ll \text{touches}, \dot{a}, \dot{b}, \dot{l}, \dot{t}, 1 \gg]$$

(where $\dot{a}$ and $\dot{b}$ are parameters for persons, $\dot{l}$ is a *LOC*-parameter, and $\dot{t}$ is a *TIM*-parameter). Now, in point of fact, as noted already in Section 3.2, the abstraction parameter $\dot{s}$ used in the above type-abstractions 'disappears' when the types S_2 and S_3 are formed, giving rise to an argument role in each of these types. Thus my reliance on the use of the same abstraction parameter to denote a reflexive constraint is purely a notational convenience to depict a notion that is really about the linking of argument roles. A more formal development would proceed otherwise, but at the present level of description there is no harm in relying on notation here. The role played by the parameters $\dot{a}, \dot{b}, \dot{l}, \dot{t}$ will be considered in just a moment.

Barwise and Perry [5, p.97] refer to constraints that stem directly from the scheme of individuation, as is the case in the above example, as *necessary constraints*.[5] For most everyday examples, necessary constraints operate in a reflexive manner.

The ringing bell means class is over. The school bell rings and the students

---

[5] Note that this is a different form of classification from that of reflexivity. To describe a constraint as 'nomic' or 'necessary' is to provide some kind of indication as to why that particular constraint obtains. To say that a constraint is 'reflexive' is to stipulate the manner in which that constraint operates.

know it is time for class to end. The systematic relation that links these two types of situation, the ringing bell on the one hand and the end of class on the other, may be explained to the students by the teacher, or they may become aware of (or attuned to) it simply by observing (or adapting to) the way the one situation follows directly from the other. In any event, it is this constraint that causes the ringing of the bell to carry the information that class is over, and it is awareness of, or attunement to, the constraint that enables the students to pick up this information whenever they hear the sound of the bell.

The constraint here is essentially one of convention. If the bell breaks down, or goes off at the wrong time, or if the teacher decides to ignore it, then the linkage may be broken. Reliance on the constraint could then result in the conveyance of *mis*information — say the belief that the class is over when in fact it is not. No fundamental laws of nature are violated by the amendment or abandonment of this constraint, though the smooth functioning of a society depends, of course, upon everyone being made aware of any change in such *conventional constraints*.

This constraint may be represented thus:

$$S_4 \Rightarrow S_5$$

where

$$S_4 = [\dot{s}_4 \mid \dot{s}_4 \models \ll \text{rings}, b, \dot{t}, 1 \gg]$$

$$S_5 = [\dot{s}_5 \mid \dot{s}_5 \models \ll \text{over}, \dot{c}, \dot{t}, 1 \gg]$$

where b is the bell and $\dot{c}$ is a parameter for a class (i.e. a session of the class).

'Cookie' means cookie. The word COOKIE means cookie. If mother utters this word, four year old Alice may be expected to react the way small children do when being offered a cookie, that is, to come running with hand outstretched in order to accept the object the word COOKIE denotes. This, of course, is linguistic meaning, and as such involves a conventional constraint. By and large, the conventional constraints that govern linguistic meaning are observed by much larger groupings than are the kinds of constraint considered in the previous example. Language is only able to function in the way it does as an efficient conveyor of information, because the relevant constraints are observed throughout the given linguistic community. When a linguistic constraint is abused, as it may be, the result could be the conveyance of misinformation (if, for example, mother says COOKIE when there is no cookie) or no information at all (say, if Alice does not know the meaning of this word, or mother has simply made it up).

Exactly how linguistic meaning fits into our formalisms will be examined fully in the chapters on situation semantics. But to give some indication of what is involved, consider the sentence

HERE IS A COOKIE.

According to our present definition, the meaning of this sentence is a binary relation

‖HERE IS A COOKIE‖

that links the type of an utterance of the sentence (S_4) to the type of the described situation (S_5):

$$S_4 = [\dot{s_4} \mid \dot{s_4} \models \ll \text{says}, \dot{p}, \text{HERE IS A COOKIE}, \dot{l}, \dot{t}, 1 \gg]$$

$$S_5 = [\dot{s_5} \mid \dot{s_5} \models \ll \text{present}, \dot{c}, \dot{l}, \dot{t}, 1 \gg]$$

(where $\dot{p}$ is a parameter for a person and $\dot{c}$ is a parameter for a cookie).[6]

Thus, at this level of analysis, the linguistic meaning of this simple assertive sentence is a constraint

$$S_4 \Rightarrow S_5$$

(Though it might be argued that this particular constraint is reflexive, the issue is by no means clear cut, and in fact there are good reasons for *not* treating linguistic constraints as reflexive. In any event, I have not represented it here as a reflexive constraint.)

4.3   Meaning and information

How is it that a constraint

$$C = [S \Rightarrow S']$$

can give rise to a flow of information? The general picture is this. Relative to the constraint C (which I will always assume to be factual), a situation s will carry information provided $s : S[f]$, where f anchors the parameters in S and S'. In which case, the information carried by s *relative to* C is that there is a situation s', possibly extending s, of type $S'[f]$. (In the case of a reflexive constraint, the information carried is that the situation s itself is of type $S'[f]$.)

---

[6] See Chapter 8 for a more detailed discussion of this notion. In particular, the notation ‖Φ‖ will there be used to denote the binary relation between *situations* that is induced by the link between the type of the utterance and the type of the described situation, rather than this link itself, for which an alternative notation will be introduced.

For example, take the (factual) constraint *smoke means fire* that we expressed earlier with the formalism $S_0 \Rightarrow S_1$, where

$$S_0 = [\dot{s}_0 \mid \dot{s}_0 \models \, \ll \text{smoke-present}, \dot{l}, \dot{t}, 1 \gg]$$

$$S_1 = [\dot{s}_1 \mid \dot{s}_1 \models \, \ll \text{fire-present}, \dot{l}, \dot{t}, 1 \gg]$$

A situation s_0 will be informational relative to this constraint if s_0 is of type $S_0[f]$, where f anchors the parameters $\dot{l}$ and $\dot{t}$ to a location l_0 and a time t_0, respectively. That is to say, there must be a location l_0 and a time t_0 such that

$$s_0 \models \, \ll \text{smoke-present}, l_0, t_0, 1 \gg$$

In this case, the information carried by s_0 relative to C is that there is a situation s_1 of type $S_1[f]$; that is

$$s_1 \models \, \ll \text{fire-present}, l_0, t_0, 1 \gg$$

Thus, if you are walking along the road and you see smoke billowing up ahead (situation s_0), then, being aware of the constraint

$$S_0 \Rightarrow S_1$$

and observing that s_0 is of type $S_0[f]$, where $f(\dot{l}) = l_0$ is the location up ahead where you see the smoke and $f(\dot{t}) = t_0$ is the time at which you see the smoke, you may conclude that there is, at that very moment t_0, a fire at location l_0 (situation s_1, of type $S_1[f]$).

Of course, there is an alternative reading of the constraint *smoke means fire* that does not entail that the fire is either spatially or temporally coincident with the smoke. For instance, you step out of your house one morning to find the air filled with smoke that is drifting over from a fire that burnt earlier on the other side of town, but which has since been extinguished. In this case, the relevant constraint is of the form

$$S_0' \Rightarrow S_1'$$

where

$$S_0' = [\dot{s}_0 \mid \dot{s}_0 \models \, \ll \text{smoke-present}, \dot{l}_0, \dot{t}_0, 1 \gg]$$

$$S_1' = [\dot{s}_1 \mid \dot{s}_1 \models \exists \dot{l}_1 \exists \dot{t}_1 \ll \text{fire-present}, \dot{l}_1, \dot{t}_1, 1 \gg]$$

where $\dot{t}_1 = \dot{t}_0 \!\upharpoonright \ll <, \dot{t}_1, \dot{t}_1, 1 \gg$, a parameter for a time prior to $\dot{t}_0$. Now, the type S_1' here involves a construction that has not appeared before, namely existential parameter-quantification of an infon. This notion will be considered fully in the next chapter; in the meantime, the type S_1' may simply be read as the type of all situations in which there is a fire at *some* location and *some* previous time.[7] In this case, if s_0 is the situation you see, namely smoke in the air at location l_0 and time t_0, that is to say, $s_0 : S_0'[f]$ where $f(\dot{l}_0) = l_0$ and $f(\dot{t}_0) = t_0$, then you can conclude, on the basis of this constraint, that s_0 is part of a larger actuality s_1 of type $S_1'[f]$; that is to say, s_1 is such that at some location l_1 and some time t_1 prior to t_0, there was a fire:

$$s_1 \models \ll\text{fire-present}, l_1, t_1, 1 \gg$$

I leave it to the reader to perform a similar analysis of the use of the constraint *kissing means touching*. In this case, the use of the same parameters $\dot{l}$ and $\dot{t}$ in the types S_2 and S_3 ensures that the touching takes place at the same place and time as the kissing. Likewise the use of the same parameters $\dot{a}$ and $\dot{b}$ ensures that the kisser is the toucher and the one kissed is the one touched. The *notational* use of the same situation parameter $\dot{s}$ captures the fact that any situation, s, that is a kissing (i.e. is of type $S_2[f]$) will *itself* be a touching (i.e. of type S_3).

Turning now to the constraint *the ringing bell means class is over*, we represented this as

$$S_4 \Rightarrow S_5$$

where

$$S_4 = [\dot{s}_4 \mid \dot{s}_4 \models \ll\text{rings}, b, \dot{t}, 1 \gg]$$

$$S_5 = [\dot{s}_5 \mid \dot{s}_5 \models \ll\text{over}, \dot{c}, \dot{t}, 1 \gg]$$

where b is the bell and $\dot{c}$ is a parameter for a (session of the) class. Given a particular session, c, of the class, if the bell rings at time t (situation s_4) then the class c will be over at that time t (situation s_5). The constraint applies to the situations s_4 and s_5 by way of the anchoring f given by $f(\dot{s}_4) = s_4$, $f(\dot{s}_5) = s_5$, $f(\dot{c}) = c$, $f(\dot{t}) = t$. Situation s_4 is informational with respect to this constraint because $s_4 : S_4[f]$, and the information carried by s_4 relative to this constraint is the proposition $s_5 : S_5[f]$.

Finally, there is the linguistic constraint COOKIE *means cookie*. More precisely, consider the constraint corresponding to the meaning of the sentence HERE IS A COOKIE, namely:

$$C = [S_6 \Rightarrow S_7]$$

---

[7] As it stands, this constraint is still not quite right, since there is no link at all between the smokey situation and the firey situation. What is intended is that the smoke should be *caused* by the fire. This requires a modification to the type S_1' to take account of this causality, and indeed a similar modification should be made to each of the previous examples. Unfortunately, causality is by no means a simple matter to come to terms with, so I do not make this move now. Causality is discussed in Chapter 7 and subsequently.

where

$$S_6 = [\dot{s_6} \mid \dot{s_6} \models \ll \text{says}, \dot{p}, \text{Here is a cookie}, \dot{l}, \dot{t}, 1 \gg]$$

$$S_7 = [\dot{s_7} \mid \dot{s_7} \models \ll \text{present}, \dot{c}, \dot{l}, \dot{t}, 1 \gg]$$

(where $\dot{p}$ is a parameter for a person and $\dot{c}$ is a parameter for a cookie). In this case, use of the constraint C requires the anchoring of four parameters, $\dot{p}$, $\dot{c}$, $\dot{l}$, and $\dot{t}$. Now, in order to be an utterance of the above sentence, a situation, s_6 say, will have to contain an individual p such that at some location l and some time t

$$s_6 \models \ll \text{says}, p, \text{Here is a cookie}, l, t, 1 \gg]$$

Thus, if $f(\dot{p}) = p, f(\dot{l}) = l, f(\dot{t}) = t$, then $s_6 : S_6[f]$. But the anchor f is not enough to bring the constraint into play, since it does not provide an anchor for the parameter $\dot{c}$. The construct $s_6 : S_7[f]$ is not a proposition but a *parametric* proposition.

Now, one obvious way to proceed at this point is to replace the type S_7 by

$$S_7' = [\dot{s_7} \mid \dot{s_7} \models \exists \dot{c} \ll \text{present}, \dot{c}, \dot{l}, \dot{t}, 1 \gg]$$

in a fashion similar to the second smoke and fire example. But this is not quite right. People do not say "Here is a cookie" to mean "There is some cookie here," which is what the type S_7' corresponds to. Rather, the normal use of the English sentence Here is a cookie requires reference to a *specific* cookie, one that is present at the location and time of the utterance. (Actually, a picture of a cookie would serve as well in certain circumstances, such as when a father is teaching his child the meaning of the word 'cookie'.) What this amounts to in terms of our formalism is that a proper use of the constraint C involves the provision of an anchor f for *all* of the parameters $\dot{p}$, $\dot{l}$, $\dot{t}$, and $\dot{c}$ that figure in C.

Now that I have described the general mechanism by which one situation can provide information about another, we can take stock of the modifications we made to the fundamental notion of an 'infon'.

Initially, these were taken to represent basic items of information about the world. Then, however, as our theory developed, we introduced parameters into the picture. *Parameter-free infons* (or 'states of affairs') became the term attached to these basic items of information. *Infons*, that is *parametric infons*, were taken to be the basic 'informational units' that our theory used to study information flow — our main aim.

This is the usage that will be retained from now on. Thus, *parameter-free infons* are the basic items of information about the world; (*parametric*) *infons* are the basic units that we utilize in the study of information flow. The parametric infons are able to fulfill this role by virtue of their obvious close connection, via anchors, with parameter-free infons.

Of course, there is a certain tension in the way we speak of 'item or unit of information' in discussions such as the present one. Our theory treats *information* as *propositional*. That is to say, a single 'item' of information about the world comes in the form of a proposition

$$e \models \sigma$$

where e is a situation and σ is a parameter-free infon. On the other hand, it is natural to speak of the infon, σ, as providing 'information' about the situation e, indeed, of σ itself *being* an 'item of information'. I see no way to avoid this duplicity and at the same time retain a readable style of presentation. So I do not make such an attempt.

At this stage it is perhaps worth emphasising a point that may well not have escaped the reader. Namely, having started out with the intention of examining the manner in which one situation can contain information about or *mean* another (Section 4.2), we were led rather rapidly into a formulation of the relationship of one situation *type* involving another situation *type*. For it is by virtue of the very general connections between situation-types that we called *constraints* that information flow is made possible. When someone says that one particular situation s *means* another situation s', what they are claiming is that there is a very general relationship linking two *types* S and S', and that the situations s and s' are, modulo an appropriate anchoring, of types S and S', respectively. This approach precludes spurious 'meaning relations' that arise through 'accidental' or extensional connections.

For example, you look at your watch and you see that it says 12 o'clock. Being aware of the constraints that govern the way watches operate, and knowing that your watch is functioning correctly, you conclude that the time is 12 o'clock. The specific situation of your watch showing a reading of 12 o'clock at that very instant *means* that the time actually is 12 o'clock. Your conclusion is justified because there is a very general constraint that whenever a working watch says that the time is t, then in fact the time is t. Contrast this with the situation where your watch is broken, so that it says 12 o'clock all the time. Now a particular reading of the watch no longer *means* that it is 12 o'clock, *even if it happens to be 12 o'clock at the time.* The two specific situations are the same, namely your looking at the watch and seeing that it says 12 o'clock on the one hand, and the time actually being 12 o'clock on the other. What is missing on this occasion is the systematic relationship between types that would provide an informational link between these two situations.

Likewise the worrisome mathematical 'implication' on page 9 may be disposed of as just a spurious coincidence of truth values, lacking the informational support that would be provided by a constraint. (Though trying to pin down just what kind of constraint would suffice here does not seem easy. Indeed, there may be no simple constraint — the issue as to when a valid mathematical implication is 'meaningful' could well reduce to one of a subjective judgement of a mathematician.)

4.4   Attunement to constraints

Among the situations in the world are the 'mental states' of cognitive agents. These *internal* situations are systematically linked to *external* situations that the agent perceives and/or experiences. For instance, if you see a football on the lawn in front of you, your mental state is such as to reflect this fact. If the football forms but a small part of what you actively see, then its effect on your mental state will be quite small. If, on the other hand, you concentrate on the football and nothing else, then your conscious mental state will be focused upon that one image — a state that you may well describe as 'thinking about a football'. Exactly what constitutes such a mental state *in physical terms* need not concern us at this stage.[8] But it is clear that such states must and do exist and that they are intimately related to the seemingly more concrete situations in the world that they correspond to. (If you disagree, then just what are you doing looking at this page? Come to that, what is your disagreement but a mental state?)

I shall use $\sharp s$, $\sharp s'$, etc. to denote mental situations (i.e. particular mental states)[9] and $\sharp S$, $\sharp S'$, etc. for types of mental situations.

The following account is not intended to (necessarily) *describe* what is *actually* involved in attunement to a constraint by an agent. Rather it illustrates one way in which our framework can provide a mechanism that is at least adequate to be taken as a useful *model* of that process.

In order for a given agent, $\mathscr{A}$, to be able to discriminate situations

---

[8] Such questions form part of what is known as the *microstructure of cognition*, whereas situation theory is designed to deal with the *macro*structure. As you might expect, the two disciplines are not without a bearing upon each other.

[9] This tacit identification of 'mental situations' with 'mental states' is not quite correct, but will suffice for the present intuitive discussion. A more complete treatment of mental states is given in Chapter 6.

of type S, there must be a type $\sharp S$ of mental state that, under normal conditions, excluding hallucinations and the like, means (in the sense of the relation *involves*) that there is a situation of type S. That is, there must be a factual constraint $\sharp S \Rightarrow S$. The factuality of constraints of this form is clearly one of the requirements that must be satisfied by any agent that may be classified as cognitive. (There will also have to be some constraints that go the other way: $S \Rightarrow \sharp S$. In general, these will be subject to more stringent conditions.)

Attunement to, or behavior-guiding awareness or knowledge of, a constraint $C = [S \Rightarrow S']$ by an agent, $\mathscr{A}$, may now be described as follows. First the agent must be able to discriminate the two types S and S'. (As usual, this use of the word 'discriminate' is not intended to convey more than the most basic of cognitive activities.) Secondly, there has to be a link $\sharp S \Rightarrow \sharp S'$ between the corresponding mental types such that the following diagram commutes:

$$ S \quad \Rightarrow \quad S' $$
$$ \Uparrow \qquad\qquad \Uparrow $$
$$ \sharp S \quad \Rightarrow \quad \sharp S' $$

For example, suppose $S \Rightarrow S'$ represents our familiar *smoke means fire* constraint. Agent $\mathscr{A}$ sees a situation s of type S. This creates in $\mathscr{A}$ a corresponding mental state $\sharp s$ of type $\sharp S$ (i.e. a mental state appropriate to a perception of smoke). The internal constraint $\sharp S \Rightarrow \sharp S'$ then gives rise to a mental state $\sharp s'$ of type $\sharp S'$ (i.e. a state that could be described as embodying the thought 'there must be a fire'). The constraint $\sharp S' \Rightarrow S'$ then enables $\mathscr{A}$ to conclude correctly that there must in fact be a fire.

Notice that, from our standpoint, it is not important here to know just what, in either physical or mathematical terms, constitutes the mental states $\sharp s$ and $\sharp s'$ here. What matters is that there are constraints $\sharp S \Rightarrow S$ and $\sharp S' \Rightarrow S'$ that link these mental states to corresponding situations in the world. Formation of the link $\sharp S \Rightarrow \sharp S'$ by the agent then amounts to what I am calling *attunement* to, or behavior-guiding *awareness* of, the (non-mental) constraint $S \Rightarrow S'$.

Notice that the top level constraint $S \Rightarrow S'$ might be a reflexive constraint, but this does not mean that there need be any form of reflexivity in the corresponding mental constraint $\sharp S \Rightarrow \sharp S'$.

What else can we say at this stage? Well, there is obviously a great deal of difference between the three kinds of constraint involved in the above diagram.

The top constraint $S \Rightarrow S'$ is one that, at least in the case of the example given, represents a basic fact of the world, one that obtains irrespective of whether or not there are cognitive agents around to recognize any of the types or the situations involved.

The two vertical constraints $\sharp S \Rightarrow S$ and $\sharp S' \Rightarrow S'$ are what link the agent $\mathscr{A}$ to its environment, and what makes the mental states $\sharp S$ and $\sharp S'$ *meaningful* with respect to the environment. Failure to respect such a constraint would amount to an instance of breaking such a link to reality. In the case of humans, such a failure would probably be described as a case of *hallucinating*.

The remaining constraint, $\sharp S \Rightarrow \sharp S'$, is the purely internal one that connects two mental states. The main reason why a discussion such as this one might seem, on the surface, to lead nowhere is that descriptions of mental states and the constraints that link them are inevitably couched in terms of their external significance. For instance, we use S, S', and $S \Rightarrow S'$ in order to discuss their mental counterparts. Even if we were to give complete, rigorous mathematical descriptions of $\sharp S$, $\sharp S'$, and $\sharp S \Rightarrow \sharp S'$, which would be possible in principle if the agent concerned were an electronic computer, it would still be necessary to make reference to the external significance of these descriptions in order to carry out any meaningful discussion. (The positive side to these remarks is that they indicate how the theory of situations enables us to classify mental states in terms of their external significance — a topic I take up later in Chapters 6 and 7.)

4.5   A simple robot

In this section I make use of a fairly basic robotic device in order to illustrate some of the issues raised so far.

SID, a *simple illustrative device*, is a mobile robot with a visual detection system. *SID* can move forward in the direction of his visual field, but cannot turn or move sideways (or to the rear). When he moves, it is at a constant speed. The visual system consists of a single lens with a motor-driven auto-focus mechanism that keeps the lens in constant focus on any planar surface towards which it is directed.

SID is placed facing a wall in the center of a rectangular room. His task is to move to a distance exactly 1 meter from the facing wall and then stop.

What we need to do is investigate just what information processing abilities *SID* requires in order to perform this task.

The only thing *SID* needs to know about his environment is whether or not he is 1 meter from the facing wall. So let us provide him with a single binary state register device *W*. This register is to contain a 1 if *SID* is exactly 1 meter from the facing wall, a 0 otherwise. The initial value in *W* is to be 0.

In addition I shall supply *SID* with a motion control register, *M*, also binary. If *M* contains a 1 then the motor controlling *SID*'s motion is to be switched on, if the stored value is 0, the motor is to be switched off. The initial value of *M* is to be 0.

Our interest in *SID* is not in his input/output mechanisms, but rather the 'mental activity' that mediates between these two. In these terms, *SID*'s entire mental apparatus is based upon just the two registers *W* and *M*. In the absence of any constraints, this means that *SID* has a total of precisely $2 \times 2 = 4$ possible internal states. Our study concentrates upon the information-processing behavior of these states.

Faced with the construction of a device such as *SID*, how might we proceed? Well, as far as the motion control is concerned, things seem pretty straightforward. Simply arrange that the register *M* acts as a switch for the motor, so that if the content of *M* is a 1 then current flows through the motor, and if *M* has the value 0, then no current flows through the motor. Making the necessary connections inside *SID* provides the state variable *M* with an informational significance (in terms of *SID*'s activity) or *meaning*. Until the connection has been made, the content of register *M* has no meaning as far as the external behavior of *SID* is concerned. (Though it presumably does have some significance as far as the movement of electrons through the register circuit is concerned, etc. As always the crucial issue is that information is relative to the relevant constraints.) Once the connections have been made, there is a constraint linking the content of *M* and the state of the robot in its environment. The content of *M* being 1 now *means* that the robot is moving; the content being 0 *means* that the robot is stationary. There is a regular correspondence between those 'mental situations' where *M* has value 1 and those 'world situations' where *SID* is moving : a relation between types and types. In terms of our formalisms, *SID*'s behaving correctly (as specified by our design) amounts to respecting the constraint

$$C = [S \Rightarrow S']$$

where

$$S \;\; = \;\; [\dot{m} \mid \dot{m} \models \; \ll M{-}\text{value}, 1, TIM_1, POL_1 \gg]$$
$$S' \;\; = \;\; [\dot{s} \mid \dot{s} \models \; \ll \text{moving}, SID, TIM_1, POL_1 \gg]$$

Notice that there is no requirement made that *SID* is in any way *aware* of the external significance of his internal M-state — his mental capacity is, after all, pretty limited. Nevertheless the manner in which the register M is connected to *SID*'s motor does result in the value stored in M having the *meaning* that it does, as there is a definite informational link between the two. Knowing the value of M by some means or other, and being aware of or attuned to the constraint C, an observer would be able to reliably conclude that *SID* either was or was not in motion at that instant, according to which is the case. (For this particular example, the converse is also true, of course. The informational link goes both ways.)

Turning now to the connection between the register W and the visual input mechanism, we can make use of the auto-focus mechanism of the lens, attaching to it a switch that is activated when, and only when, the focus mechanism settles on a distance exactly 1 meter away. This switch then triggers, or indeed could *be*, the register W.

Now, it can hardly have escaped your attention that use is being made here of some fairly sophisticated technology in order to wire-up our purported 4-mental state robotic device. "Why ignore all the states involved in the silicon chip that controls the auto-focus device?" you might ask. The answer is that, complex though such devices are, they are essentially peripherals as far as the mental activity of *SID* is concerned. Our robot is only concerned with motion and avoiding crashing into the wall. *How* that is achieved is in itself not important. Just as when you are thirsty you don't concern yourself with the complex biochemical processes that led to that state. Nor do you try to analyze just what constitutes that state. You may, conceivably, just say to yourself "I'm thirsty." Usually though, you simply go and get a drink, and think no more of it.

However it is achieved then, once the register W is wired-up to the input sensor (eye) in a suitable fashion, the state of W acquires *meaning*. If W contains a 1, then *SID* must be 1 meter from the facing wall. The content of W being 0 means that this distance is more than 1 meter.[10] Making the connections in *SID*'s circuitry amounts to giving the state variable W this external significance. As long as *SID* is functioning correctly, this connection ensures that the type of external situation where

---

[10] What happens if we start off with *SID* less than 1 meter from the wall? In this case our robot will simply crash into the wall. This state of affairs amounts to reliance on constraints that for some reason or another do not apply in the given circumstances, a topic I consider in due course.

SID is more than 1 meter from the wall will be correlated to the type of mental situation where *W* has value 0.

So now we have managed to connect the input mechanism to the register *W* and the output mechanism to *M*. This has endowed both *W* and *M* with external significance (*meaning*), but does not provide *SID* with any means of controlling his behavior. In order to do this we need to supply an informational link between the two registers *W* and *M*. It is here that I take note of the intended behavior of our robot. Namely, I want *SID* to start to move towards the wall, and continue to do so until he is precisely 1 meter away, whereupon he should stop.[11]

It is, of course, an easy matter to achieve this. All that is required is to link registers *W* and *M* so that

$$M := 1 - W$$

To see that this works, consider the behavior of the robot. Initially, when we first switch *SID* on, both registers have value 0. In particular, *SID* is stationary. Being more than 1 meter from the facing wall, the register *W* retains the value 0. This causes register *M* to flip to value 1, and the robot starts to move forward. This motion continues until *SID* is exactly 1 meter from the wall. At this point, the value of *W* changes to a 1. So *M* becomes 0, and *SID* comes to a stop.

Notice that, for all the simplicity of this particular step, it is only when we come to connect together the two registers *W* and *M* that *SID* becomes capable of 'intelligent' (in terms of its environment and allotted task) behavior. It is this final connection that ensures that *SID* may maneuver himself towards the wall, and is attuned to the constraint that says an agent should stop before running into a wall. In imposing this pattern of behavior on our robot, we are, of course, restricting the number of mental states that *SID* may actually achieve: from a maximum possible of four to an achievable two plus the initial start-up state that is never returned to. Of course, if *SID* suffers some internal mental damage, he may be able to achieve states other than the two intended ones. In which case he may start crashing into walls, or refusing to budge altogether. People can suffer similar breakdowns of constraints. Computers do so with frustrating regularity.

With *SID* at our disposal now, let us see how the construction and

---

[11] I assume that he starts in the center of the room, remember, which is presumably at a distance considerably more than 1 meter from any wall. This point is related to the previous footnote.

behavior of this device fits into the overall development of situation theory so far.

First of all, *SID*'s input mechanism involves a clear conversion of information from analog to digital representation. The optical lens perceives a vast amount of information from the environment. But only one infon of that incoming information gets encoded (digitalized) by *SID*, namely

$$\ll 1\text{-meter-apart}, SID, \text{wall}, t, i \gg$$

where t is the time and $i = 0$ or 1.

In terms of *SID*'s own individuation capacities (as we might perceive them), the single infon 'recognized' by *SID* could be written as

$$\ll 1\text{-meter-from-wall}, t, i \gg$$

SID is not able to 'recognize' any other feature of his environment — he has no further mental concepts with which to do so. In particular, though his sensory input mechanism will perceive the (let us suppose) rectangular grid pattern on the walls, *SID* does not know[12] that the wall is so decorated. That particular piece of information is one of the many that are lost in the analog-to-digital conversion that forms part of *SID*'s perceptual–cognitive process.

Turning to the output mechanism (i.e. the motion control), the state variable M ensures that *SID* knows whether or not he is stationary or in motion at any given instant. He also knows any information nested therein. Thus, *SID* knows at any instant whether or not he is approaching the wall or whether or not he is getting further away from his starting point. In each of these cases there is a systematic informational link between the status of register M and the relevant world situation.

"But surely," the attentive reader will ask, "doesn't this last remark have the unfortunate, if not downright contradictory, consequence that a finite agent such as *SID* may 'know' an infinite number of facts — indeed, anything that is nested in the finitely many informational items that the system designer explicitly caters for?" Well, true enough this does follow from our definitions. But this is neither unfortunate nor contradictory. According to the basic tenets of situation theory, all information is relative to constraints. Identifying 'information possessed' with syntactic items in a database (a common practice) is to miss entirely

---

[12] For our present purposes I am using the word *know* synonymously with *having the information that*. In due course I shall have need to make a careful distinction between these two related notions.

this relative nature of information, and is an instance of what Barwise and Perry [5, p.38] refer to as *the fallacy of misplaced information*.[13] All that is required in order for an agent to 'know' (in the sense of having, or encoding, the information) that X, is for the agent to be in a state that is linked to X via a prevailing constraint, a constraint to which the agent may or may not be attuned. Since there will be infinitely many constraints that prevail in the agent's environment, this means that the agent will be in possession of an infinite amount of information. This indicates one reason why we should be careful to make the distinction between 'knowing' and 'having the information that'. For whereas the relative nature of information allows for a finite agent to be in possession of an infinite amount of information, common use of the word 'knows' would normally prevent this. (The confusion between these two notions is presumably the reason why the idea of being in possession of an infinite amount of information seems to cause problems for many people.)

So what, exactly, do we mean by *knowing*? Well, this is by no means an easy question to answer. A glance at any one of a number of books on this issue (see, for example [18]) will indicate that the nature of and relationship between the notions of information, knowledge, and belief is a profound and difficult one. Dretske [8, Chapter 4], whose approach to the entire domain of knowledge, information, and communication takes, as I do here, information as the basic notion (and whose work had a significant influence on the early development of situation theory), adopts as his working definition [8, p.86]:

Agent $\mathscr{A}$ knows that X if A's belief that X is caused (or causally sustained) by the information that X.

So in order to understand knowledge, an analysis of belief is required, and at once we seem to be entering a realm far removed from the mundane activity of our simple robot *SID*.

Fortunately for our development, however, it is not necessary to proceed down this tortuous analytic path at this juncture.[14] The distinction between *knowledge of* and *having the information that* that is relevant to our discussion of devices such as *SID* can be drawn by a consideration of the different ways in which these two notions affect behavior.

---

[13] In fact the reference cited is to a different instance of the fallacy.

[14] Though were we to do so, a tempting place to start would be by taking as *believed* just those informational items that are 'explicitly stored' by the agent, and which the agent is capable of taking 'cogniscence' of (in its own terms), and then taking Dretske's definition of *knowledge*. One problem then would be to make sense of that phrase 'explicitly stored'. I shall have more to say on this issue in Chapter 6.

According to the definition of information as being relative to constraints, being in possession of information is essentially passive. If an agent $\mathscr{A}$ is in a state that is linked to an informational item X by some prevailing constraint C, then we say that $\mathscr{A}$ *has* (or *encodes*) that information X. For $\mathscr{A}$ to *know* X, on the other hand, involves considerably more. In particular, it requires that $\mathscr{A}$ be 'aware' of the possession of this information, and takes cogniscence of this information in determining or guiding future activity. For example, if *SID* is functioning correctly, then when he reaches a distance 1 meter from the wall he stops. Why does he stop? Because, within his rather limited framework, he *knows* (we shall say) that he is that close to the wall. Now suppose that the link between *SID*'s internal state registers W and M is broken, but that these two registers otherwise function correctly, with the result that *SID* careers into the wall and self-destructs. Since the register W is still operating properly, it is still the case that, at the appropriate moment, *SID has the information* that he is only 1 meter from the wall, but he fails to act upon this piece of information. He does not (we shall say) *know* that particular item of information.

It should be emphasized again that I am not claiming to have in any sense *defined* what it means for an agent to *know* something. Nor for that matter do I think I have managed to come up with a notion that *really* gets at the distinction between knowing and merely having information. Rather I am saying that one factor that serves to distinguish between knowing and simply having information, that is adequate *for our present purposes*, is whether or not that information has any non-vacuous effect upon the agent's behavior. If there is an effect, I shall say that the agent *knows* that particular informational item; if not, then the agent merely *has* (or *encodes*) that information.

Returning to the previous discussion of *SID* now, what more can be said concerning the connection between the two registers W and M? Just this, in the light of the above discussion. It is this connection that enables *SID* to operate in the manner for which he was designed, namely to move towards the wall until a certain distance from it, and then to stop. It is precisely because the content of the register W affects the behavior of *SID* as it does, that we may say that *SID knows* when he is 1 meter from the wall and when he is not. (This is, of course, not to say that *SID* has any concept of '1 meter' in any real sense, let alone that he could refer to it with the phrase 'ONE METER'.) It does not follow that *SID* 'knows' any particular item of information that might be nested in the fact that he is 1 meter from the wall (or not, as the case may be). Knowing something by no means implies knowledge of nested information. Indeed simple finiteness considerations provide a cast-iron *proof* that this cannot be the case.

What happens if *SID* is set in motion at a distance less than 1 meter from the wall? As mentioned in an earlier footnote, in this case he simply runs straight into the wall. What does our theory have to say about this? How can it be that a machine whose design leads to what might well be called 'rational action' (i.e. stopping before hitting a wall) is capable of such 'irrational' behavior?

The point is that if we initially place *SID* at a distance of less than 1 meter from the wall, he is being forced to operate under circumstances for which he was not designed, circumstances under which the constraints to which he is attuned do not apply. Of course, in this particular case it would be easy to modify *SID*'s construction so that this problem does not arise — simply arrange for the register *W* to contain a 1 if the distance to the wall is 1 meter or more, and a 0 otherwise. (I deliberately did not do this, in order to bring out the present issue.) But even then it is easy to imagine scenarios where *SID* still behaved in an 'irrational' manner. The reason being that, outside of mathematics, it is in fact very rare to encounter a constraint that obtains universally, at all times and locations, and under all circumstances.

For instance, it is a constraint to which all humans are attuned that if an object held in the hand is released, it will start to move (downwards). But of course, reliable though this constraint is under normal circumstances, it does not obtain universally — it may not be relied upon in outer space for example. Part of the training program of astronauts involves their having to attune themselves to a quite different set of constraints involving the behavior of free objects, including themselves.

Likewise the distressing occurrence of birds flying headlong into plate-glass windows is an example of reliance on constraints that do not apply under all circumstances. In the glass-free world in which birds evolved it was a reliable constraint that if there were no object visible ahead then forward flight was safe. But in the presence of glass that constraint is no longer reliable. Indeed, many of the changes that various lifeforms have undergone in the course of their evolution may be regarded as adaptations to changes in the reliability of the constraints that govern activity.

In general then, any constraint *C* will be subject to a set *B* of *background conditions*, conditions under which that constraint will convey information rather than *mis*information, and thus may be relied upon by an agent attuned to C. This is not to say that the agent needs or is at all able to recognize the conditions that make up the collection B, or even be aware that such conditions are necessary in order for C to be informational. It is enough simply that the conditions in B obtain under the particular circumstances under which the agent functions. Thus the bird in the forest need have no awareness of the absence of glass in order to navigate safely. The very fact that there is no glass in the forest makes the relevant constraint a reliable one.

Likewise, the familiar constraint that if an egg is dropped it will fall and break, is not one that obtains universally. It only applies to eggs dropped within the Earth's gravitational field; and then only for eggs dropped more than some minimal distance; and then only for eggs that are not hard-boiled; though even then if the distance is great enough there will be a breakage. And then there is the question of the surface onto which the egg is dropped. And then ... In fact, this example illustrates that it is in general extremely difficult, if not impossible, to specify with any degree of certainty or exactitude just what are the background conditions under which a given constraint obtains. That does not render the constraint unreliable. All that matters is that the background conditions, *whatever they may be*, are met at the time and place the constraint is utilized.

In general, the only occasions when it becomes necessary to take cogniscence of background conditions and investigate what they are, are when a previously reliable constraint suddenly leads to error, or it is anticipated that a change in circumstances would result in a previously reliable constraint leading to error. Thus, for example, the background conditions pertaining to gravity are of no concern to the vast majority of mankind, who never experience anything other than the 'normal' effects of the Earth's gravity, but to the astronaut or to the team designing the space-ship and its equipment, these background conditions are of the utmost importance, and need to be specified as accurately as possible.

As far as our overall development is concerned, the dependence of constraints upon background conditions means that when we wish to to investigate the 'logic' that governs various activities (such as robot behavior), it is necessary to incorporate an extra parameter to allow for the background. Thus, a constraint C will in general involve three things, the two situation-types as before, together with a set of background conditions. This could be written as

$$C = [S \Rightarrow S'] \, / B$$

indicating that C is the constraint S involves S', the constraint being dependent on the background conditions in B being met.

In terms of infons, the constraint C could be written as

$$\ll \text{involves}, S, S', B, 1 \gg$$

One final remark. It should be noted that the simplicity of *SID* is a little misleading. Once you have a theory that can deal with a device that is capable of starting and stopping a particular activity, then in principle the only difference between that example and a more realistic and useful device is one of complexity. Of course, this is to oversimplify matters quite considerably, but it does indicate that the issues discussed in this section are no less relevant when it comes to the design of 'real life' robots for use in industry or wherever. For instance, the absence of any need to incorporate prevailing background conditions in a robot's knowledge base is a point that has been emphasised on numerous occasions by, among others, Stanley Rosenschein, whose own research is concerned with the design of actual, working robots; see for example [22].

5

Some Logical Issues

So far in our discussions I have said nothing about details of the logical processing of information. How, for instance, may two related infons be combined to yield a third infon? Indeed, is this the way we wish to view 'logic' within our infon-framework? To answer such questions I review once again the basic viewpoint that underlies the current work.

5.1 The standpoint

Our goal is to develop a mathematical theory of information — information as it is picked up, processed, and utilized by agents such as ourselves, other living organisms, and computers of one sort or another. Quite clearly, at the very outset this task requires our having available some reasonably fixed notion of what we mean by the word 'information'. This does not entail our saying just what *information* (really) is — indeed it seems highly unlikely that such could be achieved in any absolute sense. Rather we need to formulate some *notion* of 'information' that is sufficiently close to what we have in mind when we speak of 'information', and at the same time is sufficiently well-defined to allow the development of a scientific theory.

This much is, of course, common to any scientific theory. In developing their model of the atom at its various levels of refinement, physicists need not claim that matter *actually is* that way. Rather the *model* of the 'atom' provides an extremely useful way of thinking about certain aspects of matter at a certain level of detail. Again, and this example is very close to the way our theory handles information, the study of light often proceeeds by regarding it as a stream of *photons*, but its well-known behavior as a 'wave in the aether' indicates that neither the particle nor the wave picture is anything more than a way of looking at things, a means of getting a particular handle on some aspect of the phenomenon. Similarly, postulating the existence of objects called *gravitons* can facilitate study of gravity, and flowing *electrons* provides a useful picture of electric current. Though the success of such theorizing may often lead to our regarding such *models* of (aspects of) reality as 'true' pictures of what is going on, this is, of course, purely self-deception, as the history of science has demonstrated time and time again. At best such theories can provide good 'approximations' to what is going on.

In our study of *information* then, our first task is to formulate some notion of what it is we wish to study — some formal concept of *information* as we see it. Our starting point is that the very concept of information only becomes salient in the presence of information *processors* of one form or another. So we develop a (simple) model of the world as it relates to an information processing agent in that world.

We begin by observing that any cognitive agent[1] will behave in a manner that discriminates, and may even be equipped with the ability to individuate, objects (i.e. *individuals*), spatial and temporal *locations*, certain *properties* that apply to those entities and *relations* that link them, and structured parts of the world (*situations*). Our theory is built upon an initial collection of *individuals, locations, properties, relations,* and *situations*. Since the exact collection of such basics will depend upon the agent, or possibly the species of agent, our theory remains largely agnostic as to what is and what is not taken as an *individual, location, property, relation,* or *situation.* Rather we simply assume at the outset, the existence of a *scheme of individuation* that provides us with this ontology.

In order to facilitate a scientific study, we concentrate our attention on individual packets of (conceptual) information, which we call *infons,* determined by the scheme of individuation. This is not to say that 'information' really does consist of such 'packets' or that they have any kind of physical existence. It is simply a maneuver that gives us something upon which to build a theory. Thus the ontological question *'What is information?,* remains unanswered (and probably unanswerable) in any absolute sense. Instead we have provided ourselves with a *definition* of what we shall *take for* 'information'.

I shall commence by taking a close look at the fundamental objects that form the basis of our concept of 'information' — the properties and relations.

---

[1] This 'observation' really amounts to a specification of properties required of the kind of agent I shall be considering.

5.2   Properties and relations

Suppose I utter the sentence

Jon sold the house.

This seems perfectly informational. Hearing me, and, let us suppose, being aware who Jon is, you learn something about this individual. In fact, you probably learn quite a lot as a result of the utterance: the fact that Jon had a house for which he had no further need, the fact that someone else wanted to buy this house, and so on, plus additional information about me as the speaker, in particular the fact that I have this information to impart. But the main item of information you acquire is the item I intend my utterance to convey, namely its propositional content.

So what is the propositional content of my utterance? The sentence I utter introduces explicitly precisely these uniformities: the individual Jon, a certain house, and the relation of *selling*. So a reasonable suggestion would be to take the propositional content to be

$$e \models \sigma$$

where e is the described situation and

$$\sigma = \ll \text{sells, Jon, } h, 1 \gg$$

where h is the house concerned. This certainly seems to capture the principal item of information conveyed by my utterance, but is it correct as far as our theory is concerned? More specifically, is σ a properly formed *infon*? Well, it will be provided the relation *selling* takes precisely two arguments, one of which may (should) be a person and the other some individual capable of being sold. Leaving aside for the moment the issue as to the type of objects that may fill a particular argument role in a relation, is it in fact the case that *selling* is a two-place relation?

What about the time at which the selling is carried out? Though my utterance contained no explicit reference to the time of selling, my use of the word 'sold' indicates that this particular act of selling must have taken place at some time in the past. But what time? Ten minutes ago? Yesterday? Last year? The sentence used in my utterance does not make this clear. But that does not prevent the utterance being informational. The actual wording simply constrains the time of the selling to be some time in the past. So perhaps we should modify the infon σ above to:

$$\sigma' = \ll \text{sells, Jon, } h, t, 1 \gg$$

where t is some time prior to the utterance, the time the selling took place.[2] By taking note of tense, this infon seems to have a better claim on the content of my utterance.

So now we are taking *selling* to be a three-place relation, one that has time as an argument. But what about the location at which the selling takes place? Should not account be taken of that? It may not be irrelevant. For instance, if it were not a house that Jon was selling but marijuana, the location could make all the difference between life, liberty, and even death as far as Jon is concerned. In which case, ought not the infon used to determine the propositional content be:

$$\sigma'' = \ll \text{sells, Jon, } h, l, t, 1 \gg$$

where l is the location at which the selling took place (wherever that location might be)? Admittedly, my utterance made no mention of the location of the selling, not even an oblique reference. But *selling* does seem to involve a location argument, so maybe we should include it in the infon nevertheless.

If we do, that makes *selling* a four-place relation. But then what about the person to whom the house was sold? Surely, by the same token there should be an argument place for that individual, without whom there could be no selling? In which case maybe our basic infon here should be

$$\sigma''' = \ll \text{sells, Jon, } p, h, l, t, 1 \gg$$

where p is the person who bought the house.

And then what about the amount of money that changed hands as part of the transaction? Should there be an argument place for that too? It is certainly easy to imagine cases where this argument would be important — say if the sale gave rise to a future legal suit.

And maybe there are other arguments — arguments that in general are not mentioned but which under special circumstances become highly relevant. This possibility merely serves to emphasize the point I am trying to make: that everyday, run-of-the-mill, 'real world' relations generally comprise fairly complex interlinkages between a whole range of possible arguments — though it is not at all necessary to know how each and every argument place of a relation is filled in order for an utterance involving that relation to be informational.

---

[2] I have mentioned already in this essay the fact that it may not always be possible to stipulate some particular time or location in terms of standard means of reference, so this use of the time t is not problematical for us — its definition as the time of the selling is perfectly adequate.

Consequently, it is important that in formulating our theory, some kind of allowance be made for, or account be taken of, any such 'hidden' arguments when we use relations as constituents of infons. The question is, how do we achieve this goal?

There are three plausible routes to take. One is to allow duplication of relations to facilitate different usages. For example, in the case of *selling*, there would be a two-place selling relation, a three-place selling relation, a four-place selling relation, a five-place, maybe a six-place, and so on.

A second possibility is to work with 'relations' that may take a whole range (possibly infinite) of numbers of arguments. Thus, *selling* would be a single relation that could take anything from two to five (or maybe six, seven, or whatever) arguments on any one occasion.

Or, a third alternative is to work with relations having a single, fixed number of argument places, but to allow the use of relations with unfilled argument roles. Thus, *selling* would have a fixed number of argument places (let us say six), but each of the objects $\sigma, \sigma', \sigma'', \sigma'''$ above would be a well-formed infon. (When I speak of unfilled roles here, I mean unfilled in the sense of the theory. Clearly, any state of affairs or activity in the world involving a particular relation can only occur with every argument role filled. If I am eating, then I must be eating *something*, though you could have the information that I am eating without in any way having the information as to what I am eating. Since our main interest here is with information that agents can pick up about situations in the world, our theory has no need to insist upon information about every argument of a relation.)

Of these three alternatives, the last one is, I think, the one that most closely reflects common usage, and consequently this is the approach that will be adopted in this account.

From now on, therefore, I shall assume that every relation has a fixed number of argument places that cover all the possible arguments the relation has (in any usage), including location and time arguments where appropriate. Postponing for a moment an explanation of the terms *appropriate for, argument place*, and *minimality conditions*, we have the following, formal definition of an infon.

If R is an n-place relation and $a_1, \ldots, a_m$ ($m \leq n$) are objects appropriate for the argument places $i_1, \ldots, i_m$ of R, and if the filling of argument places $i_1, \ldots, i_m$ is sufficient to satisfy the minimality conditions for R, then for $i = 0, 1$, the object

$$\ll R, a_1, \ldots, a_m, i \gg$$

is a well-defined *infon*.

If $m < n$, the infon is said to be *unsaturated*; if $m = n$ it is *saturated*.

For example, take the relation *selling*. I shall assume this relation has six argument places: a seller, a buyer, an object sold, a price, a location of selling, and a time of selling.

Then the object

$$\ll \text{sells, Jon, David, } h, \text{ \$350,000, Palo Alto, 1.1.88, 1} \gg$$

is a (well-formed) saturated infon, while each of the following is a (well-formed) unsaturated infon:

$$\ll \text{sells, Jon, } h, 1 \gg$$
$$\ll \text{sells, Jon, David, } h, \text{ 1.1.88, 1} \gg$$
$$\ll \text{sells, Jon, David, } h, \text{ Palo Alto, 1980, 0} \gg$$

But wait a moment. The above notation does not seem to distinguish between the various arguments the relation has. Rather I am relying on the reader's understanding of the particular example used, in order to figure out that it is Jon who does the selling, David the buying, the house h the item sold, and so on, and not David that is being sold for a price of Palo Alto at a location 1980, or some such nonsense. Indeed, such reliance on the reader has been the case with all the examples given in the book so far. Clearly, this approach is not at all appropriate for a theory with the ambitious aims of this one. At least, it would not be appropriate if it were anything more than just a convenient device to present clear examples. But in fact it is not. Rather what is going on is this.

Each relation has a fixed collection of *argument roles* — 'slots' into which appropriate objects can be placed. These argument roles are not ordered in any way, and certainly not linearly ordered as a finite sequence $a_1, \ldots, a_n$. Rather the relation is a structured, abstract object, and part of its abstract structure concerns the argument roles of the relation. That is the way things are, and one of our tasks as theorists studying these abstract objects is to devise some notation that enables us to talk about them.

The most straightforward method, and the one I adopt here, is to denote each argument role by the 'role' it plays in the relation. That is to say, in the case of the relation *selling*, the argument roles are:

seller, buyer, object-sold, price, location, time.

The relation of *selling* then provides a structure linking these argument roles.

Specification of a relation within our theory thus requires a listing of the argument roles along with the relation of which they are part. For example, we can specify the *selling* relation like this:

⟨ sells | *seller, buyer, object-sold, price, location, time* ⟩

Of course, there is still a certain ordering involved in our notation, in that we have to write down the various roles in *some* order. But this is now very clearly a notational question. Though in the above example I have adopted an ordering that corresponds fairly closely with the kind of word order that arises in English sentences concerned with the relation of *selling*, it is obvious that any other order would do as well.

With this approach to relations, we clearly need a corresponding change in the manner in which we denote infons. The following seems fairly natural. What was formerly written as

≪sells, Jon, David, *h*, 1985, 1 ≫

may be written instead in the form

≪sells, *seller* ↝Jon, *buyer* ↝David, *object-sold* ↝*h*, *time* ↝1985, 1 ≫

or possibly in the form

≪sells, *time* ↝1985, *buyer* ↝David, *object-sold* ↝*h*, *seller* ↝Jon, 1 ≫

or any other rearrangement of the argument roles.

Thus I am using the notation *role* ↝a to denote that the object 'a' fills the argument role '*role*'.

All of which having been said, for most of the discussions and examples, I will in fact continue to employ the suggestive, reader-dependent notation used all along, since this provides for ease of understanding. But the above observations indicate that this is indeed a purely notational convenience that could be dispensed with if there were some need for a more formal precision. Such precision might in fact be required when dealing with our next point.

What is the status of an object such as

≪sells, *seller* ↝Inglebørough, *object-sold* ↝*h*, *time* ↝1.1.88, 1 ≫

Given that Ingelborough is a small mountain in Yorkshire, and hence is quite unable to sell a house on January 1, 1988, or indeed at any other time, is this simply a false infon or does it not even qualify as an infon in the first place? If the former, then by simply changing the polarity from a 1 to a 0, we obtain a true infon (i.e. a fact), of course. Do we want such an object to be amongst the 'facts' of our theory?

It is, very largely, a matter of taste. The approach I adopt is that an object such as the above is *not* an infon. The reason for making the distinction is that there seems to be a very clear difference between the information content of an utterance

Jon did not sell a house

and an utterance of

Ingleborough did not sell a house.

As a person, Jon is the kind of individual that is eligible to fill the *seller*-role of the relation *selling*, whereas Ingleborough, being a mountain, is not. Consequently, the information content of an utterance of the first sentence is significant, that of the second effectively zero. (Indeed, totally zero in the Shannon sense of 'suprisal value'.)

This distinction is reflected in our theory by the way we treat relations and the objects that are eligible to fill their various argument roles. Each argument role has associated with it a certain *type*, the type of object that may legitimately fill that argument role. The association of a type with each argument role is regarded as still another facet of the relation, that has to be taken account of in our notation just as do the argument roles in the first place.

For example, in the case of *selling* let us amend our previous notation so as to read something like this:

$$\langle sells \mid seller:S, \; buyer:B, \; object\text{-}sold:K, \; price:P, \; location:LOC, \; time:TIM \rangle$$

where S is the type of all individuals that are capable of selling things (presumably the type of all persons and all human organizations), B is the type of all individuals capable of buying things (presumably the same type as S), K is the type of all sellable objects, and P is (let us assume) the type *MONEY*. (Selling being a worldly relation, these types can be defined as object types relative to the world as the grounding situation.)

In order to qualify as a well-formed *infon*, any object assigned to fill an argument role of the relation of that 'infon' must be of the appropriate type, or else must be a parameter that can only anchor to objects of that type.

Thus the very definition of 'infon' distinguishes between falsity and nonsensity, in that the filling of argument roles with inappropriate objects is completely ruled out.

To return to the issue of saturated and unsaturated infons, introduced a short while ago but temporarily abandoned while we fixed our definitions and notations, what exactly is the informational import of an unsaturated infon?

To take a simple example, what information is encapsulated in the unsaturated infon

$$\sigma = \ll \text{eats, John}, t, 1 \gg$$

where *eating* is the four-place relation

$\langle$ eats | *eater:ANIMAL, thing-eaten:EDIBLE-SUBSTANCE,*
location:LOC, time:TIM $\rangle$

(In σ, the argument roles of *eater* and *time* are filled thus: *eater* ⤳ John, *time* ⤳ *t* , while the other two argument roles, *thing-eaten* and *location*, are left unfilled.)

If *t* is the present time, then typically an utterance of the sentence

John is eating

could have σ as its principal information content. (By which I mean that the propositional content of the utterance is $e \models \sigma$, where *e* is the described situation.) If you were to hear me utter this sentence, you would have no difficulty in understanding what was going on. This character John is currently eating. He is obviously eating *something*, but I have not indicated what it is, so you don't bother to think about this aspect of the eating. (Unless there are contextual factors that make the thing-eaten relevant. But this is another issue.) You simply concentrate on John's act of eating, going on right now. Likewise, John must be eating *somewhere*, but I have not mentioned his location either, so you do not bother about that. (Again, contextual factors apart.)

In terms of the sentence I utter, if we fill in the things I leave unsaid, we therefore obtain something like this:

John is [now] eating [something] [at some location].

This is not to say that my utterance is somehow *shorthand* for this expanded sentence. Rather, in using the sentence I do, I am providing you with certain information about John's current situation — information which is *partial* with regards to the eating relation as it concerns John, but which is genuine information for all that.

Thus, unfilled argument roles, such as the *thing* John is eating and the *location* at which he is doing it, bear some resemblance to existentially quantified variables. (This is for the case of an infon with polarity 1. If the polarity is 0, unfilled argument roles act like universally quantified variables — see presently.) If the infon σ above is a fact, then *there must be* an object *a* and *there must be* a location *l*, such that the (saturated) infon

$$\sigma' = \ll \text{eats, John}, a, l, t, 1 \gg$$

is a fact.

But it should be stressed that, this connection notwithstanding, unsaturated argument roles are *not* the same as existentially quantified roles. The facility to leave one or more argument roles unfilled allows us to get at the meaning of an utterance such as

John is eating

and this is quite different from the meaning of an utterance of the sentence

John is eating something.

Because there is a prevailing reflexive constraint to the effect that if an agent is eating then that agent is eating something, any situation in which John is eating will be a situation in which John is eating something. Consequently, the propositional content of an utterance of *'John is eating'* will be equivalent to that of an utterance of *'John is eating something'*. What Jon is doing is the same in both cases. Nevertheless, these two sentences do appear to have a different effect on the listener: in the first case attention is focused solely on John, in the second on both John and the unknown something that is being eaten. The exact distinction between these two utterances as far as their propositional contents are concerned depends on the notion of an existentially quantified infon, to be discussed in Section 5.5. The propositional content of an utterance of the sentence *'John is eating'* is

$$e \models \ll \text{eats, John}, t, 1 \gg$$

where t is the time of utterance, while that of an utterance of the sentence *'John is eating something'* is

$$e \models \exists \grave{a} \ll \text{eats, John}, \grave{a}, t, 1 \gg$$

Notice that the same sort of problem need not arise in other, superficially similar cases. For example, consider utterances of *'John is telephoning'* and *'John is telephoning someone'*. In this case, though there is a constraint to the effect that if a person is telephoning then they must be telephoning someone, this constraint is not reflexive, and consequently the receiver of the telephone call is not *forced* to be part of the telephoning situation.

One issue that has not arisen in any of the examples so far is that in order for a relation, R, to give rise to an 'item of information', that is to say, a well-formed infon, it is necessary that a certain minimal collection of argument roles of R be filled. For example, in the case of the relation *selling* considered above, neither of the following is 'informational' and hence is not a properly formed infon:

$$\ll \text{sells}, 1 \gg \quad , \quad \ll \text{sells}, \textit{seller} \leadsto \text{John}, 1 \gg ;$$

on the other hand, the following are informational and hence are well-formed infons:

$$\ll \text{sells}, \textit{object-sold} \leadsto h, 1 \gg$$

$$\ll \text{sells}, \textit{seller} \leadsto \text{John}, \textit{object-sold} \leadsto h, 1 \gg$$

In particular, notice that an utterance of '*John sells*' is not normally informational, but an utterance of '*The house is sold*' is informational.

This example highlights the fact that just which argument roles must be filled in order to result in a well-defined infon, is very much dependent upon what the relation is. Part of the complex structure that constitutes a 'relation' is the collection of conditions that determine which particular groups of argument roles need to be filled in order to produce an infon. I refer to these conditions as the *minimality conditions* for the relation.

To sum up, then, if R is an n-place relation with argument roles $r_1, \ldots, r_n$, and if $a_1, \ldots, a_m$, $m < n$, are appropriate fillers of the roles $r_1, \ldots, r_m$, respectively, such that $\ll R, a_1, \ldots, a_m, 1 \gg$ is an infon, and if

$$s \models \ll R, a_1, \ldots, a_m, 1 \gg$$

then there must be a situation s' extending s, and objects $x_{m+1}, \ldots, x_n$ in s' that are appropriate for the roles $r_{m+1}, \ldots, r_n$, respectively, such that

$$s' \models \ll R, a_1, \ldots, a_m, x_{m+1}, \ldots, x_n, 1 \gg$$

(This assumes a property of infons known as *persistence*. Though I have been tacitly assuming this property all along, the issue has not really arisen until now. I take it up in the following section.)

It should be stressed that, throughout the preceding discussion, I have been concentrating on infons with polarity 1. In the case of infons with polarity 0, unfilled argument roles behave as universally quantified variables. Thus, if $R, r_1, \ldots, r_n, a_1, \ldots, a_m$ are as before, and if $\ll R, a_1, \ldots, a_m, 0 \gg$ is an infon, then if

$$s \models \ll R, a_1, \ldots, a_m, 0 \gg$$

it must be the case that for all situations s' extending s and all $x_{m+1}, \ldots, x_n$ in s' that are appropriate for the roles $r_{m+1}, \ldots, r_n$, respectively,

$$s' \models \ll R, a_1, \ldots, a_m, x_{m+1}, \ldots, x_n, 0 \gg$$

(Persistence is also assumed here.)

I end this section by asking what the situation is with regard to argument roles in infons being filled by parameters? The answer is simple. As far as saturation of an infon is concerned, there is no difference between filling an argument role with an object and filling

it with a parameter for such an object. The cases where a parameter
will fill a role typically arise in the context of some information-bearing
structure that cuts across situations or situation-types, such as in the case
of constraints. This is best illustrated by means of some simple examples.

I start with an utterance of the sentence[3]

$$\Phi : I\ am\ eating.$$

Uttered by David, at time t, the propositional content of the utterance
is that David is eating at time t. That is to say, if u is the utterance
situation, so in particular

$$u \models \{\ll\text{speaking, David}, t, 1 \gg , \ll\text{saying, David}, \Phi, t, 1 \gg\}$$

and if e is the described situation (namely the situation David implicitly
refers to by his utterance, a situation of which he himself is an integral
part), then, provided David's utterance is truthful:

$$e \models \ll\text{eats, David}, t, 1 \gg$$

In terms of our theory of linguistic meaning, the connection between
the two situations u and e is provided by the *meaning* of the sentence Φ.
The meaning together with (certain features of) the utterance, determine
the type of the described situation and hence the propositional content
of the utterance.

More precisely, the meaning, $\|\Phi\|$, of the sentence Φ is the link between
the two situation-types

$$U = [\dot{u} \mid \dot{u} \models \{\ll\text{speaking}, \dot{a}, \dot{\imath}, 1 \gg , \ll\text{saying}, \dot{a}, \Phi, \dot{\imath}, 1 \gg\}]$$

$$E = [\dot{e} \mid \dot{e} \models \ll\text{eats}, \dot{a}, \dot{\imath}, 1 \gg]$$

To be an utterance of Φ, a situation u must be of type U. In which case
the propositional content of the utterance is that the described situation
is of type E; that is to say, u is part of a larger actuality in which the
speaker is eating.

The fact that it is the speaker that is eating, as stipulated by the use
of the pronoun 'I', is determined in our theory by the use of the same
parameter $\dot{a}$ in both types U and E. Likewise the fact that the eating
is going on at the time of the utterance, stipulated linguistically by the
tense of the verb ('*am* eating'), is accounted for by the use of the same

---

[3] In fact I could make essentially the same points using the previous sentence *John is
eating*, but the use of the first person singular pronoun 'I' brings out the various issues
more clearly. I am grateful to Stanley Peters for making this suggestion.

parameter $\dot{\imath}$ in both types. Thus the parameters play a significant role in the way the sentence meaning gives rise to a flow of information, by providing a means of representing specific links between features of the utterance situation and features of the described situation.

It is because of the crucial role played by parameters in the flow of information that I use the word 'infon' to refer to the parametric objects rather than just the non-parametric objects that were initially referred to by this name in Chapter 1. Non-parametric infons, or 'states of affairs' are the basic items of information about the world; parametric infons are the basic units our theory uses in order to study the transmission of information.

Of course, choosing to represent informational links by means of parameters, though convenient, does carry a price. According to our present way of doing things, if the parameters $\dot{a}$ and $\dot{\imath}$ in the above types U and E were replaced by different parameters $\dot{a}'$ and $\dot{\imath}'$, then different types would result, say U' and E', and then surely the link between U' and E' ought also to qualify as being the meaning of Φ. Thus it would seem that there is a whole family of technically distinct 'meanings'. Which one do we choose?

The answer is that all of these different pairs of types U, E are, in a sense, equivalent. The actual choice of parameters is not important. The parameters merely keep track of certain *linkages* between the two types. The *meaning* of the sentence is the composite connection between the types, a constraint, and as such it is a holistic entity that does not involve parameters. The parameters only appear when we *pull apart* the meaning into two separate types, the type of the utterance and the type of the described situation.

Similar remarks apply to all my uses of parameters. They provide tracking devices or markers that our theory uses to represent various abstract, informational links. As such, there is nothing to prevent different parameters being used in connection with the same link, just as in our everyday lives we often use several names to refer to the same person or object. A formal mathematical development of situation theory would introduce axioms that reflect this fact, in much the same way that the 'exchange of free variables' rules operate in first-order predicate logic.

Notice that both parameters $\dot{a}$ and $\dot{\imath}$ have to be anchored in order to pass from an utterance situation to the corresponding propositional content. On the other hand, neither of the types U, E is determined by a saturated infon. No mention has been made of the location of either the utterance or the eating, nor do we have any idea just what

David is eating. These argument roles are unfilled, either by objects or parameters, and as such have a certain 'inaccessibility', playing no part in this particular information flow.

Filling an argument role with a parameter makes that particular role a salient feature which then has to be taken account of. In particular, all parameters in, say, a (parametric) infon have to be anchored in order for that infon to provide information about the world. Unfilled argument roles may be left unfilled.

The significant role played by parameters becomes even more apparent when we carry out a deeper study of situation semantics. I pre-empt material considered more fully later, in order to provide my second illustration of parametric role-filling.

In going straight from the *utterance* of a sentence Φ (via the *meaning*, $\|\Phi\|$) to the described situation, I am able to arrive at the propositional content of *the utterance of* Φ, but along the way something has been lost, a feature that occupies a position somewhere between the meaning of Φ and the propositional content of an utterance of Φ. This semantic feature is connected to Φ and its meaning, rather than to any particular utterance of Φ.

Consider again my example

$$\Phi : I \; am \; eating.$$

My fundamental standpoint of working with specific *utterances* of Φ obscures, to some extent, one obvious feature that all utterances of Φ have in common — a semantic uniformity across all utterances of Φ: namely, the parametric infon

$$\ll eats, \dot{a}_s, \dot{t}_n, 1 \gg$$

where $\dot{a}_s$ is a parameter for the *speaker* and $\dot{t}_n$ is a parameter for the *present time*. The corresponding (parametric) type

$$F = [\dot{e} \mid \dot{e} \models \; \ll eats, \dot{a}_s, \dot{t}_n, 1 \gg]$$

will be called the *descriptive content* of the sentence Φ. (Actually this is not quite right. The descriptive content is really a function not of Φ but of the *type* of an utterance of Φ, since it is this type that provides the parameters $\dot{a}_s$ and $\dot{t}_n$. But the type of an utterance of Φ is to all intents and purposes entirely determined by Φ itself, so I shall systematically blur this distinction. This issue will be taken up more fully in Chapter 8.)

Whilst self-evidently related to the type, E, of the described situation considered above, the descriptive content is not exactly the same, in that the parameters in E are not restricted in the way they are in F. This reflects the different uses we make of these two types. In determining the propositional content, the utterance situation provides the anchors for the parameters in E. In the case of the type F on the other hand, we are not concerned with specific utterances, but rather we are trying to get at that '*parametric*' information content of the *sentence* — that semantic feature of Φ that is somehow prior to the propositional content of any utterance of Φ.

The descriptive content of Φ supplies 'parametric information' about the described situation. This 'parametric information' is uniformly associated with (the *type* of an utterance of) Φ, rather than with any specific utterance thereof, and captures what it is that all propositional contents of all utterances of Φ have in common. Given appropriate anchorings for the parameters, the descriptive content yields a particular propositional content.

Of course, given the way the machinery is set up, we could avoid having two different types E and F here, by replacing the type E in $\|\Phi\|$ by F. This would still lead to the same propositional content of any utterance of Φ. Indeed, a more detailed development of situation semantics might well adopt such an approach. But at this preliminary stage, with the various definitions as they have been developed so far, having the two different types around serves to emphasize the distinction between the two concepts. (In other linguistic studies, the separation of semantics from pragmatics results in an analogous distinction.)

To finish, let me stress again that the appearance of a parameter in an infon does not represent some form of quantification. An occurrence of a parameter, $\dot{x}$, in an infon with polarity 1 does not constitute an existential quantification over objects of the type to which $\dot{x}$ may be anchored, nor does its occurrence in an infon with polarity 0 constitute a universal quantification over such objects. Rather, in both cases the parameter acts as a kind of 'proxy' for some particular, but unspecified, object of the appropriate type. The situation is different regarding unfilled argument roles in relations. Parameters and argument roles are quite distinct notions, having quite different functions in our theory. Argument roles are 'slots' in relations, slots that may be filled by either objects or parameters. Parameters are 'representatives' for objects, used by our theory in order to capture informational linkages between one situation and another. An unfilled argument role in a relation represents a feature of that relation that is not being considered. Filling that argument role with a parameter makes that feature salient and able to contribute to information flow. In order to supply information about the world, all parameters in, say, an infon must be suitably anchored. There is no such requirement on unfilled argument roles.

5.3   Persistence

Any infon is assumed to have the property of *persistence*. This means that if

$$s \models \ll R, a_1, \ldots, a_n, i \gg$$

for any situation, s, and appropriate objects $a_1, \ldots, a_n$ in s, then

$$s' \models \ll R, a_1, \ldots, a_n, i \gg$$

whenever s' is a situation that extends s.

Persistence of infons is closely connected to the minimality conditions mentioned in the previous section. I give a couple of examples, starting with the relation of being *alone*. It is quite possible for an individual, a, to be alone in a situation s (at some time t), and not alone in some larger situation s' (at time t). Thus if the relevant objects were infons, we could have:

$$s \models \ll \text{alone}, a, t, 1 \gg$$

and

$$s' \models \ll \text{alone}, a, t, 0 \gg$$

where s' extends s. But the objects involved here are not properly formed infons, since not enough argument roles are filled to satisfy the minimality conditions. In the case of the relation *alone*, in order to be informational, and thus give rise to an infon, reference must be made to some location or some situation. *Aloneness* only makes sense (i.e. is only informational) with reference to the location or situation concerned. Sitting in my office at CSLI, I can say I am alone if I am referring to my office location (or situation), but in terms of the larger location (or situation) that comprises all of CSLI, I am by no means alone.

Thus, an object of the form

$$\ll \text{alone}, a, t, 1 \gg$$

is not a well-formed infon. To obtain a genuine infon, we need an additional argument for the location or situation that the *aloneness* implicitly refers to. Thus, either of the following will be well-formed infons:

$$\ll \text{alone}, a, l, t, 1 \gg \quad , \quad \ll \text{alone-in}, a, s_0, 1 \gg.$$

Both of these are clearly persistent.

How do we regulate matters so that all infons are persistent? By dictat, via the minimality conditions on relations. Just as we require that 'infonhood' requires the filling of argument roles only by objects that are *appropriate* for those roles, so too we demand that enough argument roles are filled (possibly by parameters) in order for that infon to be informational — that is to say, to be persistent.

In some cases, care has to be exercised in recognizing the minimality conditions of a given relation. For instance, on the face of it, the object

$$\ll present, a, 1 \gg$$

would seem to be a well-formed infon. It is clearly persistent. If the object a is present in some situation, s, it will be present in any larger situation, s'. However, this is not a well-formed infon, since the minimality conditions of the relation *present* require a location argument be filled. To see this, consider the dual 'infon'

$$\ll present, a, 0 \gg$$

having the opposite polarity. This is clearly not a well-formed infon. In order to make this particular object into a genuine infon, we would have to stipulate (either absolutely or parametrically) the location or situation where a is not present. Whereas the 'proposition'

$$s \models \ll present, a, 1 \gg$$

would make perfect sense, the putative 'dual'

$$s \models \ll present, a, 0 \gg$$

makes no sense at all; for if the object a is not present in the situation s, then s is not able to provide any (*internal*, or infonic) information about a. As far as s is concerned, no questions about a arise to be resolved; there is no such object a. The non-presence of a in s is an observation about the relationship between a and s that can only be made from a broader perspective *outside* of s. Thus, a situation, s' that includes both s and a could give rise to either of the propositions

$$s' \models \ll present, a, l, 0 \gg \quad , \quad s' \models \ll present\text{-}in, a, s, 0 \gg$$

where l is some location appropriate for s.

Thus the persistence, and hence apparent infonhood, of

$$\ll present, a, 1 \gg$$

was heavily dependent upon the polarity — an occurrence I do not wish to allow. Rather the minimality conditions of a relation should depend solely on the relation, not on the polarity of any putative infon. In the case of the relation *present*, some form of location argument must be filled. Both of

$\ll$present, $a, l, i \gg$, $\ll$present-in, $a, s, i \gg$

are well-formed infons for $i = 0$ or 1.

5.4   Agent logic versus theorist's logic

Our present standpoint commits us to two 'logics' that require study, corresponding to the two schemes of individuation. First there is the *agent logic* : our account of the inference mechanisms that form part of the information processing activity of the agent. (In so far as it is possible to give such an account. In many cases it amounts to an *ascription* of a logic to the agent — see presently.) The ontology for this logic is provided by the agent scheme of individuation. Second there is the *theorist's logic*, the logical framework adopted by the theorist in studying the flow of information pertinent to the agent or species of agent concerned. This uses the ontology given by the theorist's scheme of individuation. I commence by taking a look at the processes that constitute the *agent logic*.

The first thing to observe is that there is no reason to suppose that the theorist's account of what justifies an inference made by an agent, that is to say, the agent logic, should at all resemble the manner in which the agent actually performs that inference. That is to say, there is, in general, no reason for supposing that the agent itself *uses* the agent logic. Rather, what we are calling the agent logic is just that logic we, as theorists, attribute to that agent in order to provide an account (from the outside) of its information processing mechanisms. What *is* required is that the *internal* 'logic' employed by the agent, and the agent logic as stipulated by the theorist, both *be consistent with* the way the world is.

Consider the simple[4] case where an agent cognitively picks up the two pieces of information $\ll R, a, l, t, 1 \gg$ and $\ll S, a, l, t, 1 \gg$. (More precisely, these infons are our theorist's representation of the information acquired. So in particular, each of the uniformities R, S, a, l, t are in the agent ontology, that is to say, are individuated within the agent scheme. As mentioned just a moment ago, we may have no way of knowing how things *really* appear to the agent. This comment is pertinent to this entire discussion.) Then both items of information are in the agent's possession, and both may influence the agent's activity, either independently or by virtue of their conjunction. But is it necessarily the case that the agent

---

[4] What makes this example particularly simple is that the two infons not only refer to the same individual a, but both the location and time are the same in each case.

is able to combine these two items of information to obtain the single infon

$$\ll R\&S, a, l, t, 1 \gg$$

Clearly not. For the ability to pick up or store this item depends upon the property *R&S* being amongst those uniformities individuated by the agent. And simply because the agent is capable of independently individuating the two uniformities *R* and *S*, it does not follow automatically that it is capable of individuating the (single, complex) uniformity *R&S*.

An excellent illustration of the above point is provided by research into the cognitive behavior of monkeys, carried out by Klüver (see the account by Eleanor Gibson in [10]). Klüver successfully trained monkeys to recognize the larger of any two rectangles they were presented with, regardless of their actual size. That is to say, the monkeys were, after a period of training, able to individuate, or at least discriminate, the uniformity *larger-than* as applied to a pair of rectangles,[5] and thus to extract from a visually presented scene an infon of the form ≪larger-than, *b, a, i* ≫, where *a* and *b* are rectangles. (I am ignoring the issue of location and time here.) However, no amount of training resulted in the monkeys being able to pick out the intermediate of three different sized rectangles. Given rectangles *A, B* and *C* with *A* smaller than *B* and *B* smaller than *C*, they could not be trained to pick out *B* as the one of intermediate size, despite being able to pick out *B* as the larger of *A* and *B*, and *C* as the larger of *B* and *C*. That is to say, they were incapable of discriminating the uniformity *between-sized* as applied to the relative sizes of rectangles, and hence could not extract from an appropriate scene an infon of the form ≪between-sized, *a, b, c, i* ≫. (Though chimpanzees could be trained to perform this task.)

What then can be said about one of Klüver's monkeys *vis à vis* the possession of information about the three rectangles?

It will be of assistance at this stage to make an additional assumption concerning the monkey's performance, one for which I have no supporting evidence (indeed, I suspect it to be false), but which nevertheless facilitates the present discussion. I shall suppose that, on any given occasion, the monkey is able to *remember* which of two given rectangles is the larger. That is, upon being presented with rectangles *A* and *B*, it recognizes that *B* is the larger and makes a mental note of that fact.

---

[5] That is to say, they discriminated *some* uniformity that we would normally refer to as one rectangle being larger than another.

Then, when subsequently shown rectangles *B* and *C* together, the animal makes a similar mental note that *C* is the larger of the two.

Thus the monkey picks up and stores two items of information: the information that *B* is larger than *A* and the information that *C* is larger than *B*. Now, the information that *B* is intermediate in size between *A* and *C* is *nested* in the conjunction of these two items by virtue of what, in Section 4.2, was called a *necessary constraint* — in this case the constraint that arises from the individuation of the uniformity *between-sized*. Since, under my current assumption concerning the monkey's memory, the monkey's mental state encodes both the information that *B* is larger than *A* and the information that *C* is larger than *B*, it follows that the monkey's state also encodes the information that *B* is intermediate in size between *A* and *C*.

But the monkey is not attuned to this particular constraint – indeed it neither individuates nor discriminates the relation *between-sized*. Consequently, the monkey is not able to 'recognize' or in any way utilize its possession of the information that *B* is intermediate in size between *A* and *C*.

In terms of the discussion in Section 4.5 concerning the distinction between knowing and merely having information, we would say that the monkey *has the information* that *B* is intermediate in size between *A* and *C* but that it does not *know* this fact (and indeed, in this case, does not even discriminate the uniformity involved).

Before leaving Klüver's monkeys, what is the situation if, as I suspect is the case, the monkey is in fact unable to remember which of two given rectangles it correctly picked out as the larger? Under these circumstances, at no time does the monkey's mental state encode the two items of information that rectangle *B* is larger than rectangle *A* and rectangle *C* is larger than rectangle *B*. Consequently, there is no stage at which the monkey could be said to have, or encode, the information that *B* is intermediate in size between *A* and *C*, though at some time it does have the information that *B* is larger than *C*, and at some other time the information that *C* is bigger than *B*.[6] Thus the issue as to whether or

---

[6] It is, however, possible to imagine scenarios whereby, despite its lack of memory capacity, the monkey's state does nevertheless encode this information, say if the rectangles are each made of different edible materials having distinctive effects on the monkey's state, and the animal is trained to take a bite out of the larger of any given pair. But examples such as this simply supply some alternative means of storing past information, using different constraints, and so as far as the present discussion is concerned, are not really any different from the case where the monkey actually remembers the information.

not the agent logic allows the monkey to conclude that B is intermediate in size between A and C does not arise.

To return then to the general situation, if an agent is able to individuate the two uniformities (properties) R and S, and picks up the two items of information $\ll R, a, l, t, 1 \gg$ and $\ll S, a, l, t, 1 \gg$, so that the internal state of the agent simultaneously encodes these two items of information, then that agent will be in possession of (i.e. its internal state will encode) the consequent information $\ll R\&S, a, l, t, 1 \gg$. But this does not imply that this particular item of information is available to the agent — say in order to affect its behavior. The ability of the agent to make the logical step from the two individual infons $\ll R, a, l, t, 1 \gg$ and $\ll S, a, l, t, 1 \gg$ to the infon $\ll R\&S, a, l, t, 1 \gg$ depends, *inter alia*, upon the composite property $R\&S$ being one individuated by the agent.

In the case of Man, this does not seem to present any difficulties. Given any two properties we are, at least in principle, able to individuate their conjunction as a single, complex property — or at least, this appears to be the case for the kind of properties that arise in everyday life. But for more primitive agents, such as monkeys or computers, this is not at all the case, and for such agents the discrepancy between agent logic and theorist's logic can be quite significant.

5.5 Infon logic

As I tried to indicate in the previous section, for a given cognitive agent there can be a difference between what I called the agent logic, corresponding to the way the agent processes information, and the theorist's logic that reflects our theorist's view of the world. Whether this is advantageous or a problem to be overcome depends upon your goal. For instance, for the psychologist trying to understand the mental processes of people or animals by analyzing their observed behavior, over-reliance on, say, the rules of predicate logic could lead to quite erroneous conclusions. On the other hand, from the point of view of the engineer trying to design an efficient robot, the difference between the agent logic and the theorist's logic can be exploited, in that there is no need to equip the robot with the knowledge and ability to carry out every inference step that is involved in the theorist's logic of its intended behavior. This observation may lead to considerable saving of memory and computation time; see, for example, the paper of Rosenschein [22].

In this section, I develop a logical calculus of infons to provide a framework for studies from either standpoint.

First of all, I wish to be able to form the *conjunction*, $\sigma \wedge \tau$, of two infons, σ, τ. (It should be noted that I am not declaring this conjunction as itself an infon. Rather it is an instance of what I shall refer to as a *compound infon*.)

The informational meaning of the conjunction operation is fairly clear. The compound infon $\sigma \wedge \tau$ is the informational 'item' that comprises both σ and τ.

By definition, for any situation, s, we have

$$s \models \sigma \wedge \tau \text{ if and only if } s \models \sigma \text{ and } s \models \tau.$$

In terms of theorist's logic, the following equivalences obtain for any situation s:

$$s \models \,\ll R, \mathbf{a}, 1 \gg \wedge \ll S, \mathbf{a}, 1 \gg \,\Leftrightarrow\, s \models \,\ll R\&S, \mathbf{a}, 1 \gg$$

$$s \models \,\ll R, \mathbf{a}, 0 \gg \wedge \ll S, \mathbf{a}, 0 \gg \,\Leftrightarrow\, s \models \,\ll R \vee S, \mathbf{a}, 0 \gg$$

where $\mathbf{a}$ abbreviates $a_1, \ldots, a_n$.

However, no single one of these implications need feature in the agent logic. In particular, an agent may individuate the two uniformities R and S without individuating either of the two properties $R\&S$ and $R \vee S$, and conversely, an agent may individuate a uniformity T that is the same as $R\&S$ or $R \vee S$, without individuating either (or both) of the uniformities R, S. And even in the case where all the relevant uniformities are individuated, the agent may not be able to make the link between them.

Likewise, the *disjunction* of two infons, σ, τ, is a compound infon, $\sigma \vee \tau$, such that for any situation, s,

$$s \models \sigma \vee \tau \text{ if and only if } s \models \sigma \text{ or } s \models \tau \text{ (or both)}.$$

It should however be noted that the informational status of an infon disjunction is not as clear cut as that of a conjunction. For although $\sigma \vee \tau$ is the informational 'item' that at least one of σ, τ is the case, this is not information of quite the same form as that provided by a single infon.

For example, if we were to analyze the claim

Melissa believes that her new bicycle will be red or blue

then (and here I am pre-empting — and greatly simplifying — material on belief to be covered more fully later) the content of Melissa's belief will be, roughly, that a certain situation, s, will be of type:

$$E = [\dot{s} \mid \dot{s} \models \,\ll \text{red, bicycle, } 1 \gg \vee \ll \text{blue, bicycle, } 1 \gg]$$

(Strictly speaking, our type-formation machinery does not, as it stands at present, provide for the formation of this type, since it requires abstraction across a disjunction of infons. I shall deal with that matter in the next section.) But what exactly is the status of a proposition of the form

$$s \models \ll \text{red, bicycle, } 1 \gg \vee \ll \text{blue, bicycle, } 1 \gg$$

A situation can support one infon or it can support another infon, but to say it supports a 'disjunction' of two (incompatible) infons is in some ways at odds with the fundamental informational role we have attached to infons (and to the supports relation).

Now, it may on occasion be possible to form the disjunction of two *relations*, R and S, and consider the infon involving that new complex relation $R \vee S$, but in the case of the above example this seems unreasonable, since *'red-or-blue'* is not something that most people would regard as a 'property' in our sense of an 'agent-individuated uniformity'.

Things go the other way in the case of the Melissa-individuated relations *father-of* and *mother-of*. Here she also individuates the disjunction relation, *parent-of*. Thus her individuation scheme provides for infons of the three forms

$$\ll \text{father-of, } x, y, 1 \gg \quad , \quad \ll \text{mother-of, } x, y, 1 \gg \quad , \quad \ll \text{parent-of, } x, y, 1 \gg .$$

Clearly, the information content of the single infon

$$\ll \text{parent-of, } x, y, 1 \gg$$

is the same as that of the disjunction

$$\ll \text{father-of, } x, y, 1 \gg \vee \ll \text{mother-of, } x, y, 1 \gg$$

but only the former has infon status, because of its basic nature, involving as it does a single Melissa-individuated relation. (Recall Klüver's monkeys, discussed in the previous section.)

Disjunctions of infons, therefore, should be regarded as 'items' of information of a less specific, less concrete variety than the infons themselves. A disjunctive compound, $\sigma \vee \tau$, provides information that *restricts* the ways the world is, but it does not provide the specific, concrete information about the world that a single infon does. (This issue also arises in quantum physics, in the guise of the famous Shrödinger's Cat.) I shall have more to say on it in the next section.

Notice that, as I have introduced them, the notions of conjunction and disjunction of infons have been defined as operations on infons. However, we require our logical calculus of compound infons to allow for the repeated application of these operations. Consequently, we should regard the above definitions as clauses in a recursive definition of compound infons. A similar remark holds for the quantification of infons, considered next. For reasons of persistence analogous to our earlier considerations concerning the property *present*, we should only allow *bounded* quantification of infons.

I start with existential quantification. If σ is an infon, or compound infon, that involves the parameter $\dot{x}$ and u is some set, then

$$(\exists \dot{x} \in u)\sigma$$

is a compound infon, and for any situation, s, that contains, as constituents, all members of u :

$s \models (\exists \dot{x} \in u)\sigma$ if and only if there is an anchor, f, of $\dot{x}$ to an element of u, such that $s \models \sigma[f]$.

Notice that the anchor, f, here may involve some *resource situation* other than s. That is to say, f must assign to the parameter, $\dot{x}$, an appropriate object in some anchoring situation, e, that supports the various infons that figure in the structure of $\dot{x}$. (See the example below.) There is no requirement that the situations e and s be one and the same, though $f(\dot{x})$ must *be* a constituent of s, of course.

Notice also that in the infon σ, $\dot{x}$ is, or at least may be, a *free* parameter, in the sense that we may freely anchor $\dot{x}$ to an appropriate object in any given appropriate situation. In the quantified infon $(\exists \dot{x} \in u)\sigma$, $\dot{x}$ is not *free* to be anchored; rather it is *bound*.

As an example, let σ be the compound infon

$$\ll \text{tired}, \dot{c}, t_0, 1 \gg \wedge \ll \text{hungry}, \dot{c}, t_0, 1 \gg$$

where $\dot{c}$ is a parameter for a cat. If s is a room situation at time t_0 and u is the set of individuals in s, we shall have

$$s \models (\exists \dot{c} \in u)\sigma$$

if and only if there is an anchor, f, of $\dot{c}$ to some fixed object, c, in u (c will necessarily be a cat) such that $s \models \sigma[f]$, i.e. such that

$$s \models \ll \text{tired}, c, t_0, 1 \gg \wedge \ll \text{hungry}, c, t_0, 1 \gg$$

That is to say, $s \models (\exists \dot{c} \in u)\sigma$ if and only if there is a cat, c, in u that at time t_0 is tired and hungry in s.

Notice that the existence of the anchor, f, entails the existence of an associated *anchoring* (or *resource*) situation, e, such that, in particular,

$$e \models \ll \text{cat}, c, 1 \gg$$

In particular, c is a constituent of e. This is the way anchors work. However, the object c has to be in the (room) situation, s, at time t_0 in order for the proposition

$$s \models \ll \text{tired}, c, t_0, 1 \gg \wedge \ll \text{hungry}, c, t_0, 1 \gg$$

to obtain.

As with infon disjunction, existential quantification across infons, while at times a useful device, results in an informational 'item' that is not as basic as a simple infon. An assertion of the form

$$s \models \ll R, a_1, \ldots, a_n, i \gg$$

provides a basic item of information about the objects $a_1, \ldots, a_n$ *within* the situation s, and as such provides *internal, structural* information about s. Quantification over s, on the other hand, is to some extent an *external* property of s, that says something about what kinds of objects are to be found within s.

Now, in the case of existential quantification, this issue does not seem too problematical. In particular, even the *unbounded* existential quantification of an infon would, if we were to allow this operation, clearly produce a compound that is persistent. But unbounded universal quantification would be quite different, resulting in a compound that may well not be persistent.

Turning now to that issue of universal quantification across infons, if σ is an infon, or compound infon, that involves the parameter $\dot{x}$, and if u is some set, then

$$(\forall \dot{x} \in u)\sigma$$

is a compound infon, and for any situation, s, that contains, as constituents, all members of u,

$$s \models (\forall \dot{x} \in u)\sigma \text{ if and only if, for all anchors, } f, \text{ of } \dot{x} \text{ to an element of } u,$$
$$s \models \sigma[f].$$

It is obvious that a compound infon of this form is persistent.

It should be noted that in the cases both of existential and universal quantification, I do not exclude the possibility that the bounding set u consists of all the objects of a certain kind that are in the situation s. Consequently, our definitions do provide a notion of 'unrestricted' quantification, but it is very definitely a notion of *situated* quantification.[7] This seems to be 'right'. Given a situated view of language, a natural-language assertion involving an unbounded existential or universal quantifier surely makes implicit reference to the domain over which the quantifier ranges.

For example, when I truthfully assert

All citizens have equal rights

---

[7] Set-theoretic modeling of such a construct might require non-well-founded set theory, but that has long been accepted by the majority of people working on situation theory.

I am presumably quantifying over some country such as the United States, not the entire world, for which such a claim is not true. Consistent with this observation, I shall often write

$$s \models \exists p\sigma$$

as an abbreviation for

$$s \models (\exists p \in s)\sigma$$

and

$$s \models \forall p\sigma$$

as an abbreviation for

$$s \models (\forall p \in s)\sigma$$

One final remark before I leave this topic of infon logic. We do not have a 'negation operator' on infons. The polarity of an infon serves to handle the one aspect of negation that makes sense in the present enterprise.

5.6 Types and propositions

So far, our framework can only handle information of an essentially 'atomic' nature. That is to say, information at the level of the relations provided by the individuation scheme.

Let me make this a little more precise. In the theory of information I am developing, information is regarded as essentially *propositional*; that is to say, 'information' is information *about* some situation, s, (possibly the whole world). This either has the form

$$s : S$$

where s is a situation and S is a situation-type, or else

$$x : T$$

where x is an object and T is an object-type defined over some grounding situation, u. In this latter case, notice that if

$$T = [\dot{x} \mid u \models \sigma]$$

then $x : T$ if and only if

$$u \models \sigma[f]$$

where $f(\dot{x}) = x$. Thus all propositions are essentially of the form

$$<\text{situation}> \models <\text{infon}>$$

We observe that constraints are structured to convey information about situations in precisely the propositional form.

Thus, the logical complexity of information, relative to a fixed scheme of individuation, is dependent on the complexity of the types of our theory. At the moment, our machinery only allows us to form types using the abstraction procedures described in Section 3.2. In order to handle more complex forms of information, we need to extend the collection of types that can be formed to cover types abstracted across the new case of compound infons.

If σ is an infon or a compound infon and $\dot{s}$ is a *SIT*-parameter, there is a corresponding *situation-type*

$$T = [\dot{s} \mid \dot{s} \models \sigma].$$

Similarly, given a situation u, a parameter $\dot{x}$, and an infon or compound infon σ, there is an *object-type*

$$T = [\dot{x} \mid u \models \sigma]$$

I call u the *grounding situation* of the type T.

If T is a situation-type of the form $[\dot{s} \mid \dot{s} \models \sigma]$, where σ is an infon or a compound infon, I call the proposition

$$s : T$$

an *infonic proposition*; in which case, it can clearly be written in the equivalent fashion

$$s \models \sigma.$$

If σ is in fact a single infon, the proposition is said to be *basic infonic*, or simply *basic*.

Apart from the infonic propositions, the other propositions are those of the form $x : T$ for T an object-type of the form

$$T = [\dot{x} \mid u \models \sigma]$$

where σ is an infon or compound infon and $\dot{x}$ occurs in σ. The object x here may itself be a situation.

For an example of a proposition of this form, let T be the type of all football games seen by a Stanford professor in the Bay Area during 1988. That is, set

$$T = [\dot{s} \mid u \models \exists \dot{p} \ll\text{sees}, \dot{p}, \dot{s}, 1988, 1 \gg]$$

where $\dot{s}$ is a parameter for a football game (situation), $\dot{p}$ is a parameter for a Stanford professor, and u is the Bay Area. By the convention established a short while ago for quantifiers, this is an abbreviation for

$$T = [\dot{s} \mid u \models (\exists \dot{p} \in u)\ll\text{sees}, \dot{p}, \dot{s}, 1988, 1 \gg]$$

Let s be a football game. Then

$$s : T$$

if and only if there is an anchor, f, of $\dot{p}$ to some object, p, necessarily a Stanford professor, such that

$$u \models \ll \text{sees}, p, s, 1988, 1 \gg$$

Thus, $s : T$ if and only if s is a football game that is seen by *some* Stanford professor in the Bay Area during 1988.

Again, the anchor f will anchor $\dot{p}$ to the appropriate object p in some *anchoring situation* e such that, in particular,

$$e \models \ll \text{Stanford professor}, p, 1988, 1 \gg$$

Since

$$u \models \ll \text{sees}, p, s, 1988, 1 \gg$$

p is necessarily in the Bay Area situation, u, at the appropriate time.

So what exactly *are* types? Well, they are the abstractions by means of which the agent classifies certain aspects of the world. More precisely, the theorist uses types to depict certain uniformities that appear to be pertinent to the agent's behavior; as such they are simply uniformities of a higher order than the individuals, locations, and situations. That is to say, they are abstract objects that either figure in the cognitive activity of the agent under study, or else are used in the study of the behavior of that agent. Thus as far as our ontology is concerned, the types rank alongside the individuals, locations, and situations.

For example, the *type* of all cats and the *type* of all dangerous situations are both genuine objects, achieving this status as a result of being individuated by some agent, either the agent under consideration or else the theorist studying that agent.

These two examples should indicate just what it is I conceive types to be: namely a type is an intentional object that cuts across the class of all those objects that share some feature or possess some common property. As such, a type is neither an infon nor a property, though all three notions are closely related, as we shall see presently.

Though of a higher order, types are no less 'real' than any of the other entities in situation theory. Being the kinds of agent we are, we naturally regard the individuals, the temporal and spatial locations, and (possibly) the situations as having some form of independent 'existence', being somehow 'out there'. But this is simply a reflection of our own status as situated agents, restricted to build our theories using our own individuation capacities. One can conceive of other intelligent agents, of a completely different kind, carving things up quite differently, in ways that we could not recognize at all. So we should not equate 'higher order' with 'less real'.

Of course, one of the difficulties faced when trying to establish the intuitions in a new area such as this, is that some, or maybe even most, of the basic notions cannot adequately be defined or explained in terms of already familiar concepts. Rather the basic notions have to be devloped in their own terms, referring to each other. This was the case with the basic notion of a 'uniformity', and is also true of the types as well. The actual words chosen help to some extent, but ultimately the basic notions can only be understood in the theory's own terms.

It should be observed that types are not the same as properties, though there is an obvious close relationship between the two. The distinction lies in the roles played by types and propositions in our study of the behavior of the agent. There is a *property* of being a cat, and a *property* of being a dangerous situation, but these are quite distinct from the corresponding types. Properties are things that *hold* of certain objects, types are things that *are* (in the sense that individuals, locations, and situations 'are'). This, of course, is a distinction of role, not ontology — both properties and types are abstract objects within our ontology. A clear distinction between these two notions as far as the mechanics of our theory is concerned is that if P is a property (or a relation), then P can occur either as the head of an infon or in the body of an infon (as an argument); whereas if T is a type, T can occur in the body of an infon, but not in the head.

If T is a type, then there may be an associated property, namely the property of *being of* the type T. Conversely, given a property, P, there may be a corresponding type, the type of all objects with property P. But even if there is a correspondence, that does not make the two concepts identical in that instance: one is still a type, the other a property. (I said "*may* be" in the previous sentences, since it depends upon what the theory takes to be the 'propositions' in the ontology and what type-abstractions are available.)

Another important distinction is that, for a type T, the truth or falsity of the proposition

$$a : T$$

for a given object a, is determinate; that is to say, it is a fact of the world that either a is of type T or a is not of type T. (If this were not the case, we could not, of course, refer to $x : T$ as a *proposition*, propositions being things that are true or false.) On the other hand, given a (unary) property, P, and an appropriate object a, the infons

$$\ll P, a, 1 \gg \quad , \quad \ll P, a, 0 \gg$$

are neither true nor false. Infons are not the kind of thing that can be 'true' or 'false'. Rather a situation, s, is required in order to produce a proposition

$$s \models \ll P, a, i \gg$$

and thereby obtain a truth evaluation.

As higher-order uniformities across various classes of objects, types provide the main means of classification in our theory. In particular, we take *propositions* to be claims of the form that such and such an object is of such and such a type. Thus both types and propositions are abstract objects that arise as a result of the intentionality of an agent's mental states, with the types being uniformities across the propositions.

In the case of situation-types, a robotic analogy might help. In designing a mobile, autonomous office robot, there can be several different 'layers' of control. One of these, the 'motor level', handles the tasks of recognizing objects in the robot's path, making sure the device does not run into walls, knock over hatstands, or bump into passing secretaries. This level corresponds to the individuation of individuals, locations, and situations.

The next higher level of control involves the strategic behavior of the robot, fixing goals to be achieved (e.g. the delivery of a letter to a certain office), and designing plans (e.g. figuring out the route) to achieve that goal. This level corresponds to the individuation of types.

Thus, for instance, the overall behavior patterns of an agent will vary according to the *types* of situation in which it is located, or with which it is faced; the detailed, moment-by-moment behavior of the agent will involve the individuation and discrimination of the individuals and locations in its environment.

Of course, like all simple analogies, this picture only takes us so far. For instance, the detailed behavior of the robot will vary according to the *type* of individual it is faced with. For example, a door might be pushed open, but a secretary has to be either circumvented or asked to move out of the way. The acceptable behavior of the robot clearly requires that it be able to distinguish between these two kinds of situation; that is to say, it should be equipped to recognize the types involved, the type of a person and the type of a door.

Type abstraction is intended to correspond to the cognitive process of abstracting a 'type' from a given property, a process that comes naturally to humans at least. The combinatorial logic I have developed for infons provides for a rich ontology of types. But notice that it is at the level of infons that this 'logic' applies, not at the type level. That is to say, I have not allowed for any logical combinations of types. This is at variance with the stance adopted by Barwise and Perry in [5], but it seems to me that this is 'correct' — that is to say, corresponds more closely to those aspects of cognition that types are intended to represent. Cognitive agents manipulate information, which our theory takes to be in infon or compound infon form; the types are just reified abstractions across properties, not appropriate for logical manipulation.

Thus we have the following picture. Agents either individuate, or else their behavior discriminates, *types*. Agents such as ourselves are able to make *propositions*, claims about the world or some part thereof, which our theory takes to be of the form

$$x : T$$

where x is an object and T is a type. Thus, given the intentionality of an agent's mental states, to be discussed in Chapter 6, types are uniformities across propositions. *Infons* are the basic items of information or misinformation (what I call 'structural' information) about situations in the world. The inclusion in the ontology of a particular infon depends upon the scheme of individuation. But whether a given infon is a *fact* in the world, or whether it is supported by some situation, depends upon the way the world, or that situation, is. Infons are the abstract objects our theory uses to classify situations according to their 'internal' structure.

And what then of the compound infons? The first thing to observe is that these only occur within the body of a type abstraction. Thus they play a functional role within the way our theory models propositions. In fact we can regard compound infons as 'uniformities' across types, 'uniformities' that reflect the logical structure of the type concerned.[8] As such, it would of course be possible to avoid the introduction of compound infons altogether, and develop the required combinatorial logic at the level of types. But this, I feel, is not quite right, given the rationale that lies behind situation theory. Agents that are capable of individuating types do not manipulate them logically the way they do, say, sentences. Rather they simply individuate them as uniformities across their environment. Thus any logical structure in a type is essentially *internal* to that type, that is to say, *prior* to its abstraction as a type.

---

[8] The quotes around 'uniformities' are to indicate that this is not exactly our formal use of this word, though the meaning is fairly close.

Thus it is at the informational level of infons and compound infons that the combinatory logic is appropriate.

5.7   Two points of information

The treatment so far has resulted in at least two issues that could be a source of confusion with regard to the nature of information.

First, there is the question as to what we mean by the phrase 'an item of information'? Do we mean a parameter-free infon, σ, or do we mean a basic infonic proposition $s \models \sigma$? The same phrase has been used in both contexts.

Now, information is intrinsically information *about* some portion of the world, that is to say, it is information about some situation. Thus there is a sense in which information is essentially *propositional*. Propositions are either true or false, and a true proposition is an item of information. If the proposition is basic infonic, this item of information is of the form

$$s \models \sigma$$

where s is a situation and σ is a single infon. In the case of such a proposition, it is natural to speak of the infon, σ, as providing 'an item of information' about the situation s, and to say further that this item of information about s is either true or false, according to whether the proposition is true or false. (Note that an infon is not something that of itself has a truth value. Only when applied to some situation — possibly the world — via the supports relation, does a truth value arise.)

Both meanings seem to accord with common readings of the word 'information', and I see no reason to make for awkward circumlocutions by suppressing either. But note should be taken of the two distinct, though connected, meanings we are thus ascribing to this word.

The second issue concerns the distinction between information being given about a situation by virtue of that situation being of a certain type, and information which that situation carries by means of some constraint.

For example, suppose I walk into the kitchen and see cat hair in the butter. I turn to my wife and say

A cat has been in here.

Let u be the situation to be found in the kitchen when I make my utterance. Thus, u has physical location bounded by the walls of the kitchen, and temporal duration the span of my utterance (say). Salient constituents of u include me, my wife, and the butter dish.

Some feature of the situation u provides me with the information that a cat has been in that room some time in the recent past. What feature? Well, the cat hair in the butter. That is, direct perception gives me access to the following informational item:

$$u \models \ll \text{in, cat hair, the butter, } l_0, t_0, 1 \gg$$

where l_0 is the location of the kitchen and t_0 is the time of the utterance. This is a typical instance of information about a situation by virtue of that situation *supporting* an infon.

But this proposition is not what I report with my utterance. That is to say, this proposition is not the propositional content of my utterance. In particular, my utterance makes no reference to either cat hair or butter. Rather, I refer to 'some' cat, a cat that is not, let us suppose, a constituent of the situation u. Seemingly, the propositional content of my utterance is that some situation is of the type T , where T is the type

$$T = [\dot{s} \mid \dot{s} \models \exists \dot{c} \exists \dot{t} \ll \text{present, } \dot{c}, l_0, \dot{t}, 1 \gg]$$

where $\dot{c}$ is a parameter for a cat and $\dot{t}$ is a temporal parameter for some time in the recent past.[9] But just what situation is it that my utterance claims to be of type T ? That is to say, for what situation, s, is it the case that my utterance has as its propositional content the proposition $s : T$?

Certainly not the situation u. This situation does not contain the cat, nor does it have a temporal extent that reaches back sufficiently to include the time when the cat was present. In particular, it cannot be the case that $u : T$, since there is no way the parameters $\dot{c}$ and $\dot{t}$ can be anchored to appropriate objects in u.

Rather, my utterance refers to a different situation, namely the situation to be found in the kitchen over a time span extending further back in time than does u, a situation having the same spatial extent, l_0, as u, but a temporal duration that began some time before t_0, the time of my utterance. Call this situation v.

How do I manage to refer to this situation? By my use of the words 'here' and 'has been'. Having picked out the requisite situation, with sufficient precision to make my utterance informational, the propositional content of my utterance is then

$$v : T$$

---

[9] I do not want to be too specific about issues such as what constitutes the 'recent past' at this stage.

Thus, the situation u manages to provide me with information about another, closely-related situation v.

But of course, there is a natural sense in which my utterance nevertheless does convey information about u, the situation in the room as I witness it. Indeed, since my only source of the information my utterance imparts is what I see before me, this information 'about' v must in some sense be information 'resident' in u. We might say that u must somehow manage to *carry* this information. How does it do this? By means of various constraints, constraints that I shall not bother to write down formally, but which amount to the fact that if there is cat hair around, then a cat must have been there.

Now, my intention here is not to go over familiar ground as to how constraints function. Rather I am trying to draw attention to the distinction — which everyday language conflates — between a situation 'having' or 'providing' information by virtue of that situation supporting various infons or, more generally, being of a certain type, and 'having' or 'providing' (or better, 'carrying') information by means of some constraint. The former relates to information that is in a sense 'part of' the situation, internal information pertaining to the structure of that situation; the latter depends upon the way constraints allow one situation to provide information about another. It is by virtue of the internal information of the former, propositional variety that constraints can enable one situation to carry information about another.

6

Mental States

This book does not set out to develop a theory of mind, and that is not the purpose of this chapter. However, no book that tries to come to grips with information can ignore the issue of mental states. In particular, the account of situation semantics presented in Chapters 8 and 9 depends upon a number of features of mental states. This should not come as a surprise; practically any instance of linguistic communication is an attempt of one mind to affect another.

So there is one reason to say something about mental states. But there is another: an empirically-based account of information such as the one I have been developing ought to provide a mechanism for a functional discussion of mental states. That is to say, our situation-theoretic framework should enable us to say something about the behavior of the human mind (in particular), when viewed as an information processor. From this viewpoint, an account of mental states provides an illustration of the way situation theory may be used as a framework for a study of certain aspects of mind.

6.1   Cognition

A standard way to approach a theory of mental phenomena, and the one that motivated a lot of the early work in artificial intelligence, is described in the following passage from the book *Understanding Computers and Cognition*, by Winograd and Flores [31, p.73].

At its simplest, the rationalistic view accepts the existence of an objective reality, made up of things bearing properties and entering into relations. A cognitive being 'gathers information' about those things and builds up a 'mental model' which will be in some respects correct (a faithful representation of reality) and in other respects incorrect. Knowledge is a storehouse of representations, which can be called upon for use in reasoning and which can be translated into language. Thinking is a process of manipulating representations.

In essence, what Winograd and Flores mean by the phrase 'rationalistic view' is the general consensus of approach that underlies the vast majority of the contemporary physical and social sciences. It may reasonably be summed up in terms of the following three steps [31, p.15].

1. Characterize the situation in terms of identifiable objects with well-defined properties.
2. Find general rules that apply to situations in terms of those objects and properties.
3. Apply the rules logically to the situation of concern, drawing conclusions about what should be done.

By and large, [31] amounts to an argument *against* this 'rationalist' approach to mind. Now, as an attempt to flesh out a *mathematical* theory, the present endeavor falls very definitely into the 'rationalist' approach Winograd and Flores claim to be inappropriate. Consequently, we should give careful consideration to the arguments they use to justify their conclusions.

The main thrust of *Understanding Computers and Cognition* comes from the work of the philosopher Martin Heidegger and the biologist Humberto Maturana. Generally speaking, the viewpoint advanced in [31], and in many ways typified by the writings of Heidegger, is that of the so-called *phenomenologist* school of philosophy, *phenomenology* being the study of experience and action.

Heidegger (see [31, Chapter 3]) claims that it is a mistake to approach the study of cognition from the standpoint of an agent observing and representing an objective reality. Rather the agent is inseparably *linked* to the environment — what Heidegger refers to as *Dasein* (*being-in-the-world*).[1] For Heidegger, an agent does not operate by manipulating some internal *representation* of reality, rather it is an integral part of that reality, and that reality is in a certain sense an extension of that agent.

To take a familiar example of Heidegger [31, p.36], if you are engaged in the process of hammering a nail into wood, you do not control your actions in terms of an internal representation of a 'hammer', any more than you have internal representations of the muscles and tendons in your arm. None of these, including the hammer, need be granted the status of an 'existing object' in your mind as the hammerer. The hammer

---

[1] As Winograd and Flores go to some pains to point out, it is difficult to put across Heidegger's precise viewpoint in terms easily accessible from within the rationalistic tradition it seeks to overthrow. Rather one has to take fundamental terms such as *Dasein* as defined by the theory they help to determine.

only presents itself as an 'object' when there is some kind of breakdown, such as its breaking or slipping from your grasp.

Again, as I sit here entering these words at my keyboard, none of the sophisticated electronic apparatus I am making use of has a representation, and therefore the status of an existing object in my mind — until, that is, I chose to use this particular example to illustrate the point I did. Before then they were just a part of the background of what Heidegger calls *readiness-to-hand*, taken for granted without explicit recognition or identification as objects.

Maturana takes a biological stance somewhat parallel to the more theoretical, phenomenological ideas of Heidegger. For Maturana, the essence of a living system is characterized by what he calls an 'autopoietic system'. As Winograd and Flores quote from Maturana and Varela [16], an *autopoietic system* is

... a network of processes of production (transformations and destruction) of components that produces the components that: (i) through their interactions and transformations continuously regenerate the network of processes (relations) that produced them; and (ii) constitute it (the machine) as a concrete unity in the space in which they (the components) exist by specifying the topological domain of its realization as such a network.
—Maturana and Varela [16, p.79], Winograd and Flores [31, p.44].

In essence, and ignoring the various technical terms involved in the above definition, an autopoietic system is a closed, evolving collection of components. It grows, evolves, adapts, and eventually dies, through a process Maturana refers to as *structural coupling* with the environment (which may include other systems). Again, requoting Maturana from [31, p.45], for an autopoietic system:

Learning is not a process of accumulation of representations of the environment; it is a continuous process of transformation of behavior through continuous change in the capacity of the nervous system to synthesize it. Recall does not depend on the indefinite retention of a structural invariant that represents an entity (an idea, image, or symbol), but on the functional ability of the system to create, when certain recurrent conditions are given, a behavior that satisfies the recurrent demands or that the observer would class as a reenacting of a previous one.
—Maturana, [14, p.45].

According to Maturana [14, p.13]:

A cognitive system is a system whose organization defines a domain of interactions in which it can act with relevance to the maintanance of itself, and the process of cognition is the actual (inductive) acting or behaving in this domain.

A classic example is the work of Maturana and others on frog vision [15]. One of the results reported in this paper was the identification of one particular type of optic nerve fiber that was triggered by a dark spot surrounded by light. The result of such triggering was behavior of the frog appropriate for catching a fly at the location corresponding to the spot. The significant point to note here is that it is the excitation of a single type of nerve fiber that causes the frog to react in the way it does. The frog does not form a *representation* of a fly. (Unless, that is, you take the word 'representation' to include such an example. This move can certainly be argued for, but the resulting notion of 'representation' is then quite a bit more general than the one commonly understood, at least in AI circles.) Rather, as a result of structural coupling, the structure of the nervous system exhibits a certain kind of behavior. That this behavior results (assuming it does) in the frog catching a fly, is purely a consequence of the history of perturbations of the frog (and its ancestors) as an autopoietic system dependent on a steady supply of flies for its continued existence.

For Maturana, a nervous system is a closed network of interacting neurons where activity in one collection of neurons can propogate change in the same or other collections of neurons. There are no 'inputs' and 'outputs' in the usual sense of the words. Rather the system can be *perturbed* by structural changes in the network itself, and this will affect its activity. (As with the usage of the word 'representation' above, a more general reading of the word 'inputs' than that commonly in use could include such perturbations to the system.) The perturbation can be caused by light striking the retina, as in the case of the frog, or by other means, such as the chemical or manual irritation of the network. Trigger the right nerves and the frog will react in the manner appropriate to catching a fly, regardless of how that excitation was brought about, and independently, therefore, of the existence or otherwise of a fly in the vicinity.

At this stage I should stress that there is little hope of my being able to put across in three or four pages what requires some sixty or so pages in Winograd and Flores [31]. Indeed, as the authors of [31] point out, their own coverage of the work of Heidegger, Maturana, and others is itself of necessity abbreviated. I hope that readers of this essay will be prompted to study [31] for themselves. But, at the very least, it is important at this stage to be aware of the theories sketched above, in order to provide a perspective on the present enterprise — a task I now turn to.

At the outset, I have to admit to finding myself attracted towards the thesis sketched above. It seems reasonable to me that 'cognition' and 'intelligence' are intrinsically biological and not mechanizable. In particular, if the aim of artificial intelligence is, as it once seemed to be, the design of computer systems that mimic human intelligent behavior, then it seems to me that there is no hope of success.

But I do not regard this as the goal of AI, nor I believe do many others working in the field; rather the aim is to build computer systems that exhibit certain features of 'intelligence', features that make those systems both more reliable and easier to use. Moreover, and more pertinent to the subject matter of this book, I do not regard the the possible validity of the phenomenological stance as rendering pointless a mathematical theory of information and cognition as is being attempted here. What is important, however, is to be very clear just *what* it is that is being attempted: what are the aims and claims of the proposed theory? Let me try to provide that clarity.

Mathematical theories are supremely abstract and idealized. Indeed, it is the very idealization and accompanying rigor that makes such theories *mathematical*. The points, lines, and surfaces of geometry are abstract idealizations that are not to be found in nature, and the real world provides only approximations to the exact theorems of that subject. Again, the continuity of three-dimensional Euclidean space and the infinitesimal calculus it supports have only approximate counterparts in the real three-dimensional spatial universe in which we live.

By dealing solely with rigorously defined idealized concepts and using totally rigorous methods, the mathematician is able to develop extremely powerful, and supremely reliable theories. That the mathematician's results so often prove to be of real use in our everyday lives (to say nothing of the everyday lives of the likes of astronauts, airline pilots, engineers, journalists, writers, and so on), stems from the fact that the initial idealizations of the theory are in fact just that: idealizations of phenomena *observed in the real world*, not arbitrary figments of the mathematician's imagination.

Clearly, in attempting to set up a new 'mathematical model' of some aspect of the world, as I am doing here, great care has to be taken to ensure that the idealizations adopted are appropriate for the desired goal. Any consistent collection of postulates can give rise to a rigorous mathematical theory, possibly one of great beauty and elegance. But that theory's ability to tell us anything about the world, or to assist us in our lives, depends very much on how well its initial postulates tie in to reality.

How then do we judge this initial modeling phase of the enterprise? Not by rigorous mathematical means, that much is clear. Rather, intuition and reflective analysis must be relied upon — there simply is nothing else. (Though once the theory is sufficiently developed, there is always the check of how well the theory's results match observation.) This is why, in this book, so much attention has been paid to intuitive motivation of each step.

Here then, is the basic, metaphysical standpoint adopted by our present enterprise.

The theory assumes a basic ontology of individuals, temporal and spatial locations, relations, situations, and types, determined by a scheme of individuation dependent on the agent or species of agent under consideration.

More precisely, we commence our study with some particular kind of agent in mind. For many of our examples, and in particular for applications of situation theory to natural-language semantics, the agent is Man, but it could equally well be some other species of cognitive organism or some form of computing device, for example, the robot *SID* of Section 4.5. Associated with this agent or species of agent will be two *schemes of individuation* that carve up the world into entities such as individuals, locations, relations, situations, and types: the *agent scheme* and the *theorist's scheme*. Using the ontology provided by the theorist's scheme of individuation, we can define a formal notion of *information*: namely, discrete informational units known as (parameter-free) *infons*. From the standpoint of the theory, cognitive activity is the manipulation and utilization of infon-information by an agent, in general for the purpose of guiding behavior.

This is, of course, a particular and restricted use of the phrase 'cognitive activity'. So too my use of the word 'cognition' in Section 2.2, where I defined *cognition* as the process whereby the agent acquires infon-information by some perceptual means. In the case of visually acquired information, for instance, the 'digitalization', to use Dretske's word, of perceived, conceptual information may be performed by the perceptive apparatus itself, as in the case of frog vision described above, where a particular optic nerve fiber is sensitive to one specific kind of signal, or it may be performed at some higher-order level in the agent's cognitive structure, as would appear to be the case with much of the conceptualized (i.e. infon) information picked up by human beings.

Of course, if one accepts the views Winograd and Flores express in [31], then this entire infon approach to (*real*) cognitive activity will be an idealized, artificial one, in much the same way as the postulation of 'photons' provides an idealized view of light. There is, however, a good, intuitive argument to be made in support of infons *as a basis for a mathematical theory*.

From our information-theoretic viewpoint, the world is a kapok-like mass of information (or 'potential information' — it could be argued that we should not even use the word 'information' at this stage in the development, which is prior to the formulation of a theory of information. But this stage is, remember, one of trying to develop *intuitions* on which to ground that theory.) Much of this information may be *perceived* by the agent; a great deal may not (because the agent is not equipped for its perception). The agent scheme of individuation provides a regularization that carves up the world into various uniformities, and 'conceptually filters out' discrete items of conceptual information (infons) about those uniformities. This process is analogous to the transition from analog to digital coding of information as described by Dretske in [8]. Indeed, it is precisely Dretske's arguments for the relevance of the analog–digital distinction to cognition in *his* theory of information, that provide the principal motivation for the analogous move in *our* infon-based theory of cognitive behavior: namely that digitalization is, for the kinds of agent we are considering, the essence of cognitive activity (of the kind we are considering).

This strategy of taking infons as the basic informational currency, means that the form of cognitive activity we consider is, arguably, only a *part* (more precisely, an idealization of a part) of what Winograd and Flores would regard as genuine cognitive activity. In which case, the present aim should, and will, be to make this part as large as possible.

This is reflected in my approach to 'mental states', in particular the issues of perception, action, knowledge, belief, desire, and intentions, that are so critical to the AI enterprise. The following section establishes the framework within which I shall handle these notions.

6.2 Intentionality

From either the rationalist or the phenomenological standpoint, a cognitive agent is, at any moment, in a certain *state*. (I shall think in terms of a *mental* state.) That state results from the agent's history, in particular its history of interactions with the world and other agents therein. In order for that agent to function in the world, there is evidently some systematic way the state of the agent relates to the state of the environment — regularities in state correspond to regularities in the environment. Our theory does not concern itself with the exact nature of these states —

at least, not at this stage in the development. But it does assume their existence, and in particular it assumes that they have *external significance* in terms of the agent's history, the state of the environment, and the future behavior of the agent.

Thus, if I *know* it is raining[2] then it is a fact of the world that it is raining; if I *believe* it is raining, then my belief is true or false depending on whether or not it actually is raining; if I *desire* that it will rain, then my desire will be fulfilled if and only if it actually rains; and if I *intend* to take my umbrella to the game, then my intention will be fulfilled only if I do in fact take my umbrella to the game.

In each case, the relevant mental state has *external significance*; that is to say, it is linked to the world in terms of what that state is *about*. The technical term for such *aboutness* is *intentionality*. (This notion should not be confused with that of *intention* in the sense of intending to do something. The two concepts are related, but are not identical; the exact relationship between them will be considered in due course. Care should also be taken not to confuse *intentionality*, spelt with a 't', and *intensionality*, spelt with an 's', this second notion being the opposite to extensionality. Again, the two notions are related but not at all identical.)

As a starting point for our discussion of intentionality, let me take the opening passage from the highly readable account of this phenomenon provided by John Searle in his book *Intentionality* [26]:

As a preliminary formulation we might say: Intentionality is that property of many mental states and events by which they are directed at or about or of objects and states of affairs in the world.[3] If, for example, I have a belief, it must be a belief that such and such is the case; if I have a fear, it must be a fear of something or that something will occur; if I have a desire, it must be a desire to do something or that something should happen or be the case; if I have an intention, it must be an intention to do something.
—Searle [26, p.1]

In essence, this quotation spells out what it is that I shall mean by the word 'intentionality' in this essay.

Exactly how it can come about that mental states can *be* intentional is not something this theory attempts to answer. Rather I simply assume that there are such things as intentional mental states. This can be

---

[2] I shall always understand this to mean in my, or the agent's, environment.

[3] This does not mean that there must in fact *be* such objects or states of affairs in the world. For instance, consider a belief that Santa Claus has a white beard. Though there is no such object in the world as Santa Claus, the belief is nevertheless directed at the world in an appropriate fashion. See later for a further discussion on this point.

regarded as an attempt to capture within the rationalist framework some of the pnenomenologist's view of cognition, as outlined in [31]. Adapting Searle, we have:

On my view mental phenomena are biologically based: they are both caused by the operations of the brain and realized in the structure of the brain. ... It is an *objective* fact about the world that it contains certain systems, viz. brains, with *subjective* mental states, and it is a *physical* fact about such systems that they have *mental* features.
—Searle [26, p.ix]

It may be, of course, that (real) cognition is essentially *biological* in nature. But what exactly is meant by this word 'biological' in this context? This, surely, is precisely the issue Maturana tries to capture with his definition of an autopoietic system. In computational terms relevant to our theory, the following seem to be crucial attributes for any 'biological' system:[4]

a rich collection (relative to the purposes of the system) of input–output mechanisms that link the agent to the environment (e.g. sight, hearing, touch, smell, taste, temperature sensors, balance mechanisms, sound production, and various forms and degrees of action);

a computational architecture that exhibits a high degree of complexity (relative to the input–output mechanisms and to the purposes of the system);

adaptability of the computational architecture, or at least the behavior patterns, of the system as a result of interactions with the environment (possibly including other such systems), most likely including some form of memory.

Note that none of the above requirements is at all absolute. For instance, different organisms or agents having different purposes will exhibit/require different input–output mechanisms and different degrees of complexity in their mental architecture. The simple robot *SID* described in Section 4.5 has just one input channel and one motor channel, but these suffice for its (minimal) purpose. Likewise, though *SID*'s total number of possible mental states (namely, 4) is numerically small, in terms of the purposes of this robot (which consists of moving towards a wall and then stopping) the number of mental states is *exponential* in

---

[4] That is to say, any artificial system would have to satisfy these criteria before we could begin to contemplate referring to its activity as 'cognitive'. For reasons that I have already made clear, I do not believe that these conditions fully capture the essence of cognition, so their use to provide a 'definition' of 'cognitive activity' would be a stylized one.

the number of external states $(4 = 2^2)$. Thus *SID* could be said to lie at one end of the spectrum of systems that fulfill the above three criteria.

At the other end of this spectrum would be Man. Certainly our criteria would seem to point to the vast computational gap between human intelligence and attempts at artificial intelligence. In particular, however you enumerate the input–output mechanisms and 'purposes' of a human being, the computational complexity of the brain is clearly exponential in those parameters — something that has not yet been achieved, or even approached, in the artificial realm, except in very simple cases not significantly more complex than *SID*.

The above criteria are, it seems to me, sufficient to support the phenomenon of *cognition* (i.e. cognitive activity) and its potential to result in the *intentionality* of certain mental states, in so far as these terms directly pertain to the present theory. Thus my earlier use of the word 'biological' could, as far as we are concerned, be taken as coextensive with the satisfaction of these criteria.[5] In any event, I do not perceive any kind of insoluble 'mind–body problem' lurking in the background.[6] Mental phenomena are both caused by the operations of the brain (or other computing device) and realized in the structure of that brain (or computing device).[7] To see this as problematical, as many seem to have done, can only arise because of a confusion of levels.

To take my own favorite example, and the one used by Searle in [26, p.265], consider the property of water that it is wet. At the molecular level, it makes no sense to talk of a single water molecule being wet. The wetness property is at a higher level than the molecular. You cannot point to any part of the water and say "This is where the wetness is." Nevertheless, the wetness is *caused by* molecular behavior and is *realized in* the molecular structure. So too with the brain and mental activity.

Another familiar example also serves to illustrate how abstract mental activity, construed now as a higher level feature of the brain, can bring about physical movement of the body, a significant component of the 'mind–body problem'. The *expansion* of a gas in the cylinder of an automobile engine causes the physical motion of the piston, and yet the

---

[5] Of course, there is considerable vagueness in the criteria as expressed. But then it is not altogether clear what 'biological' means either in terms of 'simpler' concepts.

[6] In essence, the 'mind-body problem' asks where exactly in the body the mind is located, and if it is not so located, then what exactly is it, and how can it figure causally in physical activity of the body.

[7] This sentence is a modification of one in the final chapter of Searle [26, p.265].

property of the gas that it is *expanding* is a higher level one, not one that makes sense when applied to individual gas molecules. Again, the *expansion* is both caused by and realized in the molecular behavior. The situation is analogous for the brain and the mind. There is nothing mysterious, *per se*, about the fact that higher-level properties of the brain that we call 'mental states and acts' can figure causally in the physical activity of the agent.

Where the brain–mind case differs from the water–wetness and gas-expansion examples, is that in the latter cases we have fully worked-out theories that tell us how the lower level structure gives rise to the higher-level phenomena; in the case of the human brain-mind situation, no such theory has yet been fully developed. That may, of course, simply be a matter of time. It probably is.

Certainly, the capacity of the human mind to contemplate and to some extent control its own behavior does not, of itself, it seems to me, place it on an altogether different spectrum from other organisms or computational devices, including *SID*. Of course, this is not at all to say that it is likely, or even possible, to construct ever more sophisticated AI systems that will eventually achieve the mental sophistication of the human mind. The complexity issue alone will probably prevent that from happening.

To summarize then, I regard mental activity, and in particular the kind of mental activity involving mental states that possess *intentionality*, as being realized as concrete structures in the brain, though at a higher level than the molecular or neuron-synapse. *Intentionality* is that property whereby mental states can be directed at or about or of objects or states of affairs in the world. Accepting the *real* existence of such a property allows the rationalist scientist (such as ourselves) to come part way towards meeting the demands made by the phenomenologist school. With this notion available, I am now able to commence my examination of the particular mental states of relevance to our present overall aims.

6.3   Belief

A *belief* is an intentional mental state. That is to say, if an agent, $\mathscr{A}$, has a belief, B, then B is an actual cognitive structure, realized in the brain of $\mathscr{A}$.

Clearly, the above is a description rather than a definition. It does not say what it is about a belief that makes it different from any other mental state such as a doubt, a suspicion, or a desire. Indeed, as with the notion

of intentionality just discussed, an exact definition of 'belief' in terms
of more basic notions does not seem possible. Belief is a fundamental
cognitive state, and the best that can be done within the framework of
a rationalist, mathematical framework is to describe the properties of
belief, in particular its logical properties, as precisely as possible. This is
the approach which I shall begin in this section.

To maintain consistency with our overall framework, I shall restrict
attention to beliefs that correspond to our notion of information. That
is, I shall only consider beliefs whose *external content* (see presently) is a
proposition.

I shall not be concerned with the manner in which such a belief is
realized in hardware, and only in one context will I have recourse to
consider the internal logical structure of beliefs. Rather my approach
will be to classify such beliefs by 'what they are about'.

Considered in this light, what is required in order to determine a
particular belief? That it is in fact a belief, and not some other mental
state, certainly, and I shall have more to say on this in due course. What
else? Well, as just mentioned, *what it is* that is believed — the external
significance — must play a role. I shall take this to be a *proposition*, and
it is this proposition that I shall refer to as the *external content* of the
belief.

Thus the external content of a belief will be a proposition, that is to
say, an entity of the form

$$x : E$$

where x is an object and E is a (parameter-free) type.

For example, if John believes that it is raining, then the external
content of this belief is the proposition

$$s : E$$

where s is John's immediate environment at the time, t_0, that he holds
this belief, and

$$E = [\dot{s} \mid \dot{s} \models \ll \text{raining}, t_0, 1 \gg]$$

(As earlier, I assume that this belief refers to rain in the immediate
environment.) This belief will be satisfied (i.e. be a true belief) if and
only if this propositional, external content is true.

Is this enough to characterize a particular belief? That is to say, is it
enough to know:

    (a) that the mental state concerned *is* a belief; and

(b) what the external content is ?

The answer is 'no', as I now show.

Consider my belief, B, that it is grimbling. 'Grimbling', I should explain, is the phenomenon whereby small purple objects called 'grimbles' fall from the sky. Of course, you have never heard of 'grimbles'. They do not exist; there is no such thing as 'grimbling'. Nevertheless, I have, let us suppose, a number of sincerely held beliefs about these objects, and in particular I believe that there really are such things as grimbles, and that grimbling is a genuine phenomenon. To my mind, the 'content' of my belief, B, is the 'proposition'

$$s : E$$

where s is my immediate environment at the time, t_0, I hold this belief, and

$$E = [\dot{s} \mid \dot{s} \models \ll \text{grimbling}, t_0, 1 \gg]$$

But there is no such phenomenon as grimbling. More precisely, the scheme of individuation with which we are working (in this case one appropriate for the agent-species Man) does not give rise to such a relation. So surely, the above is not a properly formed proposition. In such a case, what I would say is that the belief, B, has no *external content* — it is what will be called an *ungrounded* belief. But it is a belief for all that.

Ungrounded beliefs will be considered in due course. In the meantime, I shall restrict my attention to beliefs that *do* have an external content — the grounded beliefs. This disposes of examples of the 'grimbling' variety, and the natural question then is: is it the case that for all *grounded* beliefs the external content serves to classify that belief adequately; or is the extreme simplicity of my earlier example (i.e. John's belief that it is raining) masking some difficulties? In fact, even for grounded beliefs there is still a problem, and the following well-known example shows that there is more to the concept of belief than my account so far has indicated.

In [12], Kripke describes the Frenchman, Pierre, who, on the basis of what he has been told by others, has the belief *Londres is pretty*, a belief which he continues to hold even when, in 1990 say, he travels to London for the first time and forms the belief *London is not pretty*. Seemingly, therefore, Pierre holds two contradictory beliefs, whose external contents are:

$$w \models \ll \text{pretty}, x, 1990, 1 \gg \quad \text{and} \quad w \models \ll \text{pretty}, x, 1990, 0 \gg$$

where x is the city of London. And yet one would be reluctant to conclude, on the basis of this, that Pierre was an irrational sort of fellow, happy to tolerate contradictory beliefs. Rather the explanation is surely that Pierre has two different *notions* of London, one acquired from conversations with his friends back in France (when the city was referred to as 'Londres'), the other formed by his direct perception from being in London (when he learns to call his ugly new surroundings 'London'). Should he ever be informed that 'Londres' is in fact just the French name for London, then presumably he would at once revise his earlier belief about 'Londres' being pretty, trusting perception above linguistically acquired information. (Perception will be considered in the next chapter.)

Beliefs then, it would seem, ought not to be classified solely in terms of their external content. Rather, account should be taken of the *internal* structure of the belief, in so far as it involves *notions* of objects. As with belief states themselves, it is not my present intention to say what exactly constitutes a *notion*, though I shall presently introduce a suggestive notation for such an entity. I do, however, conceive of notions as being realized as certain configurations in the structure of the brain, configurations that are (sometimes) associated with certain objects in the world, and which are involved in the structures of belief states.

Thus, Pierre has two beliefs, each involving a particular *notion* of a certain city. Or does he? Would it not be more accurate to say that one belief, the one he formed in France, involves a *notion* of a certain city, but the other belief, the one formed as a result of his actual experience in that city, is a belief that involves *that very city*? My answer is that this is not the case, and that such a claim would amount to a confusion of what is meant by the two terms 'about' and 'involves' in this context. Beliefs, as intentional mental states, can be *about* things in the world. For example, Pierre has two beliefs *about* the real, actual city London. But as mental states, beliefs will have a structure that *involves* notions of those things in the world. The belief does not *involve* the objects in the world any more than the belief is *about* those notions.[8] Pierre's two beliefs *involve* different notions of London. *About* and *involves* are getting at two different things here.

In order to understand how notions can be acquired, in particular inappropriate ones such as Pierre's first notion of London, it is necessary

---

[8] Though beliefs *can* be about notions; for example my belief that Pierre's notion of *Londres* was inappropriate is a belief *about* one of Pierre's notions of London. But this is a different issue from the one under discussion here.

to recognize that a belief (or other mental) state cannot be considered in isolation, but is an integral part of a whole 'intentionality network' of other mental states, skills, practices, and general know-how, set against a 'background' of ways the world is.[9] I look at each of these two factors in turn.

First of all the *intentionality network*. Suppose I believe (belief B) that Professor Bright will get a Nobel Prize for his work on ectoplasmic synthesis. Now, I have never met Professor Bright, nor do I know anything about ectoplasmic synthesis other than what I have read in *Scientific American*. My belief B is only linked to the world by way of a number of other beliefs, beliefs I have acquired from reading the literature, literature that I *believe* to be reliable. As part of this network of other beliefs about Professor Bright and his subject, my belief B seems reasonable, and is certainly intentional, its intentionality deriving from the other beliefs in that network. But without that network of related beliefs, there is no way my particular mental state can be an intentional belief state. That is to say, suppose neuroscience had reached a sufficiently advanced state that it was possible to give an exact physical description of the brain state corresponding to a particular belief, and moreover that state could be accurately simulated on some computing device.[10] Thus this device would be in exactly the same state as my brain *vis à vis* the belief *Professor Bright will get a Nobel Prize for his work on ectoplasmic synthesis*. Nevertheless, the state of the device could not be said to be a belief *about* Professor Bright and his work, nor indeed is it an *intentional* state at all. For, in the absence of the rest of the network of interrelated beliefs (and other intentional states), this particular mental state is just that, an isolated state.

A helpful analogy is provided by the example of a perfect counterfeit hundred-dollar bill. Suppose someone manufactured a perfect counterfeit, identical in all respects to a real one, other than the fact that one is real the other counterfeit. Then of course the counterfeit bill is just that: a counterfeit. Being identical to the real thing, does not make it genuine currency. To be genuine, a hundred-dollar bill must be produced at an

---

[9] The terms 'network' and 'background' are also used in this context by Searle [26], but his usage is different. Part of what I include in the 'network' Searle refers to as 'background' and what I refer to as 'background' is not referred to by name at all in [26].

[10] Whether or not one can in fact 'isolate' that precise belief state, even in principle, is another matter. I suspect that such is not even theoretically possible. But the supposed fiction I am entering into here should nevertheless serve well enough to indicate the point I am trying to make.

authorized plant — that is to say, it must occupy an appropriate position in the network of human society. A counterfeit bill, even though identical in all respects to a real one, nevertheless fails to be genuine because it does not fit into this network in the correct fashion — it is produced by unauthorized means.

In addition to the other beliefs — and possibly other intentional states as well — the intentionality network involves a whole array of interlinked mental and bodily skills, abilities, and general know-how, exhibiting varying degrees of intentionality. An example involving an intentional act is perhaps best suited to illustrating this part of the network, though it is equally important to a great many, if not all, intentional states and acts, such as belief, desire, intention, perception, speech, and so on; indeed in some ways the holistic nature of the network is the very essence of intentionality as the link between an agent and the environment that evolves over a history of interactions of the agent with that environment.

Suppose then, I am driving down to the Big Sur coastline. This act is a consequence of a prior *intention* I formed, the intention to make such a trip. In turn, this intention is presumably a result of a number of other intentional states: a *desire* to make such a trip, the *knowledge* that I had no other commitments at this time, the *belief* that the good weather will continue to hold, and doubtless a whole host of other intentional states as well.

This is not to say that I was or am necessarily aware of all these various intentional states, much less that I performed some kind of logical deduction leading from them to the formation of my intention to drive to Big Sur. The relevance of the particular mental states just listed might become apparent to me if I were asked to explain what had led to my deciding to make my trip, but there will be other intentional states whose relevance I could only perceive, if at all, as a result of a fairly detailed analysis. To take one seemingly trivial example, presumably my intention was dependent upon a belief that it is possible to drive from Palo Alto to Big Sur, but this is a belief that I had certainly never been conscious of until this very moment of writing.[11]

Even more extensive than the conscious or unconscious beliefs, etc. that figure in the way the network supports my action (and the intention that led to it) are a whole spectrum of other features, features that while

---

[11] As it happens, at the time of writing this particular passage I have just returned from Big Sur, so my having now become aware of this particular belief does not affect my argument as it applies to that particular trip.

not *intentional*, at least not to the extent of states such as belief, desire, intention, are nevertheless connected to my being a part of the world.

For instance, both my act of driving and the intention to perform this act depend, each in their own way, upon my ability to drive, and this in turn consists of a whole array of skills involving my hands, legs, eyes, ears. None of these 'low-level' skills seem to justify the description of 'intentional acts', nor does my intention to make my trip seem to depend upon a whole series of beliefs that I can perform such basic bodily actions; rather they are just what the word says they are: basic *skills*.

And going even further, each of these relevant basic skills depends upon the way my nerves, tendons, muscles, and skeleton function, but again these do not figure in my beliefs about my ability to drive down to Big Sur. Nor does this task require that I have any knowledge or beliefs about the laws of gravity, of mechanics, and so on, though again there are many such laws that are highly relevant to my action, and my body certainly needs to be attuned to, and perform in accordance with, those laws. (The relevance of this seemingly endless array of such non-intentional network features is one of the things that makes the aims of artificial intelligence so very difficult to achieve using the methods adopted by the early pioneers in this field.)

Turning now to the *background*, this consists of all those ways the world is, without which an intentional state such as a belief could not exist (as an intentional state — though as indicated above it is at least fictionally possible for the state itself to have an independent, non-intentional existence). Thus, for example, if it were not the case that Alfred Nobel had established the Nobel Prizes in the first place, and if these were not regularly awarded, on the basis of highly meritorious scientific research work, then the actual state of my brain that constitutes my particular belief about Professor Bright, which, let us suppose, could still arise or be artificially simulated, could not have the external significance it in fact does.

Thus in particular, while intentional states are realized in the brain as concrete, cognitive structures, and thus *belong* to the agent, the external significance of an intentional state depends also upon the way the world is, and on the history of interactions of the agent with the world.

At this stage, lest the reader throw up her hands in horror at the sheer complexity of all of this, I should point out that I shall not concern myself greatly with detailed issues of the network and the background. My development does, however, make reference to the existence and role played by these structures, so we do need to have some awareness of how they function in supporting intentional states and acts. Moreover, in view of the overall theme of our theory, namely the relative nature of information, it does no harm to be aware that the same is the case for intentional mental states.

In general, the identification of an individual in the world by an agent, either by perceptual means or otherwise, is dependent on both the agent's intentionality network and the background. From our theoreticians' standpoint of independent observers, if x is an object individuated by an agent, $\mathscr{A}$, then the x-representing cognitive structure realized in the brain of $\mathscr{A}$ as a result of that individuation or identification, is called a *notion* of x.

Thus, conversations with his colleagues in France enable Kripke's Pierre to form a notion of a particular city, which he knows as 'Londres', and his subsequent experience in London enables him to form another notion of a city he knows as 'London'. Two processes of identification, each one producing a specific *notion* of a city. In point of fact they are both notions of *the same* city, but Pierre does not know that. He does know that each is a notion of *some* city, that in each case the city is in England, that it is a large city, and so on. His notion of 'Londres' may indeed be sufficiently rich that he is eventually able to figure out for himself that this is in fact the city, 'London', in which he now finds himself, at which point he will be able to *merge* his two notions into one. But until that occurs his two notions remain quite separate.

Similar remarks apply to *notions* of relations, locations, situations, and whatever else in the world the agent individuates. I refer to the various kinds of notion as *individual-notions, relation-notions*, and so on.

Notions are concrete structures realized in the brain. Exactly how they are realized is not relevant to our present discussion. They can arise as a result of perception (visual, aural, tactile, and whatever), or communication from another agent, or a combination of various means, and in all cases they depend upon the intentionality network of the agent, and in turn contribute to that intentionality network. As a part of that intentionality network, an individual-notion acts as an 'individual'; that is to say, the part it plays in mental states and acts, such as belief or desire or doubt, is that of an individual. And likewise for relation-notions, location-notions, and so on. There may or may not be an actual uniformity in the world corresponding to such a cognitive structure. If a given notion, n, corresponds to some actual uniformity, x, in the world I say that n is a notion *of* x. If there is no uniformity x in the world to which the notion n corresponds, then n is said to be an *empty* notion, and is not a notion *of* anything. Examples of notions that are notions *of* something in the world are the notion I have of the terminal in front of me, the notion I have of the sun, the notion I have of London, and my notion of the relation raining. Examples of empty notions (that are not *of* anything) are my notion of the unicorn my neighbour claims to have seen in my garden, my notion of the flying carpet described on the front page of the magazine I saw in the supermarket checkout line, and my notion of the relation 'grimbling'. (I shall reserve unqualified use of the word 'notion' for notions that are of something, and use the phrase 'empty notion' for notions that are not of anything in the world.)

Of course, we have a problem of language here, in that even in the case of our examples of notions that are not *of* anything in the world, we nevertheless use phrases such as 'notion *of* the unicorn … ,' 'notion *of* the flying carpet … ,' and so on. Given that our only means of describing mental states is through their external significance, this seems unavoidable. A notion of a unicorn may be formed as a result of seeing pictures in story books, or by suitably combining two prior notions, one of a horse, the other of a horn. To the individual agent, all notions are notions 'of' something, but this use of 'of' pertains to the way the notion fits in to the rest of the agent's intentionality network. The other use of 'of', the italicized one above, is an *empirical* one, concerned with the way the notion links to the world.

Clearly, notions acquired by experience or direct perception are always notions *of* something in the world, whereas notions acquired through other means may or may not be. But it does not follow that an experientally or perceptually acquired notion is necessarily a *reliable* notion about the object it is a notion of, in the sense of giving rise to true beliefs about the object concerned.

For example, suppose you are in Hollywood, and you see a particularly fine looking house. You might form the belief that a only a wealthy film star could afford to live there. On the other hand, if a colleague points out to you that you are in fact on a studio back lot, and that what you are looking at is not a house but a mere façade, part of a film set, you will not form the same belief. In both cases, what you are looking at is exactly the same. If you know, or believe, you are looking at an entire house, that is what you will 'see', and that provides the notion that will figure in your beliefs. If you know or believe it is a façade, that is what you will 'see' and that will be the notion that figures in your subsequent beliefs. In either case, what you perceive in an *aspect* of some object;

your network and background contribute to the notion that figures in your beliefs.

Since perception of an object is always perception of some *aspect* of that object, even in the 'reliable' case of visual perception, the notion of the object thus acquired may turn out to be a poor one, giving rise to false beliefs about that object. For example, a belief that what was 'seen' as a house would be a nice place to live, when in fact all that exists is a façade.

What now of the part played by notions in belief states? Provided we keep clear in our mind the premise that intentional states are concrete cognitive structures realized in the brain (i.e. properties of the brain at a suitable level), the answer seems fairly clear.

For simplicity, I shall henceforth concentrate on what I shall call *basic* beliefs, that is to say, beliefs whose external content is a basic infonic proposition, i.e. of the form

$$s \models \sigma$$

where s is a situation and σ is a basic infon.

Suppose that as I sit at my desk at CSLI, I believe that across campus, Mark is working in Tanner Library. This particular (basic) belief is a mental state, B. The *external content* of B is the proposition

$$e \models \ll\text{working, Mark, } t, 1 \gg$$

where e is the situation that exists in Tanner Library (i.e. Tanner Library conceived as a situation) and t is the present time.

As a mental state, my belief, B, involves various notions: a notion, $e^{\#}$, of the Tanner Library situation, a notion, working$^{\#}$, of the activity of working, a notion, Mark$^{\#}$, of Mark, and a notion, now$^{\#}$, of the present time.[12] I shall denote the 'structure' of B, $\mathscr{S}(B)$, by:

$$\mathscr{S}(B) = \langle Bel, \ e^{\#}, \text{working}^{\#}, \text{Mark}^{\#}, \text{now}^{\#}, 1\rangle$$

This is not to make any claim as to the way the state B is realized in the brain, nor about the manner in which the notions $e^{\#}$, working$^{\#}$, Mark$^{\#}$, now$^{\#}$ are brought together to form this belief. Rather I am simply indicating the basic components of the belief as relevant to our standpoint of external significance. The initial parameter *Bel* in $\mathscr{S}(B)$ signifies that the mental state B is in fact a belief — see presently when I set beliefs in the context of other mental states.

---

[12] This last notion of 'the present time', is atypical in that it is an *indexical* notion, dependent for its referent upon contextual factors in the same way as the pronouns 'I' and 'you'.

But consider now another of my beliefs as I sit at my desk, namely the (basic) belief, C, that it is raining. The external content of this belief is the proposition

$$e \models \ll \text{raining}, t, 1 \gg$$

where e is the environment outside my office and t is the present time.

So far, everything is much the same as in the previous example. Where there is a difference is in the structure, $\mathscr{S}(C)$, of this belief. For surely, though C involves notions raining$^{\#}$ for the condition of raining and now$^{\#}$ for the present time, it does not involve a notion for the situation e. This is reflected in the very way I would describe my belief. I do not say "I believe it is raining *around here*." I simply assert "I believe it is raining." The context, that is to say, *my* context, provides the location of the raining. In other words, what puts the environment situation, e, into the external content of my belief, is *my location* as I have the belief.

This is quite different from the previous example, where the only way that Tanner Library could get into the external content was by way of my notion thereof figuring as a component of the structure of that belief.

The point to note is that beliefs are not just 'mental states' but rather mental states possessed by agents who are *situated in* and *linked to* the world. And that very situatedness can supply the situation that gets into the external content of a belief.

I shall denote the structure, $\mathscr{S}(C)$, of the belief C by:

$$\mathscr{S}(C) = \langle Bel, \, - \, , \text{raining}^{\#}, \text{now}^{\#}, 1 \rangle$$

The dash is not meant to suggest that there is something *missing* from my belief structure, that some parameter has been left out. Rather that this particular belief simply does not involve a notion of the situation, e, that figures in the external content, that part of the external content being determined instead by my being in the situation I am when I have this belief. In going from my situation to the content situation, e, the relation that figures in the external content can play a role. For a relation such as raining, this situation will generally be my immediate environment, as I assumed above. In many other cases, and in particular cases involving beliefs with an essentially unlocated content, the content situation, e, will be the world. (Pierre's beliefs about London fall into this latter category, as I shall indicate in just a moment.)

I refer to beliefs such as the belief, C, that pick up the situation in their external content by way of contextual factors rather than via a notion, as *situated beliefs*. (Since all mental states are of necessity 'situated', this is a purely stylized use of the word 'situated', intended to signify one particular aspect of such beliefs.)

In general then, suppose I have a (basic) belief, B, that p, where p is the proposition

$$s \models \ll R, a_1, \ldots, a_n, i \gg$$

Thus R is some relation (which may have more than n argument places) and $a_1, \ldots, a_n$ are objects in the world (of the kinds appropriate for R). Then this belief, i.e. this particular intentional mental state B, has as its *external content* the proposition p, and a *structure*, $\mathscr{S}(B)$, of one of the two forms:

- $\mathscr{S}(B) = \langle Bel, s^\#, R^\#, a_1^\#, \ldots, a_n^\#, i \rangle$

- $\mathscr{S}(B) = \langle Bel, -, R^\#, a_1^\#, \ldots, a_n^\#, i \rangle$

where Bel signifies that the state is a belief state, $s^\#$ is my notion of the situation s, $R^\#$ is my notion of the relation R, $a_1^\#, \ldots, a_n^\#$ are my notions of $a_1, \ldots, a_n$, respectively, and i is the polarity indicator, which corresponds to the polarity of the infon in the content type, E. $\mathscr{S}(B)$ denotes the 'structure' of the belief B in the sense relevant to our analysis, namely in terms of external significance. In the former case, the situation s gets into the external content proposition, p, by virtue of my notion $s^\#$. In the latter case, s arises from my own situatedness as the agent holding this belief. In both cases the external content of my belief is a *proposition*.

Returning now to the first example of my belief that Mark is working in Tanner Library, let B_1 denote this belief held by me as I sit at my desk in CSLI on one particular day, and B_2 the 'same' belief held, under the same circumstances, the following day. Clearly, these two beliefs have a lot in common, as reflected in that use of the enquoted word 'same'. On the other hand, there is a definite sense in which B_1 and B_2 are not the same belief; they are held on different days, and one may be true, the other false. So just what is it that these two beliefs have in common, and how do they differ?

Clearly, both beliefs have the same structure, namely:

$$\mathscr{S}(B_1) = \mathscr{S}(B_2) = \langle Bel, \ e^\#, \text{working}^\#, \text{Mark}^\#, \text{now}^\#, 1 \rangle$$

In both cases, $e^\#$ is a notion of the Tanner Library situation, e, working$^\#$ is a notion of the property of working , and Mark$^\#$ is a notion of Mark. Where there is a difference is in the way the notion now$^\#$ relates to the world. In B_1, now$^\#$ is a notion of t_1, the time at which the belief B_1 is held, whereas in B_2, now$^\#$ is a notion of t_2, the time at which the belief

B_2 is held. This difference in the denotations of the notion now$^\#$ results in the two different external contents:

$$\text{Content } (B_1): \quad e \models \ll \text{working, Mark, } t_1, 1 \gg$$

$$\text{Content } (B_2): \quad e \models \ll \text{working, Mark, } t_2, 1 \gg$$

Our inclination to say that I have the *same* belief on the two days reflects our tendency to report beliefs in terms of their structure. (See presently regarding the *de re* and *de dicto* distinction in belief reports.) The different external contents of the two beliefs would probably result in our declaring that the beliefs *refer to*, or are *about*, two different situations.

The fact that the same belief structure can give rise on different occasions, to different external contents, means that beliefs are what Barwise and Perry [5] refer to as *efficient* mental states.

Part of the very essence of the intentionality of (grounded) belief states is that some or all of the notions they involve are tightly linked to objects in the world — they are notions *of* something in the world. I shall represent this linkage in our theory by introducing the basic relation *of*.

An agent being in possession of a belief, together with the links between all the notions in that belief and the objects they are notions of (assuming there are such objects) constitutes what I shall call a *belief situation*. The belief situation, s, that arises as I sit in my office at CSLI and think about Mark, is such that:

$$s \quad \models \quad \ll \text{has\_belief, Keith\_Devlin, } B, \text{CSLI}, t_B, 1 \gg$$
$$\wedge \ll \text{has\_structure, } B, \langle Bel, e^\#, \text{working}^\#, \text{Mark}^\#, \text{now}^\#, 1 \rangle, 1 \gg$$
$$\wedge \ll \text{of, } e^\#, e, \text{CSLI}, t_B, 1 \gg$$
$$\wedge \ll \text{of, working}^\#, \text{working, CSLI}, t_B, 1 \gg$$
$$\wedge \ll \text{of, Mark}^\#, \text{Mark, CSLI}, t_B, 1 \gg$$
$$\wedge \ll \text{of, now}^\#, t_B, \text{CSLI}, t_B, 1 \gg$$

where CSLI denotes my location and t_B the time at which my belief is held. The appearance of the location (CSLI) and time (t_B) in the various *of* infons in this example, is required because the same notion may be linked to different objects on different occasions.

The belief situation associated with a particular belief captures everything there is concerning that belief, its structure, the denotations of the various notions involved, and the external content of the belief.

Many of the traditional puzzles about belief can be explained by concentrating on the way the *of* relation links notions to objects in the world. In the case of the example above, the same belief structure, $\mathscr{S}(B)$, was linked, on two separate occasions, to two distinct contents. On the other hand, it is possible for two beliefs to have different *structures* and yet the same *external content*.

For example, to modify the scenario concerning our Frenchman, Pierre, suppose he regards the city (London) he comes to live in as a very pretty place, but still does not realize that this is the very city (Londres) that was described to him so glowingly by his friends in France. Thus he has two basic beliefs, B_1 and B_2, having the structures

$$\mathscr{S}(B_1) = \langle Bel, \; - \, , \text{pretty}^{\#} , n_1, 1990, 1 \rangle$$

$$\mathscr{S}(B_2) = \langle Bel, \; - \, , \text{pretty}^{\#} , n_2, 1990, 1 \rangle$$

where pretty$^{\#}$ is Pierre's notion of the property pretty, n_1 is his notion of London acquired from his friends in France, and n_2 is his notion of London acquired by direct perception of the city in which he now finds himself. Though these two beliefs clearly have a lot in common, they are quite definitely not the same belief (i.e. they are not the same cognitive structure), since they involve different notions, and notions are themselves cognitive structures; $\mathscr{S}(B_1) \neq \mathscr{S}(B_2)$, therefore $B_1 \neq B_2$. But the two beliefs have the same *external content*. Since n_1 is a notion of London (denote it by L) and n_2 is also a notion of L, we have

$$Content(B_1) = Content(B_2) = \pi,$$

where π is the proposition

$$w \models \, \ll \text{pretty}, \, L, 1990, 1 \gg$$

In this case, the distinction between the two beliefs, B_1 and B_2, comes not from the external content of their beliefs but from their structures, more specifically from the two different *notions* of London that Pierre has.

To take a different example, what about that unicorn my neighbour claims to have seen in my garden? As a result of talking to my neighbour, I acquire an (empty) notion, u, of a 'unicorn', together with a number of (ungrounded) beliefs involving that notion. In particular, I form the ungrounded belief, B, having the structure

$$\mathscr{S}(B) = \langle Bel, \; - \, , \text{white}^{\#}, u, 1 \rangle$$

What is this a belief *about*? Nothing, since u is not a notion *of* any actual object in the world. What is the external content of this belief? It has none. It is an ungrounded belief, and thus, whilst it can fit into my intentionality network in much the same way as any other belief, it cannot have an external content, since it is not properly linked to the world.

Now, in the case of basic beliefs, this observation is a special case of the more general fact that a grounded, basic belief cannot involve an empty notion. This is easily seen. But in the case of non-basic beliefs, things are not so straightforward. Consider, for example, my daughter's belief that:

If Santa Claus does not exist, then my parents buy my Christmas presents.

This belief involves the empty notion of 'Santa Claus', and yet it is clearly a perfectly acceptable, grounded belief. Indeed, it is a true belief! But of course, it is not a basic belief. The empty notion of 'Santa Claus' occurs as part of a conditional. Beliefs of this complexity are outside my present scope.

How are notions acquired? Through direct perception, certainly. Also, as in the case of my daughter's 'Santa Claus', Pierre's 'Londres', and my unicorn, through communication with other agents. And by internal mental construction, such as when I form the notion of the grand house I might one day live in. Notice that the Pierre example, where an intentional notion is acquired by communication with other agents, illustrates how the *link* between an intentional notion and the object in the world it is a notion *of* — the very essence of intentionality — is one that can be passed on from one agent to another. Both of Pierre's notions are *about* the same city, London. What might not be passed on in this process is sufficient means for the recipient to recognize that two notions (say one acquired by communication, the other by perception) are in fact notions of the same object.

Of course, it is quite possible for an agent to have a notion that fails to be a notion *of* something because of a confusion of identification. The receptionist at CSLI might have a notion of the tall Israeli visitor who checks his mail twice every morning, whereas in reality there are two Israelis, Uri and Saharon, who look remarkably similar, and whom the receptionist has failed to recognize as two separate individuals. In such a case, her belief that 'the visiting Israeli' speaks some German fails to have a content, because her notion fails to be a notion of an individual. Just as Pierre might eventually *merge* his two notions of London, so too the CSLI receptionist might one day have to replace her single notion of 'the Israeli visitor' by two notions, one of Uri, the other of Saharon.

I finish this section by making a few remarks on the nature of (grounded, basic) belief as a particular kind of mental state. Though for the most part we are taking 'belief' as a fundamental concept, some things can be said.

First of all, to say that an agent $\mathscr{A}$ *believes* a basic, infonic proposition p is to say that $\mathscr{A}$ has a belief whose external content is p. Thus, if p is the proposition

$$s \models \ll R, a_1, \ldots, a_n, i \gg$$

then $\mathscr{A}$ must have notions $R^{\#}, a_1^{\#}, \ldots, a_n^{\#}$ of $R, a_1, \ldots, a_n$, respectively, and possibly a notion, $s^{\#}$, of s as well, such that either

$$\mathscr{S}(B) = \langle Bel, s^{\#}, R^{\#}, a_1^{\#}, \ldots, a_n^{\#}, i \rangle$$

or else, in the case of a situated belief,

$$\mathscr{S}(B) = \langle Bel, -, R^{\#}, a_1^{\#}, \ldots, a_n^{\#}, i \rangle$$

Having such a cognitive structure entails an awareness of the conditions of satisfaction of the belief, namely that the belief is satisfied if and only if the proposition p is true in the world, together with an awareness of what Searle [26] refers to as the *direction of fit*, which in the case of a belief is 'mind to world'. Roughly speaking, this last condition means that the onus as to whether or not the belief is satisfied is upon the belief, not the world: the world is the way it is, and to be satisfied a belief has to conform to that world. This contrast with an intentional state such as desire, where the fulfillment of a desire requires that the world (come to) match that desire, an example of 'world-to-mind' direction of fit. This issue will be taken up more fully in the next section.

This direct linkage between a belief state and the world means that beliefs are in general completely *extensional*: that is, a belief does not depend (for its satisfaction) upon any particular description of the objects it is about. If Pierre believes that *Londres* is pretty, then Pierre believes that *London* is pretty. *What* Pierre believes constitutes the *external content* of his belief state, and the external content of a belief is a proposition; that is to say an entity in the public domain, involving actual objects in the world. No particular description of those objects is involved.

This is quite different from, though often confused with, the situation concerning a *belief report*. For instance, suppose I utter the sentence

Pierre believes that London is pretty.

Theoretically, this has two possible readings, the *de re* and the *de dicto*, though in practice, normal English usage seems invariably to favor the *de dicto* reading. (This paragraph assumes the reader is familiar with the *de re, de dicto* distinction, and may be ignored by readers without the necessary background — though to some extent the paragraph itself gives some indication of the issue.) Under the *de re* reading, my utterance reports the *external content* of Pierre's belief. Under the *de dicto* reading, I am making a claim about Pierre's *mental state*. His belief is about a city. My claim is about his belief. Under the *de re* reading, I report his belief in terms of its *external content*. Under the *de dicto* reading, I describe his actual belief *state* (in terms arising from its external significance). Given a *de re* reading, the reference to 'London' in my utterance is to the city of London. Given a *de dicto* reading, the reference is to Pierre's *notion* of London. In this latter case, depending on which notion I refer to, my claim may be either true or false. This explains the difference between *de re* and *de dicto* belief reports, and shows how, in the case of the *de dicto* reading, a single belief report can seemingly give rise to contradictory claims.

6.4   Other mental states

Not all mental states are intentional. For example, instances of joy and sorrow are not necessarily intentional, though they may be. Belief is intentional, as are desire and intention.

The intentional states of belief, desire, and intention are usually regarded as the most 'basic' intentional states. It certainly seems to be the case that all other intentional states can be regarded as refinements of modal combinations of these three using the modal operator $\diamond$ ('it is possible that'). For example, *fear that p* is a refinement of the combination

$$Believe(\diamond p) \wedge Desire(\neg p)$$

sorrow that p is a refinement of

$$Believe(p) \wedge Desire(\neg p)$$

and *hope that p* is a refinement of

$$\neg Believe(p) \wedge \neg Believe(\neg p) \wedge Believe(\diamond p) \wedge Desire(p)$$

Of course, these (and other) examples put a considerable loading on that word 'refinement'. Nevertheless, they do indicate the sense in which belief, desire, and intention are basic amongst the intentional states. (In point of fact, modal combinations of belief and desire alone suffice for almost all the intentional states except for intention itself.)

Having adopted belief as the exemplary intentional state, my aim in this section is simply to indicate how that study of belief fits into a more general framework of a theory of intentional states. Since *intention* is closely bound up with the concept of *action*, which is dealt with in the following chapter, I take as my paradigm example here the intentional state of *desire*; more precisely, desire in the sense of desire that some proposition be true, rather than desire of some individual. (So, for example, I would allow the example whereby David desires that he own a pink Cadillac, but not the example whereby David desires a pink Cadillac, though it is not clear that there is any real distinction between these two.)

As I did for belief, I shall concentrate on mental states whose external content is a *basic, infonic* proposition, referring to such states as *basic*.

For my purposes, a basic intentional state, I, having the *propositional* external content

$$s \models \ll R, a_1, \ldots, a_n, i \gg$$

has the 'structure'

$$\mathcal{S}(I) = \langle M, s^\sharp, R^\sharp, a_1^\sharp, \ldots, a_n^\sharp, i \rangle$$

or else, in the case of a *situated* state where the context supplies the relevant situation,

$$\mathcal{S}(I) = \langle M, -, R^\sharp, a_1^\sharp, \ldots, a_n^\sharp, i \rangle$$

where

M is the *psychological mode* of the state (see presently);
$s^\sharp$ is a situation-notion;
$R^\sharp$ is a relation-notion;
$a_1^\sharp, \ldots, a_n^\sharp$ are individual-notions;
i is a polarity.

Examples of psychological modes are *belief* (denoted by *Bel*) and *desire* (denoted by *Des*). The psychological mode says precisely what kind of mental state I is, and thus governs the way the state fits into the rest of the agent's intentionality network, and what role the state plays in guiding the behavior of the agent. In particular, it determines the manner in which the intentional state may be satisfied, as considered in just a moment.

In order for I to be grounded and thus have an external *content*, the notion $s^\sharp$ must, in the case where this notion figures in the structure, be a notion of some situation, s, the notion $R^\sharp$ must be a notion of some relation, R, and the notions $a_1^\sharp, \ldots, a_n^\sharp$ must be notions of some individuals $a_1, \ldots, a_n$, respectively, appropriate for the argument places of R. In which case, the *external content* of the state I is the proposition

$$s \models \ll R, a_1, \ldots, a_n, i \gg$$

where s is supplied by contextual factors in the case of a situated state.

As in the case of belief, for a *basic* mental state to be grounded it is necessary that it involves no empty notions.

The psychological mode determines, among other things, a *direction of fit* for the state. In the case of belief, the direction of fit is 'mind to world': in order that a belief, *B*, be satisfied, an agent must tailor *B* to fit the way the world is. In the case of desire, the direction of fit is 'world to mind': in order that an agent's desire, *D*, be fulfilled, the world must be, or come to be, the way *D* requires.

The direction of fit is one of the ways the psychological mode governs the way a mental state fits into the agent's intentionality network and guides the behavior of the agent. Thus, if I believe it will be dry and sunny, I will dress accordingly. If the day subsequently turns out to be wet and cold, my decision not to wear my raincoat will remain a rational one *given my earlier belief*, but I will conclude that my belief was mistaken. I will not declare that the weather made a mistake in not matching my belief. Nor will I express dismay at my failure to make the weather match my belief.

On the other hand, if I desire to run a five-minute mile,[13] then if I want to see this desire fulfilled, I will head for the track and start running. If my best efforts only succeed in my clocking 5 min 20 s for the mile, it is not that the desire was 'wrong'. (Though it may have been formed as a result of a false belief!) What went wrong is that I was not able to perform the action necessary for the fulfillment of that desire. The only way to fulfill that desire was to run a five-minute mile. Given the desire, the onus of fulfillment is on me, and in particular my physical actions.

To be in an intentional state, *I*, of the kind under present consideration, entails an awareness of the external content of that state (i.e. the conditions of satisfaction of the state) and of the direction of fit whereby that propositional content may be satisfied.

An intentional state can only exist *as an intentional state* within the agent's 'intentionality network' and set against the agent's 'background'. In particular, the network helps to determine any *notions* that may figure in the state.

It should perhaps be remarked that mental states are just that: *states*, and not *acts*. Imagining the Golden Gate Bridge is a mental *act*, not a state. Hoping the Golden Gate Bridge does not fall down is a *state*, not an act.

---

[13] A feat well within my capabilities, at least until a few years ago.

In a sense, intentional mental states are *representations* of parts of the world. For example, a belief *represents* its content under a certain psychological mode, the belief mode.

As indicated already, *notions* can arise in a number of ways: direct perception, communication with other agents, the gradual accumulation of a number of attributes, or simply imagination. In each case, the final notion is a certain configuration in the brain — a form of network linking together a whole array of features. As with mental states, the precise nature of this configuration is not of any significance to us; rather it suffices that we introduce a simple notation that reflects those features of notions that are relevant to our development.

I shall represent a notion, n, as a triple of one of the two forms

$$\langle D, \dot{n}, T \rangle \quad , \quad \langle I, \dot{n}, T \rangle$$

where $\dot{n}$ is a parameter of the appropriate basic type, and T is a parametric type with sole free parameter $\dot{n}$.

Intuitively, $\langle D, \dot{n}, T \rangle$ is the *definite* notion of *that* entity $\dot{n}$ of type T, and $\langle I, \dot{n}, T \rangle$ is the *indefinite* notion of an *arbitrary*, or *generic*, entity $\dot{n}$ of type T. (In the case of the definite notion, the type T should logically entail the uniqueness of any object of that type.) Notions of *relations* are assumed to be *definite*.

For example, in the case where n is my 1989 notion of the Golden Gate Bridge, we might take

$$n = \langle D, \dot{n}, T \rangle$$

where $\dot{n}$ is an *IND*-parameter and T is a parametric type of the form

$$T = [\dot{n} \mid w \models \ll \text{bridge}, \dot{n}, \text{California}, 1989, 1 \gg$$
$$\wedge \ll \text{red}, \dot{n}, 1989, 1 \gg$$
$$\wedge \ll \text{connects}, \dot{n}, \text{San\_Fransisco}, \text{Marin\_County}, 1989, 1 \gg$$
$$\wedge \ll \text{named}, \dot{n}, \text{GOLDEN GATE BRIDGE}, 1989, 1 \gg$$
$$\wedge \ldots]$$

For the notion of an (unspecified) unicorn, we could take

$$n = \langle I, \dot{n}, T \rangle$$

where $\dot{n}$ is an *IND*-parameter and T is a parametric type of the form

$$T = [\dot{n} \mid w \models \ll \text{horse\_like}, \dot{n}, 1 \gg \wedge \ll \text{has\_horn}, \dot{n}, 1 \gg \wedge \ldots]$$

These two examples should indicate what it is that my notation is intended to capture: namely, those features of the notion that pertain to the particular usage, and which can therefore be assumed to be *characteristic* of the notion.

It should be noted that a complete, extensional specification of the type T would, in general, not be possible, since notions are *intensional* in nature. Indeed, those infons that we do list in the type of a notion are essentially *default* attributes that could be violated. For instance, a typical notion of a dog might involve a type, T, that includes the condition

$$\ll\text{four-legged}, \dot{n}, 1 \gg$$

but this would not preclude there being a dog that an accident has left with only three legs.

Thus our notation for notions is designed more to facilitate our study, rather than to provide an accurate reflection of any aspect of genuine cognitive activity.

Notice that some notions are so sparse in their information content that our notation captures very little at all. For instance, suppose that as I cycle in to CSLI one morning, I notice a black cat. Later on, I have cause to reflect on this particular cat. All I recall is that there was a black cat; I remember nothing else about it. Then it seems that the notion I have of this particular individual can only be represented as $\langle D, \dot{n}, T \rangle$, where

$$T = [\dot{n} \mid \ll\text{cat}, \dot{n}, t, 1 \gg \wedge \ll\text{black}, \dot{n}, t, 1 \gg$$
$$\wedge \ll\text{sees, Keith\_Devlin}, \dot{n}, l, t, 1 \gg]$$

where l, t are the location and time of my seeing the cat.

It should be pointed out that in representing notions in terms of *types*, I am allowing only a fairly restricted form of *notion*, one that does not involve any other *notions*. A treatment that better reflects the way notions seem to work in human cognitive activity, would be obtained if the definition of an *infon* were extended, in this context at least, to allow for notions to figure in the argument places of relations, and the definition of *types* extended accordingly. However, the simplified version given here should suffice for our present purposes.

As an illustration of the different roles played by the two kinds of notion, the definite and the indefinite, consider the following famous example of Quine [21, Chapter 17]. Suppose I say that I desire a sloop. This has two possible readings. First of all, there may be a particular sloop I desire — this passage being written in California, let us say the sloop John-B. Then my desire has the structure

$$\langle Des, -, \text{own}^{\#}, \text{Keith\_Devlin}^{\#}, \text{SJB}^{\#}, 1 \rangle$$

where $\text{SJB}^{\#}$ is a definite notion, my notion of the sloop John-B. The external content of this desire is the proposition

$$w \models \ll \text{own, Keith\_Devlin, SJB, 1} \gg$$

If, on the other hand, my desire is not for some particular sloop, but rather, as Quine puts it, is merely a desire to be relieved of slooplessness, then my desire has the structure

$$\langle Des, -, \text{own}^{\#}, \text{Keith\_Devlin}^{\#}, S^{\#}, 1 \rangle$$

where $S^{\#}$ is an indefinite notion, my notion of an unspecified, generic sloop. The external content of this desire is the proposition

$$w \models \exists \dot{b} \ll \text{own, Keith\_Devlin}, \dot{b}, 1 \gg$$

where $\dot{b}$ is a parameter for a sloop. So this is an example of a desire that is *not* basic.

The definite notion $SJB^{\#}$ in the first desire here, is necessarily linked to the specific object in the world it is a notion of, namely the actual sloop John-B. The indefinite notion $S^{\#}$ in the second desire is not linked to any particular object in the world. Rather it puts into the external content an existentially quantified parameter for an object of the appropriate type (i.e. the type in the notion), in this case a sloop.

Notice that, in the case of the desire for a particular sloop, the external content comes very close to what we would subjectively describe as the 'experience' of having the desire. When I desire to own the sloop John-B, I experience a definite wish to own that boat — my desire is directed at that particular boat. But for the other case, where I simply desire *any* sloop, there is not such a close resemblance, in that what I experience by way of my desire does not, it seems to me, involve any kind of existential quantification. I do not experience a wish *that there be* a sloop that I come to own. Rather it appears to be just one of those features of human agents that they can have desires directed at 'generic' objects of a given type.[14] The existential quantifier does, however, seem appropriate in the *external content*, since this I have defined to be the 'conditions of satisfaction' of that desire, i.e. what must occur in the world in order for the desire to be fulfilled. And my desire to own a (that is to say, *some*) sloop will be fulfilled precisely in case there is some sloop that I will come to own.

---

[14] It could be argued that a better fit between the experiental aspect and the external content is achieved by removing the existential quantifier in the external content, leaving this as a parametric proposition, with the unanchored parameter, $\dot{b}$, representing the 'generic' sloop. But, this strikes me as little better, since parameters (at least as I have been using them) do not really correspond to 'generic mental notions'.

Now, finally, I am in a position to say more about the distinction between *grounded* and *ungrounded* beliefs, desires, and so on. Take the case of belief.

What marks out a particular mental state as a *belief*, and not some other form of mental state, is what I have called the *psychological mode*. By including this 'mode' in the 'structure' of the belief, I was ackowledging its essentially internal nature. Broadly speaking, the psychological mode is intended to indicate the way the state fits in to the rest of the agent's intentionality network, and the role it plays in guiding the agent's behavior.

In particular, the following characteristic features of beliefs all contribute to a particular mental state *being* a belief, basic or otherwise:

(i)   a belief represents the way the agent takes the world to be;
(ii) an agent acting rationally will act in accordance with its beliefs, so that in a world in which those beliefs are satisfied it may achieve its desires and fulfill its intentions;
(iii) beliefs tend to persist until overthrown;
(iv) beliefs may be held unconsciously;
(v)   an agent may simultaneously hold more than one belief.

Notice that it is not the case that what an agent believes will necessarily be true. But it is the nature of belief that the agent *takes* its beliefs to be true, and acts, under normal circumstances and assuming complete rationality of the agent, in a manner that would be to the agent's advantage, given its goals and desires, if the world were in accordance with its beliefs. Thus beliefs play a significant causal role in guiding the agent's behavior, which means that a given belief situation can provide information about the future behavior of that agent. If I believe it will rain, I will probably take my umbrella. If Bob believes that Alice has missed her train, he will delay cooking dinner. And so on. The *truth* of the belief is not a prerequisite for these causal relations.

Notice also that no mention was made above of the mental state being *grounded*, that is to say, linking in to actual entities in the world in the appropriate manner. Rather the various features listed are all structurally *internal* to the agent. This has the consequence that *ungrounded* mental states may also satisfy the various criteria, that is to say, may occupy the same kind of position in the agent's intentionality network, and play the same kind of role in guiding the agent's behavior, as do grounded beliefs. For example, my belief that it is grimbling will have a structure of the form

$$\langle Bel, -, grimbling^{\#}, now^{\#}, 1 \rangle$$

What prevents this particular (basic) belief from being grounded, and thereby having an external content, is the absence of any real world phenomenon *grimbling* corresponding to my notion grimbling$^{\#}$. This particular notion has presumably arisen either as a result of internal mental activity on my part, or by my having mistakenly acquired this notion from someone else. But this ungrounded mental state can still satisfy all the *internal* requirements for a belief that comprise the psychological mode. For instance, such a state can guide my actions: my belief that it is grimbling could lead to me taking my umbrella when I leave for work.

Likewise for my notion of the unicorn my neighbour claims to have seen in my garden, and my belief that this creature is white. The notion can occupy the same kind of position in my cognitive activity as does, say, my grounded notion of my neighbour's horse, and my belief that the unicorn is white can be cognitively indistinguishable from my true belief that this particular horse is brown.

The difference between grounded and ungrounded beliefs is one that is *external* to the agent. Since ungrounded beliefs are not properly linked to the world, they cannot have an external content. What they do have is what we propose to call an *internal content*. This is what the agent *takes* to be the content of the belief. For our purposes, the *internal content* of any mental state may be identified with what I have called the 'structure' of the belief.

Thus, the internal content of my belief that Mark is working in Tanner Library is

$$\langle Bel, e^{\#}, \text{working}^{\#}, \text{Mark}^{\#}, \text{now}^{\#}, 1 \rangle$$

where $e^{\#}$ is my notion of the Tanner Library situation, e. The internal content of my belief that Mark is eating grimbles in Tanner Library is

$$\langle Bel, e^{\#}, \text{eating}^{\#}, \text{Mark}^{\#}, \text{grimbles}^{\#}, \text{now}^{\#}, 1 \rangle$$

The first of these two beliefs is grounded, with external content

$$e \models \ll \text{working, Mark}, t_0, 1 \gg$$

where t_0 is the time the belief is held.

The second is ungrounded, since the notion grimbles$^{\#}$ does not correspond to anything in the world. Nevertheless, both beliefs, if held sincerely, could occupy similar positions in my intentionality network. For instance, if I needed to speak to Mark urgently, either belief could lead to my going over to Tanner. And likewise, both beliefs could be overturned by my observing Mark walk past my office at CSLI.

Similar considerations apply to desire. Thus, if I desire to ride a unicorn, the non-existence of unicorns prevents my desire being grounded, but given that I have a notion of a unicorn, my desire has an internal content, namely the desire structure

$$\langle Des, -, \text{ride}^{\#}, \text{Keith\_Devlin}^{\#}, \text{unicorn}^{\#}, 1 \rangle$$

where unicorn$^{\#}$ is an indefinite notion of a unicorn. This contrasts with my desire to ride a horse, which is a grounded desire with the structure

$$\langle Des, -, \text{ride}^{\#}, \text{Keith\_Devlin}^{\#}, \text{horse}^{\#}, 1 \rangle$$

where horse$^{\#}$ is an indefinite notion of a horse. This desire has the external content

$$w \models \exists \dot{h} \ll \text{ride}, \text{Keith\_Devlin}, \dot{h}, 1 \gg$$

These two mental states are both classified as *desires* by virtue of the role they play in my intentionality network. For instance, the following features are characteristic of desires:

(i)   a desire represents the way the agent would like the world to be;

(ii)   an agent acting rationally may form intentions to attempt to satisfy its desires (i.e. to make the world come to be the way its desires represent it);

(iii)   desires may conflict with beliefs;

(iv)   desires may be held unconsciously;

(v)   an agent may simultaneously have more than one desire;

(vi)   desires tend to persist, but they can be dropped without any external stimulus.

In fact, the above observations pertain to desires in general, not just the basic ones that have formed the main focus of the discussion in this section.

Notice that I have not enlarged the basic ontology to include such entities as notions, beliefs, desires, and so on. This is because each of these, being realized as a certain neural configuration, is in fact a *situation* — albeit one of considerable complexity. The situation that comprises a brain in a certain belief state B, together with the links connecting the notions involved in that belief to the objects in the world they are notions *of*, is what I have earlier called a *belief situation*. Analogously, there are *desire situations*, *doubt situations*, and so on, for each intentional mental state.

This observation highlights the fact that classifying intentional mental states by means of their external significance, or external content, makes use of certain constraints that allow one situation to provide information about another.

For instance, let B be a belief state with external content p, where p is the proposition

$$e : E$$

As a situation, what do we know about B? That it is of type *Mental_Situation*, certainly; indeed, that it is of the subtype *Bel*. And beyond that, we know that B is a *Bel*-situation of a type that is *about* a situation of type E. Making all of this precise within our formalism would clearly involve considerable effort, so I shall content myself with a simple example.

Let

$$E = [\dot{e} \mid \dot{e} \models \ll \text{raining}, t, 1 \gg \wedge \ll \text{present-in}, \dot{I}, \dot{e}, t, 1 \gg]$$

where t is tomorrow afternoon (as a time interval) and $\dot{I}$ is a parameter for 'self'.

Suppose I am told that Jon has a belief, B, whose content is that some situation is of type E, and that this is all we are told about B. Now, I have no knowledge of what constitutes a belief state (as a situation) in the case of my own mental activity, let alone that of Jon. In particular, I do not know how this belief is realized in Jon's brain, nor how that realization brings about various changes in the way Jon behaves. And yet I would still feel confident to make a number of fairly reliable predictions concerning his future activities: for instance, that he is unlikely to cancel tomorrow afternoon's seminar and go for a picnic.

The reason for this confidence is that, while largely ignorant of situations such as B, I am very familiar with situations of type E. I know what it means for a situation to be of type E, and what is more I know what effect it would have on my own behavior, if I had a belief whose content was that the situation the belief is about is of type E, in which case the indexical parameter $\dot{I}$ would anchor not to Jon but to me. Since Jon's belief, B, is thus of a type T (say) I am myself familiar with, I can make a reasonable prediction as to how B will influence Jon's future behavior. The type T does not classify B in terms of its structural realization as a brain state. Rather it is a uniformity that is individuated in terms of the external significance of certain intentional mental states, namely: T is the type of situation, s, such that:

(i) s is a mental state;
(ii) s is a belief;
(iii) s has as external content the proposition that the situation, e, which the belief is about, is of type E.

This type T is one that my own experience has equipped me to recognize, and I know what it means for an agent to have a mental state of this type. But of course, *my* only means (though presumably not *the* only means) of stipulating the type T is in terms of the type E. Thus a type of world situation is used to specify a type of mental situation.

This is what I mean by saying that we classify intentional mental states in terms of their external significance, and provides a vivid example of the way we can use one situation to provide information about another, utilizing the informational constraints that link the corresponding types.

Finally, notice that propositions have now gained an ontological status within our theory. Propositions, that is to say, entitites of the form

$$x : E$$

where x is an object and E is a type, are the *external contents* of intentional mental states. That is to say, they are the objects in the public domain that are created by the mental activity of cognitive agents, and which we commonly think of as 'claims made about the world or some part thereof'. Thus, propositions are uniformities across intentional mental states.

6.5 Knowledge

It is arguable that this topic should not figure in a chapter entitled 'Mental States'. For whatever knowledge is, and, as I shall indicate, it is a tricky concept to pin down, *knows that* is not simply a mental state in the way that *believes that* is, though it clearly involves a mental state. Whereas an agent can *believe* any proposition she cares to choose, and can *desire* any proposition she wishes, she can only *know* propositions that are true. Thus, *knowledge* involves the world, and in particular the concept of truth, in a fundamental way.

Still, in view of the obvious close connection between knowledge and belief, this seems to be as good a time as any to see what the concept involves.

As a first step, let us ask ourselves what exactly the connection is between knowledge and belief?

Certainly, if I *know* something, then I will *believe* it, though I might not be consciously aware that I believe it. But belief does not entail knowledge. Indeed, belief does not even entail truth. Nor is true belief sufficient to yield knowledge.

For example, suppose that, unbeknownst to me, my watch has stopped. I look at it and see that it says ten o'clock. Being unaware that my watch is not working, I thereby come to *believe* that it is ten o'clock. Clearly, given that this belief stems solely from the evidence supplied by my watch, I cannot be said to *know* that it is ten o'clock, even if, quite by chance, *it happens to be ten o'clock*, so that my belief is in fact true.

In the above case, the problem obviously concerns the manner in which the belief was acquired. Glancing at my watch did not supply me with the *information* that it was ten o'clock, because my watch, having ceased to function correctly, no longer encoded this information (via the usual constraints that govern timepieces and their use). Suppose then we require that, to constitute knowledge, a belief should be formed as a direct result of the acquisition of information.

Certainly, what we then get will be knowledge, but now the conditions are too stringent, since knowledge does not *of necessity* have to originate with information.

For example, suppose that, as a result of reading my horoscope in a cheap magazine, I come to believe that I will shortly be wealthy. Then, subsequently, my publisher calls me to inform me that *Logic and Information* has risen to the number 1 position on the *New York Times* Bestsellers List, with the result that I will shortly become a wealthy man. Clearly, as a result of this acquisition of information I now *know* that I will soon become wealthy. And yet my *belief* has not changed at all. I *believed* I was about to become wealthy *before* I received the call from my publisher. My belief did not *originate* with the acquisition of this particular piece of information. It originated with the magazine horoscope, which certainly did not provide me with *information* about my imminent wealth.

So what exactly *do* we require in order that a belief qualify as *knowledge*? An examination of the last example suggests the approach I shall adopt.

Knowledge of some proposition, *p*, consists of a belief that *p*, which is either *caused by*, or else *causally sustained by*, the acquisition of the information that *p*.

This surely comes close to what we want. It incorporates the fact that, in order to qualify as knowledge, belief must have a dependency on information, but does not insist that the belief be *caused by* information. So let us try to firm things up a little, and see what this definition entails.

First of all, I assume that knowledge is knowledge of some proposition. Thus, I consider a three-place relation

$$Knows\,(a, p, t)$$

between an agent, a, a proposition, p, and a time interval, t :

a knows that p at time t.

Our analysis of this is as follows. $Knows(a, p, t)$ holds if and only if, at time t, agent a has a belief, B, whose external content is p, and B was either caused by, or else causally sustained by, a acquiring the information that p at some time t' prior to t.

Thus, *knows* is not an intentional mental state in the sense of belief or desire. It is a relation. The mental state involved in *knows* is that of *belief*. What makes a belief state give rise to a *knowing*, is the way that state was either caused by, or else causally sustained by, information.

But what is meant by those requirements 'caused by' and 'causally sustained by'? I start by trying to reduce the latter to the former.

Intuitively, a mental state B is *causally sustained* by an event E if E is sufficent to cause B. That is to say, suppose that the state B were in fact caused by an event E_0, and then subsequently the event E occurs. Then E is said to *causally sustain* B if, had the event E_0 not occurred, the occurrence of E would have caused the state B.

The trouble with this 'definition' is the use of the counterfactual. What exactly do I mean by 'if the event E_0 had not occurred'? The event E_0 might have all kinds of effects on the agent, spreading throughout the agent's intentionality network. Do I neglect all of those when trying to decide counterfactually that E would have caused B? Very likely the effect of the event E_0 on many of the agent's other states was not great, but still not negligible. Surely I do not want to neglect all of these states in my counterfactual? What I want is a sort of 'minimal' counterfactual, where I remove the event E_0 in a 'minimal way'. Unfortunately, I don't at the moment see any way to make this at all precise, and thereby solve the problem.

One solution would be to take the concept of 'causally sustains' as a basic concept, a primitive property of the world. This is indeed the approach I shall adopt to causation itself in just a moment. But whereas there seem to be good reasons for regarding causation as primitive, the same does not appear to be true for 'causally sustains'. Indeed, the intuition suggests very strongly an approach along the counterfactual line just discussed. So, given that the overall aim of this enterprise is to flesh out a basis for a mathematical model (and therefore an idealization), it seems worthwhile setting to one side any disquiet we may have about the use of the counterfactual in the definition, and simply seeing how far we can get with it as it stands. This is what I propose to do.

But what of *causation* itself? Here, it seems to me, there is nothing for it but to take as fundamental the relation of one event causing another. Since this strategy may strike some as evading the real issue, let me give briefly my reasons for this choice.

The classic example of one event *causing* another is the one involving two billiard balls on the table. Billiard ball A is set in motion towards the stationary ball, B. When A strikes B, B starts to move. The impact of A onto B *causes* the subsequent motion of B. But where exactly does the *causality* come in?

It cannot, surely, be extensional. Performing the same experiment with the two balls many times will always produce the same outcome: the event of B starting to move following directly on from the event of A impacting on B. But this regularity does not constitute the causality any more than the fact that nights are invariably followed by days means that night causes day. And yet if causality is intensional (i.e. not extensional), then there are surely only two possibilities. Either causality is something that is imposed upon the world by our intentionality as cognitive beings, a property that would not exist if we were not there to 'recognize' it; or else causality is simply there as a feature of the world, quite independent of whether or not there are any cognitive agents to observe causal chains. Of these two possibilities, the second seems to me by far the most acceptable. Billiard ball A (or asteroid A) would *cause* billiard ball B (or asteroid B) to move (or undergo an acceleration) whether or not there was anyone there to see this event or not.

Consequently, I shall assume that there is a basic relation, *causes*, in the world that links certain pairs of situations, and I shall write

$$s_1 \ \triangleright \ s_2$$

to indicate that situation s_1 *causes* situation s_2. This assumption is a simplistic one, in so far as I take *causes* to link situations. Arguably it is one situation *being a certain way* that causes another situation *to be a certain way*. But within our present framework, the choice made seems the most convenient.

As with the other basic relations of *equality* and *supports*, the *causes* relation is not extensionally determined. The situations it links will only constitute 'situations' when they are so individuated by the individuation scheme corresponding to some agent. So the agent, or, more commonly, the species of agent, determines what does and what does not constitute a situation, but the world then determines whether or not one of those situations *causes* another.

Notice that on my account of knowledge, in order for an agent, $\mathcal{A}$, to know that p, it is neither necessary nor sufficient that $\mathcal{A}$ be consciously aware of her belief that p, nor indeed have any conscious awareness of p at all.

Also, there is nothing in my account that suggests or requires that $\mathcal{A}$ *knows* that she knows p. Given the notion of causation, whether or not a belief constitutes knowledge is simply a matter of fact concerning the origin or causal support for $\mathcal{A}$'s belief that p. There is no demand that $\mathcal{A}$ have evidence for, or be aware of, that origin or support. Indeed, from her point of view, she simply *believes* that p. She may, of course, express this by declaring "I know that p," just as I, having looked at my watch, and being unaware that it has broken, might claim to 'know' that it is ten o'clock. From the agent's point of view there is nothing to distinguish a belief from knowledge, at least in the case of a belief acquired from a source taken to be reliable.

Things are, however, different when it comes to *knowing* that you know — or even just *believing* that you know. This involves the agent acquiring information *about* (the reliability of) *the evidence* upon which the belief was formed. Many common references to 'knowledge' are really to 'believing and believing-that-you-know'. A highly cautious agent, such as a scientist, might be prepared to say "I believe that p," but be reluctant to claim "I know that p" without having some additional evidence concerning the origin of that belief that p. But this issue has nothing to do with whether or not the agent actually *knows* p. Rather it concerns the agent's state of belief about her particular belief that p.

Notice that, strictly speaking, knowledge is a theorist's concept. To say an agent, $\mathcal{A}$, *knows* p is to say something *external* about $\mathcal{A}$'s belief that p, since it concerns the way that particular belief relates to the world. In this sense, there are very few propositions, p, for which an agent can accurately claim "I know p." (The most obvious such p is "I exist.")

Finally, what can be said about the relationship between knowledge and having information? This issue has already arisen in the discussion of *SID* in Section 4.5. I observed there that the possession of information that p, did not in itself qualify as knowledge that p. In particular, I suggested that one thing that was required in order for information possessed by an agent to qualify as knowledge, was that the agent should possess that information in a form capable of utilization. The treatment of knowledge given above clearly satisfies this requirement, since an agent only has *knowledge* of p if it has a belief that p, and that belief state will figure in the agent's intentionality network.

Notice that as a belief is a cognitive structure realized in the finite mental apparatus of an agent, there is a finite bound on the amount of information an agent can believe or know. In particular, there is no implication that belief or knowledge is closed under logical deduction. Knowing p and knowing q does not necessarily entail knowing $p \wedge q$. This is quite different from the situation concerning the possession (or encoding) of information. The relative nature of information, together with deductive closure, means that any cognitive agent will encode an infinite amount of information. As Abraham Lincoln might have commented had he read this book, a person might *have* all the information some of the time, but no one can *know* all the information at any time.

7

Perception and Action

7.1 Visual perception

This chapter is almost exclusively concerned with perception and action in the case of the agent Man, though one would hope that some of what we say has relevance to the study of other organisms and the design of artificial agents.

In the brief discussion of the issue in Section 2.2, I regarded 'perception', in the sense of the perceptual acquisition of information, as consisting of two stages. The first stage is the actual act of perceiving, and it was this part for which I used the term *perception*; I characterized it in terms of the analog nature of the information thus acquired. Perception is followed by what I called *cognition*, the extraction of information in digital form.

Though arguably adequate for the purpose of developing a mathematical model, this picture of events is a very simplistic one, and before proceeding any further towards a mathematical theory it might be worthwhile seeing if we cannot say just a little more.

For definiteness, my account of perception will concentrate almost exclusively on visual perception.

First of all, just what is the evidence in favor of the two-stage process of 'perception' followed by 'cognition'? Suppose I go in to give a lecture — a large one, say freshman calculus. Looking out at the class, I see a whole range of faces. Not just one face. Not just some of the faces. All of them. What I see, what I *perceive*, is a roomfull of faces. In particular, there is some number, N, such that I see exactly N faces. But I have no idea what number N is, nor even a rough idea within, say, an error of five. Though this information is clearly coded in my perceptual apparatus as it registers the scene before me, it does not make it through to the higher levels of my cognitive structure — in Dretske's terminology, it is not *digitalized*. In fact there is a rough 'Rule of Seven', that says that the largest number of individual items that can be directly recognized without counting is seven (unless the items are arranged in some special way). If I am lecturing to, say, five students, I will know at once how many are in the class; with eight or more, I will not know with any certainty unless I count them. (For a full discussion of the 'Rule of Seven', see Miller's article [17].)

This is not to say that I am not encoding the entire scene. Indeed, as research carried out in the 1960s shows, human subjects do indeed perceptively code more information than they can digitalize. As described in [30], when subjects were shown an array of nine or more letters for a period of 50 milliseconds, their resulting visual image remained for up to 150 milliseconds after the array had been removed. By prompting the subjects with randomly placed markers, it was demonstrated that this lingering image was sufficient for them to pick out accurately up to three or four of the letters they had seen, though never any more than that. The entire array was not only perceived in the sense of some form of encoding, it was retained for a discrete length of time. (This retention of a visual image is sometimes referred to as *iconic memory*.)

There is, therefore, a sense in which an agent acquires the conceptualized information involved in higher-level cognitive activity by way of a two-stage process of perceptual acquisition followed by digitalization of particular items of information from that sensory input.

Now, as is shown by the example of the frog vision mentioned in Section 6.1, this is by no means the only mechanism whereby digitalized (infon) information reaches the cognitive centers. On some occasions, the sensory apparatus itself provides the requisite 'filtering'. In addition to frogs in search of flies, today's desktop computers all acquire their information in this manner. Nevertheless, given that most of the discussion in this chapter concentrates on the agent Man, there seems to be little harm in *adopting* this two-stage process as our paradigm. After all, our ultimate goal is not to explain the actual mechanisms whereby cognitive agents acquire the information they need to function, but rather to develop a mathematical framework that can be used to study the flow and utilization of that information. And, as far as this is concerned, the crucial feature is, as Dretske pointed out, the passage from perceived, analog information to digital information.

In terms of the perception–cognition paradigm, the first stage, the perceptual acquisition of (analog) information, is cognitively *neutral*. The information simply becomes accessible to the agent. What then determines what it is the agent *sees*? (Remember that I have decided to concentrate on visual perception in this section.) Well, what we *see* are situations and individuals in those situations. And we are able to see these first and foremost because our individuation capacities equip us to see these uniformities. Indeed, so fundamental to our existence are these individuation capacities , that we *see* the world as a collection of real, honest-to-goodness 'objects'. We do not, at least not under normal circumstances, see some kind of amorphous 'soup' or else collections of molecules or large numbers of elementary particles whizzing about.

Whether or not this view of the world as a collection of 'objects' is something we are born with or else acquire at an early age, I do not know. There seems to be no *a priori* reason why such an individuation of the world should not be acquired through experience.

For instance, take the case of hearing a foreign language for the first time. At first, all you hear is a stream of practically uninterrupted sound. Only subsequently, after you have listened to it for some time, can you begin to discern the way it splits up into discrete words — though the discrete nature might not depend upon complete breaks in the sound. In engineer's terminology, what you do is, through experience, acquire the ability to *demodulate* a signal that at first sounds to be pure *noise*. Presumably the same is the case for a small child as it acquires the use of its native language. Why not a similar process, at an earlier age, for the child's visual access to the world?

In any event, what we *see* comprises situations and individuals in situations, as determined by our scheme of individuation. But that is not all the story. For one thing, just where is this italicized, post-perception *seeing* going on?

In view of the discussions of mental states developed in the previous chapter, my proposed answer to the above question should be fairly obvious. Cognitive *seeing* is a higher-order, intentional activity of the brain. The effect of a visual signal from the eyes (more realistically, the combined affect of a number of different signals from various sensing mechanisms in the organism)[1] is to produce a change in the brain state, that is to say, a concrete, structural change, an intentional mental *event*, and it is this change in mental state that constitutes an act of 'seeing'.[2]

---

[1] What we generally refer to as 'visual input' is really a product of several factors in addition to the light striking the retina — for instance, bodily motion, tilt of the head, orientation to gravity all play a role. And, once the visual signal gets in, what is *seen* is invariably dependent on a whole host of other features of the intentionality network.

[2] This way of looking at things is somewhat artificial, since it regards the brain as a passive recipient of incoming signals, but this is precisely the kind of artificiality that is involved in handling complex, biological processess within a rationalist framework.

Similarly for aural and other forms of perception. I shall refer to a visually produced change of mental state as a *visual experience*.

Our aim is to classify visual experiences in terms of their external significance, measured along the yardstick of digitalized information, in much the same way that we classified belief and other intentional mental states.

Suppose v is a visual experience. That is to say, v is an intentional mental event caused primarily by a visual input. This visual input stems from a particular situation, s_{vis}, that I shall refer to as the *visual scene*. (Clearly, there is a two-way functional dependency between the visual experience, v, and the visual scence, s_{vis}, but because this dependency *is* two-way, I choose not to make use of functional notation in either direction.)

Now it is the nature of vision that, in general, when an agent sees a *visual scene*, there are a great many things in, and going on in, that situation that the agent *sees*, or at least *perceives*. I shall remain within the framework established by the notion of *digitalized* or *itemized* information, by concentrating on particular, itemized instances of cognitive seeing as are typically described by a *perceptual report*, such as an utterance of

Jon saw Mary

or

Jon saw Mary run.

The (intentional, cognitive) *visual content* of a visual experience, v, will be an infonic proposition

$$s_{vis} \models \sigma$$

where σ is a parameter-free, compound infon.

In the case where σ is a basic infon, I shall say v is a *basic* visual experience. (*cf. basic* belief and *basic* desire.)

For example, to say that Jon sees Mary run (directly, not on film, etc.), is to say that Jon has a visual experience, v, with visual scene s_{vis}, such that (part of) the visual content of v is the proposition

$$s_{vis} \models \ll \text{runs, Mary}, t_{seeing}, 1 \gg$$

In words, (part of) the *visual content* of Jon's visual experience is that in the scene before him, the one that he sees, Mary is running. The reason for the parenthetic 'part of' here, is that, as indicated just a moment ago, the nature of visual experiences, at least in the human case, is such that rarely is just one thing seen.

Notice that we do would not normally say that Jon sees the *scene* (or situation) in which Mary is running, though we could do. We simply say "John sees Mary run(ning)." In other words, the most natural way of describing what it is that Jon sees, is to describe (the relevant part of) the *visual content* of the visual scene associated with his visual experience.

Of course, very often it is not some situation that is 'seen' but an object, as in the case described by saying simply: "Jon sees Mary." In the present framework, to say that Jon sees Mary is to say that Jon has a visual experience, v, with visual scene s_{vis}, whose visual content contains the proposition

$$s_{vis} \models \ll \text{present, Mary}, l_{vis}, t_{seeing}, 1 \gg$$

where l_{vis} is the spatial extent of s_{vis}. In words, Jon sees Mary if and only if Jon has a visual experience (part of) whose visual content is that Mary is present in the visual scene.

This example highlights the fact that I am taking the visual content of any visual experience to be a *proposition*, and not a situation or an object. This is not to say that what is *seen* is a proposition. If Jon sees Mary, then the *individual* Mary is what Jon sees, and if Jon sees Mary run then what Jon sees is the *event* of Mary running. What *is* propositional, is the visual *content* of a visual experience, and this is (part of) the external content of an intentional mental event, comparable to the external content of an intentional belief or desire. Visual contents are not the objects that are seen as part of a visual experience.

Notice that in order for Jon's visual experience to be a seeing of Mary, it is not enough that

$$s_{vis} \models \ll \text{present, Mary}, l_{vis}, t_{seeing}, 1 \gg$$

Rather, what is required is that this proposition *be part of the visual content* of Jon's visual experience. There may be a great many things present, and activities going on, in s_{vis} that Jon does not cognitively *see* (though he will, by definition of s_{vis}, *perceive* a great many of them). The visual content picks out what it is in s_{vis} that is actually *seen* by Jon in this particular visual experience.

Of course, one of the constraints respected by visual experiences is that any individual in the visual scene that figures in the visual content in any way, is itself *seen*. For instance, if Jon sees Mary run, then it must be the case that Jon sees Mary: that is, if Jon has a visual experience whose visual content contains the proposition

$$s_{vis} \models \ll \text{runs, Mary}, l_{vis}, t_{seeing}, 1 \gg$$

then of necessity his visual experience will also contain the proposition

$$s_{vis} \models \ll present, Mary, l_{vis}, t_{seeing}, 1 \gg$$

Notice that the above 'closure' property for visual experiences does not have a counterpart for beliefs. Just because I believe one thing does not imply that I believe all 'closely related' consequences thereof.

At this stage it is perhaps worthwhile making a brief comparison between visual experiences and (grounded) beliefs:

(i)   Both are intentional mental situations : a belief is a belief *about* something in the world (possibly another mental situation, i.e. a higher-order structural property of a brain), and a visual experience is a visual experience *of* something in the world (necessarily something 'concrete').

(ii)   Whereas intentional beliefs are mental *states*, i.e. essentially static situations, visual experiences are intentional mental *events*, i.e. changes in state.

(iii) Visual experiences are of necessity conscious events; a belief may or may not be conscious. I cannot have a visual experience without being *aware* of that experience,[3] but I can, and do, have many beliefs of which I am not consciously aware. (Of course, as soon as I dredge one up as an example, I immediately become aware of it, though I may soon forget it again. But the nature of beliefs is that, conscious or unconscious, they remain beliefs until overthrown for some reason.)

(iv)   A belief may be classified by its external content; the external content of a belief is a proposition. The belief will be satisfied if and only if that external content is true in the world. In Searle's terminology, the 'direction of fit' of a belief is mind-to-world. Beliefs guide future activity of the agent. A visual experience may be classified by its visual content; if v is a visual experience, there is associated with v a *visual scene*, s_{vis}, and the external content of v is a proposition of the form

$$s_{vis} \models \sigma$$

Clearly, the last, somewhat incomplete, comparison in the above list raises a number of questions about visual experiences. For instance, can we speak of a visual experience being 'satisfied', and does the notion

---

[3] Of course, it is possible to have 'visual experiences' that involve very little conscious attention, such as one's visual monitoring of the road ahead while driving to work by a familiar route. But, as should be clear by now, this form of 'passive' seeing is not the same as the *visual experiences* that forms my primary interest here.

of 'direction of fit' have any meaning in this context? Also, what effect does a visual experience have upon the rest of the agent's intentionality network? These questions form the main focus of the remainder of this section.

Though an agent can simultaneously hold a wide variety of beliefs, in the ordinary way of things, each belief will be a belief about one single thing. That is to say, one normally regards beliefs as somehow 'atomic'. Thus, we would speak of a belief that it will rain or a belief that the flowers will grow, but we would not normally regard as a single belief that 'it will rain and the flowers will grow'. Rather this latter would be classified as a conjunction of two beliefs.

But with visual experiences, things are different. Most visual experiences, at least in the human case, involve the seeing of a wide variety of things. For example, if I see David eat a pickle, then I see David, I see the pickle, I see David's face, I see his hand, I see his fingers, and so on. Consequently, the visual content of a visual experience is in general a proposition of considerable complexity. More precisely, if

$$s_{vis} \models \sigma$$

is the visual content, then the compound infon σ will be a conjunction of a great many basic infons.

And yet this very example indicates that there is nevertheless a similarity with beliefs. For though it is not possible for me to see David eat a pickle without seeing all these other things, the conscious visual experience that I have as I sit there watching David eat his pickle is of *David eating a pickle*. The other things are seen incidentally. Likewise with any other *active* visual experience where the observer consciously *looks at* something. But it is precisely the conscious, information-gathering form of active seeing that is relevant to our study.

Consequently, as far as the present enterprise is concerned, we lose little by restricting our attention to *basic* visual experiences, that is to say visual experiences whose visual content is a *basic* infonic proposition of the form

$$s_{vis} \models \sigma$$

where σ is a basic infon.

A belief does not have to be true; the content of a belief stipulates how the world *would have* to be in order for that belief to be satisfied. Likewise, the visual content of a visual experience does not have to be a true proposition; the visual experience could be a hallucination. But notice now that I have used a different word here: 'hallucination'.

For whereas we are generally happy to speak of false or ungrounded beliefs, and indeed are often quite uncertain about the status of our beliefs when challenged, we are extremely reluctant to contemplate false or 'ungrounded' visual experiences, but rather classify them as something quite apart. Visual experiences are regarded as *veridical*; that is to say, in the normal course of events, the visual content of a visual experience is expected to be a *true* proposition. And if it is not, we would say that there is not a genuine visual experience, but a hallucination. This is why I compared visual experiences with *grounded* beliefs, and not beliefs in general. A hallucination is in some ways analogous to an ungrounded belief.

Just why we place such great reliance on our visual experiences is an issue we shall investigate presently. But for the moment, let us note that from the point of view of the observer, there really is no way to distinguish between a genuine visual experience and a hallucination — that is what makes unpleasant hallucinations so scary. Now the similarity between the satisfaction of beliefs and the veridicality of visual experiences becomes a clear one. Though a believer might acknowledge the possibility that a particular belief is false, she knows what is required in order for that belief to be true; namely that the world should be the way the content of the belief stipulates. Likewise with a visual experience. Even if an observer acknowledges that a particular visual experience could be a hallucination, she knows what is required in order that the visual experience be veridical; namely that the world should be as represented by the visual content of her experience.

In both cases here, the belief and the visual experience, the 'direction of fit' is mind-to-world. If a belief is false, it is not the world that is at fault; rather the believer has simply made a mistake in forming that particular belief. If a particular visual experience is not veridical, it is not the world that is at fault, but rather the observer, whose visual experience is in fact a hallucination.

Picking up now that point about our overwhelming tendency to rely upon evidence of the world acquired via visual (and other directly perceptual) experiences, this highlights what is a considerable difference between visual (and other directly perceptual) experiences and beliefs (other than beliefs that are acquired as a direct consequence of a visual experience).

If you have a visual experience of something, if you *see* something, then that experience gives you a form of 'direct access' to what it is you are seeing. Indeed, this is reflected in the language we use to describe the acquisition of information. If you were simply informed about some situation or event, without having *seen* (or otherwise directly perceived) it for yourself, you would classify your acquisition of this particular information as *indirect*, to distinguish it from information acquired *first hand* by perceptual means. The perceptual senses are what *ties us in* to the world in an intimate fashion — indeed in a fashion so tight that, according to the phenomenologists, any attempt to regard the two as separate, the agent and the environment, cannot hope to present a true picture of cognitive activity.

But what does this 'direct access' amount to in terms of our theory? Let me make a suggestion. Suppose I have a (basic) visual experience, v, with visual scene s_{vis} and visual content

$$s_{vis} \models \ll R, a_1, \ldots, a_n, i \gg$$

Then the *structure*, or *internal content*, of this visual experience will, I claim, be of the form

$$\mathscr{S}(v) = \langle Sees, -, R^\sharp, a_1^\sharp, \ldots, a_n^\sharp, i, v \rangle$$

The dash indicates that v is a *situated* experience. Unlike the cases of situated belief and desire discussed in the previous chapter, however, there is only one situation that can occupy the corresponding role in the *external content* of v: the *visual scene*, s_{vis}.

But far more significant is the appearence of the visual experience, v, itself as a component of its own internal content. This reflects what I think is a highly characteristic feature of vision, one that accounts for the great reliance we place upon information acquired directly through vision: namely, that it is part of the visual experience of some situation *that it is in fact a visual experience* of that situation. In other words, seeing involves an experience of that seeing. (Clearly, believing does not necessarily involve an experience of belief; one simply believes. But one cannot see without experiencing that seeing.) Thus seeing is inherently circular — this circularity being reflected in the appearance of the visual experience, v, as a component of its own internal content.

What then of the visual content of v? How does this reflect the *immediacy* of seeing that manifested itself in the circularity of the internal content of v? What is it about the visual content of a *seeing* that makes us so willing to accept the information we directly perceive? The answer I suggest is the same as the one advocated by Searle in [26, Chapter 2]. Namely, what makes us so confident in the veridicality of our visual experiences is that a visual experience is directly *caused by* (what is going on in) the visual scene.

For example, suppose I see Mary run. Then what must occur in order for this to be a genuine seeing of Mary running is the following:

(i)   I have a basic visual experience, v, with visual scene s_{vis}

(ii)   the visual content of v is the proposition:

$$s_{vis} \models \ll \text{runs, Mary, } t_{seeing}, 1 \gg$$

and moreover

(iii) v is caused by s_{vis}. (I shall have more to say on this particular clause after I have completed the discussion of action later in this chapter.)

Thus the *external content* of the mental event that we call a visual experience comprises both the visual content and the fact of the relevant causality. If I have a visual experience, v, with visual scene s_{vis}, and if the visual content of v is the proposition

$$s_{vis} \models \sigma$$

(where σ is a parameter-free infon), then the *external content* of v is the proposition

$$w \models [(s_{vis} \models \sigma) \wedge (s_{vis} \rhd v)]$$

Clearly, this requires some 'translation' into the standard infon form of propositions, but the significant feature of the definition is that it is self-referential. The visual experience, v, figures in its own external content: it is part of the external content of a visual experience, *that* it is caused by what is seen. It is this self-referentiality that comprises the *immediacy* of seeing.

Of course, it is not so much the entire visual scene that causes the visual experience, but that part of the observed situation that supports the visual content of the seeing. If I see Mary run, it is the event of Mary running that gives rise to my visual experience thereof; other things that are present in, or going on in, the visual scene are not directly relevant. But in view of my previous decision to restrict attention to the primary object of a visual experience, ignoring those things that are unavoidably, but incidentally, 'seen' as part of a visual experience, it seems reasonable to think of the situation s_{vis} as constituting just that part of the perceived situation that is cognitively *seen* (and informationally classified) by the agent.

Notice that, having relativized the causality involved in seeing, in making the causality part of the content of the visual experience, I have concentrated on fleshing out just what it is that gives rise to the agent's subjective reliance on vision, what it is that makes us regard our visual senses as a reliable means of acquiring information. From a theorist's, third party point of view, there is another aspect to the matter. *Does* the agent in fact *see* what it is he thinks he sees? Is his particular visual experience veridical? Here the issue is one of straight causality in the world, not in a relativized form as part of an external content. Agent $\mathscr{A}$ really does *see* x if $\mathscr{A}$'s visual experience of x actually is caused by x. Thus, seeing in this sense is analogous to knowing. In particular, both are facts of the world, not solely part of the agent's cognitive experiences. This issue will be considered further in the next section.

7.2 Seeing and seeing that

Seeing — that is, having a visual experience — is, like all other intentional mental states and events, intensely subjective. A theory dealing with these subjective issues, such as the one I am trying to develop here, clearly has to rely on third party, external *reports of*, or *statements about*, what is subjectively *seen, believed, doubted*, and so on. In the case of seeing, this externalist viewpoint leads to an additional difficulty not encountered when dealing with non-perceptual mental states and events. Namely, the visual scene is a concrete situation that can be seen by all, and yet what the agent cognitively *sees*, may not be quite the same as reported by a third party who is witness to the agent's seeing. The possibility of confusion raised by this duality of viewpoint means that we have to exercise some care in interpreting reports of seeing events. The following example indicates the general issue.

Emma is watching the television coverage of the the 1984 Olympic 1500 meters final in Los Angeles. After the race, I say

Emma saw Sebastian Coe win the Olympic 1500 meters final.

In order to make this claim justifiably, I need to have the following information: that Emma was looking at the television screen at the appropriate time, that she saw the events being broadcast (and was not just staring blankly at the screen), that it was indeed the Olympic 1500 meters final that was being shown, and that it was Sebastian Coe that won it. The only claim my utterance entails concerning Emma's mental states at that time, is that she was having a visual experience caused by the picture on the television screen, and having as its visual content the proposition

$$s_{vis} \models \ll \text{wins}, SC, OF, l_{OF}, t_{OF}, 1 \gg$$

where SC is the individual Sebastian Coe, OF is the Olympic 1500 meters final, and l_{OF}, t_{OF} are the location and time of the race. My statement makes no claim about Emma's knowledge and beliefs concerning the events being broadcast, other than what is directly involved in her having a visual experience that has the visual content it does. (See later for further elaboration on this point.) What Emma saw, that is what it was that caused Emma's visual experience, is simply described as a fact of the world.

In contrast, consider the following statement by me:

Emma saw that *Sebastian Coe won the Olympic 1500 meters final.*

What is required in order to justify this claim? Considerably more than in the previous case. In addition to the above, I have to know that Emma *knew* that she was watching the Olympic Games and not some other athletic event, that she *knew* that the race being run was the 1500 meters final and not some other race, and that she *recognized* the winner of the race as Sebastian Coe.

Whereas my first statement is *epistemically neutral* as far as Emma's state of mind is concerned, and simply requires as justification that Emma saw the events shown on the television screen, the second statement is *epistemically positive*: it makes a claim about Emma's knowledge of the events she sees.

In the latter, epistemically positive, case, my statement makes it pretty clear just *what* objects and events Emma *cognitively saw*. That is, we know what information Emma acquired as a direct consequence of her visual experience, and can draw conclusions as to how this particular visual experience affected her behavior. For instance, since Emma is British, we can be fairly sure that she was pleased by what she saw, that she experienced some measure of pride in an accomplishment of her fellow countryman, and so on.

We can also draw certain conclusions as to Emma's state of knowledge prior to this visual experience, and how this knowledge affected the visual experience. She *knew* the event she was watching was the Olympic 1500 meters final, she *knew* what was involved in winning such an event, and she was able to *recognize* the individual named Sebastian Coe. Given that framework of prior knowledge, what she *cognitively saw* by way of her visual experience, was precisely *that* the individual she knew to be Sebastian Coe won the race she knew to be the Olympic 1500 meters final.

But what about the epistemically neutral, former case? What exactly did Emma *cognitively see* in this situation? Of course, we have no way of knowing. She *may* have cognitively seen everything as just described in the case above. The report we have, namely the first of my two statements, being epistemically neutral, supplies no information on this particular point. But that does not mean, at least it should not be taken to mean, that nothing can be said in this case. Saying that Emma *saw* such and such an event is stronger than saying she *perceived*, or *looked at*, that event. At least, the usage of the word 'sees' is intended to entail such a distinction. Provided Emma's eyes are open, functioning normally, and focused on the television screen during the broadcast, she will, we say, *perceive* the event of Sebastian Coe winning the race. That is, she will have a visual experience whose visual scene, s_{vis}, is what appears on the screen, and that visual scene will cause that visual experience. To say she *sees* this event, is, according to our framework, to say she has a visual experience that is not only caused by its visual scene, s_{vis}, but that this experience has as its visual content, the proposition[4]

$$s_{vis} \models \ll \text{wins}, SC, OF, l_{OF}, t_{OF}, 1 \gg$$

It is not part of this content that the individual SC *is* the British athlete named Sebastian Coe, nor that the race situation OF *is* the Olympic 1500 meters final, as would be entailed by the *sees that* report, which addresses the issue of Emma's epistemic state concerning the event she witnesses. But it is a prerequisite for a visual experience with this visual content, that Emma individuates SC as an individual, OF as a race situation, and 'winning' as a relation between individuals and races. In other words, Emma's *seeing* a certain event, while not dependent upon her identification of each of the individuals involved, *is* relative to her individuation scheme. What constitutes *seeing*, as opposed to mere *perceiving*, is the individuation and conceptualization of (aspects of) the perceived scene — that is to say, making the appropriate analog to digital conversion. To describe the seeing as "... *sees Sebastian Coe win the Olympic 1500 meters final,*" as I did above, is, I claim, to stipulate that this digitalization is of the form

$$\ll \text{race}, OF, 1 \gg \land \ll \text{wins}, SC, OF, l_{OF}, t_{OF}, 1 \gg$$

---

[4] Notice that we are taking s_{vis} here to be the actual race situation, not the 'television screen situation'. Thus we are regarding the television as simply a *medium* that provides Emma's visual system with a longer reach than normal. This, I think, accords with the way we actually view live broadcast television: what we 'see' is the actual event, not a picture of that event. If you disagree with this, then simply imagine our scenario changed to have Emma transported from her living room to the Los Angeles Coliseum where the event took place.

As far as Emma is concerned, what this amounts to is that she *saw that* some individual won some race. That is to say, on the basis of an epistemically neutral report that Emma

saw Sebastian Coe win the Olympic 1500 meters final,

we can make the epistemically positive report that Emma

saw that some individual won some race.

And in general, whenever we have a report that an agent *sees* Φ, we can infer that the agent *sees that* Ψ, for some Ψ, suitably related to Φ. What determines Ψ is a combination of the agent's intentionality network and the expectations the agent brings to the visual experience. This is the issue taken up in the following section.

It should be noted that throughout our discussion I have been using the phrase 'see that' in the case of direct perception only. An alternative, common usage is to mean something like 'conclude that', as in the case where you and I have an argument about some proposition Φ, and finally you convince me and I say "Ah, now I see that Φ." This kind of example clearly has nothing whatsoever to do with a visual experience, and such usage of 'see that' is not what is under discussion in this chapter.

But what about cases where a proposition Φ, while not part of a visual experience, is nevertheless a direct consequence of one? For example, I look into Jon's office and it is empty. Ordinary English usage allows me to say "I see that Jon is not in his office." Does this usage fall under the discussions in this chapter? I do not think it does. What our discussion is concerned with are visual experiences. A *sees* report describes the visual content of an agent's visual experience in an epistemically neutral way; a *sees that* report describes (or attempts to describe, perhaps only partially) the visual content in an epistemically positive way, taking account of the knowledge and beliefs about the visual scene that the agent brings to the visual experience. But in both cases what is being described is the visual content of the agent's visual experience. When I look into Jon's office and see it is empty, what I see *that*, what is the visual content of my visual experience, is that it is empty. Jon has nothing to do with this particular visual experience. So in terms of the usage of the phrase 'see that' of concern in this chapter, I do not *see that* Jon is not there. Rather I *conclude*, on the basis of my visual experience, that he is not there.

This issue should become clearer after the discussion in the following section.

7.3 Seeing and the network

Seeing is believing, they say. And so indeed it is. There is a constraint linking the visual contents of visual experiences to belief states. When you see something, you generally believe what you see (in the sense of see *that*): what you see (*that*) is added to your belief corpus.[5] But there is also a relationship going the other way. What you see *that* depends upon what you believe and what you know, and at a more fundamental level upon your scheme of individuation.

The role played by the agent's scheme of individuation in a seeing event has already been touched upon in the previous section. Because Emma individuates people, races, and winning races, when she sees the event of Sebastian Coe winning the Olympic 1500 meters final, she can see *that* some person wins some race. The basic scheme of individuation by which she sees and negotiates the world guarantees this. (Indeed, this last assertion is virtually tautological, since the very essence of a scheme of individuation is that *that* is how the world is cognitively encountered.) Of course, as mentioned earlier, she may or may not know who the individual is that wins this race, or indeed what particular race it is — that requires additional knowledge of the event she sees, above and beyond her individuation scheme. So if on the basis of a report that

Emma sees Sebastian Coe win the Olympic 1500 meters final,

we conclude that

Emma sees that some person won some race,

we are simply asserting that *at the very least* this is what Emma cognitively sees, i.e. forms a digital representation of. It may well be that she sees (that) far more than is stated in the *sees that* report, but this would require her use of knowledge above and beyond her scheme of individuation.

Now, as I indicated in Section 6.3 in connection with the house/façade in Hollywood, the individuation scheme alone does not determine what it is that an agent cognitively *sees* by way of a particular visual experience. Since anything seen is of necessity seen purely as an *aspect*, the agent's beliefs about what is seen also play a role. A simple example, taken from Searle [26, p.54], is the figure

---

[5] Though in general true, this is not always the case. For instance, when you see what you know to be a white surface, illuminated by what you know to be red light, what you *see* is a red surface, but you do not form the belief that the surface is red.

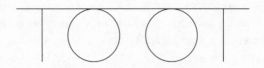

An adult human will probably see this as the word 'TOOT', thereby using linguistic information to supply the visual content. A small child, unable to read, might possibly see the figure as a man wearing a hat with a string hanging down each side, or maybe a bridge with two pipelines underneath, or then again maybe as nothing more than an assemblage of circles and lines. In the context of a computer science class dealing with the storage of numbers in computers, it could easily be the binary numeral 1001 with a bar across the top to indicate complementation. In any event, what is cognitively *seen* here, depends very much upon the prior knowledge and expectation the agent brings to the visual experience.

Again the many familiar examples of visually ambiguous pictures, such as the candlestick/talking heads, the ascending/descending staircase, or several of Eschers's 'impossible figures', all create confusion in the mind of the beholder by capitalizing on the active nature of vision. In each case, *what* is cognitively seen depends not only upon the agent's individuation scheme, but also upon the beliefs and expectations the agent brings to the visual experience. Seeing (i.e. cognitive seeing, seeing *that*) is not a straightforward, almost passive act of receiving an incoming visual signal, but rather is an active interplay of the agent's intentionality network with incoming information.

Now, according to my definitions, what the agent cognitively sees constitutes the visual content of the visual experience, namely the proposition

$$s_{vis} \models \sigma$$

for some infon σ. An immediate consequence of the above discussion is that this proposition is not necessarily true. But cognitive agents such as ourselves have an overwhelming tendency to take such propositions as true, by virtue of the immediacy of our sensory apparatus — an immediacy reflected in my taking the *external* content of a visual experience, v, to be the proposition

$$w \models [(s_{vis} \models \sigma) \wedge (s_{vis} \vartriangleright v)]$$

Only if there is strong evidence to the contrary are we likely to discount the assumed truth of the visual content.

7.4 Logic of belief, desire, and perception

In the discussion of the mental states of belief and desire (Sections 6.3 and 6.4) and of the mental event of visual perception, I restricted my attention for the most part to *basic* instances where the external significance was captured by means of *basic infonic* propositions. In this section I consider, briefly, how these basic instances build up to produce more complex forms of belief, desire, and perception. I shall not say anything about the internal structure of such complex states/events, but concentrate instead on the external significance. As will become clear, different kinds of mental state/event exhibit different forms of logical behavior.

It should be noted that while believing and seeing provide excellent illustrations of the kinds of logical behavior that can arise, they are by no means typical. Indeed, the nature of intentional states is such that each one tends to exhibit its own peculiarities. (An instructive exercise is to duplicate the analysis given here for other mental states, such as hoping or doubting.)

The first issue I consider is not one of logical behavior *per se*, but rather of truth.

Veridicality. That Naomi believes Melissa ate the cookie does not entail that Melissa actually did eat the cookie. Believing something does not mean that it is true. On the other hand, if Naomi sees Melissa eat the cookie, then Melissa certainly does eat the cookie, and likewise in the case of sees *that*. Beliefs are not necessarily true; *sees* and *sees that* are, in general, veridical.

For desire, the issue of truth does not arise, of course.

Conjunction. If Melissa believes that Santa Claus is big and has a white beard, then she believes that Santa Claus is big and she believes that Santa Claus has a white beard.

If Melissa desires a hamburger and a Coke, then she desires a hamburger and she desires a Coke.

Likewise in the case of *seeing* or *seeing that*. In general, if agent $\mathcal{A}$ believes/desires/sees/sees that $\Phi\&\Psi$, then $\mathcal{A}$ believes/desires/sees/sees that Φ and believes/desires/sees/sees that Ψ.

Notice that the situation is quite different for *doubting*. I can doubt

that I will have to teach 160A and teach 160B, but it does not follow
that I doubt that I will have to teach 160A or that I doubt that I will
have to teach 160B.

As to the converses, agents can believe/desire/see that Φ and believe/
desire/see that Ψ without believing/desiring/seeing that $\Phi\&\Psi$. Indeed,
the agent may not connect Φ and Ψ in any way in her mind, so $\Phi\&\Psi$
may be something towards which she has no attitude at all.

In the case of *seeing*, there is a partial implication. If $\mathscr{A}$ sees Φ and, *as
part of the same visual experience*, sees Ψ, then $\mathscr{A}$ sees $\Phi\&\Psi$. However,
this conclusion cannot be drawn if the two seeings take place on different
occasions.

Disjunction. Naomi can believe we will spend the night in Monterey or
we will spend the night in Carmel, without believing that we will spend
the night in Monterey and without believing we will spend the night in
Carmel. In general, believing $\Phi \vee \Psi$ does not entail belief of either of Φ
or Ψ.

With desires, things are not quite so clear cut. If an agent, $\mathscr{A}$, desires
$\Phi \vee \Psi$, then it cannot be the case that the agent is *opposed* to each of
Φ, Ψ. There must at the very least be a *latent* or *partial* desire for one
of them. But it does not necessarily follow that $\mathscr{A}$ has a definite desire
for either one of these on its own. However, if one were axiomatizing a
calculus of desires, it would, I think, seem reasonable to include the rule
that desire of $\Phi \vee \Psi$ does in fact imply the desire of at least one of Φ, Ψ.

For *sees* there is no such difficulty. An agent can only see $\Phi \vee \Psi$ if
the agent either sees Φ or else sees Ψ. If Emma sees Sebastian Coe win
the race or Steve Cram win the race, then either she sees Sebastian Coe
win the race or she sees Steve Cram win the race. This is because of the
immediacy of seeing. But this does not carry over to *seeing that*, where
the agent's beliefs become relevant. Knowing that Sebastian Coe and
Steve Cram are the only two British runners in the race, and being able
to recognize the British colors, Emma sees *that* Sebastian Coe or Steve
Cram wins the race but, because she is not able to recognize the two
runners, she does not see *that* Sebastian Coe wins the race, nor does she
see *that* Steve Cram wins the race. Seeing *that* $\Phi \vee \Psi$ does not imply that
one of seeing *that* Φ or seeing *that* Ψ must be the case.

Turning to the converses, if $\mathscr{A}$ sees at least one of Φ, Ψ, then certainly
$\mathscr{A}$ sees $\Phi \vee \Psi$, but in the case of belief, desire, or seeing that, there is
no such implication, since, as for conjunction above, the agent may not
even connect Φ and Ψ in her mind, and thus will not have any attitude

to $\Phi \vee \Psi$.

Negation. In the normal course of events we would not expect a rational agent to hold conflicting beliefs. But remember the case of the Frenchman, Pierre, who holds the two beliefs *London is pretty* and *London is not pretty*. Because all beliefs about entities in the world are structured in terms of *notions* of those entities, an agent having two different notions of the same entity can have two conflicting beliefs about that entity. Thus, an agent's belief of ¬Φ does not entail that it does *not* believe Φ.

Likewise, I can desire that it snows tomorrow and I can desire that tomorrow's temperature will be in the 80s, though the contents of these two desires are mutually contradictory. Thus a desire of ¬Φ does not entail a non-desire of Φ.

Sees is straightforward. If I see Patches not chew the slipper, then I do not see Patches chew the slipper. In general, seeing ¬Φ implies not seeing Φ. And likewise for *sees that*. If an agent sees that ¬Φ, then that agent does not see that Φ.

Existential generalization. If Fred believes *the chairman* is approaching, then there is some person, X, such that Fred believes X is approaching. (Of course, Fred may have no way of identifying X other than as 'the chairman'.)

Similarly for *desires, sees*, and *sees that*. (In the case of *sees that*, in making a report of the form 'Fred sees that X is approaching', one might in practice have to resort to some physical means, such as pointing, to pick out the individual X involved.)

In general, if an agent believes/desires/sees/sees that $\Phi(the\ \pi)$, then there is some X such that the agent believes/desires/sees/sees that $\Phi(X)$.

Instantiation. If Betsy sees *a student* fall down, then there is some X such that Betsy sees X fall down. (Again, Betsy may have no other means of identifying this X.) Similarly for *sees that*, though as with the existential generalization above, making a report of the form 'Betsy sees that X falls down', might require pointing or some such means to pick out the X that Betsy sees fall down. In general, if an agent sees/sees that $\Phi(a\ \pi)$, then there is some X such that the agent sees/sees that $\Phi(X)$.

In the case of *believes* and *desires*, the situation is different. Betsy can believe/desire that a student fell down without there being any particular X for which she believes/desires that X fell down. In general, belief/desire that $\Phi(a\ \pi)$ does not entail belief/desire that $\Phi(X)$ for some particular X.

Substitution. Suppose I believe that the Director of CSLI drives a BMW. Suppose further that, as a matter of fact, the Director of CSLI is the tallest man at CSLI. Does it follow that I believe the tallest man at CSLI drives a BMW? Most people would answer "no," and I would agree. The stated conclusion would require at least that I believe the Director of CSLI is the tallest man at CSLI. This is because the most natural reading (some would say the *only* reading that constitutes ordinary English usage) of a belief report is the *de dicto* reading that describes the structure of the belief (see Section 7.3). Given a *de re* reading that describes the external content of the belief, then of course the substitution of the phrase 'the tallest man at CSLI' for the phrase 'the Director of CSLI' is valid, since both refer to the same individual.

Similar remarks apply to *desires*.

In general, if an agent believes/desires $\Phi(a)$, and if $a = b$, then it does not follow that the agent believes/desires $\Phi(b)$. Only under the (unnatural) *de re* reading is such a substitution a valid one.

With *sees* there is no such problem. If an agent sees $\Phi(a)$, and if $a = b$, then the agent sees $\Phi(b)$. Thus, if Naomi sees Patches hide the sock, and if Patches is David's dog, than Naomi sees David's dog hide the sock.

Sees that behaves differently, as you might expect, given the dependency on belief. If I see that the Director of CSLI is approaching, it does not follow that I see that the tallest man at CSLI is approaching, even though the Director of CSLI is the tallest man at CSLI. The conclusion would only follow if I *knew*, or at least *believed*, that the Director of CSLI was the tallest man at CSLI. *Seeing that* $\Phi(a)$ does not imply *seeing that* $\Phi(b)$ whenever $a = b$.

Logical equivalence. None of the four kinds of state report under consideration are preserved under classical logical equivalence. That is to say, if an agent believes/desires/sees/sees that Φ, and if $\Phi \Leftrightarrow \Psi$, then it does not follow that (necessarily) the agent believes/desires/sees/sees that Ψ. In the case of *believes, desires,* and *sees that*, arguments such as those used above for substitutivity suffice to justify this claim. For *sees*, notice that just because Melissa sees Naomi eat a pickle, it does not follow that Melissa sees Naomi eat a pickle and [Laura run or Laura not run], since that would require that Laura be part of Melissa's visual experience, whereas there is no mention of Laura in the initial perception report.

In fact, what this last example really shows is that the classical logical notion of logical equivalence (i.e. the biconditional, or truth-value equivalence) is completely inappropriate in the kind of setting we are currently working in.

7.5 Intention and action

So far we have encountered the following variants of 'intentionality':

(i)   intentionality as that property of mental states by which they are directed at or of or about the world or objects therein;

(ii)   intention in the sense of intending to perform some act;

(iii) intensionality, spelt with an 's', which I take to be the opposite of extensionality, therefore meaning property-dependent as opposed to extensionally determined, though in the literature this is often used in more specific instances, such as to indicate non-substitutability in, say, attitude reports.

This troublesome overload of the same word (ignoring the spelling difference, which not everyone acknowledges to be significant) surely indicates that we are dealing with a deep and confusion-fraught issue — the more so since there are strong connections between all of the above uses. To add to this potential confusion, my attempts, in this section and the next, to come to grips with the phenomenon of agent action require yet another subdivision, one that cuts across the first and second of the uses listed above. A simple illustration serves to indicate the general issue, though considerable further examination will be necessary to clear up all the attendant details even in this one case.

Suppose I intend to raise my arm.[6] That is, I decide that: "I will raise my arm," and form some kind of commitment to myself so to do. Then I have what will be called a *future-directed*, or *prior intention* to perform this act. Forming, or holding, this future-directed intention does not involve my actually performing the act of raising my arm, but I am committed to do it, and my intention will be satisfied only if (though not necessarily 'if' — see presently) I do in fact come to raise my arm.

Now consider my actual performance of the act of raising my arm, either as a result of an earlier formed prior-intention, or perhaps involuntarily, say as a reflex action to protect my face against an approaching missile. Clearly, whether the act is premeditated or not, *my raising* my arm is, both as a matter of fact and subjectively, quite different from

---

[6] This is an overworked example — see for instance Wittgenstein [32, Part I, paragraph 621] or Searle [26, Chapter 3] — but one that serves my present purposes very well.

my arm *being raised* — say by means of a wire attached to my wrist, or by an externally produced stimulation of the relevant muscle group. The difference is one involving causation. In the former case, my raising my arm involves what will be called a *present-directed intention* or an *intention-in-action*: I might describe my action by saying, as I raise my arm, "I am now raising my arm intentionally." In the other case, something else raises my arm — *I* do not raise it.

The two notions, prior intention and intention-in-action, are quite different, or at least will be treated as being different. It is with intention-in-action that I shall be primarily concerned in this section, leaving prior intention to the next.

I shall distinguish between *action* and *movement*. The latter is often a component of the former, but the two are not identical. By an *action*, we mean an intentional composite involving both an intention-in-action and an associated act or movement. The intention-in-action is an intentional mental event. The associated act or movement may be a physical, bodily movement, or a speech act, or possibly an act of *not* moving the body or some part thereof, or maybe a mental act, such as imagining something. A reasonable comparison may be made with perception, which I regarded as a combination of an input stimulus and an associated mental event — what I called a *visual experience* in the case of visual perception. Like perception, action involves causal self-reference — though in the opposite direction — and for the same reason, namely the immediacy of the experience.

To continue with my basic example, when I raise my arm, what do I *experience*? That movement of my arm, certainly, but something else as well. It is also part of my mental experience that my arm is going up *as a direct result* of the intention-in-action that constitutes this experience. Which sounds all well and good until you start to analyze just what is meant by that phrase 'as a direct result of'. The ultimate aim of the work presented here being the evolution of a mathematical model, I propose to adopt the following simplistic analysis (which I know to be flawed, but which at least provides some kind of basis from which to proceed).

An *intention-in-action*, I, is a certain kind of intentional (i.e. world-directed) mental state. Its *external content*, i.e. what in the world it corresponds to, comprises an act or movement, A (expressed in propositional form — see presently), together with the fact that I *causes* A. Thus, in the case of my raising my arm, the intention-in-action, I, has as its external content, the proposition *that* I raise my arm, plus the proposition that I raise my arm by way of fulfilling the intention-in-action, I.

That is, the content of *I* is:

$$w \models [\sigma \wedge (I \;\triangleright\; \{\sigma\})]$$

where

$$\sigma = \ll \text{raise}, k, a, t_0, 1 \gg$$

for k = Keith Devlin, a = my requisite arm, t_0 = the time of the action.

This goes part way towards what is required, though admittedly it falls somewhat short of its target. Straight causation is not enough here. My intention-in-action to raise my arm should cause my arm to go up *by way of fulfilling that intention-in-action*, and not by some roundabout means. For instance, suppose my wrist is connected to a wire that runs upwards to an extremely fast electric motor, activated by my taking my hand off the table. The moment I start to raise my arm, the wire yanks it upwards. In this case, my intention-in-action clearly *causes* my arm to go up, but it does so *in the wrong way* for the resulting movement of my arm to be regarded as part of an intentional *action*. In such a case, I would say that *I* did not raise my arm, *the wire* did — though I certainly *caused* this particular raising of my arm by my initial *attempt* to raise it.

However, because of the highly contrived nature of examples such as the above, together with the fact that things are complicated enough already, I think that the overall aim to flesh out a mathematical theory justifies the adoption of the simplified account just proposed. And this is what I shall do.

Under this interpretation, satisfaction of the intention-in-action, *I*, can fail in one of two ways. First of all, my arm might fail to go up — in which case what we have is a failed *effort* to raise my arm. Or my arm might go up coincidentally with my forming the intention, *I*, but do so quite independently of *I*. In 'standard' cases, avoiding contrived examples such as the one above, this second possibility will amount to something external causing my arm to go up, not the intention.

To summarize, *action* is a composite of an intention-in-action and a corresponding movement or act. There is no such thing as an 'unintentional action', though there can be unintentional movement or acts. Intention-in-action is an intentional mental state or event, broadly similar to belief or desire. Its *external content* is the proposition asserting what must occur in the world in order for that mental state to be fulfilled (i.e. the conditions of satisfaction of the intention-in-action). Notice that once again we have classified an intentional mental state in terms of its external significance, in this case, the intentional state of intention-in-action.

7.6   Intention

The form of 'intention' dicussed in this section is future-directed, or prior intention.

In the discussion of mental states in Section 6.4, I observed that the triad of belief, desire, and intention constitutes a kind of basic or primary collection of intentional mental states. Each other intentional mental state may be regarded, to some extent at least, as a refinement of some boolean, modal composition of these three primary states. Most contemporary workers in the area agree that this basic triad cannot be reduced any further; in particular, intention cannot be reduced to a combination of belief and desire. (See, for example, Searle [26] or Bratman [7].) But in the past there have been a number of attempts to perform just such a reduction. Broadly speaking, the idea is to create an identity out of the valid implication

$$intend(A) \Rightarrow desire(A) \wedge believe(\diamond A)$$

where A is some future action. But this simply cannot be done. For what is implicit in the left-hand side of this implication (i.e. intention), but not involved in either of belief or desire, is a *commitment* to future action. Desire and belief can provide a *reason* to act a certain way, but they do not *commit* to that action as does an intention. Desires merely *influence* action; intentions tend to *control* action.

Of course, this observation does not tell us what intention *is*; it simply describes one significant feature of intention in terms of another concept — commitment — which itself then requires elucidation. But then we are not here in the business of providing reductionist *definitions*. Belief, desire, intention, and the like, are fundamental mental states, and simplistic explanatory descriptions are the best that can be hoped for, and all that we require for our overall goal. Still, there is a problem here, in that a simple initial analysis appears to demonstrate that the notions of intention and commitment are vacuous — or at least irrelevant to the activities of cognitive agents such as ourselves. Bratman summarizes the relevant argument as follows:

Consider my intention to go to Boston tomorrow. This intention cannot involve a commitment to later action in the sense that my present state itself controls my later conduct; for that would be action at a distance. But this intention also should not involve a commitment to later action in the sense that it is an unchangeable, irrevocable attitude in favor of so acting; for such irrevocability would clearly be irrational. So this intention will involve a commitment to the later action only in the sense that I will so act later if (but only if) it is later rational so to act. But then why should I bother today to form the intention about tomorrow? Why should I not just cross my bridges when I come to them? On the first horn [of the trilemma created by this scenario], future directed intentions are metaphysically objectionable; on the second horn, they are rationally objectionable; and on the third horn, they just seem a waste of time.

— Bratman [7, p.107]

The problem seems a significant one if you think purely in terms of a single mental state — an intention — in isolation. But this is not at all a reasonable thing to do; and once a more holistic approach is adopted, Bratman's trilemma simply vanishes away, as I now indicate. (In some repsects, what follows amounts to a brief summary of the detailed arguments Bratman develops in [7].)

In general, future-directed intention is, like belief and desire, an intentional mental state, though, just like belief and desire, intention can fail to be intentional, and for the same kinds of reason. My interest here will be primarily in the intentional case. Thus, an intention, I, will be assumed to have an *external content*, and that external content will involve an *action*. (Hence, since all *action* involves intention-in-action, future-directed intention requires intention-in-action; but not conversely.) If I *intend* to raise my arm, then the *external content* of this intention is the *action* of my raising my arm, and my intention will be fulfilled *only if* I subsequently raise my arm. Moreover, my intention to raise my arm will be fulfilled *if and only if* I subsequently raise my arm *by way of carrying out this intention*.

This last observation highlights an obvious similarity between future-directed intention and intention-in-action, in that fulfillment of a future-directed intention requires that the intended action be performed *by way of fulfillment of that intention*. Thus the *external content* (i.e. the conditions of satisfaction) of an intention, I, to perform an action, A, comprises both the action, A, and the fact that the performance of A is by way of carrying out I. As in the case of intention-in-action considered in the previous section, I shall simplify matters with regards to the second component here, by adopting a naive *causality* relationship, namely that the intention, I, *causes* the performance of the action, A. Again, this allows for the possibility of deviant causal chains, but the price is, I think, worth paying, in order to move forwards towards our desired mathematical theory.

Thus, an intention, I, by an agent, $\mathscr{A}$, to perform some action, b, at some time, t, in the future, is an intentional mental state whose external content is the proposition

$$w \models [\ll \mathscr{A}, b, t, 1 \gg \wedge (I \, \triangleright \{\ll \mathscr{A}, b, t, 1 \gg\})]$$

But what is it about a particular mental state that makes it an *intention* as opposed to, say, a *belief* or a *desire*? The answer, as provided by Section 6.4, is what I have referred to as the *psychological mode* of the state. In other words, how the state fits in to the rest of the agent's intentionality network, and the role it plays in guiding the agent's behavior.

To put it another way, what distinguishes an intention (or a belief, or a desire, etc.) from other mental states is the *functionality* of that state within the agent's scheme of things. In the case of intention, this functionality is in some ways stronger and more extensive than for other mental states. For instance, the nature of belief is such that we can study a single belief more or less in isolation from the agent's other mental states, but the same is not true of (future-directed) intentions, since, as I shall argue below, part of what makes them *intentions* is the way they necessarily constrain the agent's other beliefs and intentions.

A proper understanding of what constitutes a future-directed intention requires an acknowledgement that the agent has duration in time and makes its way with the aid of *plans* of future behavior. That is, intentions are a feature of *planning agents* — agents such as Man or certain of the predatory mammals. Intentions form *parts* of plans, and plans can be regarded as *intentions writ large*. (Bratman [7, p.29].)

It should be stressed here that my present use of the word *plan* follows that of Bratman, in that an agent's having a plan entails a *commitment* to follow that plan. This excludes such 'plans' as the one I have for preparing a bolognese sauce, except in the case where I am actually about to follow this plan. For most of the time, my bolognese sauce 'plan' is simply an algorithm that I store away in my memory; only when I commit myself to following it and actually prepare a bolognese sauce does it constitute a *plan* under my present usage of this word. Bratman sums up the issue like this:

... a central fact about us is that we are planning creatures. We frequently settle in advance on plans for the future. These plans help guide our conduct and coordinate our activities over time, in ways which our ordinary desires and beliefs do not. Intentions are typically elements in such coordinating plans: as such, intentions are distinctive states of mind, not to be reduced to clusters of desires and beliefs.

— Bratman [7, p.111]

A crude picture of the way in which future-directed intentions fit into the agent's intentionality network is provided by Figure 7.1.

To illustrate the various points entailed by the conception of 'intention' just outlined, consider an intention that I form in October, to run in the Big Sur Marathon the following April. This intention is formed as a result of a *desire* I have to take part in this event, plus a *belief* I have that it is possible for me to take part. But my intention does not merely consists of this desire and this belief; it involves a *commitment* to take part. As such, my attitude to the Big Sur Marathon is different from my attitude to, say, the Boston Marathon. I have for several years had a *desire* to take part in this event, and I *believe* it would be possible for me so to do but, given the amount of travelling involved in getting from California to the East Coast at the requisite time, I do not, in October, have an *intention* to run in the Boston Marathon the following April.

My commitment to run in the Big Sur Marathon the following April has considerable *stability*. Once formed, my intention remains unless something occurs to overturn it. I may, for instance, fall and break my leg while skiing at Lake Tahoe in February. Or perhaps I will just lose interest at some stage and simply change my mind about the race. But in any event, the *default* case is that my intention remains with me until fulfilled by my actually running in the race.

My intention gives rise to a number of *subgoals* (or 'sub-intentions') that I will have to fulfill. I will have to start training; I will have to get hold of an entry form and send it in; I will have to arrange a hotel in Carmel for the night before the race; and so on. Thus intentions typically *pose problems* for the agent, problems of fulfilling a range of subsidiary goals.

My intention also places *constraints* on my behavior and activities, and on the formation of other plans and intentions. I cannot plan to do anything else on the weekend of the race; I cannot take on any commitments that will prevent me from completing my training schedule; I should try to avoid contact with any viral infections in the weeks before the event; and so on.

My intention results in the formation of various beliefs and desires. For instance, a belief that I will inevitably lose some weight over the coming months; a desire that I will not injure myself when training or skiing; a belief that I will feel very tired for a few days after the event; and so on.

Once I have formed the intention to take part in the race, I regard the issue as *settled*. (This is certainly not the case with a desire.) I can

Fig. 7.1. Simplified schematic of cognition and action

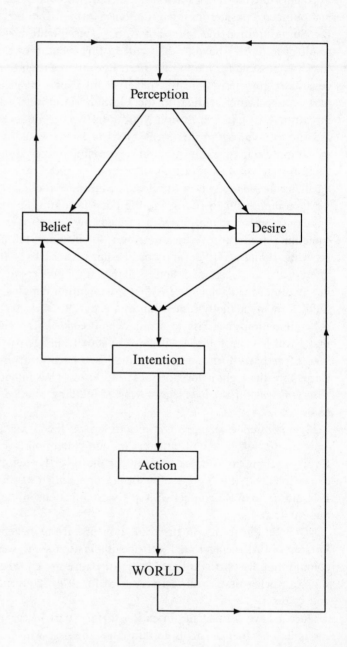

rationally form other plans and intentions on the *assumption* that my intention will be fulfilled, i.e. that I will in fact run in the race. On learning of my intention, others can take it into account in forming their own plans — for instance, my wife can avoid arranging any family trip for the weekend of the race.

Unlike desires, intentions must be consistent. I might well desire to spend next Sunday both in Yosemite and at Lake Tahoe, but I cannot rationally *intend* to be in both places at once. This requirement of intention consistency places considerable constraints on the formation of new intentions; when conflicts arise, one or more intention must be abandoned.

Notice that an intention to A does not imply a belief that A, though it does imply a belief in the *possibility* of A. My intention, formed in October, to run in the Big Sur Marathon in April can be rational, even though past experience may lead me to expect that the intensive training will probably result in some kind of injury that will keep me from taking part. So I may intend to run, but I need not believe that I will.

Finally, note that intentions create a *framework of rationality* within which the agent can formulate and follow further plans. Such plans might not be rational when viewed from outside of that framework. Thus, *given* my intention to run in the Big Sur Marathon, it is rational (relative to that intention) for me to go out and run ten miles every lunchtime. But from a broader perspective, such sustained, intensive, and time-consuming training is not a rational form of behavior for an injury-prone, middle-aged college professor with a whole range of other commitments, including the completion of a book on logic and information.

8

Situation Semantics

People use language to do many things. In addition to its use in order to convey information, language may be used to ask questions, give commands, express emotion, provide comfort, evoke mental pictures or laughter or feelings of joy, sorrow, admiration, and so on. The study of language legitimately spans a great many academic disciplines: linguistics, psychology, philosophy, computer science, artificial intelligence, mathematics and logic, cognitive science, theater studies, drama studies, creative writing, sociology, political science, law, and no doubt other examples that the reader can think of. Each one of these disciplines studies a particular aspect of language use. None can lay claim to being *the* all-embracing study of language.

Situation semantics takes an information-based approach to language, concentrating in particular on the various ways language conveys information. As the name suggests, it is a 'semantic theory', in that it tries to come to grips with the nature of 'meaning'; but in terms of the traditional linguistic distinctions between syntax, semantics, and pragmatics, situation semantics takes on board many of the issues of language use that would normally be classified as pragmatics.

8.1 Language as action

Linguistic studies often try to separate out the study of the *meaning* of language (semantics) from its use (pragmatics). My present overall standpoint and motivation leads to the completely opposite approach; namely, I will concentrate almost exclusively on language in use, including what are customarily known as *speech acts*.

Thus our main object of study will be the utterance, by some speaker, of some word, phrase, sentence, or group of sentences. Since I shall not be concerned with issues of phonology, it will be clear that practically everything I say will, when suitably reformulated, hold for written 'utterances' as well as spoken. For definiteness, I shall generally assume a single listener (or reader).

I take it as self-evident that the speech act forms the 'proper' object of a semantic theory, and I regard the *situatedness* of language use as of fundamental importance. This approach is in direct contrast to those semantic theories that follow the model-theoretic approach of Tarski. But of course, Tarski was interested in the use of language in mathematics, an altogether different and quite atypical case. In natural language use, all sorts of contextual factors are relevant, and it is possible to utter the same sentence in different circumstances to convey quite different information. Barwise and Perry [5, pp.32–39] refer to the fact that the same phrase or sentence can be used on different occasions, by different speakers, to mean different things, as the *efficiency of language*.

For example, the information conveyed by an utterance of the sentence

I am starting now

depends on several contextual features: the referent of the pronoun 'I' is determined by who the speaker is, the time referred to by the word 'now' is determined by the time of utterance, and the context must somehow determine just what it is that the speaker is starting.

8.2   Speech acts

Searle [25] has classified *speech acts* into five *illocutionary categories*:

assertives:[1] which commit the speaker to the truth of an expressed proposition;

directives: which attempt to get the hearer to do something; in addition to commands, these include questions (which attempt to get the hearer to respond with an assertive speech act);

commisives: which commit the speaker to some future course of action;

expressives: which express a psychological state about some state of affairs, such as apologizing or praising;

declarators:[2] which, when uttered by a suitably qualified person, bring about the propositional content of the speech act by virtue of the performance of that speech act, such as declaring war or pronouncing a couple 'man and wife'.

---

[1] Also referred to as 'indicatives' by some authors.

[2] Searle's original term for these was 'declaratives', but many authors use 'declarative' synonymously with 'assertive', so I shall use the name 'declarator' instead.

I shall, for the most part, concentrate my attention on the assertives, but the framework is able to handle the other four categories of utterance as well, and in due course I shall say a little about each of those.

Of course, language is an intricate and complex device. My aim here is not the development of a formal framework capable of handling all facets of language use, which is in all likelihood an unachievable goal. Rather I isolate a small number of what I believe are the most significant features from my standpoint, and work with just these. These features are as follows.

First of all there is what I shall call the *utterance situation*. This is just what the name suggests, the situation or context in which the utterance is made and received. If Jan says to Naomi

A man is at the door,

the utterance situation, u, is the immediate context in which Jan utters these words and Naomi hears them. It includes both Jan and Naomi (for the duration of the utterance), and should be sufficiently rich to identify various salient factors about this utterance, such as the door that Jan is referring to. This is probably the one in her immediate environment, but if Jan utters this sentence as part of a larger discourse, the situation u could provide an alternative door. The connections between the utterance itself and the various objects referred to are known as just that: *connections* (or *speaker's connections*).

Thus

$$u \models \ll \text{utters, Jan, A MAN IS AT THE DOOR}, l, t, 1 \gg$$
$$\wedge \ll \text{refers-to, Jan, THE DOOR}, D, l, t, 1 \gg$$

where D is a door that is fixed by u. Thus the speaker's connections link the utterance (as part of u) of the phrase THE DOOR to the object D.

In many cases, the utterance is part of an ongoing *discourse situation, d*. In cases where the utterance is made in isolation, the utterance situation and the discourse situation coincide. It is the nature of illustrative examples that in many cases they consist of isolated utterances, so many of the examples considered in this account will not distinguish between the utterance and the discourse situations.

The discourse situation is part of a larger, *embedding situation* that incorporates that part of the world of direct relevance to the discourse, in a way that will become clear as my treatment proceeds.[3]

---

[3] The question of what constitutes 'direct relevance' here is a difficult one to answer. Indeed, I do not think it is possible to provide a precise answer in *extensional* terms.

For example, what I shall presently call the 'impact' can affect the embedding situation. Thus, Jan might make the above utterance as a request for Naomi to open the door, and Naomi's subsequent compliance with this request would be a change in the embedding situation, and would constitute part of the impact of Jan's utterance. If e denotes the embedding situation at the time of utterance and e' is the embedding situation a few moments later, we could have

$$e \models \ll \text{closed}, D, l, t, 1 \gg$$

$$e' \models \ll \text{opens, Naomi}, D, l, t', 1 \gg$$

and the impact would include the transition

$$e \longrightarrow e'$$

(This is not completely accurate. See Section 8.4 for the full details.)

Next there is, or at least there may be, a *resource situation*. For instance, suppose Jan says

The man I saw running yesterday is at the door.

Then Jan is making use of a situation that she witnessed the day before, the one in which a certain man was running, in order to identify the man at the door. More precisely, let u be the utterance situation. Then for some individuals M, D,

$$u \models \ll \text{utters, Jan, } \Phi, l, t, 1 \gg$$
$$\wedge \ll \text{refers-to, Jan, THE MAN}, M, l, t, 1 \gg$$
$$\wedge \ll \text{refers-to, Jan, THE DOOR}, D, l, t, 1 \gg$$

where Φ is the sentence

THE MAN I SAW RUNNING YESTERDAY IS AT THE DOOR.

In order to refer to the individual M the way she does, Jan makes use of another situation, r, a situation that occurred the day before the utterance, and which Jan witnessed, in which there was a unique man M such that, for some appropriate values of l', t':

$$r \models \ll \text{runs}, M, l', t', 1 \gg$$

Resource situations can be part of the embedding situation, but they need not be. They can become available for exploitation in various ways, such as:

(i)   by being perceived by the speaker;

Like many of the notions in situation theory, the concept of an embedding situation is inherently *intensional*. The discussions in this book should provide some elucidation of what is meant.

(ii)   by being the objects of some common knowledge about the world or some situation;

(iii) by being the way the world is;

(iv)   by being built up by previous discourse.

Finally, there is the *described situation*, that part of the world the utterance is about. Features of the utterance situation may serve to identify the described situation. For instance, if Jan makes the above utterance while peering out of the upstairs window through a pair of field glasses, at the house across the street, then her utterance refers to the situation, *s*, that she sees, the situation at the house across the street, and we have

$$s \models \ll present,\, M, l, t, 1 \gg$$

where *l* is the location of the door and *t* is the time of the utterance.

The only other feature that I ought to say something about at this early stage is the *impact*. This is the change in the embedding situation that is brought about by the utterance. One example of this has already been given, where Jan's utterance of the sentence 'A MAN IS AT THE DOOR' has the impact of Naomi's opening the door.

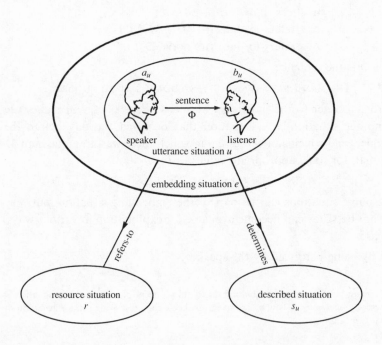

Another variety of an impact of an utterance is where some new agent or object is intoduced into a conversation. Suppose I say, as countless linguists have said before me,

The farmer bought a donkey. He beat it savagely.

Let e be the embedding situation for the discourse. Then the utterance of the first sentence introduces into the conversation a certain farmer, F, and some donkey, D. This is part of the impact of that first utterance and, after that first utterance is made, both F and D are available in e to be the referents of the pronouns 'he' and 'it'. Uttered on its own, the second sentence makes no sense; it requires the impact of the prior utterance to supply the referent of the pronouns.

The impact is particularly useful in distinguishing Searle's five illocutionary categories. I consider this issue in Section 8.4.

8.3 Meaning

In the case of assertive sentences, the basic idea behind the relational theory of meaning has already been outlined in Section 4.1. The *meaning* of an assertive sentence, Φ, is a constraint, an abstract link that connects the type of an utterance of Φ with the type of the described situation. More generally, we can describe the meaning of other kinds of sentence, and of a word or phrase, α, and in these cases too the meaning will be some kind of link between appropriate types.

It should be admitted at the outset that my treatment is an extremely simplistic one, not designed to handle the subtleties of language, or indeed all of the not-so-subtleties. It is very much a 'first approximation' to a situation-theoretic semantics of (part of) natural language, and the aim is in part to illustrate what can be done with the machinery developed so far and in part to guide and motivate the future development of the theory.

I start out by developing a formal notion of meaning for a number of basic types of word or phrase, and then turn to the meaning of sentences.

I adopt the following framework: a speaker utters the word, phrase, or sentence, α, to a single listener. I use u to denote the utterance situation, e the (larger) embedding situation, r any resource situation, and s the described situation. I denote the speaker in u by a_u, and the listener by b_u. The time and location of the utterance are denoted by t_u, l_u, respectively.

I denote by $U(\alpha)$ the situation-type of an utterance of α, namely:

$$U(\alpha) = [\dot{u} \mid \dot{u} \models \ll \text{speaking-to}, \dot{a}_u, \dot{b}_u, \dot{l}_u, \dot{t}_u, 1 \gg \wedge$$

$$\ll\text{utters}, d_u, \alpha, \overset{.}{l}_u, \overset{.}{t}_u, 1 \gg]$$

Now, there are at least two different interpretations of the word 'meaning' of relevance to our study: 'context-free meaning' and 'meaning-in-use'. The former, what I shall refer to as the *abstract meaning*, will be represented in our theory as an abstract linkage between two types. The *meaning-in-use* will be represented as a relation between pairs of objects, in general not types. The distinction between these two notions should become clear as we proceed. In essence the abstract meaning supplies the answer to the question 'What does this word/phrase/sentence mean (*in general*)?', where the word/phrase/sentence is taken out of any context, whereas the meaning-in-use answers the question 'What does this word/phrase/sentence mean (*as it is being used in this instance*)?', where the word/phrase/sentence is uttered in a particular context. The meaning-in-use is *induced* by the abstract meaning, with the former a particular instantiation of the latter. In the case of an utterance of a sentence, the meaning-in-use is closely related to the propositional content.

The abstract meaning a part of speech, α, will be denoted by $\mathcal{M}(\alpha)$; the meaning-in-use of α will be denoted by $\|\alpha\|$.

I commence with a discussion of the meaning of certain kinds of individual words. Here the meaning-in-use provides a link between the utterance situation and the object (possibly an abstract object, such as a relation) in the world that the word denotes.

It should be emphasized that this account gives a fairly crude notion of word meaning. In practice, when a word is uttered as part of a sentence or an extended discourse, the overall context of utterance can contribute features to the meaning of that word (in that context). I mention one such case in the treatment of proper names below. Further (simple) instances arise in the examples I use to discuss sentence meaning later in the chapter.

The meaning of 'I'

From a functional point of view, the meaning of the first-person singular pronoun, 'I', is quite straightforward. In any utterance, u, 'I' denotes the speaker, a_u, of u. I shall define the meaning-in-use, $\|I\|$, of 'I' to be the relation that connects u to a_u for any utterance u. So, for given objects u and a,

$$u\|I\|a \quad \text{if and only if} \quad u : U(I) \quad \text{and} \quad a = a_u.$$

Thus the meaning-in-use of the pronoun 'I' is a relation linking situations to individuals. In mathematical terms, this is expressed by saying that $\|\text{I}\|$ is a relation *on* $S \times A$, where S is the class of situations and A is the class of individuals, or alternatively that $S \times A$ is the *field* of the relation $\|\text{I}\|$.

The abstract meaning of 'I' is defined to be the link between the situation-type

$$U(\text{I}) = [\dot{u} \mid \dot{u} \models \ll\text{speaking-to, } \dot{a}_u, \dot{b}_u, \dot{l}_u, \dot{t}_u, 1 \gg \land$$
$$\ll\text{utters, } \dot{a}_u, \text{I}, \dot{l}_u, \dot{t}_u, 1 \gg]$$

and the object-type

$$E = [\dot{a} \mid \dot{u} \models \ll=, \dot{a}, \dot{a}_u, \dot{l}_u, \dot{t}_u, 1 \gg]$$

It is this link that I denote by $\mathcal{M}(\text{I})$. Notice that there is exactly one type E such that $U(\text{I})[\mathcal{M}(\text{I})]E$ here.

This abstract linkage, $\mathcal{M}(\text{I})$, induces the relation $\|\text{I}\|$ in the fashion:

$$\|\text{I}\| = \{(u,a) \mid u : U(\text{I}) \ \& \ a : E \text{ where } U(\text{I})[\mathcal{M}(\text{I})]E\}$$

The meaning of 'YOU'

This one is equally easy: in any utterance situation, 'YOU' denotes the listener. Thus the meaning-in-use of the word 'YOU' is such that

$$u\|\text{YOU}\|b \quad \text{if and only if} \quad u : U(\text{YOU}) \ \text{and} \ b = b_u$$

and the abstract meaning, $\mathcal{M}(\text{YOU})$, is the link between the situation-type

$$U(\text{YOU}) = [\dot{u} \mid \dot{u} \models \ll\text{speaking-to, } \dot{a}_u, \dot{b}_u, \dot{l}_u, \dot{t}_u, 1 \gg \land$$
$$\ll\text{utters, } \dot{a}_u, \text{YOU}, \dot{l}_u, \dot{t}_u, 1 \gg]$$

and the object-type

$$E = [\dot{b} \mid \dot{u} \models \ll=, \dot{b}, \dot{b}_u, \dot{l}_u, \dot{t}_u, 1 \gg]$$

The meaning of 'HE', 'SHE', 'IT'

Here things are not quite as simple. I start with the abstract meaning. Taking the case 'HE' for definiteness, the significant feature of the pronoun 'HE', when considered out of context, is that it is used to denote a male individual. The appropriate type then to figure in the abstract meaning is the type of any male individual:

$$F = [\dot{b} \mid w \models \ll\text{male, } \dot{b}, 1 \gg]$$

where $\dot{b}$ is an *IND*-parameter and where as usual w denotes the world.

Then the abstract meaning, $\mathcal{M}(\text{HE})$, will be the link between the situation-type

$$U(\text{HE}) = [\dot{u} \mid \dot{u} \models \ll \text{speaking-to}, \dot{a}_u, \dot{b}_u, \dot{l}_u, \dot{t}_u, 1 \gg \wedge$$
$$\ll \text{utters}, \dot{a}_u, \text{HE}, \dot{l}_u, \dot{t}_u, 1 \gg]$$

and the object-type F.

Of course, in this case, the abstract meaning does not really capture the main feature of a pronoun, which is to refer to a particular individual of the appropriate gender. Rather, pronouns really acquire meaning when used in a specific context, and accordingly it is the meaning-in-use that is the more important of the two forms of meaning in this case.

Turning to that meaning-in-use, there are two main ways a pronoun can pick up its referent: either through the speaker or else by having some other noun phrase as an antecedent. Consider, for instance, the sentence:

Jon thought he was wrong.

Uttered one way, 'HE' refers to Jon himself; that is to say, the pronoun picks up its referent *anaphorically* from a previous part of the utterance. Alternatively, the speaker could be using 'HE' *diectically*, to refer to some other person, say Jerry. This referent could be provided by the speaker pointing to Jerry, or could be supplied by some previous utterance as part of a discourse, such as:

Jerry said there was a language of thought. Jon thought he was wrong.

Thus the interpretation of an utterance of the pronoun 'HE' requires the provision of a referent by means of the utterance situation. That is to say, the utterance situation, u, must supply some individual $h = i_u(\text{HE})$ (or $h = i_u(\text{HIM})$) such that for some resource situation, r,

$$r \models \ll \text{male}, h, 1 \gg$$

and then, for any a,

$$u \| \text{HE} \| a \text{ if and only if } u : U(\text{HE}) \text{ and } a = i_u(\text{HE}).$$

Notice that the individual $h = i_u(\text{HE})$ need not be a constituent of the utterance situation. Rather the speaker uses, or relies upon, some resource situation, r, and it is that resource situation, r, that has h as a constituent. One possibility for r would be $Oracle(h)$, the oracle situation for h, as discussed in Section 3.5. (Strictly speaking, I mean $Oracle_\Gamma(h)$ for an appropriate set of issues Γ — see Section 3.5 for details. But here and throughout the remainder of this book, I shall omit any explicit mention of Γ.)

Similarly for the other pronouns, 'SHE', 'IT', etc.

Thus in this case, the manner in which the meaning-in-use is induced by the abstract meaning is a little less straightforward than in the previous two cases. The context can play a far more complex role in determining the meaning-in-use of third-person pronouns than it does for the indexicals 'I' and 'YOU'.

The meaning of proper names

Used correctly, a proper name should designate a particular individual. Since many individuals often share the same name, this means that the context should somehow identify the requisite individual the speaker has in mind. Thus for a proper use of the name 'JAN', the utterance situation, u, should provide an individual $p = i_u(\text{JAN})$ such that for some resource situation, r, usually $r = Oracle(p)$,

$$r \models \ll \text{named}, p, \text{JAN}, 1 \gg$$

and then, for any a,

$$u \| \text{JAN} \| a \quad \text{if and only if} \quad u : U(\text{JAN}) \quad \text{and} \quad a = i_u(\text{JAN}).$$

As with the case of third-person pronouns above, there is no requirement that the person Jan be present in the utterance situation. Rather Jan is a constituent of the resource situation, r, which the speaker makes use of when he makes his utterance.

And again as with third-person pronouns, the abstract meaning of a proper name does not really capture what names are about in the way that the meaning-in-use does. For example, $\mathcal{M}(\text{JAN})$ is the link between the situation-type

$$U(\text{JAN}) = [\dot{u} \mid \dot{u} \models \ll \text{speaking-to}, d_u, \dot{b}_u, \dot{l}_u, \dot{t}_u, 1 \gg \wedge$$
$$\ll \text{utters}, d_u, \text{JAN}, \dot{l}_u, \dot{t}_u, 1 \gg]$$

and the object-type

$$E = [\dot{b} \mid w \models \ll \text{named}, \dot{b}, \text{JAN}, 1 \gg]$$

To point out one particular manner in which the abstract meaning of proper names is simply at too high a level of abstraction to really capture the way names are used, notice that, if a is an individual of type E, then we shall have

$$w \models \ll \text{named}, a, \text{JAN}, 1 \gg$$

so for some temporal location t we will have

$$w \models \ll \text{named}, a, \text{JAN}, t, 1 \gg$$

So all this tells us is that, at *some* time, this individual a is named 'JAN'. But of course, people can and do change their names, whereas correct usage of proper names requires using the name that prevails at the appropriate time. And indeed this may be reflected in the meaning-in-use. In the present framework this could result from the resource situation having the appropriate temporal duration. But there are other possibilities.

For instance, if the word 'JAN' were uttered as part of a complete sentence, then features of the utterance as a whole could provide an appropriate temporal location t_0 so that in the meaning-in-use of the proper name 'JAN' (on this occasion) we have

$$r \models \ll\text{named}, a, \text{JAN}, t_0, 1 \gg$$

where r is the resource situation, perhaps *Oracle*(p).

A further example occurs in the discussion of sentence meaning that I shall come to presently.

Another weakness of the abstract meaning of proper names, also shared by the abstract meaning of third-person pronouns, is that the relevant object-type is defined over the world, w, whereas in any given instance only some small part of the world (a resource situation) will be involved in detemining the name or gender of a particular individual. Again, this simply reflects the fact that the abstract meaning is just at too high a level of abstraction for many kinds of words.

Similar comments apply also to common nouns, considered next.

The meaning of nouns

The abstract meaning of a noun, α, is the link between the type, $U(\alpha)$, of an utterance of α, and the type of the object denoted by α. For example, the abstract meaning of the noun 'APPLE' is the link between the situation-type

$$U(\text{APPLE}) = [\dot{u} \mid \dot{u} \models \ll\text{speaking-to}, \dot{d}_u, \dot{b}_u, \dot{l}_u, \dot{t}_u, 1 \gg \wedge$$
$$\ll\text{utters}, \dot{d}_u, \text{APPLE}, \dot{l}_u, \dot{t}_u, 1 \gg]$$

and the object-type of all apples:

$$[\dot{b} \mid w \models \ll\text{apple}, \dot{b}, 1 \gg]$$

where 'apple' here denotes the property of being an apple.

As for meaning-in-use, this concept applies not so much to nouns as to noun phrases. The normal usage of a noun is as part of a noun phrase, and even on those occasions where a noun is uttered in naked fashion, such as when a small child looks at her plate and says "Apple," this can be regarded, for our purposes, as an abbreviation for the noun phrase 'An apple'. I investigate the meaning-in-use of noun phrases in just a moment.

The meaning of verbs

The meaning-in-use of any verb is the link between the verb and the relation it denotes. For example, the verb 'RUNS' corresponds to the relation, R, of running, and for any utterance situation, u,

$$u \| \text{RUNS} \| R$$

I shall deal with the issue of tense presently.

To be consistent with the development so far, the abstract meaning of a verb, say 'runs', should be taken to be the link between the type of an utterance of the word 'RUNS' and the type of all relations of running. However, for simplicity I have adopted an overall framework in this book whereby I do not make use of parameters for relations and do not form relation-types. This means that the current machinery cannot accommodate such a notion of abstract meaning of verbs. A more complete development in which relation-types abstraction was allowed, would be able to handle this issue in the manner suggested, but I leave that to another time. The notion of meaning-in-use of verbs will serve all our present requirements.

Speaker's connections

Notice that, in each case so far, the meaning-in-use of a word, α, is a relation, $\| \alpha \|$, that links an utterance situation, u, with a certain object, a, either an individual in the case where α is a pronoun or name, or a relation in the case of a verb. The relation $u \| \alpha \| a$ places a constraint on the utterance situation, u, to supply or contain a suitable object.

Given different utterance situations, the same word can be linked to different objects. Around CSLI at the time of writing, the name 'John' is very much dependent on the utterance situation: does the speaker mean John Perry, John Etchemendy, or John Nerbonne (or even Jon Barwise in the case of a *spoken* utterance)? And as I have already observed, the referent of a pronoun is always dependent upon the utterance situation.

The general term I use to denote the object that the utterance situation, u, provides to correspond to a word, α, via its meaning, is $c_u(\alpha)$. Thus, in the case of a third-person pronoun or a proper name, c_u is the same as the function i_u introduced a short while ago.

In case an utterance of a word or phrase, α, in an utterance, u, makes use of a resource situation, r, I denote this resource situation by $c_u^{res}(\alpha)$. It is quite often the case that, where α denotes an individual $c_u(\alpha)$, then

$$c_u^{res}(\alpha) = Oracle(c_u(\alpha))$$

In the case where u is an utterance of a sentence, Φ, there will also be a *described situation*, that part of the world the utterance of Φ is about. I denote this situation by $s_u(\Phi)$.

Extending the terminology of Barwise and Perry [5, p.125], I use the term *speaker's connections* to mean any or all of the functions c_u, c_u^{res}, and s_u.

Thus the speaker's connections are the functional links between the words the speaker utters and those parts of, or objects in, the world she uses these words to refer to. They thus provide our theory with a mathematical realization of the intentionality of speech, the fact that agents use language to talk *about* the world.

Notice that effective communication requires that, in general, the listener is aware of the identity of the described situation, $s_u(\Phi)$, and the values of the speaker's connection function, c_u, and the onus is on the speaker to ensure that the listener is so aware. In general there is, however, no need for the listener to know the values of the resource-situation function, c_u^{res}. The role played by resource situations is simply that of a supporting background.

For instance, if, in the course of a conversation, I use the noun 'APPLE', then there must be some resource situation that supports the fact that the object referred to is indeed an apple, and if challenged my listener might well agree that there will be such a situation, but the identity of that resource situation is not in general important. (Many of the cases where the identity of a resource situation is important are among those where the resource situation is an oracle situation.)

Of course, as theorists we may well want to keep track of the various resource situations, and hence the function c_u^{res} cannot be left out of our theory. But that is our concern, not that of the speaker or the listener.

The speaker's connections also provide the interpretation of the tense of a verb, as I consider next.

Speaker's connections and tensed verbs

Consider the following sentences.

> *Mary is running.*
> *Mary was running.*
> *Mary will run.*

In each case, the meaning of the word 'run' (ignoring the morphological differences between 'run', 'runs', 'running') connects this word to the same relation, R, the relation of running. In using a particular tense of this verb, the speaker is providing a reference to a particular time, the time at which the running takes/took place. Our theory accounts for this by means of the speaker's connections function. Thus,

$c_u(\text{IS}) = t_u$

$c_u(\text{WAS}) = t$ where $t \prec t_u$

$c_u(\text{WILL}) = t$ where $t_u \prec t$.

These last two often occur in the context of an existential quantification over t.

The meaning of singular noun phrases

In my investigation of the meaning of singular noun phrases, I shall restrict attention to meaning-in-use, and leave it to the reader to supply the more general notion of abstract meaning (the link between the utterance type and an appropriate object-type, that induces the meaning-in-use).

I commence with definite descriptions. For example:

(I) THE MAN IN A BLACK HAT

(II) THE PRESIDENT OF THE UNITED STATES

(III) THE KING OF FRANCE

Each of these can be used to denote, or refer to, a specific individual. Such usage of a definite description is known as the *referential* use. I shall consider other uses in due course, following the discussion of sentence meaning. In the meantime, I shall restrict attention to the referential use.

In each of the above three examples then, if we assume the phrase is used to refer to a particular individual, the question arises: where is that individual, i.e. what situation(s) is the individual a constituent of? Clearly, he need not necessarily be a constituent of the utterance situation, or even the larger, embedding situation. In the case of example (I), an utterance of this phrase could well have the relevant individual present in the embedding situation, but most utterances of (II) will not be made in the presence of the US President. And of course no contemporary situation can include an individual that fits the description in (III), since there is no current King of France.

Rather, in making (referential) use of a definite description

$$\alpha = \text{THE } \pi$$

in the utterance situation, u, the speaker is making use of some resource situation, $r = c_u^{res}(\alpha)$, of which the requisite individual is a constituent.

So the meaning-in-use of α, $\|\alpha\|$, links u to an individual $a = c_u(\alpha)$ such that:

(i) $r \models \ll \Pi, a, l_\Pi, t_\Pi, 1 \gg$; and

(ii) a is the unique individual in r with property (i),

where Π is the property (possibly complex) that corresponds to π, namely the property of *being a* π, and where l_Π and t_Π are the location and time associated with Π if this is location or time dependent.

That is to say, for any given situation u and individual a,

$u\|\text{THE } \pi\|a$ if and only if

$\quad u : U(\text{THE } \pi)$ and a satisfies (i) and (ii), where $r = c_u^{res}(\text{THE } \pi)$.

Thus, in the case of example (I), suppose this sentence is uttered at a party, and it is this party (or maybe some time interval within this event) that we take to be the utterance situation, u. Then the legitimate utterance of this phrase, with reference to the situation u itself as resource situation, will require that there is a man in u wearing a black hat, and moreover there is only one such man.

On the other hand, if we take u to be some conversation that is going on at the party, say a conversation about the rock group playing at the other end of the room, then the phrase (I) may be legitimately uttered provided that precisely one man in the rock group is wearing a black hat, *even though at the party as a whole there may be many men wearing black hats*. This is because the conversation itself determines an appropriate resource situation, namely the situation comprising the rock group.

In either case, the entire party as a resource situation or the rock group as a resource situation, the speaker's connections provide a resource situation, r, in which there is exactly one man wearing a black hat (i.e. possessing the complex property associated with the phrase 'MAN IN A BLACK HAT', that is to say, *being* a man in a black hat), and then the meaning of the definite description (I) links the utterance situation u to this particular individual.

Returning now to example (II), this differs from (I) only in that the resource situation will in general be quite distinct from the utterance situation. In fact, for most (referential) utterances of (II), the 'default' resource situation will be the entire USA over some period of time, a situation that may include the utterance situation or be quite disjoint from it.

Finally, sentence (III) is different from the other two in that there is, currently, no individual in the world that fits this description: there is no King of France. Thus a legitimate referential utterance of this phrase can only be made with reference to a resource situation located in the past, at a time when there was such a person.

The meaning-in-use of an indefinite description (used referentially) such as

A BLACK CAT

or

A SMALL TOWN IN GERMANY

is defined in a similar way to that of a definite description, the only difference being that the uniqueness condition (clause (ii) in the above) is not required.

Other singular noun phrases are handled similarly. For instance, when used referentially, a phrase such as

MY DOG

functions very much like a definite description, in that there must be a resource situation, r, in which there is one dog, d, that, at the appropriate time t, belongs to me, KD, that is to say

$$r \models \; \ll\text{dog}, d, t, 1 \gg \; \wedge \; \ll\text{owns}, KD, d, t, 1 \gg$$

and the meaning of this phrase links the utterance situation with that dog.

In some cases the resource situation, r, here may be $Oracle(KD)$, but other features of the utterance as a whole might determine an entirely different resource situation.

The principle of compositionality

One obvious property of language is that the meaning of a larger unit, such as a sentence, is a function of the meanings of the individual parts, the words and phrases that go together to give the sentence. But what kind of function is it that combines meanings of parts to form meanings of wholes or of larger parts?

In classical, first-order logic, where the only formally defined notion is that of truth-value, and not meaning in any real sense of the word, the truth-value of the whole is defined in terms of the truth-values of the parts in a mathematically precise and uniform fashion, namely the Tarski definition of model-theoretic truth.

But for natural languages things are by no means so simple. Though I have presented formal definitions of 'meaning' for each of the basic parts of speech, the relationship between these meanings and the meanings of the more complex wholes they can be part of, is highly context-dependent and can be quite complicated, though one presumes that, for language to function as it does, there must be some such relationship, at least where fairly straightforward forms of utterance are concerned, avoiding such uses as metaphor or slang.

I shall not, at this stage of the development, investigate the compositional rules dealing with meaning. Rather, having now defined a notion of 'meaning' for the various basic parts of speech, my approach will be to proceeed straight to a discussion of the meaning of a complete sentence. The process whereby this meaning arises from the meanings of the various words that go together to make up the sentence will be left to another occasion. At the end of this chapter and in Chapter 9 I present a few examples to indicate how our machinery can be used in such an analysis.

Sentence meaning

In this section I indicate how the information-theoretic machinery developed so far can be used to analyze natural language discourse at the sentence level.

The reader anticipating anything remotely like the familiar Tarski semantics for predicate logic is in for a disappointment, or at least a surprise. Natural language is simply far too complex for that. Indeed, one of the lessons to be drawn from our analysis is just *how* complex are even very simple-looking natural language utterances, when viewed from an information-theoretic viewpoint. So much background information is assumed by the speaker in order to make a typical natural language utterance, and so much background information is required in order for the listener to resolve that utterance, that it seems inevitable that any study such as ours will be forced into the kind of convolutions that are presented below.

On the other hand, our framework does appear adequate for carrying out such an analysis, at least at the fairly crude level I pursue, and this is what I wish to convey.

I consider an *utterance situation*, u, in which a *speaker*, a_u, utters a sentence, Φ, to a single *listener*, b_u, at a time t_u and a location l_u. The situation u may be part of a larger, *discourse situation*, d. (Otherwise we take $d = u$.) The situation d is part of some (possibly larger) *embedding situation*, e, that part of the world of direct relevance to the utterance. During the utterance, the speaker may refer to one of several *resource situations*. The utterance u will determine a *described situation*, $s_u = s_u(\Phi)$.

I concentrate first of all on an utterance of a single assertive sentence, say Jan's utterance of the sentence

$$\Phi \; : \; \textit{Keith bought a dog.}$$

Factors about the utterance situation, u, should, if this utterance is to succeed in imparting to the listener the information Jan wants to convey, determine a unique individual $k = c_u(\text{KEITH})$ such that for some resource situation $r_k = c_u^{res}(\text{KEITH})$:

(1) $r_k \models \ll \text{person}, k, t_k, 1 \gg \wedge \ll \text{named}, k, \text{KEITH}, t_k, 1 \gg$

(2) k is the only such individual in r_k

where, according to the overall context, either t_k includes t_u or else t_k includes the time t introduced below.

The meaning of the word 'BOUGHT' relates Jan's usage of this word to a relation 'buys', and the usage of the past tense determines that for some time, t, preceding t_u :

(3) $s_u \models \ll \text{buys}, k, p, t, 1 \gg$

where p is as below.

Finally, for the utterance to be true, there must be an individual p and a resource situation $r_p = c_u^{res}(\text{A DOG})$ such that

(4) $r_p \models \ll \text{dog}, p, t, 1 \gg$

(5) $s_u \models \ll \text{buys}, k, p, t, 1 \gg$

I examine the various components of this analysis, beginning with the resource situation r_k.

In the absence of any circumstances to the contrary, this will be the oracle of k, $Oracle(k)$. In making her utterance the way she does, Jan presumably assumes that the listener has some (possibly quite miminal) information about r_k, in particular the information that there is an individual k' such that:

(6) $r_k \models \ll \text{person}, k', t_k, 1 \gg \wedge \ll \text{named}, k', \text{KEITH}, t_k, 1 \gg$

(7) k' is the only such individual in r_k

It is not necessary that the listener can identify the k' here with the individual, k, Jan is referring to, though Jan might well be assuming the listener has such knowledge.

The *assumption* by Jan of a certain shared knowledge about the resource situation, r_k, is what enables her to use the name 'KEITH' the way she does. Though she herself may well have a very extensive stock of information about r_k, the listener's knowledge could be quite meager. It might only amount to the two items (6) and (7) above. More likely, the listener's knowledge of the rules governing English proper names would allow him to conclude in addition that

(8) $r_k \models \ll \text{male}, k', t_k, 1 \gg$

A fairly cursory knowledge of Jan's family circumstances might also provide the listener with the further information

(9) $r_k \models \ll \text{husband-of}, k', a_u, t_k, 1 \gg$

(In the case I have in mind, it is also the case that t_k includes t_u.)

The listener then, requires only quite minimal knowledge about r_k in order for Jan's usage of the word 'KEITH' to be informational. But notice that Jan too actually needs to draw on very little information about r_k in order to make this utterance. This is, I think, a strong argument in favor of the situational approach to information processing in general, and the use of oracle situations in particular. There is indeed a situation *Oracle*(k), and Jan has informational access to it, though that access will only amount to *partial* information about that situation.

Though more traditional, AI-oriented approaches to this issue might refer to r_k as a 'Keith-*file*', this would be misleading, in that use of the word 'file' suggests a list of facts about Keith, a list to which the speaker and listener may each add new information, and through which they each search for information. This is not at all what is meant here. Rather, associated to this guy Keith is a certain situation $r_k = Oracle(k)$, and as the occasion demands, different people can draw on various items of information about r_k (in terms of our ontology, we might say they can utilize various compound infons, σ, such that $r_k \models \sigma$). The situation r_k remains constant here, a fixed situation, part physical and part abstract, intimately associated with Keith. We could, if we wished, refer to the collection of infons that the speaker and listener each know to be supported by r_k, as the speaker's 'Keith-file' and the listener's 'Keith-file', respectively. In which case *these files* are dynamic entities that change with time. But the *situation* r_k remains fixed.

There is obviously a relationship between the oracle r_k and Jan's *notion* of Keith, as discussed in Chapter 6 (see Section 6.3 and subsequent). Indeed, under ideal circumstances Jan's notion of the person k will amount to a mental aggregate of infons supported by r_k, and so too will the listener's (perhaps much leaner) notion about the person Jan refers to. Indeed, any information (infons), σ, about k that Jan uses will be part of her notion of k, in the sense of the framework for describing notions that I developed in Section 6.4. And likewise for the listener.

Turning next to Jan's utterance of the word BOUGHT, in keeping with our overall treatment of relations in this study, I assume that both the speaker and the listener associate with this word the same relation, *buys*, a complex, structured object relating a number of arguments, as discussed in Section 5.2. The usage of the past tense will be dealt with in just a moment, when I examine the informational *content* of Jan's utterance.

Now let's look at Jan's usage of the phrase A DOG. This is likewise linked to a certain situation r_p, a situation associated with the dog Keith bought, a situation that supports, among other things, the fact of that dog being a dog.

Notice that Jan may or may not have any direct knowledge of just *which* dog Keith bought. All we can say as theorists is that there must be such a p and an associated resource situation r_p. The use of the indefinite article leaves aside all questions as to the identity of the dog.

Thus, Jan's utterance refers to a situation in which there are two individuals, k and p. The individual k is referred to directly in the utterance, and facts about the resource situation r_k are required in order for the utterance to convey the information Jan intends of it (assuming the obvious intent, discussed below). The individual p is not referred to in the utterance, nor is the resource situation r_p. There must of course *be* such an individual, and associated with that individual there will *be* a resource situation, r_p. But Jan's utterance does not identify them the way it does the individual k and the situation r_k. This distinction will be highlighted in the following discussion about the informational content of the utterance.

Turning now to that informational content, in the most straightforward case, the item of information that Jan wants to convey by means of her utterance is what I refer to as the *propositional content* of the utterance. This is the proposition

$$s_u \models \exists \dot{p} \exists \dot{i} \ll \text{buys}, k, \dot{p}, \dot{i}, 1 \gg$$

where $\dot{p}$ is a parameter for a dog and $\dot{i}$ is a parameter for a time period prior to t_u, for example $\dot{i} = TIM_{56} \restriction \ll <, TIM_{56}, t_u, 1 \gg$.

Notice that this content has as constituents the described situation, s_u, the individual k, and the relation *buys*. The speaker makes explicit reference both to the individual k and the relation *buys*. The described situation, s_u, is not referred to in the utterance. Rather the speaker's connections put s_u into the propositional content. Neither the actual time of the buying nor the actual dog bought get into the propositional content.

Contrast this with an utterance of the sentence

$$\Psi : \textit{Keith bought the dog.}$$

Here the propositional content is

$$s_u \models \exists i \ll \text{buys}, k, p, i, 1 \gg$$

This time the particular dog, p, gets into the propositional content as an articulated constitutent of the utterance. But where does this individual come from? The utterance of this one sentence alone does not serve to identify p. Rather some previous utterance, or some embedding circumstance, has to pick out the particular dog Jan refers to. (This particular sentence would seem to force the referential use of the definite description 'THE DOG', but in any case I assume such usage.) Normal language use requires that an utterance of sentence Ψ is indeed either preceded by an utterance that supplies the individual, p, referred to in Ψ by the phrase 'THE DOG', or else the utterance is made in a circumstance where other factors serve to make this identification, such as the utterance being made while the speaker and listener are jointly viewing a scene in which there is exactly one dog.

Notice that in this case, provided that the utterance manages to identify the relevant dog, communication can proceed with $r_p = Oracle(p)$. This was not possible in the previous case when the indefinite article was involved ('A DOG'), since there was no way Jan could bring this particular resource situation into the listener's focus, and thereby rely upon shared information about that situation.

Notice that the fact that the person, k, referred to in any veridical utterance of Φ, is named 'Keith,' does not contribute directly to the meaning of Φ, nor does the fact that the individual bought, p, is a dog, although these are part of the *meanings* of the two words concerned. Rather these facts are reflected in our framework by virtue of the way parameters operate. Any veridical utterance of Φ is constrained to have the word 'KEITH' refer to a person named 'Keith' and the word 'DOG' refer to a dog.

The propositional content of the utterance of an assertive sentence is our theory's way of getting at the principal item of information that, under normal circumstances, the speaker intends to convey by the utterance. As such it is closely related to the meaning of the sentence, which I turn to next.

Now, the abstract meaning of a sentence is an extrinsic feature of the sentence, independent of any particular context of utterance. For the present example, the *abstract meaning* of the sentence Φ is an abstract link, $\mathscr{M}(\Phi)$, that connects the situation-type

$$U = [\dot{u} \mid \dot{u} \models \ll \text{speaking-to}, \dot{a}_u, \dot{b}_u, \dot{l}_u, \dot{t}_u, 1 \gg \wedge$$
$$\ll \text{utters}, \dot{a}_u, \Phi, \dot{l}_u, \dot{t}_u, 1 \gg \wedge$$
$$\ll \text{refers-to}, \dot{a}_u, \text{KEITH}, \dot{k}, \dot{l}_u, \dot{t}_u, 1 \gg]$$

and the situation-type

$$E = [\dot{s} \mid \dot{s} \models \exists \dot{p} \exists \dot{i} \ll \text{buys}, \dot{k}, \dot{p}, \dot{i}, 1 \gg]$$

where $\dot{k}$ is a parameter for a person named 'Keith', $\dot{p}$ is a parameter for a dog, and $\dot{i}$ is a parameter for a time period preceding $\dot{t}_u$, say $\dot{i} = TIM_5 \upharpoonright \ll \prec, TIM_5, \dot{t}_u, 1 \gg$.

The meaning-in-use of Φ, $\|\Phi\|$, should link any particular utterance of Φ with the fact of the world (or relevant part thereof) being the way Φ says it should be. That is to say it is the relation between situations u and v, induced by $\mathscr{M}(\Phi)$, such that:

$$u\|\Phi\|v \quad \text{if and only if} \quad [u : U] \ \& \ [s_u(\Phi) \subseteq v] \ \& \ [v : E]$$

where $U[\mathscr{M}(\Phi)]E$.

As indicated briefly in Section 5.2, the parametric, compound infon that determines the type E above is known as the *descriptive content* of Φ, denoted by $\mathscr{C}(U)$. That is:

$$\mathscr{C}(U) = \exists \dot{p} \exists \dot{i} \ll \text{buys}, \dot{k}, \dot{p}, \dot{i}, 1 \gg$$

I denote this by $\mathscr{C}(U)$ rather than $\mathscr{C}(\Phi)$, since the descriptive content is really a function of the type of an utterance of Φ, rather than the sentence Φ. In particular, it is U that provides the link between the word 'KEITH' in Φ and the parameter $\dot{k}$ in $\mathscr{C}(U)$. In practice, however, I often blur this distinction and simply write $\mathscr{C}(\Phi)$, it being understood that what is really meant is the descriptive content of Φ *with respect to the type of an utterance of* Φ.

The descriptive content captures the 'information template' that produces the principal item of information conveyed by any veridical utterance of the sentence (that is to say, the information about the described situation that consitutes the propositional content of the utterance) when the various parameters are anchored to the appropriate objects.

Thus the descriptive content provides an intermediate layer between the syntactic unit Φ and the propositional content of an actual utterance of Φ. It allows us to account for Barwise and Perry's *efficiency of language*; in this case the fact that the same sentence Φ can be used over and over again, by different speakers, referring to different Keiths and different dogs, to convey the 'same' item of information each time, namely that the particular Keith referred to bought some dog. The descriptive content is thus a uniformity across all propositional contents of all veridical utterances of Φ.

Notice that the descriptive content transcends the actual syntax of Φ. Rather it gets at something deeper than syntax. For example, translations of Φ into different languages will all have the same descriptive content. The sentence is a string of symbols, constructed in accordance with certain rules; the descriptive content is a parametric, compound infon, a genuine object in our ontology. A veridical utterance of the sentence provides anchors for the various parameters in the descriptive content, and the result is that item of information about the described situation that constitutes the propositional content of the utterance.

In other words, if $\sigma = \mathscr{C}(\Theta)$ is the descriptive content of an assertive sentence Θ, then for any utterance, u, of Θ, if f_u denotes the anchor that u provides for the parameters in σ, then the propositional content of this utterance is

$$s \models \sigma[f_u]$$

where $s = s_u(\Theta)$ (the described situation).

The anchors for the parameters in $\mathscr{C}(\Theta)$ are clearly related to what I have called the speaker's connections for some of the words that go to make up Θ. If α is a word or phrase in Θ and if the speaker's connections link α to the individual $c_u(\alpha)$, and if $\dot{a}$ is the parameter in $\mathscr{C}(\Theta)$ that corresponds to α, then

$$f_u(\dot{a}) = c_u(\alpha)$$

The descriptive content of a sentence is essentially a parametric object. According to the convention I have adopted in this book that there are no parameters for relations, any descriptive content will involve relations, but by and large all other constituents will be parameters. Exceptions would be where a word or phrase has a fixed meaning, independent of context of utterance, such as 'Earth' or 'Mars' or 'Principia Mathematicae'. (Though it is possible to argue for the context dependency of each of these.)

Further discussion of sentence meaning requires the concept of 'impact' of an utterance, introduced in the next section.

Attributive uses of definite and indefinite descriptions

Hitherto our discussion of both definite and indefinite descriptions has been in terms of what is generally known as the *referential* use, where the description is used to refer to a particular individual — a uniquely specified individual in the case of a definite description, not uniquely identified in the case of an indefinite description.

However, there are other uses of noun phrases and, though a detailed examination of such usage is beyond our present scope, I provide some indication of the issues involved.

Starting with definite descriptions, consider the following sentences, all involving one of our original examples of a definite description:

(i)   *The President of the United States lives in Washington.*
(ii) *George Bush is the President of the United States.*
(iii) *George Bush, the President of the United States, lives in Washington.*

Sentence (i) has two quite distinct readings. When the noun phrase is used referentially, to refer to the particular individual who happens to be the President of the United States at the relevant time, the propositional content of the utterance (u) is of the form

$$s_u \models \ll \text{lives-in}, p, c, t_u, 1 \gg$$

where

$$p = c_u(\text{THE PRESIDENT OF THE UNITED STATES})$$

and

$$c = c_u(\text{WASHINGTON}).$$

[In fact c is the city of Washington D.C. (a situation in our ontology) and, if the utterance is made at the time I am writing this, in 1990, p is President George Bush (an individual in our ontology).]

In using the phrase 'THE PRESIDENT OF THE UNITED STATES', the speaker makes use of a resource situation r, possibly the whole of the United States, to identify the particular individual p, that is to say, to determine the value of the function c_u for this particular noun phrase.

The second reading of (i) is the *attributive* reading, where the sentence has a meaning roughly the same as:

The President of the United States, whoever it is, always lives in Washington.

Under this reading, the phrase 'THE PRESIDENT OF THE UNITED STATES' does not refer to a particular individual, but rather to the general property of *being* a President of the United States. Under this reading, an utterance,

u, of sentence (i) expresses a constraint, and the propositional content of u is:

$$s_u \models (S \Rightarrow T)$$

where

$$S = [\hat{s} \mid \hat{s} \models \ll \text{US-President}, \hat{p}, \hat{t}, 1 \gg]$$

$$T = [\hat{s} \mid \hat{s} \models \ll \text{lives-in}, \hat{p}, c, \hat{t}, 1 \gg]$$

where s_u, the described situation, is probably the entire United States, and where c is the city of Washington D.C., as before.

Turning now to sentence (ii), there is clearly no meaningful reading of this sentence in which the definite description 'THE PRESIDENT OF THE UNITED STATES' is used referentially, since that would just amount to the triviality

George Bush is George Bush.

Under the attributive reading, the phrase 'THE PRESIDENT OF THE UNITED STATES' determines a predicate, the property of being the President of the United States, and the propositional content of an utterance, u, of (ii) is:

$$s_u \models \ll \text{US-President}, p, t_u, 1 \gg$$

where $p = c_u(\text{GEORGE BUSH})$ is the individual (President) George Bush.

Finally, sentence (iii) provides an example of an *appositive* use of a definite description. Uttering the phrase 'THE PRESIDENT OF THE UNITED STATES' as part of sentence (iii) provides additional information about the individual named 'GEORGE BUSH' referred to by the subject of the sentence. Among other things it serves to specify precisely *which* George Bush the speaker has in mind.

The propositional content of an utterance, u, of sentence (iii) will be:

$$s_u \models \ll \text{lives-in}, p, c, t_u, 1 \gg \wedge \ll \text{US-President}, p, t_u, 1 \gg$$

where $p = c_u(\text{GEORGE BUSH})$ is the individual (President) George Bush and $c = c_u(\text{WASHINGTON})$ is the city of Washington D.C.

Notice that, in the case of the attributive reading of (i), the definite description picks out a *function*, $\mathscr{P}$, the function that associates with each time t the current President of the United States at time t, and the propositional content amounts to the claim that for any time t:

$$s_u \models \ll \text{lives-in}, \mathscr{P}(t), c, t, 1 \gg$$

A particularly striking example of such a *functional* use of a definite description arises in connection with the so-called Partee Puzzle. This purports to show that it is not always possible to substitute equals for equals, by considering the pair of sentences:

The temperature is ninety.
The temperature is increasing.

A naive substitution of equals for equals in this pair of sentences produces the absurdity

Ninety is increasing.

Of course, such a substitution is not possible, and the question then is "Why not?"

The answer is that in the first sentence, the definite description 'THE TEMPERATURE' is used referentially to refer to the actual temperature at the time of utterance, whereas in the second sentence the same definite description is used functionally to refer to the function that links the time to the temperature at that time.

Broadly similar remarks to all the above can be made about indefinite descriptions. For example, paralleling the three examples of sentences involving definite descriptions, the following exhibit the same overall features:

(i)   *A Scotsman wears a kilt.*
(ii)   *Angus is a Scotsman.*
(iii) *Angus, a Scotsman, lives in Oxford.*

I leave it to the reader to carry out the appropriate analyses of these three sentences.

8.4   Impact

Hitherto our study of sentence utterances has concentrated on the utterance of an assertive sentence. We focused on the propositional content to capture that item of information the speaker intends to convey by the utterance.

The other feature of sentence utterance that I shall consider is the *impact*. Every sentence utterance has an impact, regardless of whether that sentence is assertive or not.

I adopt a framework broadly similar to the one used already. Thus, u is an *utterance situation*, in which a *speaker*, a_u, utters a sentence, Φ, to a single *listener*, b_u, at a time t_u and a location l_u. In general, u is part of a larger, *discourse situation*, d. The discourse, d, is part of a (possibly larger) *embedding situation*, e, that part of the world of direct relevance to the discourse. The sentence Φ is not necessarily an assertive sentence.

I denote by t_u^+ some time following the utterance. At the current level of generality, it is not possible to say exactly how much later than t_u this time t_u^+ is, nor what its duration is. It depends very much on context. In the case of a command that should be obeyed immediately, t_u^+ could be an interval immediately following the utterance, the time when the command should be obeyed. In the case of the utterance, u, made as part of an ongoing discourse, d, a common value for t_u^+ will be t_v, where v is the next sentence utterance in the discourse.

The *impact* of u, $\mathscr{I}(u)$, consists of compound infons, σ, built up from basic infons of the form $\ll R,\ldots,t,i \gg$, where $t \leq t_u^+$, such that:

$$e \models \sigma$$

$$u \rhd [e \models \sigma] \quad \text{(more precisely, } u \rhd \{\ll \models, e, \sigma, 1 \gg\} \text{)}.$$

Intuitively, the impact of an utterance is the (relevant) change in the embedding situation that the utterance brings about. (The parenthetic use of the word 'relevant' here is to exclude such 'irrelevant' changes as the movement of molecules in the air caused by the utterance, etc.)

For example, in the case where Φ is an assertive sentence, where the speaker (a_u) has the straightforward intention of conveying to the listener (b_u) the information comprising the propositional content, p, of u, and where this intention is fulfilled (i.e. the listener does acquire that information), $\mathscr{I}(u)$ contains the infon

$$\ll \text{has-information}, b_u, p, t_u^+, 1 \gg$$

Notice that the speaker's intention here is in terms of the listener having certain information. We do not refer to the belief or knowledge of the listener. To do so would be quite inappropriate. There are many cases where information is conveyed without the listener, or indeed the speaker, either knowing or believing that information. For example, the speaker or listener might be a computer, which can acquire and dispense vast amounts of information but which neither believes nor knows anything. Or again, one suspects that a great many television newsreaders neither know nor believe all the information they read to camera. Conveying information does not require belief or knowledge of that information, though it does of course require that the speaker *has* that information — a condition I assume throughout.

One obvious property of the impact is that it serves to distinguish between certain of Searle's five illocutionary acts, catalogued in Section 8.2

In the case of a directive, one might imagine that the impact will include the listener's act of compliance or non-compliance to the command.

For example, if Naomi says to Melissa

Close the door

then in the case where Melissa obeys the command, the impact of this utterance, u, could include the infon

$$\ll \text{closes, Melissa, } D, l_D, t_u^+, 1 \gg$$

where $D = c_u(\text{THE DOOR})$, or, if Melissa does not obey the command, it could include the infon

$$\ll \text{closes, Melissa, } D, l_D, t_u^+, 0 \gg$$

However, this is not quite right. For as far as the act of communication is concerned, the utterance of a directive has succeeded if, as a result of the utterance, the listener forms the intention to perform the requisite action. Some other factor(s) might frustrate the fulfillment of this intention, but that is independent of the success or failure of the speech act.

Accordingly, what the impact of Naomi's utterance, u, *will* contain is either the infon

$$\ll \text{of-type, } Melissa, I(D), t_u^+, 1 \gg$$

or the infon

$$\ll \text{of-type, } Melissa, I(D), t_u^+, 0 \gg$$

where $I(D)$ is the object-type of having an intention to close the door D. (See Section 7.5 for an elaboration of this kind of type.)

Whether the directive is in fact obeyed or not is not reflected in the impact. The impact is concerned exclusively with the effects of the utterance *as a speech act*. But notice that it is the nature of a directive that exactly one of the above two intentional-state infons must be in the impact. There is no 'neutral' position, whereby the impact is void of any infon pertaining to Melissa's intention regarding the closing of the door.

That is to say, one feature of a directive is that if u is an utterance of a command 'Do $\mathscr{K}$' then precisely one of

$$\ll \text{of-type, } b_u, I(\mathscr{K}), t_u^+, 1 \gg$$

or the infon

$$\ll \text{of-type, } b_u, I(\mathscr{K}), t_u^+, 0 \gg$$

is in $\mathscr{I}(u)$, where $I(\mathscr{K})$ is the object-type of having an intention to perform the action $\mathscr{K}$.

For a commisive, the impact will be the formation by the speaker of the intention to perform some future action. Thus if Melissa says to Naomi

I will close the door

then the impact of this utterance, u, will include the infon

$$\ll \text{of-type, Melissa, } I, t_u^+, 1 \gg$$

where I is the object-type of having an intention to close the door.

The impact of a declarator will be that act brought about by the utterance. Thus, if Keith says to Dale:

You are now in charge of the department

then the impact of this utterance, u, includes the infon

$$\ll \text{in-charge-of, Dale, D}, t_u^+, 1 \gg$$

where $D = c_u(\text{THE DEPARTMENT})$.

The above examples illustrate the prominent and characteristic role played by the impact in an utterance of a directive, commisive, or declarator. The impact is not such a prominent feature of the utterance of an assertive or an expressive.

Indeed, at the present level of treatment, the impact does not distinguish between assertives and expressives. Both assertives and expressives are considered purely in terms of the information conveyed, in the sense of propositional content.

But this does not mean that the utterance of assertive or expressive sentences does not have an impact, as the following discussion indicates.

From the point of view of discourse analysis, one important feature of the impact is that it enables us to handle the way that, as a discourse proceeds, referents are supplied for subsequently used pronouns and otherwise ambiguous proper names.

For instance, consider the example mentioned earlier, where I say:

The farmer bought a donkey. He beat it.

The discourse, d, here comprises two sentences. Let u_1 be the utterance of the first sentence, u_2 that of the second. The embedding situation, e, extends the discourse and includes the farmer and a donkey. The utterance u_1 introduces the two objects

$$F = c_{u_1}(\text{THE FARMER}) \quad \text{and} \quad D = c_{u_1}(\text{A DONKEY})$$

into the discourse situation. Then, the utterance u_2 may take

$$c_{u_2}(\text{HE}) = F \quad \text{and} \quad c_{u_2}(\text{IT}) = D$$

In this case, the impact of u_1, $\mathscr{I}(u_1)$, includes the infons

$$\ll \text{salient-in, } F, d, t_{u_1}^+, 1 \gg$$

$$\ll \text{salient-in, } D, d, t_{u_1}^+, 1 \gg$$

In general, if u is an utterance of a word/phrase/sentence, α, such that one or more of $c_u(\alpha), c_u^{res}(\alpha)$, or (in the case where α is a sentence) $s_u(\alpha)$ is defined, then if a is any one of these objects, we have

$$\ll \text{salient-in, } a, d, t_u^+, 1 \gg \in \mathscr{I}(u)$$

which implies that

$$e \models \,\ll\text{salient-in}, a, d, t_u^+, 1 \gg$$

Moreover:

if $a = c_u(\alpha)$ is an individual that is referred to by α in u, then

$$\ll\text{refers-to}, a_u, \alpha, a, t_u, 1 \gg \,\in \mathscr{I}(u)$$

if $a = c_u(\alpha)$ and $r = c_u^{res}(\alpha)$, then

$$\ll\text{resource-for}, r, a, t_u, 1 \gg \,\in \mathscr{I}(u)$$

if α is a sentence and $s = s_u(\alpha)$, then

$$\ll\text{speaking-about}, a_u, \alpha, s, t_u, 1 \gg \,\in \mathscr{I}(u)$$

The function $\mathscr{I}$ is such that, if u_1 is a subutterance of u_2, then $\mathscr{I}(u_1) \subseteq \mathscr{I}(u_2)$, whenever both these sets are defined.

Consider now the following discourse:

Ed : *Did you see the 49ers game yesterday?*

Jan: *Yes, I think Montana is wonderful.*

Ed : *Yes, his last pass to Rice was amazing.*

Let u_1 be the first utterance, that of Ed, let u_2 be the second, Jan's, and let u_3 be Ed's final utterance. Let t_1, t_2, t_3 be the time intervals corresponding to each of these utterances, respectively, and let Φ_1, Φ_2, Φ_3 be the three sentences uttered.

The impact of u_1 includes the introduction into the discourse situation of the San Fransisco 49ers. Indeed, though formulated as a question, it is this first utterance that identifies

$$\text{SFO} = Oracle(\text{the San Fransisco 49ers})$$

as the resource situation, and

$$G = \text{yesterday's 49ers game}$$

as the described situation, the focus of the ensuing discourse.

Thus, $\mathscr{I}(u_1)$ includes the following infons:

$$\ll\text{salient-in}, \text{SFO}, d, t_1^+, 1 \gg$$

$$\ll\text{salient-in}, G, d, t_1^+, 1 \gg$$

$$\ll\text{refers-to}, \text{Ed}, \text{THE 49ERS GAME}, G, t_1, 1 \gg$$

$$\ll\text{resource-for}, \text{SFO}, G, t_1, 1 \gg$$

where in this case t_1^+ denotes the time interval comprising both t_2 and t_3.

In asking the question he does, Ed is assuming that Jan is familiar with the 49ers, that she has access to the situation SFO. In making the

initial 'Yes' response she does, Jan confirms that she does indeed have
such access. Otherwise, a more appropriate response would have been
"Who?" Likewise, her initial "Yes" shows that she is also familiar with
the situation G, since she would otherwise have responded "No."

Now, among the facts that Jan knows about the situation SFO is that
the quarterback is named Joe Montana. Thus, in making her response,
u_2, Jan can take

$$c_{u_2}(\text{MONTANA}) = M \quad \text{and} \quad c_{u_2}^{res}(\text{MONTANA}) = \text{SFO}$$

where M is the individual Joe Montana.

In turn now, the impact of u_2 includes the introduction of the individual
M into the discourse situation. That is to say, $\mathscr{I}(u_2)$ includes the infon

$$\ll\text{salient-in}, M, d, t_2^+, 1 \gg$$

where t_2^+ denotes the time interval t_3.

So, in making the utterance u_3, Ed can take

$$c_{u_3}(\text{HIS}) = M$$

in order to make his comment on the pass made by Montana to wide-
receiver Jerry Rice.

In the absence of Ed's first utterance however, Jan's remark could
equally well have been about the State of Montana. It was the utterance
of u_1, with its impact including the introduction of the situation SFO
into the embedding situation, that prevented any such breakdown in
communication due to the ambiguity of the word 'Montana'.

Likewise, Ed's knowledge of the situation SFO included the fact that
its star wide-receiver is a man, R say, called 'Rice', and thereby allowed
him to take

$$c_{u_3}(\text{RICE}) = R$$

The success of u_3 (in terms of the conveyance of information) depends
upon Jan, the listener, also knowing that the 49ers have a player called
'Rice'. Otherwise, she might have taken the referent of the word 'rice' to
be the white, granular substance found on the supermarket shelves, and
not the person R Ed was talking about. (Well, this is conceivable — the
word is ambiguous. More likely though, Jan's background knowledge of
ball games would have forced her to conclude that Ed's use of the word
'rice' must refer to some person by that name, even if she had never heard
of that person before. The present framework can handle this possibility
as well.)

It is, of course, easy to pursue the above investigation to far greater
depths. But my intention here is not to carry out a linguistic analysis.

Rather I am trying to indicate how the formal tools of situation theory, including the impact of an utterance, can be used to perform such an analysis. And that, I would hope, has now been achieved.

8.5 Meaning and the Searle Classification

The meaning of an assertive sentence has already been defined and investigated. But what is the meaning of other forms of sentence in the Searle classification, the directives, commisives, declarators, and expressives? The machinery we now have available is not only adequate for dealing with utterances of each of these types, it also provides features that distinguish utterances of one category from those of another.

As before, u is an *utterance situation* in which a *speaker*, a_u, utters a sentence, Φ, to a single *listener*, b_u, at a time t_u and a location l_u.

Let U be the type of an utterance of Φ by a_u to b_u, namely:

$$U = [\dot{u} \mid \dot{u} \models \ll\text{speaking-to}, \dot{a}_u, \dot{b}_u, \dot{l}_u, \dot{t}_u, 1 \gg \wedge$$
$$\ll \text{utters}, \dot{a}_u, \Phi, \dot{l}_u, \dot{t}_u, 1 \gg]$$

I start with the expressives, since from the standpoint of our theory these turn out to be very similar to the assertives.

Suppose that the sentence Φ is an expressive:

'I am Π'

where Π is some psychological state, such as sorrow or anger. Let E be the situation-type

$$E = [\dot{s} \mid \dot{s} \models \ll\text{of-type}, \dot{a}_u, B(\Pi), \dot{t}_u, 1 \gg]$$

where $B(\Pi)$ denotes the object-type of being in the state Π.

Then $\mathscr{M}(\Phi)$, the abstract meaning of Φ, is the link between the types U and E.

Turning to the meaning-in-use of Φ, this will be a relation linking utterances of Φ (i.e. situations of type U) to situations extending the described situation that are of type E. So one question to answer is what are the possible described situations? The answer is implicit in the nature of an expressive. In uttering an expressive, the speaker, a_u, describes her own state, so the described situation, $s_u(\Phi)$, will be part of the oracle-situation, $Oracle(a_u)$.

Then, given situations u and v we shall have

$u \| \text{I AM } \Pi \| v$ if and only if

$$[u : U] \ \& \ [s_u(\Phi) \subseteq v] \ \& \ [v \models \ll\text{of-type}, a_u, B(\Pi), t_u, 1 \gg]$$

In the three remaining categories of utterance, the directives, commisives, and declarators, the main function is not the conveyance of information, as was the case with the assertives and expressives; rather it is the regulatory effect the utterance has on action, either of the speaker or the listener. For such sentences, the impact of the utterance is the most significant feature, not the propositional content.

I consider first the case where the sentence Φ is a directive:

$$\text{'Do } \mathcal{K}.\text{'}$$

Let E be the type

$$E = [\dot{s} \mid \dot{s} \models \ll \text{of-type}, \dot{b}_u, I(\mathcal{K}), i_u^+, 1 \gg \wedge$$
$$\ll \vartriangleright, \dot{u}, (\dot{s} \models \ll \text{of-type}, \dot{b}_u, I(\mathcal{K}), i_u^+, 1 \gg), 1 \gg]$$

where $I(\mathcal{K})$ is the object-type of having an intention to perform the action $\mathcal{K}$.

Then the abstract meaning of the sentence Φ, $\mathcal{M}(\Phi)$, is defined to be the link between the two types U and E. The intention here is that the meaning of a directive is that link which, for a given utterance of the directive, connects the utterance with its compliance (in the sense of forming the intention to do as instructed). This explains the second component in the definition of the type E, which I have expressed in an abbreviated fashion for clarity. The meaning must reflect the fact that the intention to perform the action $\mathcal{K}$ that figures in Φ has to arise by way of complying with the directive.

The meaning-in-use of Φ, induced by $\mathcal{M}(\Phi)$, is a relation, $\|\Phi\|$, between utterances, u, of Φ and certain situations v that extend the described situation, $s_u(\Phi)$. Now the situation $s_u(\Phi)$ is identified by features of the utterance itself. For assertives it can be any situation whatever. For expressives the described situation is constrained to be part of the speaker's oracle, $Oracle(a_u)$. In the case of a directive, the described situation must be part of the listener's oracle, $Oracle(b_u)$. Then for any two situations u and v:

$u\|\text{Do }\mathcal{K}\|v$ if and only if

$$[u : U] \,\&\, [s_u(\Phi) \subseteq v] \,\&\, [v \models \ll \text{of-type}, b_u, I(\mathcal{K}), t_u^+, 1 \gg \wedge$$
$$\ll \vartriangleright, u, (v \models \ll \text{of-type}, b_u, I(\mathcal{K}), t_u^+, 1 \gg), 1 \gg]$$

Suppose now that Φ is a commisive:

$$\text{'I will } \mathcal{K}.\text{'}$$

Let E be the type

$$E = [\dot{s} \mid \dot{s} \models \ll \text{of-type}, \dot{a}_u, I(\mathcal{K}), i_u^+, 1 \gg]$$

where again $I(\mathcal{K})$ is the object-type of having an intention to perform the action $\mathcal{K}$.

The abstract meaning of Φ is again defined to be the link between the two types U and E.

Turning to $\|\Phi\|$, if we are given a particular utterance, u, of the commisive Φ, the described situation, $s_u(\Phi)$, will be a part of the speaker's oracle, $Oracle(a_u)$, and the meaning-in-use of Φ relates the situation u to those situations v extending $s_u(\Phi)$ in which the speaker forms the intention to do as promised in Φ:

$u\|\text{I WILL } \mathcal{K}\|v$ if and only if:

$$[u : U] \ \& \ [s_u(\Phi) \subseteq v] \ \& \ [v \models \ll\text{of-type}, a_u, I(\mathcal{K}), t_u^+, 1 \gg]$$

Finally, suppose Φ is a declarator:

$$\text{'I declare } \mathcal{K}.\text{'}$$

Let E be the type

$$E = [\dot{s} \mid \dot{s} \models \ll T(\mathcal{K}), i_u^+, 1 \gg]$$

where $T(\mathcal{K})$ expresses that fact that things are as the utterance of Φ declares them to be. For example, if

$$\mathcal{K} = \text{'You are in charge'}$$

then

$$T(\mathcal{K}) = \text{in-charge}, b_u$$

Then $\mathcal{M}(\Phi)$ is the link between U and E.

For $\|\Phi\|$, if we are given an utterance u of Φ, then there is no general rule as to what is the described situation, $s_u(\Phi)$. It depends very much on $\mathcal{K}$. In the case of the example just given, $s_u(\Phi)$ will be whatever it is the listener is put in charge of, say, the department. Then, given situations u and v, we have:

$u\|\text{YOU ARE IN CHARGE}\|v$ if and only if

$$[u : U] \ \& \ [s_u(\Phi) \subseteq v] \ \& \ [v \models \ll\text{in-charge}, b_u, t_u^+, 1 \gg]$$

8.6 Compositionality

As indicated earlier, it is not my intention to provide a full-blown account of the way that the meaning of a composite sentence or utterance is built up from the meanings of the various components. Certainly the high degree of context dependency of this process would seem to render as a hopeless dream any kind of development analogous to Tarski's semantics of predicate logic. But the tools I have developed do appear to be adequate for an analysis of particular instances of compositionality, so it will be a useful exercise to investigate two of the simplest, and most basic kinds of example: conjunction and disjunction. I restrict attention to meaning-in-use.

I start with conjunction. I let u be an utterance situation, in which a speaker a_u utters a conjunctive sentence $[\Phi$ AND $\Psi]$ to a single listener b_u at a time t_u and a location l_u. In general, u is part of a larger, discourse situation d. The discourse d is part of a (possibly larger) embedding situation e, that part of the world of direct relevance to the discourse. Let u_1 be the utterance situation in which the clause Φ is uttered, u_2 that pertaining to Ψ.

Naively, one might expect that, given assertives Φ and Ψ, the meaning-in-use of the sentence $[\Phi$ AND $\Psi]$ is given by

$$u\|\Phi \text{ AND } \Psi\|v \text{ if and only if } u_1\|\Phi\|v \text{ and } u_2\|\Psi\|v$$

This is indeed the case, but the superficial resemblance this has to the analogous Tarskian rule obscures some considerable complexity.

Suppose for instance the sentence uttered is:

Sid loves Nancy and she loves him.

Then the above reduction gives

(*) $u\|$SID LOVES NANCY AND SHE LOVES HIM$\|v$ if and only if

$u_1\|$SID LOVES NANCY$\|v$ and $u_2\|$SHE LOVES HIM$\|v$

The first conjunct here is straightforward enough. The speaker's connections should fix two individuals, $S = c_{u_1}(\text{SID})$ and $N = c_{u_1}(\text{NANCY})$, such that (in particular)

$$u_1 \models \ll\text{refers-to}, a_{u_1}, \text{SID}, S, l_{u_1}, t_{u_1}, 1 \gg \wedge$$
$$\ll\text{refers-to}, a_{u_1}, \text{NANCY}, N, l_{u_1}, t_{u_1}, 1 \gg$$

and

$$v \models \ll\text{loves}, S, N, t_{u_1}, 1 \gg$$

The second clause involves two pronouns, 'SHE' and 'HIM'. The referents for these pronouns must be supplied by the utterance. The most natural case would be where

$$c_{u_2}(\text{SHE}) = N \text{ and } c_{u_2}(\text{HIM}) = S$$

and then part of the requirement on v imposed by (*) is

$$v \models \ll\text{loves}, N, S, t_{u_1}, 1 \gg$$

In this case the impact of the utterance u_1 provides the relevant individuals to act as referents for the pronouns used in u_2. But there are other possibilities. The utterance could pick out other individuals to be referents for these pronouns. I leave it to the reader to investigate this matter further.

The meaning of disjunctive sentences, [Φ OR Ψ], is similar to conjunctions. Thus:

$$u\|\Phi \text{ OR } \Psi\|v \quad \text{if and only if} \quad u_1\|\Phi\|v \text{ or } u_2\|\Psi\|v$$

Remarks analogous to those made in the case of conjunction apply here as well.

Of course, there is no need to restrict attention to just these two binary sentence connectives. Though these are the two logicians are most familiar with, the English language has many others; for example, the connective 'BUT'. A detailed examination of a whole host of such issues would be outside the scope of the present work, but in order to indicate the manner in which the tools developed here can be used to carry out such an analysis, in the next chapter I make a few remarks about the particular question: what is the distinction between an utterance of a conjunctive sentence [Φ AND Ψ] and a sentence of the form [Φ BUT Ψ] ?

Informationally there is no distinction, at least not at the level of our present investigation. The abstract meanings of these two compound sentences are identical, as are their meanings-in-use. Moreover, an utterance, *u*, of either sentence will result in the same propositional content.

As we shall see, the distinction lies in the intention of the speaker and the resulting impact of the utterance. In making an utterance of

[Φ BUT Ψ]

the speaker is both asserting the conjunct of Φ and Ψ and at the same time emphasizing the *contrast* between Φ and Ψ.

This involves a notion that has not appeared in any of the analyses so far: the *speaker's intentions*, that part of the utterance situation that concerns the effect the speaker wants the utterance to have on the listener, reflected in the impact of the utterance. In the present case, this will be to draw attention to the *distinction* between Φ and Ψ.

Another instance where the speaker-intention is highly relevant is where the impact of an utterance is quite distinct from the propositional content. For example, where Keith says to Jan

It is cold in here

and the impact is, as Keith intended, that Jan closes the window.

The issue of speaker's intention is taken up in Section 9.4

Three other examples of compositionality that come to mind, at least to the mind of someone trained in formal logic, are negation, implication (i.e. conditionals), and quantification. Again each of these is dealt with in the next chapter.

9

Topics in Situation Semantics

In this chapter I present a selection of specialized topics in situation semantics. As with the coverage in the previous chapter, this is not intended as a linguistic study, but rather is an illustration of how we can apply the techniques of situation theory and situation semantics to investigate issues in natural language.

9.1 Quantification

One of the most significant uses of parameters in situation theory arises in the semantics of natural language quantification. For example, let Φ be the sentence

Every logician admires Quine.

Let u be an utterance of Φ. The first question I ask is what is the described situation, $e = s_u(\Phi)$? Well, in the absence of any previously established context this will surely be the world, w, or at least some part of the world that pertains to, and in particular includes, all logicians — say the academic world. In any event, the propositional content of the utterance u will be of the form

$$e \models <compound\ infon>$$

The question is, just what compound infon occurs here? I present two answers. The first answer is an obvious one, but it turns out to be too restrictive for our purposes, and I shall end up opting for the second alternative.

The first approach takes as the propositional content of the utterance, u, the proposition:[1]

$$e \models (\forall \dot{p})\ll admires, \dot{p}, Q, t, 1 \gg$$

---

[1] For pedagogic reasons I concentrate on the propositional content in this account, but this is of course closely related to the meaning, both abstract and in-use.

or, more precisely (recall the convention regarding quantification in compound infons):

$$e \models (\forall \dot{p} \in e) \ll admires, \dot{p}, Q, t, 1 \gg$$

where $\dot{p}$ is a partameter for a logician, Q is the individual W.V.O. Quine, and t is the present time. (Taking t to be the time of utterance, t_u, would be inappropriately restrictive in this connection. The time interval t will include t_u but have considerably longer duration. The utterance makes no specific reference to time, though it is clearly intended to be about 'the present time' or perhaps 'the present epoch'.)

By virtue of the manner in which quantifiers operate on infons, this means that for any anchor f for the parameter $\dot{p}$ to an object p in e, it must be the case that

$$e \models \ll admires, p, Q, t, 1 \gg$$

Now, in order for f to be an anchor for $\dot{p}$, there must be a resource situation, r, such that:

$$r \models \ll logician, p, t, 1 \gg$$

But there is no requirement that r should be the same situation as e, or indeed bear any particular relation to e. (Though if e is the world, then r will be a subsituation of e, of course.) Indeed, all that is required is that to each p in e to which $\dot{p}$ can be anchored, there will be *some* such resource situation $r = r_p$ that depends on p.

Consider now the sentences

$$\Phi_1 : \textit{Every player touched the ball.}$$

$$\Phi_2 : \textit{Every player ate a cookie.}$$

Let u_1 be an utterance of Φ_1, u_2 an utterance of Φ_2.

Starting with Φ_1, the described situation, $s_{u_1}(\Phi_1)$, will be some ball game, say e, and the propositional content of u_1 will be

$$e \models (\forall \dot{p})(\exists \dot{t}) \ll touch, \dot{p}, b, \dot{t}, 1 \gg$$

where $\dot{p}$ is a parameter for a player, $b = c_u(\text{THE BALL})$, and $\dot{t}$ is a parameter for a time preceding t_{u_1}. The game situation e will provide the resource situation for all the individuals p to which the parameter $\dot{p}$ can be anchored. That is to say, for any anchor f of $\dot{p}$ to an individual p in e, it will be the case that for some time t within the time-span of e:

$$e \models \ll player\text{-}in, p, e, t, 1 \gg$$
$$e \models \ll touch, p, b, t, 1 \gg$$

The resource situation for the fact that t precedes t_{u_1} is, as always, the world:

$$w \models \ll <, t, t_{u_1}, 1 \gg$$

since this is the nature of the basic type $<$.

Turning now to the second sentence, Φ_2, assuming the players eat the cookies during the game, the described situation, $s_{u_2}(\Phi_2)$, will be the game e, as before, and the propositional content of u_2 will be

$$e \models (\forall \dot{p})(\exists \dot{c})(\exists \dot{t}) \ll \text{eats}, \dot{p}, \dot{c}, \dot{t}, 1 \gg$$

where $\dot{p}$ is a parameter for a person and $\dot{t}$ is a parameter for a time preceding t_{u_2}, much as before, and where $\dot{c}$ is a parameter for a cookie. (The reading of Φ_2 whereby every player eats the *same* cookie is too implausible to consider. Rather I assume the reading whereby to each player there corresponds a cookie which that player, and only that player, eats.)

Clearly, there is no reason to suppose the game situation e supports the facticity of any particular individual being a cookie. Nor is it necessarily the case that every cookie eaten by some player is of the same variety, with its cookieness being supported by one and the same resource situation. Rather, for each individual p in e to which $\dot{p}$ may be anchored and each corresponding time t to which $\dot{t}$ is anchored, and for which, therefore

$$e \models \ll \text{player-in}, p, e, t, 1 \gg$$

there will be an individual c and a resource situation r_c, such that

$$r_c \models \ll \text{cookie}, c, t, 1 \gg$$

(The default for the situation r_c will be *Oracle*(c).)

Given my assumption that the players eat the cookies during the game e, then the cookie c will be a constituent of e. But this is not necessarily the case. The cookies could be eaten at some other time. For instance, they could be eaten in the locker-room after the game is over at some time t' preceding t_{u_2}. To be definite, consider the case where a previous utterance has established, by way of its impact, a speaker's connection to a time t' when the cookies were eaten. Then the described situation e' will be a situation different from the game e, and the propositional content of u_2 will be:

$$e' \models (\forall \dot{p})(\exists \dot{c}) \ll \text{eats}, \dot{p}, \dot{c}, t', 1 \gg$$

Whatever the described situation turns out to be, the two points to notice are, firstly, that the described situation may or may not provide the scope and resource situation for the quantified parameters, and secondly, the resource situation for an instance of the quantifier $(\exists \dot{c})$ is not necessarily the same as that for the instance of $(\forall \dot{p})$ to which it corresponds.

In the case where the cookies are eaten during the game, then the described situation provides the scope of the quantifier $(\forall \dot{p})$ and the resource situation for each anchor of $\dot{p}$ being a player in e. The described situation also provides the scopes for the quantifiers $(\exists \dot{c})$ and $(\exists \dot{t})$, but for neither of these quantifiers does it provide the appropriate resource situation.

If, on the other hand, the cookies are eaten at some other time determined by the speaker's connections associated with some prior utterance, then the described situation provides the scope for the quantifier $(\forall \dot{p})$ but not the resource situation for any anchor of $\dot{p}$ being a player in the game.

Thus, our theory places no restrictions on the possible scope of quantifiers or on the situations that can provide a resource for the anchor of a particular parameter. It is up to the speaker to ensure that the context of utterance provides the right connections to the scope of any quantifier and to the appropriate resource situations, where relevant. In the case of a cookie, this is clearly of little importance, at least in the majority of cases. But establishing the relevant game situation e and whether the cookies were eaten during the game or at some other time is critical to the success of the utterance as a conveyance of information. Our theory allows for, and reflects, all possibilities, but leaves the responsibility for effective communication where it belongs — with the speaker.

So far I have considered just two kinds of quantifiers, *for all* and *there exists*. In order to handle other quantifiers, some further development of the situation-theoretic framework is necessary.

One solution is to enlarge the collection of compound infons by introducing various generalized quantifiers. For example, we could allow the following constructions to figure as compound infons:

$$(M\dot{x} \in u)\sigma \quad \text{and} \quad (F\dot{x} \in u)\sigma$$

where σ is a compound infon, where $(M\dot{x} \in u)$ denotes 'for most $\dot{x}$ in u', and where $(F\dot{x} \in u)$ denotes 'for few $\dot{x}$ in u'. Some form of definition of what these quantifiers actually mean would then be necessary of course.

But this approach seems to be at odds with the way I decided to regard our ontology, and in particular the *basic* nature of infons as informational *units*. Though there are good arguments in favor of allowing restricted universal and existential quantification to figure in the formation of compound infons (I present two such arguments below), the same cannot be said for allowing other kinds of quantifiers, at least not given the present state of our ability to handle such quantifiers with mathematical rigor. Rather the aim here is to provide a sound mathematical framework *within which one may investigate such natural language generalized quantifiers.*

An alternative approach, consistent with the last remark, is to regard quantifiers (at least those that arise explicitly in natural language — see presently) not as operators acting on infons, but rather as relations within the theory's ontology; in particular, as relations between types.[2] Thus, for example, among the relations we might have the basic five-place relations $\forall, \exists, M, F$, and then the following would be infons:

$$\ll \forall, u, S, T, l, t, i \gg \qquad \ll \exists, u, S, T, l, t, i \gg$$
$$\ll M, u, S, T, l, t, i \gg \qquad \ll F, u, S, T, l, t, i \gg$$

where u is a set or situation and S and T are one-place types.

The first of these is the informational item that: if $i = 1$ then *all* objects in u of type S are of type T, and if $i = 0$ then it is not the case that all objects in u of type S are of type T (at location l and time t).

The second is the informational item that: if $i = 1$ then *there is* an object in u of type S that is of type T, and if $i = 0$ then there is no such object (at l, t).

The third is the information that: if $i = 1$ then *most* objects in u of type S are of type T, and if $i = 0$ then this is not the case (at l, t).

Finally, the fourth infon is the informational item that: if $i = 1$ then *few* objects in u of type S are of type T, and if $i = 0$ then this is not the case (at l, t).

Notice that since quantification is now of the infonic form

$$\ll Q, u, S, T, l, t, i \gg$$

a situation is required in order to obtain a proposition

$$e \models \ll Q, u, S, T, l, t, i \gg$$

so the quantification is situated in, and hence restricted to, e. Thus the argument u is not required in order to ensure that the quantification is restricted; the situation e will do that. Rather the argument u is included in the infon to fulfil a different function: namely to guarantee persistence. Without such a restriction on the quantification we could have, for example,

$$e \models \ll \forall, S, T, 1 \gg$$
$$e' \models \ll \forall, S, T, 0 \gg$$

where $e \subseteq e'$.

---

[2] This kind of approach was first suggested by Barwise and Cooper in their paper [3].

Using this new framework, I shall take a second look at the two previous examples. The first of these is an utterance u_1 of the sentence

$$\Phi_1 \ : \ \textit{Every player touched the ball.}$$

Under the new framework, the analysis of this utterance goes as follows. As before, the described situation, $s_{u_1}(\Phi_1)$, is the game, say g. Let S, T be the following object-types:

$$S = [\dot{p} \mid g \models \ll \text{player-in}, \dot{p}, g, 1 \gg]$$

$$T = [\dot{p} \mid g \models (\exists \dot{t}) \ll \text{touches}, \dot{p}, b, \dot{t}, 1 \gg]$$

where $\dot{p}$ is a parameter for a person, $\dot{t}$ is a parameter for a time prior to t_{u_1} and $b = c_{u_1}(\text{THE BALL})$. Then the propositional content of the utterance u_1 is:

$$g \models \ll \forall, g, S, T, 1 \gg$$

Notice that the use of the same parameter $\dot{p}$ in the two type-abstractions was in order to help the reader. In practice, since the abstraction parameter in a type-abstraction becomes 'absorbed', leaving solely an 'argument role', it does not matter which parameter is used in each abstraction. Rather, it is the nature of the relation $\forall$ that it links the argument roles of the two types.

Notice also that, in this particular example, there was no mention of a time or spatial location in the propositional content. The minimality conditions for quantification relations require that, in order to yield an infon, the arguments for the bounding set or situation and for the two types must be filled, but the time and place arguments need not be. Indeed, it is often the case that they are left unfilled.

One further remark that needs to be made at this juncture concerns the quantification of the time parameter $\dot{t}$ in the definition of the type T. This was done using the quantification mechanism for forming compound infons, rather than in terms of our new quantifier framework. This reflects the fact that an unarticulated quantification over time that arises by virtue of verb tense, is what might be called a 'structural' quantification. That is to say, verb tense mechanisms are part of the basic structure of language that our ontological framework is intended to handle: our ontology includes temporal locations and quantification over temporal locations in compound infons, and verb tense relates directly to this temporal aspect of our framework. Such implicit quantification is not at all the same as an articulated quantification, even one over time, such as an utterance u_1' of the sentence Φ_1':

Every player touched the ball many times.

In this case, the analysis would be as follows.

Let M be a 'many' quantifier. Let T_b be the type

$$T_b = [\dot{t} \mid g \models \ll \text{touch}, \dot{p}, b, \dot{t}, 1 \gg]$$

where $\dot{t}$ is a parameter for a time prior to $t_{u_1'}$ and $\dot{p}$ is a parameter for a person. T_b is the parametric type of all instances at which some person touches b $(= c_{u_1'}(\text{THE BALL}))$ during the course of the game g.

T_b is a parametric type with parameter $\dot{p}$, so we can form the type

$$T = [\dot{p} \mid g \models \ll M, g, TIM_1, T_b, 1 \gg]$$

the type of all persons for which there are many instances in g at which that person touches b. Then the propositional content of u_1' is:

$$g \models \ll \forall, g, S, T, 1 \gg$$

where S is as before.

Notice that the present framework allows for a quantifier such as 'for many' to be defined locally. In the case of the above example, the 'many' quantifier M could be specially tailored to ball games. This is, I believe, a strong argument in favor of treating quantification as a relation within the ontology, rather than as part of the underlying framework. Indeed, we may use our framework to *investigate* such quantifiers. This is one of the two arguments promised earlier in favor of the present approach to quantifiers. The other argument is connected with my earlier remarks concerning the treatment of implicit quantifiers such as the temporal quantifiers associated with verb tense. For instance, the framework chosen distinguishes between unarticulated temporal quantification resulting from verb tense and articulated temporal quantification, a distinction that I feel is important from the standpoint of the theory I am trying to develop.

The second of our two original examples is an utterance u_2 of

$$\Phi_2 : \textit{Every player ate a cookie.}$$

Let e be the described situation, $s_{u_2}(\Phi_2)$, whether this is the game g or some other situation. Let T_d be the type

$$T_d = [\dot{c} \mid e \models (\exists \dot{t}) \ll \text{eats}, \dot{p}, \dot{c}, \dot{t}, 1 \gg]$$

where $\dot{t}$ is a parameter for a time preceding t_{u_2}, $\dot{c}$ is a parameter for an edible individual, and $\dot{p}$ is a parameter for a person. Thus T_d is the type of all edible individuals that, in the situation e, are eaten at some time prior to t_{u_2} by some person. Noting that T_d is a parametric-type with parameter $\dot{p}$, let T_p be the type

$$T_p = [\dot{p} \mid e \models \ll \exists, e, T_c, T_d, 1 \gg]$$

where T_c is the type of a cookie. Thus T_p is the type of all those persons for which, in the situation e, there is a cookie eaten by that person at some time preceding t_{u_2}.

With S as before, the propositional content of u_2 is:

$$e \models \ll \forall, e, S, T_p, 1 \gg$$

The only question that remains to be answered is what is the described situation, e ? The naive answer is that e is simply the situation in which the cookies were eaten. But this does not work here, since the infon in the propositional content of the utterance involves the type S, which is an object-type with grounding situation g, and there is no reason to suppose that the situation in which the cookies were eaten supports an infon that concerns the game situation g. (If e and g coincide there is no problem. This is what happened with the previous example concerning the players touching the ball many times.) So we must look further for our answer.

In fact, the resolution to the problem involves a shift in the way we regard quantification, since the approach I have adopted provides us with a view of quantification that more traditional definitions do not. Given that quantification is essentially a relation (indeed, a quantitative comparison) between two types, the utterance of any sentence involving a quantifier must be *about* those two types, among other things. That is to say, the described situation must include those two types.

Thus in the present example, the described situation, e, must include both the game situation, g, and the situation in which the cookies are eaten, say h. Then what the utterance does is describe a relation between the two situations g and h, namely the quantitative comparison between the individuals in g that are players and the individuals in h that ate a cookie. In this case the fact that all individuals of the former type are of the latter type.

Notice that, although this was not the original aim, our investigation has led to an alternative conception of the nature of quantification: it is simply a particular kind of relation between types. Indeed, we can apply this to the 'traditional-style' quantifiers we allow in the formation of compound infons. Although our theory treats these quantifiers as logical operators on compound infons, we may apply our 'quantifiers-as-relations' conceptualization at a meta-theoretic level in order to regard these quantifiers as relations too.

It should be noticed that the new framework has not been achieved at the cost of our earlier freedom of choice of resource situations for the quantified objects. But the mechanism for handling (or reflecting) this freedom has shifted from the manner in which parameters function to the free choice we have in choosing the types that figure in quantifier infons. In particular, the grounding situations for the various types provide the necessary resource situations.

Thus our new framework explicitly incorporates the requisite background information source for each quantifier into the quantifier infon. Since all quantifications are necessarily made with reference, either explicit or implicit, to some domain, it seems right that our mathematics should reflect this fact. For although a particular utterance might not stipulate the various domains of quantification, the semantics should. This is not always the case with the more traditional accounts of quantification in logic, where it is often left to the context to determine the range of quantification.

Of course, so far all I have done is establish the framework and look at one or two simple examples. I have not investigated the structural and logical properties of the various quantifer-relations. But that is the stuff of 'applied situation theory', and the intention here is simply the setting up of the requisite machinery. However, the following section does have some bearing on the logical properties of quantification, and accordingly contains further examples of natural language quantification.

9.2   Negation

There are a number of ways that a sentence can involve negation. The most straightforward of these is verb phrase negation. This is easily handled in situation semantics by means of a polarity change and a possible quantifier switch. For example, let u_1 be an utterance of the sentence

$$\Phi_1 : \textit{John did not see Mary.}$$

Let e be the described situation, $e = s_{u_1}(\Phi_1)$. Then the propositional content of u is

$$e \models (\forall i) \ll \text{sees}, J, M, i, 0 \gg$$

where i is a parameter for a time prior to t_{u_1}, $J = c_{u_1}(\text{JOHN})$, and $M = c_{u_1}(\text{MARY})$.

There is, however, one question that needs to be answered. What is the described situation e ? In the case of an utterance of the positive sentence *'John saw Mary'* there is no problem. In the absence of any context that determined otherwise, the described situation will be the act of John seeing Mary, the situation in which the seeing takes place. In other words, for a positive utterance, in the absence of any other contextual features, the utterance itself determines the described situation. But for a negative utterance this is not the case. There will be a great many situations in which John did not see Mary. Just which one is the speaker referring to?

The answer is that it is up to the speaker to fix the described situation. At least, this is what the speaker's obligation amounts to in our theory's terms. In everyday language, what the speaker must do is ensure that the listener is aware just *what* the utterance is about. To make the utterance u_1 without having set the relevant context results in a failure to communicate. Uttered on its own, without there being either a predetermined described situation or else an obvious 'default' situation, the sentence Φ_1 does not convey information, at least not the information that would be captured by the propositional content. (Most obvious scenarios for such an utterance do in fact supply an obvious default described situation.)

Since there will be a great many situations in which John did not see Mary, in order for the utterance u_1 to convey the right information, the speaker must ensure that some aspect of the context of utterance determines the described situation e. The utterance should convey the same information, in the sense of propositional content, as an utterance of the 'sentence'

$$\sharp \; John \; did \; not \; see \; Mary \; in \; e$$

where the $\sharp$ indicates a sentence that is not part of normal English (in that one does not normally mention a situation).

The above remarks apply to a great many negative utterances. Of course, in the vast majority of cases the utterance of a positive sentence too is made with reference to a predetermined described situation. Speakers generally speak about some part of the world. Indeed, this is one of the main motivating factors behind situation theory.

Negated quantifiers are also handled quite easily. For example, let u_2 be an utterance of the sentence

$$\Phi_2 : Not \; every \; student \; passed \; the \; quiz.$$

Let $q = c_{u_2}(\text{QUIZ})$, let t_q be the time of taking the quiz q, and let e be the situation comprising the taking of the quiz.

Presumably the speaker is referring to some particular class, k, the class that took the quiz q. Let $c = Oracle(k)$. Let $\dot{p}$ be a parameter for a person, and let

$$S = [\dot{p} \mid c \models \ll \text{student-in}, \dot{p}, k, t_q, 1 \gg]$$

$$T = [\dot{p} \mid e \models \ll \text{passes}, \dot{p}, q, t_q, 1 \gg]$$

Then the propositional content of u_2 is:

$$d \models \ll \forall, k, S, T, 0 \gg$$

where d is the described situation.

Recalling the discussion of the previous section concerning quantifiers, note that the utterance states a relationship between the type of all students in k and the type of all persons who passed the quiz q, and accordingly the described situation d will extend both c, the grounding situation for type S, and e, the grounding situation for type T.

A seemingly more problematical form of negation is exemplified by an utterance, u_3, of the sentence

$$\Phi_3 : \textit{No sailors were there.}$$

Assuming u_3 is part of a discourse about a particular dinner party, say d, the natural assumption is that d is the described situation. In which case, how can a proposition of the form

$$d \models \sigma$$

have anything to say about sailors? There are no sailors at the party!

Clearly, it cannot. But a few moments reflection should indicate that this issue has nothing to do with negation. Consider an utterance, u_4, of the positive sentence

$$\Phi_4 : \textit{There is a sailor that was there.}$$

Though on this occasion a sailor will be a constituent of the party, it is unlikely that this situation will have anything to say about this particular person being a sailor, and so once again the propositional content cannot be of the form

$$d \models \sigma$$

So what has gone wrong?

The answer is that nothing is wrong, except for the assumption that d is the described situation for an utterance of Φ_3 or Φ_4. For both sentences involve quantifiers, and as I observed in the previous section, an utterance of a quantifier sentence states a relationship between two types, so the described situation must include the grounding situations of those two types.

Both u_3 and u_4 are about sailors: they describe a relation that connects the collection of all sailors and the dinner party d. The grounding situation for the type of all sailors is the world, or at least enough of the world to ground this type. So, if i is a parameter for a time preceding the utterance in each case, and if

$$S = [\dot{p} \mid w \models \ll\text{sailor}, \dot{p}, i, 1 \gg]$$

$$T = [\dot{p} \mid d \models \ll\text{present-in}, \dot{p}, d, i, 1 \gg]$$

then the propositional content of u_4 is

$$w \models (\exists i)\ll \exists, d, S, T, i, 1 \gg$$

and the propositional content of u_3 is

$$w \models (\forall i)\ll \exists, d, S, T, i, 0 \gg$$

(or possibly

$$w \models (\forall i)\ll \text{No}, d, S, T, i, 1 \gg$$

if the quantifier 'No' is regarded as a basic relation in the ontology).

Given our present conception of quantifiers then, even though u_3 or u_4 could be uttered as part of a discourse that until then had concerned the party situation exclusively, once the property of being a sailor is introduced, the so-called described situation is extended to include the grounding situation for being a sailor. Of course, you might object to my calling the resulting situation the *described situation* in this case, and look for another name. On the other hand, given a framework in which a quantifier is interpreted as a relation between two types, rather than some form of logical operator on the second of those types, which is the case in classical logic, then it really is the case that a quantifier utterance *describes* (some feature of) both those types (and hence their grounding situations in the case of object-types): indeed, it *compares* the two types.

It should be noted that the semantics assigned to u_4 is different from the semantics that would be assigned to an utterance u_4' (under the same circumstances and with reference to the same dinner party situation d) of the sentence:

A sailor was there.

In this case, the described situation is indeed the party, d, and the propositional content of the utterance is:

$$d \models \exists\dot{p}\exists i \ll\text{present-in}, \dot{p}, d, i, 1 \gg$$

where $\dot{p}$ is a parameter for a sailor and i is a parameter for a time prior to the time of utterance.

The distinction between u_4 and u_4' amounts to a difference in focus. Uttering the sentence

There is a sailor that was there

makes a definite claim *about the collection of sailors* (namely that at least one of them was at the party). On the other hand, uttering the sentence

> A sailor was there

makes a claim *about the party* (namely that among the guests there was at least one sailor).[3]

Of course, none of my examples involves a *negation* in the sense of classical logic, where negation is a logical operator that acts on well-formed formulas. Rather they are simply utterances of sentences that involve a negative component. As we have seen, this generally requires more emphasis on the specification of the described situation than is the case for utterances where there is no such negative component, but apart from that there was no real difference between positive and negative assertions as far as the above analysis was concerned.

Far more reminiscent of the negation operator of classical logic is sentence *denial*, where a positive assertive sentence is prefixed by a phrase such as 'It is not the case that ...' For example, let u_5 be an utterance of the sentence

$$\Phi_5 : \textit{It is not the case that John saw Mary.}$$

Much ink has been used in discussing examples such as this. Let me expend a bit more.

The starting point of most discussions is to take the phrase *'It is not the case that'* as determining a denial operator that acts on the sentence *'John saw Mary'*. But it seems to me that this is not the right way to proceed. Rather Φ_5 should be regarded as a negative version of the sentence

$$\Phi_6 : \textit{It is the case that John saw Mary.}$$

In both cases, let J be the referent for the name JOHN, M the referent for the name MARY, i a parameter for a time prior to the time of utterance. Let $e_5 = s_{u_5}(\Phi_5)$, $e_6 = s_{u_6}(\Phi_6)$.

The propositional content of u_6 is:

$$w \models \ll \models, e_6, (\exists i) \ll \text{sees}, J, M, i, 1 \gg, 1 \gg$$

That is to say, the effect of the prefix *'It is the case that'* in an utterance of a sentence *'It is the case that Φ'* is to make the propositional content of the sub-utterance of Φ the infon part of a proposition about the world.

---

[3] Though our mathematics makes a distinction between these two, ordinary linguistic practice is far less clear-cut, and it is possible to give either sentence either reading. And it is not at all clear which category should include the sentence *'There was a sailor there'*.

Turning now to u_5, the most natural choice of the propositional content would seem to be:

$$w \models \; \ll \models, e_5, (\exists t) \ll \text{sees}, J, M, t, 1 \gg, 0 \gg$$

where the polarity of the world proposition has changed from a 1 in the case of u_6 to a 0 in the case of u_5. Does this accord with our intuitions?

Unravelling the notation a bit, what this proposition says is that

(∗) $\qquad\qquad\qquad e_5 \not\models (\exists t) \ll \text{sees}, J, M, t, 1 \gg$

Now, as I remarked above, in order for a negative utterance to be informational (in the intended manner), the speaker should ensure that the described situation is adequately identified. That is to say, the speaker should make sure that the listener knows what the utterance is *about*. In the present case, e_5 is the John and Mary situation, or something extending it. Now, since John's seeing Mary is a relevant feature (the speaker talks about it), it ought to be the case that the situation e_5 that constitutes the described situation completely determines whether or not John actually did see Mary or not. That is to say, it should be the case that: either

$$e_5 \models (\exists t) \ll \text{sees}, J, M, t, 1 \gg$$

or else

$$e_5 \models (\forall t) \ll \text{sees}, J, M, t, 0 \gg$$

Assuming this is the case, then by (∗), the propositional content of u_5 should entail the second of these two propositions. This is what we would have expected.

Notice that the above places a restriction on the possible described situation for utterances involving denials. The requirement I have stipulated is considerably stronger than the universally true fact that for any situation s and any infon σ, either $s \models \sigma$ or else $s \not\models \sigma$. The argument I am making here is that a cooperative use of a negative utterance such as u_5 places on the speaker an obligation to ensure that the described situation as understood by the listener (i.e. *what* the listener thinks the utterance is *about*) is sufficiently rich to *decide* the relevant issue, in this case whether John saw Mary or not, one way or the other. A similar issue arises in the following discussion (and elsewhere), and will be addressed more fully at the end of Section 9.5.

A natural question to ask in connection with sentence denial is how it affects conjunctive and disjunctive sentences. The natural expectation is that there is some form of duality between the two, as occurs in classical logic. And indeed this is the case, given that certain requirements are met.

For example, imagine a discourse between Jan and Ed about last week's 49ers game, g, in which Jan makes the following utterance, u:

It is not the case that Joe threw the ball and Roger carried the ball.

This has a propositional content of the form

$$w \models \ll \models, g, \sigma, 0 \gg$$

where σ is the compound infon

$$(\exists i_1) \ll \text{throws}, J, b, i_1, 1 \gg \wedge (\exists i_2) \ll \text{carries}, R, b, i_2, 1 \gg$$

and where $J = c_u(\text{JOE})$, $R = c_u(\text{ROGER})$, and $b = c_u(\text{THE BALL})$.

Unravelling the notation a little, this says the following:

(*) $g \not\models (\exists i_1) \ll \text{throws}, J, b, i_1, 1 \gg \wedge (\exists i_2) \ll \text{carries}, R, b, i_2, 1 \gg$

Now, since g is the actual game, either

$$g \models (\exists i_1) \ll \text{throws}, J, b, i_1, 1 \gg$$

or else

$$g \models (\forall i_1) \ll \text{throws}, J, b, i_1, 0 \gg$$

and again either

$$g \models (\exists i_2) \ll \text{carries}, R, b, i_2, 1 \gg$$

or else

$$g \models (\forall i_2) \ll \text{carries}, R, b, i_2, 0 \gg$$

So by (*) it must be the case that at least one of

$$g \models (\forall i_1) \ll \text{throws}, J, b, i_1, 0 \gg$$

and

$$g \models (\forall i_2) \ll \text{carries}, R, b, i_2, 0 \gg$$

Hence

$$g \models (\forall i_1) \ll \text{throws}, J, b, i_1, 0 \gg \vee (\forall i_2) \ll \text{carries}, R, b, i_2, 0 \gg$$

Reverting back to infon notation, this becomes

$$w \models \ll \models, g, \bar{\sigma}, 1 \gg$$

where $\bar{\sigma}$ is the compound infon

$$(\forall i_1) \ll \text{throws}, J, b, i_1, 0 \gg \vee (\forall i_2) \ll \text{carries}, R, b, i_2, 0 \gg$$

In words:

It is the case that Joe did not throw the ball or Roger did not carry the ball.

Which seems right.

The above example is related to the following notion of *infon duality*, which is important in studies of compositionality.

The *dual*, $\bar{\sigma}$, of a compound infon, σ, is defined by recursion as follows. If σ is a basic infon of the form $\ll R, a_1, \ldots, a_n, i \gg$ then

$$\bar{\sigma} = \ll R, a_1, \ldots, a_n, 1 - i \gg$$

If $\sigma = \sigma_1 \wedge \sigma_2$, then $\bar{\sigma} = \overline{\sigma_1} \vee \overline{\sigma_2}$.

If $\sigma = \sigma_1 \vee \sigma_2$, then $\bar{\sigma} = \overline{\sigma_1} \wedge \overline{\sigma_2}$.

If $\sigma = (\forall \dot{x} \in u)\tau$, then $\bar{\sigma} = (\exists \dot{x} \in u)\bar{\tau}$.

If $\sigma = (\exists \dot{x} \in u)\tau$, then $\bar{\sigma} = (\forall \dot{x} \in u)\bar{\tau}$.

I shall say a situation e is *complete* relative to the compound infon σ if at least (and hence exactly) one of the propositions

$$e \models \sigma \quad , \quad e \models \bar{\sigma}$$

is valid.

A generalization of the above argument shows that if u is an utterance of a denial

It is not the case that Φ

and if the sub-utterance of the sentence Φ has the propositional content

$$e \models \sigma$$

and if e is complete relative to σ, then the propositional content of u is

$$w \models \ll \models, e, \bar{\sigma}, 1 \gg$$

which is 'equivalent' to

$$e \models \bar{\sigma}$$

The point I made earlier is that, for an utterance of a denial to be suitably informational, the speaker should ensure that the listener is sufficiently aware of the context. In our theory's terms, what this amounts to is that the described situation as understood by both speaker and listener should be complete relative to the requisite infon. See Section 9.5 for further discussion of the constraints placed upon the described situation by the conventions governing natural language communication.

9.3 Conditionals

Conditionals, or *if–then* statements, are the bedrock of rational argument and as such are central not only to such overtly 'logical' pursuits as mathematics, computer science, the sciences in general, philosophy, and the legal system, but to large parts of our everyday life. And yet for all their ubiquity, conditionals have resisted the attempts of generations of philosophers to understand just what the devil they *are* ? What exactly does a conditional say about the world? There is a great deal that can, and has been, said. I shall simply pursue the matter sufficiently to indicate the role that situation theory can play.

In our current terminology, the issue I shall investigate is this. If *u* is an utterance of a conditional of the form

$$If\ \Phi\ then\ \Psi$$

then what is the propositional content of *u* (and hence what is the meaning of the sentence uttered)?

I shall consider four examples that, though having some similarities, lead to quite different, but in many ways paradigmatic analyses:

(i)   *If it freezes, Ovett wears a hat.*
(ii)   *If it freezes, Ovett will not run.*
(iii) *If it freezes, Ovett will be cold.*
(iv)   *If it had frozen, Ovett would not have run.*

All four examples will be understood to refer to cross-country races and the British Olympic athlete Steve Ovett.

Sentence (i) appears first because its analysis turns out to be different from the others. Indeed, although all four sentences have an *if–then* form, an utterance of any of sentences (ii), (iii), or (iv) will refer to a specific, single event, a cross-country race in this case, whereas sentence (i) can only be used to refer to such events *in general*.

In fact, an utterance of sentence (i) does not express a *conditional* at all, but rather is a statement of the validity of a certain constraint, a general connection the obtains between all those events when it freezes and all those events when Ovett wears a hat. (Actually, there is a reading of sentence (ii) that also serves to express a general link. I shall not consider this alternative reading, and the analysis I present below will exclude this possibility. As always, my main concern is with utterances of sentences, and by concentrating on utterances I avoid alternative readings of sentences.)

The remaining three sentences all do express genuine conditionals of one form or another. Sentences (ii) and (iii) are syntactically similar. Each may be used to predict some form of link between two specific future events. Sentence (iv) is different in that a speaker would normally only utter sentence (iv) after the race in question had taken place, and moreover only if, counter to the antecedent of the utterance, it had in fact not frozen. Statements made with sentences such as (iv), where the antecedent is false, are known as *counterfactuals.* Non-counterfactual, predictive-type conditionals such as examples (ii) and (iii) are often referred to as *indicative* conditionals.

My treatment of sentence (i) is quite straightforward and I shall dispose of it right away. Let u_1 be an utterance of sentence (i), which I repeat here for convenience:

If it freezes, Ovett wears a hat.

Quite clearly, this does not refer to any particular pair of events. Rather the utterance states that there is a connection between two *types* of event, the type of race situation where it is freezing and the type of race situation where Ovett wears a hat. In other words, what u_1 does is state a certain constraint. I make this precise below.

Let

$$S = [\dot{e} \mid \dot{e} \models \ll\text{present-in}, SO, \dot{e}, \dot{i}_r, 1 \gg$$
$$\wedge \ll\text{registered-in}, SO, \dot{r}, \dot{i}_r, 1 \gg$$
$$\wedge \ll\text{freezing}, \dot{i}_r, 1 \gg]$$

$$T = [\dot{e} \mid \dot{e} \models \ll\text{wears-hat}, SO, \dot{i}_r, 1 \gg]$$

where $\dot{r}$ is a parameter for a race, $\dot{e}$ is a parameter for the situation surrounding $\dot{r}$ (that is to say, the race itself, the race organization, and the environment local to the race), $\dot{i}_r$ is a parameter for the time of $\dot{r}$, and $SO = c_{u_1}(\text{OVETT})$.

Then the propositional content of u_1 is

$$w \models (S \Rightarrow T)$$

or at least

$$d \models (S \Rightarrow T)$$

for a suitably large part of the world d (enough to include all the race situations involving Steve Ovett).

The remaining three examples all have in common the fact that they are used to refer to specific events. (At least, this is true in the case of their normal uses, the ones considered here.) Nevertheless they all exhibit quite distinctive features that make it difficult to come up with any kind of unified treatment that seems appropriate for all examples.

I shall in fact present two alternative treatments, both of which have some appeal as well as some shortcomings. Though I have a preference for the second of the two alternatives, I shall point out the appeal and the shortcomings of both and leave it to you to decide which you like best.

One approach to handling conditionals in logic is the material conditional. My first treatment of the semantics of sentences (ii) through (iv) develops a version of this approach within the framework of situation semantics. It should be pointed out that the treatment I give adopts an 'extreme' form of the 'material conditional' that expresses nothing more than the contingent prohibition of two particular eventualities. Other treatments of the conditional can be developed within the framework of situation theory that could also be described as a 'material conditional' — for example, taking the relationship to link *types* rather than specific propositions as I do below.

Let u_2 be an utterance of sentence (ii) :

If it freezes, Ovett will not run.

A situation-theoretic analysis of this utterance along the lines of the material conditional goes as follows.

The utterance u_2 refers to some particular circumstance, an upcoming race and how the weather will affect the participation of Ovett. The described situation, d, therefore, comprises the organization of the race and the meteorological environment local to the race.

Note that the race is not an existing situation, nor an event that has taken place in the past, but rather is some planned, future event: indeed an event that might eventually be cancelled, and not take place at all. Thus r has an objective existence purely as a result of the intentionality network of planning agents, *to whit* Man. But this does not prevent r being a perfectly well-defined situation in our ontology. People discuss future events all the time, and frequently plan their activities around future events.

What claim does the utterance make about the situation d ? It does not state some kind of constraint, as does an utterance of (i). Nor is there a constraint of which this is an instance, as is the case in example (iii), which I consider presently. There is no generally prevailing causal link between the local temperature and Ovett running or not running. Runners can, and do, run in freezing conditions, Ovett among them. The freezing conditions might well be the *reason* Ovett decides not to run on this particular occasion, but that is Ovett's personal decision. There is no general rule, no constraint as there was in example (i).

Rather what the utterance does is claim that a certain event will not occur, namely the event of it freezing and Ovett running in the race. That is to say, if we let r be the race, l_r the location of r, t_r the time of r, and

e the environment local to l_r, then the propositional content of u_2 is:

$$d \models \ll \text{precluded}, P \wedge Q, t_u, 1 \gg$$

where P is the proposition

$$e \models \ll \text{freezing}, l_r, t_r, 1 \gg$$

and Q is the proposition

$$r \models \ll \text{runs-in}, SO, r, t_r, 1 \gg$$

and where $SO = c_{u_2}(\text{OVETT})$.[4]

Turning now to sentence (iii), let u_3 be an utterance of :

If it freezes, Ovett will be cold.

Again I develop a situation-theoretic analysis analogous to the material conditional of classical logic.

In this case the utterance u_3 expresses an instance of a general *constraint*, the constraint that if it is freezing then a person will be cold. There is a definite, generally prevailing, causal link between the antecedent *'it freezes'* and the consequent *'Ovett will be cold'*. However, it is arguable (see momentarily) that although (ii) and (iii) differ as to the reason for the validity of the expressed conditional, this difference does not affect the meaning of the sentence, and the propositional content in the case of example (iii) will be just as in (ii). Thus, if d is the described situation and t_d is the requisite time (so $t_d = c_{u_3}(\text{WILL})$ and $t_{u_3} < t_d$), then the propositional content of the sub-utterance of *'it freezes'* is

$$d \models \ll \text{freezing}, t_d, 1 \gg$$

and the propositional content of the sub-utterance of *'Ovett will be cold'* is

$$d \models \ll \text{cold}, SO, t_d, 1 \gg$$

Then the propositional content of u_3 is

$$d \models \ll \text{precluded}, P \wedge Q, t_{u_2}, 1 \gg$$

where P is the proposition

$$d \models \ll \text{freezing}, t_d, 1 \gg$$

and Q is the proposition

$$d \models \ll \text{cold}, SO, t_d, 0 \gg$$

According to the above analysis then, the reason why the semantics of (iii)

---

[4] I regard the situation r as the entire race situation, which will include all runners registered for the race, regardless of whether they actually run on the day or not. Hence r is big enough to support Ovett running or not running the race.

works out the same as for (ii) is that, although the utterance of (iii) states an instance of a general constraint, it is not part of the utterance that it is such an instance. Rather the utterance asserts a simple conditional that expresses, as a matter of fact, that a particular pair of events cannot occur in conjunction. The distinction between (ii) and (iii) is part of the general background knowledge of the world that both the speaker and listener will be aware of. The constraint of which (iii) states a particular instance is not part of the propositional content of the utterance u_3, since the utterance makes no reference to the constraint.

So far then, a material-conditional style analysis seemed to work for examples (ii) and (iii). What about the final example? Let u_4 be an utterance of the sentence (iv):

If it had frozen, Ovett would not have run.

Presumably u_4 refers to a specific event, a past race r, run at a location l_r at a time t_r where $t_r < t_u$, in an environment e. The utterance refers to properties of each of the situations r and e, the property of it freezing in e and the property of Ovett running in r. This was also the case in example (ii). If we attempt an analysis using the material-conditional approach as in example (ii), we obtain the following propositional content for u_4:

$$d \models \ll \text{precluded}, P \wedge Q, t_u, 1 \gg$$

where P is the proposition

$$e \models \ll \text{freezing}, l_r, t_r, 1 \gg$$

and Q is the proposition

$$r \models \ll \text{runs-in}, SO, r, t_r, 1 \gg$$

and where d is the described situation.

But what is the described situation? In the case of example (ii), d comprised both r and e, that is to say, both the race and the (meteorological) environment local to the race. But this cannot be right in this case. Why? Well, the use of the subjunctive in (iv) is only appropriate if in fact

$$e \models \ll \text{freezing}, l_r, t_r, 0 \gg$$

and if this is the case and we take d to extend e, then our proposed propositional content is degenerate and essentially non-informational: it would be a valid proposition regardless of whether or not Ovett ran in the race.

This is, of course, why the material conditional fails so miserably to handle counterfactuals in classical logic. The material conditional renders a proposition

$$P \to Q$$

as true whenever P is false, and consequently is unable to handle counterfactuals, which by their very nature have a false antecedent.

But a situation-theoretic framework saves us from falling into this trap, and in a way that, I believe, squares with our everyday intuitions about counterfactuals. In making an utterance of (iv) with the sincere intention of conveying information, the speaker is not referring to the situation as it was, but to some hypothetical variant thereof, a variant that resembles the actual situation in almost every way except for differing as to the fact of it freezing or not.

In other words, the described situation d is not a part of the world extending the actual race-environment situation e. It is some abstract situation postulated by the speaker. If d_a denotes the actual race organization and environment local to the race, what was the described situation in example (ii), then d and d_a will have the same constituents and the same spatial and temporal extent, and for almost all infons σ it will be the case that

$$d \models \sigma \quad \text{if and only if} \quad d_a \models \sigma$$

but

$$d \models \ll \text{freezing}, l_r, t_r, 1 \gg \quad \text{and} \quad d_a \models \ll \text{freezing}, l_r, t_r, 0 \gg$$

What justification is there for allowing a situation such as d into the ontology? Well, almost as much as for allowing a great many other situations, it seems to me. People do indeed use conditionals such as the above all the time, and if you accept the two premises that (a) when two people are engaged in a successful exchange of information, they must be talking about *something*, and (b) we use situations to represent these 'somethings', then it follows that hypothetical entities such as the d above will figure as situations.

As a situation theorist (assuming you are one by now) you cannot object to premise (b) here, but you could object to (a). Not on the grounds that we cannot provide an adequate specification of d. As I have observed many times in this essay, there are very few situations at all that can be pinned down 'uniquely' in extensional terms. Usually, all that we have is partial information about a given situation, and the description of d given above (in terms of d_a) is little better or worse than the description of many other situations that arise in discourse analysis. Stipulating that d differs from d_a only in the *minimal* way stated is not at all precise, in that had the freezing/non-freezing property really gone the other way, then doubtless a great many other things would have turned out differently as well. But this does not leave us in a significantly worse position than when we are dealing with the actual situation d_a, about which there is also a great deal we do not know.

Rather the only grounds for objecting to d as a genuine situation are not informational ones but rather that situations should be *actual* parts of the world, be those parts real or abstract. In other words, there can be no counterfactual situations, period.

At this stage in the development of situation theory, opinion is still divided on the issue of whether or not hypothetical (though internally consistent) situations should be allowed in the theory. Though I tend to be in favor of hypothetical situations, thereby allowing a treatment of fiction as well as the above account of counterfactuals, in this book I have hitherto taken a completely agnostic line on the matter, and after this present discussion is over that will once again be my approach.

Of course, to anyone who takes a firm line against hypothetical situations, the above treatment of counterfactuals is not available, and some other approach must be found. One possibility is the one described next.[5]

To summarize the above account, suppose u is an utterance of a conditional sentence of the form

$$\textit{If } \Phi \textit{ then } \Psi$$

(or equivalent) and that

$$e_1 \models \sigma_1$$

is the propositional content of the sub-utterance of Φ and

$$e_2 \models \sigma_2$$

is the propositional content of the sub-utterance of Ψ. Then the propositional content of u is:

$$d \models \ll \text{precluded}, (e_1 \models \sigma_1) \wedge (e_2 \models \overline{\sigma_2}), t_u, 1 \gg$$

where $d = s_u(\text{IF } \Phi \text{ THEN } \Psi)$ is the described situation.

In the case of an indicative conditional, the described situation, d, will include both e_1 and e_2. In the case of a counterfactual, where in fact

$$e_1 \models \overline{\sigma_1}$$

then d will be a hypothetical situation that differs minimally from what actually occurred (i.e. from a situation including both e_1 and e_2) in that:

$$d \models \sigma_1$$

---

[5] As it happens, though I am happy enough to accept hypothetical situations, and find my first account of conditionals reasonable enough, I have an overall preference for the second approach.

My alternative approach to the semantics of conditionals is not only uniform across examples of forms (ii), (iii), and (iv), as was the case with the first treatment, but in fact includes example (i) as well, in that an utterance of *any 'if–then'* statement is taken to refer to a constraint (in one way or another).

I commence with sentence (iii). As before, u_3 is an utterance of the sentence

If it freezes, Ovett will be cold.

This utterance expresses an instance of the constraint that, if a person's environment is freezing, and that person is scantily clad (such as a runner), then that person will be cold. More precisely, let S and T be the situation-types

$$S = [\dot{e} \mid \dot{e} \models \ll \text{freezing}, \dot{t}, 1 \gg$$
$$\wedge \ll \text{present-in}, \dot{p}, \dot{e}, \dot{t}, 1 \gg$$
$$\wedge \ll \text{scantily-clad}, \dot{p}, \dot{t}, 1 \gg]$$

$$T = [\dot{e} \mid \dot{e} \models \ll \text{cold}, \dot{p}, \dot{t}, 1 \gg]$$

where $\dot{e}$ is a situation parameter, $\dot{t}$ is a temporal parameter, and $\dot{p}$ is a parameter for a person.

Then the described situation for u_3 is the world and the propositional content is:

$$w \models (S \Rightarrow T)[f]$$

where f anchors $\dot{p}$ to $SO = c_{u_3}(\text{OVETT})$.

Turing now to example (ii), let u_2 be an utterance of the sentence:

If it freezes, Ovett will not run.

As noted earlier, u_2 differs from u_3 in that it does not express an instance of a general constraint. And yet it does make a *prediction* of a future event. Assuming this prediction has an informational basis, and is not just a random guess, how can this be? Surely the only informational basis on which to make such a prediction is knowledge of some uniformity that systematically links the eventuality of it freezing and Ovett's deciding not to run; in other words, a constraint.

But what constraint? As observed earlier, runners can and do run in freezing conditions. Indeed, Ovett himself has run in freezing conditions, though as a matter of fact he prefers not to. Whether or not Ovett runs in the race referred to in the utterance u_2 is purely up to Ovett to *decide*. So where is the constraint?

The answer is to be found in the discussion of intention in Section 7.6. Human beings are *planning* creatures. They form plans or intentions as to their future courses of action. And part of this plan-formation process will involve establishing what we might call *personal constraints*, constraints that govern their own action in accordance with their own desires and intentions.

Thus, Ovett, having found as a result of past experience that running in freezing conditions is unpleasant, and indeed can lead to illness and injury, might well decide that in future he will not run if it is freezing. Or it may be even more specific than this. Maybe he has just recovered from a cold and decides that, as far as next Saturday's race is concerned, the one referred to in u_2, he will not run if it is freezing. Beyond next Saturday he forms no intentions either way as far as running in cold weather is concerned. But for this one occasion he forms a personal constraint that will guide his future actions. (It is this highly restrictive case that I shall consider.)

Knowing of this constraint, a speaker may then confidently utter sentence (ii). That is to say, it is the knowledge of the constraint that provides the speaker with an informational basis for the utterance. In effect, what the utterance of sentence (ii) conveys to the listener is that 'this guy Ovett has formed the intention that *if* it is freezing on the day of this particular race, *then* he will not run'. Indeed, we may adopt the position that it is precisely this constraint that provides the propositional content of u_2.

More precisely, let S and T be the situation-types

$$S = [\grave{e} \mid \grave{e} \models \ll\text{environment-of}, \grave{e}, r, t_r, 1 \gg$$
$$\wedge \ll\text{freezing}, l_r, t_r, 1 \gg]$$

$$T = [\grave{e} \mid \grave{e} \models \ll\text{run-in}, SO, r, l_r, t_r, 0 \gg]$$

where r is the race in question, l_r is its location, t_r is its time, and $\grave{e}$ is a situation parameter.

Taking the described situation, d, to be $Oracle(SO)$ at the time of the utterance (i.e. a time-slice of $Oracle(SO)$ at the temporal interval t_{u_2}) then the propositional content of u_2 is:

$$d \models (S \Rightarrow T)$$

At which point a not unnatural question would be: why does the same treatment not work in the case of sentence (iii)? Though in the case of (iii) there was a prevailing general constraint, the actual utterance only referred to an instance of that constraint involving Ovett. So why in case (iii) did I take the described situation to be the world, and the propositional content to be

$$w \models (S \Rightarrow T)[f]$$

where $(S \Rightarrow T)$ is a general constraint and f an anchor to Ovett? Why not particularize the constraint to Ovett in the first place, as in example (ii)?

The answer is this. In case (ii), the utterance has nothing to do with Ovett's state of mind, with his desires and his intentions. There is no personal constraint of this nature. For all the speaker or listener knows, Ovett has not given a thought to it being cold on race day and his getting cold then. Moreover, there is no reason to assume that the situation *Oracle(SO)* will support the general constraint that if it is freezing a person will get cold, or even that if it is freezing Ovett will get cold. Nevertheless, if it does freeze on race day, Ovett certainly will get cold. Not because of any plan of intention he has formed. Simply because there is a prevailing general constraint to the effect that scantily clad people get cold if the temperature falls below freezing. The propositional content of u_3 has a structure that accords with this observation.

In example (ii), on the other hand, there is no prevailing general constraint, only the personal constraint (or 'contingency plan') formulated by Ovett.

In neither case does the speaker explicitly mention the constraint. But, according to the present account, the constraint is nevertheless the *content* of the utterance: the propositional content captures what it is the speaker claims to be the case.

Finally, what about the counterfactual case, example (iv)? Let u_4 be an utterance of the sentence

If it had frozen, Ovett would not have run.

In view of the treatment of the previous example, the resolution of this problem should be fairly obvious now.

The grammatical structure of the sentence makes it clear that the utterance is made after the race has taken place, and that in fact it had not frozen. The speaker is describing the personal constraint Ovett had formed prior to the race. As it happens, the conditions that would have brought that constraint into play, and resulted in Ovett's not running, did not prevail — it did not freeze. But Ovett nevertheless *had formed* that constraint, and would have acted in accordance with it. This is what the utterance claims. Accordingly, the propositional content of the utterance is almost the same as in the previous case.

What distinguishes these two cases is the circumstances of utterance.

In example (ii), at the time of the utterance, the race has not yet taken place ($t_u \prec t_r$) and the utterance describes a constraint that prevails at the time of utterance; in example (iv), the race has already taken place ($t_r \prec t_u$) and moreover it did not freeze, and the utterance describes a constraint that prevailed at the time of the race. Thus with the types S and T as before, the propositional content of u_4 is

$$d \models (S \Rightarrow T)$$

where in this case the described situation, d, is $Oracle(SO)$ *at the time of the race*.

I finish this section by examining a famous pair of examples due to Quine [20]. The traditional question is what is the status of the following two sentences?

(1) *If Bizet and Verdi had been compatriots, Bizet would have been Italian.*

(2) *If Bizet and Verdi had been compatriots, Verdi would have been French.*

A lot of the considerable discussion generated by these examples has concentrated on their counterfactual nature. But surely similar problems arise if we consider the following two indicative sentences involving the contemporary American mathematician Jon Barwise and the British linguist Robin Cooper:

(3) *If Barwise and Cooper are compatriots, then Barwise is English.*

(4) *If Barwise and Cooper are compatriots, then Cooper is American.*

I investigate both pairs of sentences first using the material conditional framework and then in terms of the constraint-based approach. The conclusion I shall draw is that the material conditional works moderately well in the case of sentences (1) and (2), but fails hopelessly when presented with (3) and (4), whereas the treatment in terms of constraints handles both pairs with ease. Indeed, my examination of these examples provides strong evidence to suggest that the constraint-based approach is the right way to handle conditionals, be they counterfactual or indicative.

Of course, unlike many of the discussions that have taken place concerning sentences (1) and (2), my approach will be in terms of utterances of these sentences. So, starting with the material conditional treatment of the first pair of sentences, let u_1 be an utterance of sentence (1). Let $B = c_{u_1}(\text{BIZET})$, $V = c_{u_1}(\text{VERDI})$, and let t be the time to which the utterance implicitly refers, i.e. the time when both Bizet and Verdi were alive. Let d denote the described situation.

According to the framework developed above, the propositional content works out to be:

(i) $\qquad d \models \ll \text{precluded}, P \wedge Q, t_{u_1}, 1 \gg$

where P is the proposition

(ii) $\qquad d \models \ll \text{compatriots}, B, V, t, 1 \gg$

and Q is the proposition

(iii) $\qquad d \models \ll \text{Italian}, B, t, 0 \gg$

and where d differs from reality, d_a, in a minimal fashion such that (ii) is valid.

Now,

(iv) $\qquad d_a \models \ll \text{Italian}, V, t, 1 \gg$

and

(v) $\qquad d_a \models \ll \text{French}, B, t, 1 \gg$

So if d is to differ from d_a minimally it must, by (i), be the case that

(vi) $\qquad d \models \ll \text{Italian}, V, t, 1 \gg$

and

(vii) $\qquad d \models \ll \text{Italian}, B, t, 1 \gg$

Thus in this case d is a hypothetical situation in which both Bizet and Verdi are Italian.

Starting with an utterance u_2 of sentence (2) we likewise end up with a hypothetical situation d' such that

(viii) $\qquad d' \models \ll \text{French}, V, t, 1 \gg$

and

(ix) $\qquad d' \models \ll \text{French}, B, t, 1 \gg$

These are the only possible outcomes if the described situation is to differ *minimally* from reality.

Is this a reasonable account? My own view is that, although it does provide a consistent semantics of utterances of sentences (1) and (2), it is not particularly convincing, and I find the alternative, constraint-based treatment, to be given presently, preferable in this case. But still, it is a solution.

On the other hand, as far as the second pair of examples is concerned, utterances of sentences (3) and (4), the material conditional approach simply does not get off the ground. An utterance of either (3) or (4) certainly does not postulate a hypothetical, alternative world the way that the subjunctive in (1) and (2) does. Rather the described situation must be (part of) the real world. But then the falsity of the antecedent renders the entire semantics degenerate.

Ultimately, it is this example, and others like it, that persuade me to

opt for the second of my two treatments, the one in which conditionals
are taken to refer to constraints, even though the material conditional
does, it seems to me, provide a good semantics for the future-directed,
predictive type of indicative conditional and an acceptable, if not wholly
convincing, semantics for counterfactuals.

The constraint-based semantics for conditionals provides a uniform
treatment for all four sentences, as well as clarifying the issues involved
in these examples.

An utterance of any one of the four sentences refers to a generally
prevailing constraint of the form:

> *If person A and person B are compatriots and person A has
> nationality N, then person B has nationality N.*

for some nationality N.

Let u_1 be an utterance of sentence (1), and let B, V, t denote Bizet,
Verdi, and the time they were both alive, as before. Let $\dot{a}, \dot{b}$ be parameters
for people, and let S_1, T_1 be the situation-types

$$S_1 = [\dot{e} \mid \dot{e} \models \ll\text{compatriots}, \dot{a}, \dot{b}, \dot{t}, 1 \gg \wedge \ll\text{Italian}, \dot{a}, \dot{t}, 1 \gg]$$
$$T_1 = [\dot{e} \mid \dot{e} \models \ll\text{Italian}, \dot{b}, \dot{t}, 1 \gg]$$

Then the described situation for u_1 is the world and the propositional
content of u_1 is:

$$w \models (S_1 \Rightarrow T_1)[f]$$

where $f(\dot{a}) = V, f(\dot{b}) = B$.

Similarly, the propositional content of an utterance, u_2, of sentence (2)
is:

$$w \models (S_2 \Rightarrow T_2)[f]$$

where

$$S_2 = [\dot{e} \mid \dot{e} \models \ll\text{compatriots}, \dot{a}, \dot{b}, \dot{t}, 1 \gg \wedge \ll\text{French}, \dot{b}, \dot{t}, 1 \gg]$$
$$T_2 = [\dot{e} \mid \dot{e} \models \ll\text{French}, \dot{a}, \dot{t}, 1 \gg]$$

and where f is as before.

Notice that this semantics for utterances u_1 and u_2 resolves the confusion that can arise between (1) and (2). Given the constraint that
figures in its propositional content, an utterance of sentence (1) will be
appropriate — that is to say it will be informational — if the listener
and speaker know that Verdi was Italian. Then the utterance makes a
valid assertion that describes this particular instance of that constraint.
Likewise, an utterance of u_2 will be appropriate given the knowledge that
Bizet was French.

Of course, an anchor, f, that assigns Verdi to the parameter $\dot{a}$ and

Bizet to the parameter b is not possible for any situation that includes both of these individuals and is of type S_1, so there can be no actual situation to which the constraint

$$(S_1 \Rightarrow T_1)[f]$$

applies.

If you accept the existence of hypothetical situations, then this is not an obstacle. Since the constraint is reflexive, it simply guarantees that in any hypothetical situation e in which Bizet and Verdi are compatriots and Verdi is Italian, then Bizet is Italian.

However, even if you reject hypothetical situations, the propositional content is still informational, in that it describes a valid constraint: the constraint itself is not invalid, it is just that it does not apply to the pair Bizet, Verdi.

Similar remarks apply in the case of the second sentence.

Turning now to the pair (3), (4), all I need to do now is observe that the above analysis works equally well in this case. Indeed, the temporal location plays no external role in the above discussion, and hence there is no distinction between the first pair and the second as far as our analysis is concerned. It applies equally to sentences that refer to past events and sentences that apply to the present, and indeed to sentences that refer to the future. I leave it to the reader to supply the details.

9.4   Speaker's intentions

Hitherto, my study of linguistic acts has concentrated on the mechanism by which a particular kind of signal, usually a word, phrase, or sentence of natural language, carries information. I suggested that the signal alone — that is to say, just a symbol structure — cannot contain information. Rather information is relative to constraints, and it is only *relative to a constraint* that a particular signal carries information.

The paradigm for this study has been an utterance by a single speaker, to a single listener, of a word, phrase, or sentence. The circumstances of the utterance, what I call the utterance *situation*, determines a great many features that contribute to the information conveyed by the signal. In the case of an utterance of an assertive or expressive sentence, the information conveyed is captured by the propositional content. In other cases — directives, commisives, declarators — the impact plays the more central role.

In all cases, a fundamental assumption has been that the speaker intends, in the case of assertives or expressives, to convey the information captured by the propositional content, or, for other types of utterance, to produce the action by the listener represented in the impact. But this need not be the case. Speakers can lie or otherwise intentionally mislead. Or they can rely on the embedding circumstances and the shared background knowledge of the speaker and the listener to convey information quite different from what would normally be the case.

For example, Nancy might say to John

It's cold in here

with the intention not of conveying to John the information (captured by the propositional content) that it is cold — which he presumably knows already — but of getting him to go close the door.

Or again, when a parent says to a child who has fallen and cut her arm

Does it hurt?

this is not meant as a question — obviously it hurts — but as a token of sympathy and comfort.

In order to account for these aspects of language use, I introduce the notion of the *speaker's intentions*. Thus, my analysis of natural (or for that matter artificial) languages is in terms of three features: propositional content, impact, and speaker's intentions.[6]

Let u be an utterance of a sentence Φ. The *speaker's intentions* associated with u is a set, $\mathscr{W}(u)$, of propositions that constitute what it is the speaker intends to be the result of the utterance.

Thus, in the case where Φ is an assertive sentence, where the speaker (a_u) has the straightforward intention of conveying to the listener (b_u) the information comprising the propositional content, p, of u, $\mathscr{W}(u)$ contains the proposition

$$e \models \ll \text{has-information}, b_u, p, t_u^+, 1 \gg$$

where e is the embedding situation (extending u), t_u is the time of the utterance, and t_u^+ is the appropriate time after t_u, as discussed in Section 8.4. (Section 8.4 also discusses the reasons for using the notion of *having information* here, rather than referring to the listener's belief.)

In the case where the speaker intends to tell a downright lie, on the other hand, $\mathscr{W}(u)$ will contain the proposition

---

[6] Actually, it is not my present purpose to carry out an analysis of natural language. Rather I am trying to establish a mathematical framework that will enable others to carry out such an analysis.

$$e \models \ll \text{believes}, b_u, \bar{p}, t_u^+, 1 \gg$$

where, $\bar{p}$ is the proposition *dual* to p, defined by: if p is the proposition $s \models \sigma$, $\bar{p}$ is the proposition $s \models \bar{\sigma}$. In this case, on the assumption that the speaker has the information that p, the intention is indeed that the listener comes to *believe* that $\bar{p}$, and not that the listener has the information that $\bar{p}$. Indeed, if $\bar{p}$ is false, there can be no question of anyone having the information that $\bar{p}$.

What about the example above where Nancy utters to John the sentence

It's cold in here

with the intention that John gets up and closes the door? Then $\mathscr{W}(u)$ will contain the proposition

$$e \models \ll \text{closes}, b_u, D, t_u^+, 1 \gg$$

where D is the door.

Notice that there is no reference to a door in Nancy's utterance. So what I have been referring to as the speaker's connections in my account will not yield the value D. Rather the door is provided by Nancy's intention — she wants John to close *that* door. It is up to Nancy to ensure that the circumstances are such that her utterance both determines the door and conveys her desire that John close it. How she does that is beyond the scope of a study such as this. I am simply providing a mechanism that *reflects*, somewhat crudely, this sophisticated use of language.

An utterance u is said to be *successful* if

$$(e \models \sigma) \in \mathscr{W}(u) \quad \text{implies} \quad \sigma \in \mathscr{I}(u)$$

that is, if all the speaker's intentions are realized, in which case they will become part of the impact of the utterance. A successful utterance is, under normal circumstances, the speaker's goal.

The notion of the speaker's intentions associated with a normal utterance of an assertive has already been considered. I consider briefly each of the other forms of utterance in the Searle classification, introduced in Section 8.2 and discussed in Section 8.5.

If u is a directive 'Do $\mathscr{K}$', and if the speaker really intends that the listener forms the intention to do $\mathscr{K}$, then $\mathscr{W}(u)$ contains the proposition

$$e \models \ll \text{of-type}, b_u, I(\mathscr{K}), t_u^+, 1 \gg$$

where $I(\mathscr{K})$ is the object-type of having an intention to do $\mathscr{K}$.

In the case of a faithful utterance of a commisive 'I will $\mathscr{K}$', the proposition

$$e \models \ll \text{of-type}, a_u, I(\mathcal{K}), t_u^+, 1 \gg$$

will be a member of $\mathcal{W}(u)$, where again $I(\mathcal{K})$ is the object-type of having an intention to perform the action $\mathcal{K}$.

For an utterance of an expressive 'I am Π', $\mathcal{W}(u)$ will contain the proposition

$$e \models \ll \text{of-type}, a_u, B(\Pi), t_u^+, 1 \gg$$

where $B(\Pi)$ denotes the object-type of being in the psychological state Π.

Finally, for a sincere (and authorized, if necessary) utterance of a declarator 'I declare $\mathcal{K}$', $\mathcal{W}(u)$ contains the proposition

$$e \models \ll T(\mathcal{K}), t_u^+, 1 \gg$$

where $T(\mathcal{K})$ expresses the fact that the world is as the utterance declares it to be. (See Section 8.5 for an example.)

In each of the above cases, if the utterance is intended to mislead, then $\mathcal{W}(u)$ contains the dual of the stated proposition.

So far I have considered two instances where the speaker's intentions are relevant: the distinction between truthful or faithful utterances and those intended to mislead; and the *ad hoc* 'It's cold in here' type of example where language is used in a manner orthogonal to the normal information content of the utterance. Other occasions where the speaker's intentions figure in a linguistic analysis are when language is used to evoke fear, pity, amusement, rage, or whatever, on the part of the listener. How to handle these within our present framework is fairly obvious, but of little relevance to the overall theme of this book, at least given my present level of treatment, so I shall not pursue the matter.

More significant to the rest of the book is the use of the speaker's intentions to capture distinctions that are essentially a matter of emphasis of one kind or another.

For example, the speaker's intentions capture the difference between the connectives *and* and *but*. Let u be an utterance of the sentence

$$\Phi \text{ AND } \Psi$$

and let v be an utterance of

$$\Phi \text{ BUT } \Psi$$

Let u_Φ be the sub-utterance of u in which Φ is uttered and u_Ψ the sub-utterance in which Ψ is uttered, and similarly for v_Φ, v_Ψ. Then, assuming a faithful utterance in each case, $\mathcal{W}(u)$ contains the proposition

$$e_u \models \ll \text{has-information}, b_u, p_u, t_u^+, 1 \gg$$

and $\mathcal{W}(v)$ contains the proposition

$$e_v \models \ll \text{has-information}, b_v, p_v, t_v^+, 1 \gg$$

where e_u, e_v are the embedding situations for u, v and p_u, p_v are their propositional contents, respectively.

The distinction between the two utterances is that $\mathcal{W}(v)$ contains the additional proposition

$$e_v \models \ll \text{contrasts}, b_u, p_{v_\Phi}, p_{v_\Psi}, t_v^+, 1 \gg$$

where p_{v_Φ} is the propositional content of v_Φ and p_{v_Ψ} is the propositional content of v_Ψ, whereas $\mathcal{W}(u)$ contains no such additional proposition.

That is to say, the speaker's intention is both to assert the joint truth of (the propositions expressed by) both Φ and Ψ, and to draw the listener's attention to the contrast between these two propositions.

9.5 Paradox and ambiguity

By and large, in the development presented in this account, my tendency has been to concentrate on the 'center region' of language use and ignore the outer fringes. Given the goal of trying to develop a mathematical framework that is able to handle more features of communication and information than can classical logic or variants thereof, it seemed sensible to adopt the criterion that what mattered was to be able to cope with the majority of everyday, run-of-the-mill examples, and ignore special cases or ingeneous counterexamples. Not that it is not important to examine all the extremal cases. Indeed, it can be crucial. But everything in its time. At the moment the priority is to get something on the table that works tolerably well, and then worry about all the niggling issues around the edges. If I am lucky, some relatively minor tinkering will make those niggling issues go away. Of course, if I am unlucky, I might discover that today's niggling fringe issue is tomorrow's major obstacle. But why not leave that until tomorrow? By then we shall have had time to develop the theory and our intuitions to a point where we might be able to overcome the obstacle.

For example, Zermelo's intuitions about Cantor's original set theory were sufficiently well developed for him to be able to develop the cumulative framework for sets, and ultimately the axiomatization of set theory, that avoids the Russell paradox.

Still, it pays not to be too cavalier about this kind of thing. If there are issues that have proved major stumbling blocks on other occasions, it would be prudent, to say the least, to examine their manifestation in the new theory being developed. It might turn out that they are no longer an issue, that features of the new theory serve to nullify their earlier potency. Or such an examination could lead to useful pointers as to how to tailor the theory to avoid trouble later.

In short, it is sensible to look at 'extreme cases' from time to time, but not to become a slave to them and attempt to dot every 'i' and cross every 't' while the game is still in progress.

This is the attitude I adopt with regards to the famous semantic paradoxes, the Liar, Russell's barber, and so forth. Since the theory is not *aimed* at being able to cope with such examples, it will not matter too much if they turn out to be beyond its capabilities. It would be nice if they could be handled, and it would be worth making minor changes to accommodate their resolution. But a perfectly reasonable response to their proving intractable would be "Okay, so the theory does not handle such cases. We must be careful not to try to apply it to them."

This is pretty well the attitude of present day set theorists to proper classes. Even within the purely set-theoretic domain of Zermelo–Fraenkel set theory, proper classes are used regularly. Paradox is avoided by the simple device of avoiding the troublesome areas, such as never considering the property of one proper class being a member of another.[7]

With the above caveats out on the table now, I first investigate how our framework deals with the famous semantic paradox, the Liar. This is most often given as a query for the truth or falsity of the sentence:

(1)   *This sentence is false.*

In this form, the problem does not arise for us. In our present framework, sentences are not 'bearers of truth'. That is to say, sentences are not the kinds of object that are either true or false. Rather they are objects that can be *used* to convey information. Thus sentence (1) just has no meaning: a sentence is not an appropriate argument for the property 'true/false'.

Indeed, our theory has had little to do with sentences in isolation. Our dealings with sentences have always been in terms of *utterances* thereof. So we could modify the question to the truth or falsity of an utterance of the sentence:

(2)   *This utterance is false.*

But again there is no paradox: this sentence too has no meaning. As

---

[7] Given my background as a set theorist, together with my overall scientific approach to the present enterprise, this should explain the views just expressed, which are quite opposed to those of many workers in philosophy and logic.

with sentences, utterances are not the kinds of things that are true or false, though we are getting closer to what is for us the real issue. For an utterance of an assertive sentence will determine a *proposition*, and in our framework it is the *propositions* that are the bearers of truth.

Thus the correct formulation of the Liar paradox in our framework is in terms of an utterance, u, of the sentence:

(3)   *The proposition expressed by this utterance is false*

or, more simply but a tad less precise, an utterance of the sentence

(Φ)   *This proposition is false.*

Let s be the described situation, $s = s_u(\Phi)$. Then, taking the basic property here to be *'true'*, with *'false'* being identified with *'not true'*, the propositional content, p, of u is:

$$s \models \ll \text{true}, p, 0 \gg$$

Notice that p is itself the proposition referred to by the phrase THIS PROPOSITION in the utterance, that is:

$$p = c_u(\text{THIS PROPOSITION})$$

The utterance claims that p is false. In other words, p claims that p is false. Which is starting to look like a paradox, but let's take the investigation just a little bit further before we start to panic.

We need to make sure we know exactly what is meant by 'false' here. Since we are taking *'false'* to mean *'not true'*, this amounts to clarifying what we mean by 'truth' in our theory.

In our situation-theoretic framework, every proposition

$$e \models \sigma$$

is either *true* or *false* (i.e. *not true*). Truth means that e does indeed support σ, which is a strong condition to place on the situation s. Falsity, on the other hand, means simply that s fails to support σ, which is fairly weak — unlike the proposition $e \models \bar{\sigma}$, which is strong, but in general quite different. This is the notion of truth and falsity that I have been working with throughout. Let's examine the proposition p above with this notion firmly in mind.

Suppose first that p is true. Thus

$$s \models \ll \text{true}, p, 0 \gg$$

is a valid proposition. Then, by persistence,

$$w \models \ll \text{true}, p, 0 \gg$$

is a valid proposition. In other words, p is false. This is a contradiction.

Hence p must be false. In other words,

$$s \not\models \ll \text{true}, p, 0 \gg$$

But so what? All this says is that the situation s does not support the infon

$$\ll \text{true}, p, 0 \gg$$

Now since p is false, we certainly have

$$w \models \ll \text{true}, p, 0 \gg$$

but again, so what? This is not necessarily paradoxical unless $s = w$. So what our investigation amounts to is a proof not of a paradox but a straightforward theorem:

Theorem 1: $s_u(\Phi) \neq w$

In words, the described situation in an utterance of the Liar sentence Φ cannot be the world.

Moreover, since we have shown that p is false, we have also established another theorem:

Theorem 2: Any utterance of the Liar sentence Φ expresses a false proposition.

In short, the Liar paradox has been resolved. Or has it? Can't we simply re-introduce the paradox by modifying Φ to read:

(Φ')   *This proposition is false in the world*

Surely in this case the described situation, $s_u(\Phi')$, will have to be $w = c_u(\text{THE WORLD})$, won't it?

In fact it will not. Indeed, analogs of Theorems 1 and 2 go through for the modified sentence Φ', so the same argument as before shows that w cannot be the described situation.

Like it or not, the conclusion then has to be that w is *not* a situation. And so we have a third theorem:

Theorem 3: w is not a situation.

This is analogous to the result in set theory that the class of all sets is not a set. But notice that this does not prevent set-theorists from discussing the so-called *universe* of sets, V, all the time, and generally treating it as if it were a set, even to the point of constructing 'extensions' of V. The trick is simply to develop enough sophistication to do this with safety.

Similarly, in situation theory we have been handling *the world* much as if it were a situation, and we shall continue to do so. We just have to bear in mind that it is not in fact a situation, and make sure we do not use it inappropriately.

Fortunately, all the references to w in this book so far, including the one used in the argument that led to Theorem 1, are technically valid. But what does this mean intuitively? Given that the principal aim of the entire situation-theoretic enterprise is to provide a sound and intuitively acceptable framework for a theory of information and communication, this question cannot be ignored.

Well, if you look at all previous references to 'the world', you will notice that it was never necessary to include absolutely everything. All uses of the *situation w* simply required that the situation concerned was big enough to include everything of relevance. And indeed it is implicit in the basic premises that underpin situation theory that this is never literally *everything*.

For remember that our entire ontology is determined by the individuation capacities and the behavior of one or more particular agent or species of agent, and since no agent can individuate *everything* or behave in a manner that involves *everything*, it seems quite obvious that our ontology cannot have need for a truly all-encompassing 'world' situation, even if we as theorists might like to have such available for convenience. Rather what we need will be 'local worlds', objects (situations) that encompass everything of relevance to the activities of a particular agent or species of agent. Such situations might even have as spatial extent the entire physical universe and duration the entire time-span of the universe, and hence include all physical matter, but they will never include *everything* there is, all the facts, causalities, and what-have-you. (Recall the remarks I made concerning *sets of issues* in the discussion of oracles in Section 3.5.)

In view of the above comments, the previous investigation does, it seems, dispose of the 'paradox' associated with the Liar sentence. What else does it tell us about the notion of truth that we are working with?

Let's look back at the key step in avoiding the paradox. We had established that p was false, and hence that

$$w \models \ll \text{true}, p, 0 \gg$$

and

$$s \not\models \ll \text{true}, p, 0 \gg$$

Now in the discussion of negation in Section 9.2 I said that there was an obligation on the part of the speaker to ensure that the listener was sufficiently aware of the described situation, and that this described situation should be adequate for the determination of the truth or falsity of the utterance. In particular, I suggested that if an infon σ was a constituent of the propositional content of an utterance whose described situation was e, then either $e \models \sigma$ or else $e \models \bar{\sigma}$. In the present case, this would clearly imply that either

$$s \models \ll \text{true}, p, 1 \gg \quad \text{or else} \quad s \models \ll \text{true}, p, 0 \gg$$

This leads at once to the conclusion that

$$s \models \ll \text{true}, p, 0 \gg$$

But this is just the proposition p. Hence p is true and we have a contradiction, and the paradox has re-emerged.

So what has gone wrong? The answer is nothing, except for our regarding a generally useful *convention* as a universally valid *rule*.

Natural language is a highly structured and rich device by which individuals can communicate with each other. In particular, it allows for considerable exploitation of contextual factors to load simple symbol structures with large amounts of information. The reliance on context in a communicative act places on the speaker a considerable obligation to ensure that the listener is aware of the relevant features of that context. Otherwise communication fails. This is what Austin calls the *demonstrative conventions* of language use, and is a feature of what Grice refers to as *cooperative communication*. In terms of our theory, what this amounts to is the fact that the speaker should ensure that the listener is aware both of the described situation and the various speaker's connections, and moreover that the described situation in particular is adequate to support what is being said.

None of this is a *rule*, notice; just a set of conventions to ensure that efficient communication may take place. Here, as in most other situations in life, a slavish adherence to the conventions — elevating them to the status of rules that have to be followed to the letter — will likely lead to absurdity or error.

What the above discussion of the Liar shows is that adherence to the normal conventions of communicative acts is not compatible with an utterance of the Liar sentence. That is to say, an utterance of the Liar sentence made in accordance with the normal conventions will not produce a meaningful proposition. This is not a paradox, just a reminder that natural language consists of a huge balancing act with enormous degrees of freedom.

Of course, our formal 'resolution' of the Liar paradox shows that our mathematical *formalism* is not contradictory, which is obviously important. Thus we can continue to use that formalism. But we have to ackowledge that there must be considerable slack in the conventions that govern the communicative acts that we study using that formalism. Mistakes can and do occur in attempts to communicate, for all sorts of reasons. Nothing we do can prevent that. But we can at least continue to develop tools to investigate not only the mechanisms of information transfer but also the causes of such breakdowns.

Turning to another example now, let u be an utterance by Bertrand Russell of the sentence

(4) *The barber shaves all and only those who do not shave themselves.*

I shall adopt the usual convention concerning this example, that the barber in question is male. Assuming that the utterance u expresses a true proposition, the question now is who shaves the barber? Classically this leads to a paradox. What results in our case?

The utterance expresses a proposition involving a universal quantifier, and the propositional content will be of the form

$$(*) \qquad e \models \ll \forall, v, S, T, 1 \gg$$

where v is the set of all those individuals referred to in the utterance, S is the type of those individuals that do not shave themselves, T is the type of those individuals that are shaved by the barber, and e is the described situation.

I shall flesh this out a little more, taking care not to make any unwarranted assumptions.

In making the utterance, the speaker is clearly referring to some particular community, say a village, v. Then the individual $b = c_u(\text{THE BARBER})$ is the village barber for v. Let

$$s = Oracle(b)$$

Then the type of all people shaved by b is:

$$T = [\dot{p} \mid s \models \ll\text{shaves}, b, \dot{p}, 1 \gg]$$

where $\dot{p}$ is a parameter for an adult male person.

The type of all people in v who do not shave themselves is:

$$S = [\dot{p} \mid v \models \ll\text{shaves}, \dot{p}, \dot{p}, 0 \gg]$$

The described situation, e, must extend the grounding situations of both types T and S, that is to say e must extend both s and v.

Now we are in a position to ask ourselves what conclusions may be drawn from the proposition $(*)$, and in particular does this lead to the classical paradox of the barber both shaving himself and not shaving himself?

Well, to obtain this paradox, it would be necessary for the individual b to be of type S, and this requires b to be a member of v. But there is no reason to assume that this is the case. Indeed, the straightforward conclusion to be drawn from the facticity of the proposition (∗) is that b is not a member of v. That is to say, the barber does not live in the village.

Of course, this resolution of the problem is hardly new. But it does fall quite naturally out of our framework, and in this sense confirms the adequacy of the choice of features we made with which to carry out our study.

And as far as I know, the present framework is adequate to resolve all of the other classical semantic paradoxes as well. But that would take us too far from our path. For a more complete account of this issue I refer the reader to Barwise and Etchemendy's excellent little book [4], where the above resolution of the Liar paradox first appeared (in a slightly different form).

The discussions of demonstrative conventions above lead naturally to the issue of ambiguity in natural language, which I take up next.

Given my standard scenario of an utterance u of a sentence Φ by a speaker a_u to a single listener b_u at a time t_u and location l_u, there are a number of ways that communication can go wrong, and in particular several forms of ambiguity that can result in a failure to communicate.

I shall restrict my attention to the case of an assertive sentence Φ, where the speaker is referring to a described situation $s = s_u(\Phi)$, and where the speaker's intention is to communicate to the listener the information about s captured by propositional content of u:

$$s \models \sigma$$

One failure arises if the listener is not able to identify correctly the described situation s. For example, the assertion "I waited by the edge" made in connection with a visit to the local swimming pool has quite different meanings depending on whether the described situation has the speaker in the water or outside the pool. In either case the speaker's connections will correctly associate with the phrase THE EDGE, the edge of the swimming pool, say k, and the propositional content will be of the form

$$s \models (\exists i) \ll \text{waits}, a_u, l_k, i, 1 \gg$$

where l_k is the location of k and i is a parameter for a time period prior to t_u. But if the speaker fails to communicate to the listener just what the situation s is here, the in-the-pool situation or the outside-the-pool situation, then there will be a communication breakdown, even though the listener might have correctly identified every other feature in the propositional content.

Or again, suppose I call you on the phone, and during the course of our conversation I say "It's six o'clock, I have to go eat." When you put the phone down, you rush off to get to an appointment scheduled for six-thirty, only to notice that it is in fact only just gone three o'clock. There are two obvious ways this misunderstanding could have arisen. First I might simply have got the time wrong. In that case what I pass on to you is misinformation. Given that there is no way we can prevent people or machines making mistakes from time to time, there is nothing more to say about that case. But perhaps I am not mistaken, and it was indeed six o'clock when I called you up, but that I was in Boston and you were in San Fransisco. Then my utterance of the sentence 'It's six o'clock' has the propositional content

$$s \models \; \ll \text{six o'clock}, t_u, 1 \gg$$

where s is my environment in Boston; but for you in San Fransisco the following proposition obtains

$$s' \models \; \ll \text{three o'clock}, t_u, 1 \gg$$

where s' is your environment.[8] My failure to communicate to you in this case arises because you were not aware that I was referring to my situation s, and not to your situation, s'. Unless there were good grounds for my believing you knew where I was, I should have commenced our conversation by telling you that I was calling you from Boston.

Of course, on most occasions such an explicit identification of the described situation is not necessary. There are all sorts of ways that the speaker can communicate to the listener what it is that is being discussed: mention of key-words, glances and gestures (in the case of face-to-face contact), and so forth. In the case of the above telephone conversation, if you were aware of the time of day, my observation that it is six o'clock could itself serve to alert you to the fact that I must be elsewhere than on the West Coast, and thereby serve to identify the situation s to you. Very often the identity of the described situation is progressively determined as the conversation proceeds.

Our theory is not able to handle all of the identification features mentioned above, nor does it try to do so, but the inclusion of the described situation as a parameter in our treatment reflects the role of

---

[8] I regard properties such as 'being six o'clock' and 'being three o'clock' as ordinary, everyday properties of local environments, having a definite, albeit fuzzy-edged duration.

these features in communication, and it is my view that any attempt at a theory of information flow that does not in any way reflect these crucial aspects of communication is doomed to fall far short of the mark.

Assuming the speaker does succefully communicate to the listener the identity of the described situation, there are several other ways that a communication breakdown can arise.

The most superficially obvious case is where an ambiguous word is used, such as 'bank' or 'letter'. The enormous differences that can result from word ambiguity is well illustrated by Chomsky's famous example:

Time flies like an arrow.
Fruit flies like a banana.

In this example it takes a considerable amount of background knowledge in order simply to identify the various parts of speech and parse these sentences correctly, let alone use them to convey information.

Our theory allows for this kind of ambiguity, in that we do not demand that each word have a unique referent. Rather a particular *use* (utterance) of a word associates with that word a particular object. In the case of the Chomsky example above, features of the utterance would distinguish between the two different sentences, and avoid any ambiguities. Of course, once again our theory does not even attempt to explain this disambiguation mechanism. It simply reflects it.

Amiguity can also arise as a result of pronoun referents. For instance, when John says

Fred thinks he is wrong

there are two possible interpretations according to whether the pronoun 'he' has Fred himself as its referent or else some other person. It is, as always, up to the speaker, in this case John, to avoid possible misunderstandings by providing enough circumstancial information to make the intended meaning clear. Our framework is able to track the most common mechanisms speakers use to do this, but again it is not my goal to try to explain the cognitive processes that make it work.

10

Retrospect and Prospect

In this final chapter I take a look at what has been achieved so far and where we should go next.

10.1 A science of information

As yet there is no science of information of the kind envisaged in this book. It remains a goal to be achieved at some later date. Likewise the mathematical theory presented here is still in, at best, an embryonic form. Indeed, some might say it is not *mathematics* at all. It depends, of course, on what you mean by 'mathematics'.

If your definition of mathematics is theorem-proving, then indeed what you find between the covers of this book is not mathematics. But that is to take an extremely narrow view of the rich and vibrant field that I see as constituting mathematics. If what is being tried here turns out to be 'right', theorems will come soon enough. And even if this approach proves not to work, it will still have been mathematics, and maybe even a necessary first step towards a mathematics that *does* work.

It is often said that mathematics is the study of patterns. And this is what I have been trying to do in this book: identify and mathematicize the relevant abstract patterns that are important in a scientific study of meaning and information. In terms of this definition, what is presented here is mathematics. It just does not look like it (yet).

In fact one should always be very cautious in trying to judge in advance what any scientific theory should look like. As Searle says in [27, p.25]:

It is a persistent mistake to try to define 'science' in terms of certain features of existing scientific theories. But once this provincialism is perceived to be the prejudice it is, then any domain of facts whatever is a subject of sytematic investigation. ... In fact if [a new development] runs counter to a certain definition of 'science', then it is the definition and not [the new development] which we will have to abandon.

As with science, so too with the mathematics that is required to underpin that science. It would be a mistake to set out with a fixed idea of what the requisite mathematics should look like.

Still, there has to be some starting point, some particular angle to bring to the problem. Having been trained as a logician, it is natural for me to take a logician's approach to the topic. In fact, having worked in logic for over twenty years, I have little choice but to take this approach. It is what I know best. As it happens, I think it is the right approach. More precisely, I think it is *one* of several 'right' approaches that will eventually coalesce to produce the kind of mathematical theory that will be required for a science of information.

10.2 A new logic?

A combination of its immense success and the influence of a number of prominent logicians, most notably among them Quine, has led to the virtual identification of 'logic' with 'first-order logic'. Most of the other 'logics' that have been studied in recent years, both by logicians and computer scientists, are little more than variants of first-order logic.

But success in the domain of mathematics, where first-order logic succeeded in providing a powerful and elegant model of the all-important notion of mathematical proof, does not necessarily translate to success in other areas. In particular, first-order logic has proved woefully inadequate at providing either an explanation of linguistic meaning or a theory of information adequate for information processing and artificial intelligence.

For some, this has been taken to imply that logic is simply not the appropriate place to start looking for a theory of meaning. But that is to accept that there can be little more to logic than first-order logic, with perhaps the occasional bell and whistle hung from the side.

This point is addressed by Barwise in the concluding remarks to his collection [2, pp.294–295]:

... An enormous amount of heat and antipathy between rival approaches to semantics is similarly grounded in inadequacies in the FOL [first-order logic] model. The attacks strike me as the worst sort of argument.

Suppose someone is trying to build a house and needs to cut a board. He picks up his hammer, only to discover he can't cut the board. So he makes two mistakes: he throws away the hammer, and he doesn't buy a saw. These dismisals of mathematical attempts to characterize meaning are just wrong-headed and defeatist. FOL was developed as a model of the axiomatic method. It is a pretty good model of it, too. Only if one thinks that the axiomatic method is all there is to meaning would one suppose that FOL would be an adequate model of meaning.

My own work in logic has always been on the 'semantic' side. Indeed, coming to the subject from mainstream mathematics, my interest in logic (in particular set theory and the application of model-theoretic techniques within set theory) was always that of a mathematician seeking new tools with which to attack problems of mathematics: questions about the real numbers and topological spaces, problems in combinatorics, and the like.

My work in constructibility theory confirmed my belief in the incredible power of what I can only refer to as 'semantic' (or even less informatively 'mathematical') methods, as opposed to the formalism and proof-theory that are often identified as 'logic'. To me, techniques of first-order logic provided useful tools, alongside various other mathematical methods, but the power always seemed to be in the mathematics, not the first-order logic.

First-order logic provides useful models of mathematical proof, but it does not, I maintain, correspond to the way people reason, even mathematicians doing mathematics (and for that matter, even logicians doing logic). At least it does not correspond very well, and certainly not in a manner adequate for a theory of meaning and information.

Time then to add a saw to use alongside Barwise's hammer. Or even better, a complete toolkit.

10.3 What next?

A scientific study cannot become a genuine 'science' until there is a mathematical backbone to sustain it. Until then there are just observations, techniques, and theories. Developing the appropriate mathematics involves a long and tortuous process of identifying and fleshing out the right features on which to concentrate, investigating the role played by these features, and constructing mathematical structures that model the way those features interact.

This 'fleshing-out' process is best carried out in a two-pronged fashion. One prong consists of a study of the target domain — not in the fashion of an expert in the field but in the overtly naive way that is a prerequisite for any piece of mathematics. Discover what are to be the 'dimensionless points', the 'widthless straight lines', the 'frictionless planes', and what-have-you of the new mathematical theory. This is, broadly speaking, what I have been doing in this book.

The other prong comprises the development of 'formal' mathematical models that seem appropriate for the task in hand, or parts of that task, in so far as this has been determined by the first prong. This is what I intend to do in the successor volume to this. At the time of writing, only a few parts of this second volume have been written. Large parts of it exist only in the form of general ideas of how to proceed. In all likelihood even greater parts have yet to be discovered: feedback from readers of this book will probably lead to new ideas.

So what is next? I really don't know. That is the nature of research, what makes it at the same time immense fun and intensely frustrating.

10.4   Historical note

The term *situation semantics* first appeared in Jon Barwise's 1981 paper 'Scenes and Other Situations' (reprinted as Chapter 1 of [2]). *Situation theory* followed soon after, as the beginnings of the mathematical theory required to sustain situation semantics.

It was as he was working on this paper that Barwise began to collaborate with John Perry, and it was largely their subsequent joint work that brought situation semantics to the point where the first book on the subject appeared, their 1983 volume *Situations and Attitudes* [5].

The appearance of this work coincided (roughly) with the opening of the Stanford based *Center for the Study of Language and Information* (CSLI), with Barwise as its first director. (Perry took over as the second director, two years later.) This proved to be both a boon and, to some extent, a liability for the development of situation theory.[1]

Bringing together a large number of workers from linguistics, philosophy, psychology, computer science, artificial intelligence, and mathematical logic, the subject advanced at a far greater pace than would otherwise have been the case, though often not in the direction that had originally been envisaged. On the other hand, the award of $25 million from the Systems Development Foundation that brought CSLI into being, led to expectations that could not possibly be fulfilled, and after the initial excitement had died down there developed a general feeling among those not directly involved in CSLI of "Well, when are all those results going to start pouring out?"

Of course, they could not — not after a mere three or four years' work. No new science comes that easily, not even if you throw millions of dollars at the problem. But real advances there have been for all

---

[1] A commonly held misconception is that CSLI was established purely to investigate situation semantics. This is far from the truth. The work on situation semantics, and later situation theory, was just one of a number of research projects that were funded through CSLI. However, the development of situation semantics and situation theory was undoubtedly helped immensely by the rich intellectual environment provided by CSLI.

that. For the most part they have been 'small steps for a man' rather than 'giant leaps for mankind'. But then that is how science generally develops.

And what of the work presented in this book? How does this fit into the overall situation theory picture?

Well, this book does not pretend to be a straight account of situation theory as developed by Barwise and Perry, or anybody else for that matter. For one thing, my goal is not the foundation of a semantic theory of natural language, as was the case with Barwise and Perry. And for another, what you find here is very much my own slant on the matter.

I started to think seriously about the issues discussed in this book back in 1983 or thereabouts, before I knew anything of situation theory or situation semantics, so when I attended a lecture on situation semantics given by Barwise in Manchester in 1984, I was already laden with my own set of prejudices and expectations on the matter.

I came away from that lecture with a sense of elation. A talk I had given to my colleagues at Lancaster (my then university) on the subject a short while before, had produced responses that ranged from incomprehension to incredulity, and I had begun to fear that my thinking must have gone way off track. So it was gratifying to find in Barwise's lecture ideas that very much echoed my own thoughts. At least there were two of us in this boat!

Reading *Situations and Attitudes* and various other papers emanating from CSLI, followed by my own sojourn at CSLI from August 1987 to July 1989, led to my completely revising a lot of my ideas, so that in the end, what is presented here is the result of a conglomerate effort, filtered through those of my own prejudices that survived my time at CSLI (a place where one is confronted by one's own prejudices all the time).

Parts are pure Barwise–Perry. Other parts are adaptations of Barwise–Perry. Still other parts are somewhat at odds with Barwise–Perry. (At times, even Barwise or Perry is at odds with Barwise–Perry.) One of the consequences of working at an intensive research institute such as CSLI is that everyone's ideas become intermingled.

So this book should not be taken to represent *the* latest word on 'situation theory'. As yet there is no such single voice, no acknowledged central theory, though there are signs of a gelling in certain directions. It does, however, provide the best approximation currently available to such a latest word, if for no other reason than that it is the only 'textbook' currently available on the topic other than the now well-out-of-date *Situations and Attitudes*.

Throughout the writing of this book, I consulted regularly with others at CSLI in order to ensure that what I wrote was for the most part in agreement with the consensus view, but in the final anaysis what gets onto the page is very much an account of the way I myself see matters. So what appears here can be thought of as my own account of what started out as Barwise and Perry's situation theory but, given that the version presented is my own, any blame can justifiably be laid firmly at my door!

10.5   Personal note

I complete this book with three regrets and a great deal of hope.

The first regret is that it does not go anything like as far as I originally intended as far as the mathematics is concerned. I set out to write a book on mathematics, a contribution to the development of a new 'logic', a logic that would facilitate a genuine theory of information. Looking back, I see now that this was an incredibly naive ambition. Large parts of this book are the result of my struggles to come to grips with issues I had never thought to become embroiled in, questions of intentionality, mental states, and so forth.[2] My original, naive ambition has now been transferred to the production of a sequel volume.

My second regret is that as yet very few of my fellow logicians have started to work on the problems investigated here. Though a great many logicians have turned their attention to issues in computer science, most of the work has been directed towards the application of existing techniques of logic. The really big question has been largely left alone.

I can understand why this is the case. As alluded to a moment ago, the sheer scope of the problem has meant that there is as yet precious little 'hard' mathematics in the subject. (By 'hard' I mean something like 'concrete', since there is no doubt that the enterprise as a whole is extremely hard in the sense of being difficult.) For those of us brought up in the contemporary mathematical tradition, used to obtaining our intellectual kicks by solving technical problems of mathematics and proving new theorems, this state of affairs can be highly frustrating. It always bothers me when I give a talk on this work to a group of fellow mathematicians, and at the end one of them asks me "Yes, we see all that, but where are the theorems?" It bothers me not because I think mathematics should be identified with theorem-proving — far from it — but because I too want to get to the part where the mathematics flows and there are technical problems to solve and theorems to formulate and prove.

---

[2] Barwise expresses similar feelings in the closing remarks to [2].

Still, wishing for that stage will not in itself bring it into being. But nor, I fear, will continuing to try to make classical logic fit the bill. Attempts to use first-order logic in order to ground a theory of meaning and information remind me of the man who, upon losing his house keys as he steps from his car late one night, walks along the road a bit and starts to crawl around on the pavement under the street light. He knows, of course, that he is unlikely to find his keys there. After all, he dropped them by the car. So why does he continue to look where he does. "Because," he will say, "the light is better here."

Undoubtedly there will one day be a theory of meaning and a science of information. Whether this will bear any resemblance at all to the work presented here is another matter. But we certainly will not find it all the time we continue to crawl around under the one available street-lamp, however brightly it might shine on one particular patch of pavement.

My third regret is that the adoption of a narrow-minded and idiotically shortsighted view of what constitutes 'desirable' research meant that the completion of this book could not be achieved at the university where it had been started — but that issue was already mentioned in the Acknowledgements, so does not need to be repeated here.

And the hope I mentioned at the start of this section? That an increasing number of logicians will start to wrestle with the big issues of meaning and information. After all, the concept of meaning is the very essence of logic, and it is a search for meaning in one form or another that has led to every advance that has been made in logic. The success of first-order logic in one particular domain, namely mathematics, is no reason to stop now. On the contrary, it should act as a spur towards future developments.

As I said a moment ago, there *will be* a science of information, and 'logic' of some form or other will be a major part of that science. We just have to find it.

I finish this book the way I began it: with a quotation. This one is appropriate in a number of ways, on several different levels, and therefore it is a marvelous example of the manner in which different constraints enable a particular symbol structure to convey different information.

Einstein's space is no closer to reality than Van Gogh's sky. …The scientist's discoveries impose his own order on chaos, as the composer or painter imposes his; an order that always refers to limited aspects of reality, and is biased by the observer's frame of reference, which differs from period to period, as a Rembrandt nude differs from a nude by Monet.

— Arthur Koestler
The Act of Creation

REFERENCES

[1]   Barwise, J. Information and Circumstance, *Notre Dame Journal of Formal Logic* 27 (1986), pp.324–338, reprinted in [2, pp.137-154]

[2]   Barwise, J. *The Situation in Logic*, CSLI Lecture Notes 17 (1988)

[3]   Barwise, J. and Cooper, R. Generalized Quantifiers and Natural Language, *Linguistics and Philosophy* 4 (1981), pp.159–219.

[4]   Barwise, J. and Etchemendy, J. *The Liar*, Oxford University Press (1987)

[5]   Barwise, J. and Perry, J. *Situations and Attitudes*, Bradford Books, MIT Press (1983)

[6]   Bollobas, B. *Littlewood's Miscellany*, Cambridge University Press (1986)

[7]   Bratman, M. E. *Intention, Plans, and Practical Reason*, Harvard University Press (1987)

[8]   Dretske, F. *Knowledge and the Flow of Information*, Bradford Books, MIT Press (1981)

[9]   Dretske, F. Private communication, Jan 29, 1988

[10]   Gibson, E. J. *Principles of Perceptual Learning and Development*, Appleton–Century–Crofts (1969)

[11]   Kac, M., Rota, G.-C. and Schwartz, J. T. *Discrete Thoughts*, Birkhäuser Boston (1985)

[12]   Kripke, S. A Puzzle About Belief, in Margalit, A. (ed.) *Meaning and Use*, Reidel (1979), pp.239–283

[13]   Maturana, H. R. Neurophysiology of Cognition, in Garvin, P (ed.) *Cognition: A Multiple View*, Spartan Books (1970), pp.3–23

[14]   Maturana, H. R. Biology of Cognition (1970), reprinted in [16], pp.2–62

[15]   Maturana, H. R., Lettvin, J. Y., McCulloch, W. S., and Pitts, W. H. Anatomy and Physiology of Vision in the Frog, *Journal of General Physiology* 43 (1960), pp.129–175

[16]   Maturana, H. R. and Varela, S. *Autopoiesis and Cognition: The Reaslization of the Living*, Reidel (1980)

[17]   Miller, G. A. The Magical Number Seven, Plus or Minus Two: Some Limits on Our Capacity for Processing Information, *Psychological Reviews* 63 (1956), pp.81–97

[18]   Pollock, J. L. *Contemporary Theories of Knowledge*, Hutchinson (1986)

[19]   Putnam, H. Philosophy of Logic (1971), *Mathematics, Matter and Method: Philosophical Papers, Vol. 1*, Cambridge University Press (1979)

[20] Quine, W. V. *Methods of Logic*, Holt, Rinehart, and Winston (1959)

[21] Quine, W. V. *The Ways of Paradox and Other Essays*, Harvard University Press (1966)

[22] Rosenschein, S. J. Formal Theories of Knowledge in AI and Robotics, CSLI Report 84 (1987)

[23] Schmandt-Besserat, D. Oneness, Twoness, Threeness, *The Sciences*, pp.44–48, New York Academy of Sciences (1989).

[24] Searle, J. R. The Philosophy of Language, in B. Magee (ed.) *Men of Ideas*, Oxford University Press (1978), pp.153–172

[25] Searle, J. R. A Taxonomy of Illocutionary Acts, in *Expression and Meaning*, Cambridge University Press (1979), pp.1–29

[26] Searle, J. R. *Intentionality*, Cambridge University Press (1983)

[27] Searle, J. R. *Minds, Brains and Science*, Harvard University Press (1984)

[28] Seligman, J. and Chater, N. Devlin on Information and Cognition, Working paper, Centre for Cognitive Science, University of Edinburgh (1988)

[29] Shannon, C. E. The Mathematical Theory of Communication, *Bell System Technical Journal*, 1948, reprinted by University of Chicago Press (1949)

[30] Sperling, G. The Information Available in Brief Visual Presentations, *Psychological Monographs* 74, Number 11 (1960)

[31] Winograd, T. and Flores, F. *Understanding Computers and Cognition*, Addison–Wesley (1987)

[32] Wittgenstein, L. *Philosophical Investigations*, Blackwell (1953)

INDEX

INDEX OF SYMBOLS